The Tale Of
The Devil

Publisher's Cataloging-in-Publication
(Provided by Quality Books, Inc.)

Hatfield, Coleman.
 The tale of the devil: the story of Devil Anse Hatfield : from manuscripts of Devil Anse Hatfield's grandson Coleman A. Hatfield / by Coleman C. Hatfield and Robert Y. Spence
 p. cm.
 Includes bibliographical references and index.
 LCCN 2003104970
 ISBN 0-9724867-1-2 (Hardbound)
 ISBN 1-891852-54-X (Quality Bound)
 ISBN 978-1-891852-54-1 (Quality Bound)

 1. Hatfield, Devil Anse, 1839-1921.
 2. Hatfield-McCoy feud. 3. Hatfield family. 4. West Virginia--Biography. I. Hatfield, Coleman A. II. Spence, Robert Y. III. Title.

HV6452.W42H372 2003   975.4'44'092
                              QB103-700252

THIRD PRINTING
Copyright © 2007 by *Hatfield Historical Associates, Inc.*

Third Printing. All rights reserved. Written permission must be secured from the publisher to use or reproduce any part of this book in any form or by any means – graphic, electronic, or mechanical, including photocopying, recording, taping, or by any information storage retrieval system — except for brief quotations in critical reviews or articles.

Published In Beautiful Chapmanville, West Virginia
Woodland Press, LLC.
Appalachian Stories. Appalachian Authors. Appalachian Pride.
Paperback edition is licensed to Quarrier Press, Charleston, WV

SAN: 2 5 4 – 9 9 9 9

The Tale Of The Devil
The Biography of Devil Anse Hatfield

*From Original Manuscripts By
Grandson Coleman A. Hatfield*

By Coleman C. Hatfield
And Robert Y. Spence

Woodland Press, LLC

*In mountains there is freedom.
The earth is perfect
everywhere except where man
comes with his torment.*

— J.C.F. von Schiller

CONTENTS

Chapter One
THE YOUNG DEVIL
The Early Life of Anse Hatfield — Page 17

Chapter Two
ANCESTORS OF THE DEVIL
The Hatfields in American History — Page 33

Chapter Three
THE DEVIL IN THE FIGHTIN'
Anse Hatfield in the American Civil War — Page 61

Chapter Four
THE DEVIL IN HIS MOUNTAIN LAIR
Anse Hatfield and the Timbering Industry — Page 89

Chapter Five
THE RAGE OF THE DEVIL
The Beginning of the Hatfield and McCoy Feud — Page 115

Chapter Six
THE DEVIL BEDEVILED
The Hatfield and McCoy Feud Roils Up — Page 137

Chapter Seven
HELLFIRE OF THE DEVIL
Anderson Hatfield and the End of the Feud — Page 163

Chapter Eight
THE CHILDREN OF THE DEVIL
The Younger Hatfields Come of Age — Page 221

Chapter Nine
THE DEVIL TURNED TO STONE
Anderson Hatfield's Old Age and Death — Page 249

Epilogue
THE DEVIL'S HISTORIAN
The Lifework of Coleman A. Hatfield — Page 281

FOREWORD
By Dr. Coleman C. Hatfield

The Land

GEOGRAPHY explains people.

Inland, a hundred miles, give or take, from the Atlantic seaboard, stretching from northern Georgia to northern New York, is the Appalachian mountain chain. One of the oldest ranges on Earth, it is thought to have been higher than the Himalayas at one time, though it is much eroded and much altered by time. Though not as high as mountains of the world go today, the Appalachians were quite formidable to the pioneers. Once those pioneers crossed the mountain ranges west of Shenandoah Valley, they faced the Allegheny Plateau, thought to be the most formidable land in North America east of the Mississippi River and south of the St. Lawrence River.

Only a few rivers that cut through our land — a short list that includes the North and South Branches of the Potomac, the Greenbrier, the New River, the Kanawha, the Guyandot, and the Tug Fork of the Big Sandy River — could penetrate the Appalachian Mountains and the Allegheny Plateau. The rivers of Appalachia once flowed north to Hudson's Bay. But geological alterations of time have uplifted or reversed this ancient flow. Only the New River — which ironically is thought by some to actually be the world's oldest river — remains flowing north. Its splendid gorge splits through our mountains until the river is captured by the more recent Kanawha River and thence flows to the Ohio River.

Eons of erosion have created an endless series of hills and valleys, n properly called "hollers," in this ancient land. Spread over the hills was some of the richest hardwood forests of the world and that timberland was almost impenetrable. The huge trees rose twice one hundred feet. The undergrowth was more than dense. Daylight was dim on the forest floor. It has been said that a squirrel could have traveled from the Atlantic to beyond the Ohio River without touching the ground. The forests' mast of nuts and fruits supported colossal flocks of passenger pigeons, turkeys, deer, elk, bear, buffalo, and so on. Wolves, mountain lions, and other predators were common.

A horse was an impediment to one traveling in that land. If a mountain could be found clear enough of underbrush for a horse to travel, it would probably be too steep for the animal to negotiate — hence, the name "Horse Pen Fork" of Gilbert Creek, the locale of much of our tale. Further, the horse was easy prey for the natural predators of the forest. A horse was too valuable to waste in this fashion. With later settlement, horses were used for transportation, with the creek bottoms serving for roads. But youngsters who wanted to warn a friend of curious strangers could easily outrun a horse by going up and over the ridges, rather than the longer way around the creek bottoms.

Geologists claim that the land has an average slope of 45 percent — a steep place. The ridge tops are so narrow that it is not unusual to stand on top of a hill with a foot on either slope. The desirable farming land was, of course, along river and creek bottoms. There was also land at the heads of the small creeks. These were "coves," but that rich land was often covered with chestnut groves above and valued ginseng below. The narrowest "hollers" had small streams that could be jumped easily, changing from one slope to the other.

From place to place, salt would crop out as a lick or saline spring in the days of game hunting for subsistence (which still persist, by the way), providing valuable minerals. In the early days of the settlement of the land, outcrops of coal and burning springs of natural gas were merely curiosities. But nowhere was our land entirely level. The steep slopes gave all the rivers swift drops. Lakes and swamps were almost nonexistent.

A heavy rain combined with melting snows in the spring would result in a "tide" on our streams. The long-awaited "tide" was the means by which timber men floated logs to markets along the less-turbulent Ohio River. Several hundred logs, six to eight feet or more in diameter, would be "bored and pinned" — tied together with withes or splits of young hickory. As long as the logs were wet, the pins remained tight and the withes secure.

Tales of rafting make for quite an interesting series of stories. The "tide" created many sections of white water. "Shooting the shoals" in the cumbersome rafts was indeed fearsome. One mistake and a huge raft along with several raft-hands could be destroyed in the swift, relentless water. One such spot was Leatherwood Shoals on the Guyandot River. It was bordered by cliffs so sheer and high that one old raft-hand declared that it took the efforts of two men just to look up. One would look up the cliff as far as his eyes could carry, then the second man would begin looking at that point until he could see the tops.

The steepness also makes access difficult, even today. The forest floor is bound tightly with a fabric of roots. Stone is only a few inches or — at most — a few feet below the surface. Without roads and afoot in heavy timber, it is very inaccessible. When fire or excessive cutting of timber damages the forest, erosion occurs and all the soil is swept away.

Yet, for all its wildness, it was then and is now a land of incredible beauty. In winter, there are so many boulders visible on the mountaintops that it looks like they were placed there to keep the land from falling away. The trees, with their lace-like branch tips, look like a woven fringe decorating the mountaintops. When frosted with winter, these tree-trimmed mountaintops gleam in the clear morning sunshine. As the official State Song "West Virginia Hills" describes it, our mountains have "summits bathed in glory like our Prince Emmanuel's land."

Spring is almost indescribably beautiful, with the mountains that are awash with color as though splashed from a huge artist's brush, with redbud, dogwood, and "sarvis" giving an isolated flash of white and purple here and there across the hills. As the leaves open, there seems to be a thousand varied shades of green. These shades blend to create a rather uniform, seemingly endless, green of summer. Summer is my least favorite mountain season, but I won't hesitate to admit it is awesome. The green ridges are overlaid with a blue hue, which, I am told, is the result of selective light filtration by water vapor. I am told that a mature tree can evaporate or transpire on the order of one hundred gallons of water daily. There are tens of thousands of such trees in our woods. Autumn almost matches spring with the palette of colors: reds of sourwood, dogwood, sumac, and the golden tulip or yellow poplar trees. No color seems quite the same all day, and all change in the play of sunlight.

Such is our geography. The fierceness of the terrain with its inaccessibility is smoothed and made beautiful by the overlying forest vegetation, much like beauty and the beast. Though we have been forced to accept the city folk who have wanted our timber, coal, oil, and gas, and have left their reminders as a memory in sawdust, gob piles, and scarred and torn mountains, the hurt that smarts the most comes from the type that wants to take our good name. Yet, if you are going to talk about us, at least get our name correct. "Appalachia" sounds like "apple at cha." Do leave us our good name for the memory of unspoiled days gone by.

The People

WE WERE once a group of wilderness-hardened pioneers who had no grandiose dreams of vast lands, estates, or ranches, but rather enjoyed the privacy and isolation of the wilderness. We were content with the rich provisions of the wild to grant a plentiful subsistence. Game and fish abounded, and the land was rich in the river bottoms and mountaintop "coves." Our people scattered to populate the mountains and have become the present indigenous mountain people.

"Scattered" is not a casual word. As a general rule, any neighbor within shouting distance was too close. To be a good neighbor, you kept to yourself and allowed others the same privacy. Yet all neighbors would be expected to rally to the aid of others, whether it was in times of trouble or times of plenty, as in corn shuckin' or house-raisings or so forth.

In spite of the toughness of our ancestors, we are sensitive in many ways. Often misunderstood and ridiculed by the media, we are driven closer together and become more suspicious of "strangers." We often flinch at the name "hillbilly," although, as Robert Burns told us, the term is honorable enough.

"Billy" was the Scottish word for friend. We are your friends from the hills. It is my hope here that these words cast a new light on my people.

We are a window back in time.

Until the perfection of electronic media arrived in our hills, the Elizabethan language more familiar to Shakespeare was common. Our customs are those frequently held over from earlier times. To understand our ways, our customs, our habits of mind, and our history, you must look at our land and the days of the American wilderness, when the frontiersmen first pulled equal to the Indians as masters of the forest.

To make our story more coherent, it is needful to know who these people are, from whence they came, and with what fire and forge they were tempered. We must know the forces that have made their children, and their children's children, loathe to leave their land.

The people came first from the British Isles, but with strong additions from France, Germany, and other areas of Northern Europe. They were people of the land, farmers, hunters, and simple tradesmen. Life was hard in Europe, unless you were one of the elite. Anyone who departed from the status quo was persecuted. The opportunity to rise in wealth and status was impossible. One was rather frozen in the social order.

As the new world opened its arms, there was the lure of opportunity. One could provide his family, and a man's home was his castle. It was not needful to be beholden to anyone. There were, of course, those representing the power, order, and wealth that wished to extend their domain to these new colonies. But the mass of people arrived, as they were able, spending all they had for passage. Others sold themselves as indentured servants to gain passage — anything to escape the dull, hopeless life they endured.

Parallel to and part of this social unrest was the early industrial revolution in England. The woolen mills needed wool. Wool meant a need for sheep. Scotland was ideal sheep pasture. The proudly independent Scot clansmen, who had long defied the English authorities, were who had made an effort to subdue the unruly Irish across the narrow Irish Sea. What better remedy, they thought, than the enclosure acts to seize the Scots' farms for pasture and dump the Scottish people in Northern Ireland, thereby letting one problem solve the other. The Scots could not live with the Irish in Northern Ireland then, nor can they do so today. So the Scots left Ireland in great numbers for the colonies — hence, the Scot-Irish.

The new world was a vast wilderness near at hand. Work was freely available on any settled lands. Those who were ambitious pushed on to the edge of a settlement to claim land for their own. It was such ambition that brought them to the Allegheny Plateau. The only threat was the "savage" inhabitants of the land. Having faced the whipping post, the rack, hanging for theft of a loaf of bread, or other such "just" laws from established authority, there was no great terror in the threat of being scalped. Many other factors contributed to the unrest that drove emigration; religious freedom is often noted as another right forbidden from the established order.

One hundred years passed after Jamestown was founded, and scarcely a hundred miles inland from the Atlantic seaboard had been settled when our history began. At that time French, Spanish, and English politics spilled over into the new world. George III, King of England, set a proclamation line at the mountaintops to divide the Indians and the frontiersmen. But few of the land-hungry Scot-Irish and none of the Indians could have read his proclamation. The people of the wilderness edged slowly forward into openings in the mountains toward the west. The valley of Virginia was one such opening and the first explorers crossed the mountain and moved down the valley. Though it took longer than forty years to fill the valley, a new, toughened, hardy, intrepid people were born of the experience. They kept the Sabbath — and everything else they could get their hands on.

Some of the emigrants did find work and a new lifestyle, and they found religious freedom. But the more venturesome, the more independent, and the more fearless or heedless, were those ambitious souls who pushed on to the no-man's land that fell between the colonies and the Indian lands. A piece of land there could be cleared and corn could be planted. Game was so plentiful that fur became a source of money, barter, or trade with the colonies. Rumors of gold west of the mountains also persisted, as a lure somewhere to the west. Dreams drove the pioneers across the continent until they did, indeed, find gold at Sutter's Mill in California.

A number of roots and herbs were also of value in the west. Chief among these was ginseng, ultimately designated for the Chinese trade. Its very name derives from the Chinese phrase "image of a man," a rather ribald reference to the three prongs of the ginseng root that perhaps implies a higher form of virility. "Sang," as it became known, was a wild harvest of great value. It was more worthwhile than furs and less disquieting to the Indians because only squaws dug herbs and roots. A pound of dried "sang" today is worth approximately one ounce of gold, a comparative value held sway in former days. With horses scarce or unavailable, a man could carry a much more valuable load of "sang" from the wilderness than he could furs.

Thus they swore to cross the mountains.

Near the time of the American Revolution, the "wilderness" was Tennessee, Kentucky, Western Virginia, and the Ohio country further west. Depending on the definition one uses, the limit of "civilization" was somewhere near Roanoke, Virginia. After the collapse of the French support of the Indians in 1760, the frontier people were able to spill westward through Cumberland Gap into Kentucky, and also down the Clinch, Holstein, and Powell Rivers into Tennessee and on westward. Davy Crockett, Sam Houston, and Jim Bowie were of that ilk.

Hence, the first westerners, the men and women who tamed the Wild West, were also of the type that remained in Appalachia. The first historian of my neck of the woods recorded some one hundred family names whose tales should be saved forever. Hatfield and McCoy are just two of those names. My hope is that the tale of one Hatfield serves to illustrate the history of my people.

In trying to organize the stacks of manuscripts written by my father, Coleman A. Hatfield, I became aware of what a large task it was, and how little time and talent that I could bring to bear upon it. I pondered what to do and where to start. A common bit of folklore told me that if you spoke of the devil, his imps would appear. One such imp did appear. His name was Robert Yie Spence.

The Writer

ROBERT YIE SPENCE is of Logan, West Virginia, where most of this tale is set. Some years ago he undertook to write the general history of our home — an effort that resulted in his book, *The Land of the Guyandot*. A most stubborn soul, he kept working on the history of this land until he wrote a four-hundred-some page manuscript that includes some four hundred photographs of this place.

There is no easy way to describe him quickly, and I will not try. He is, in part, a free spirit whose main drive is his imagination; but he is also a painstaking researcher who will not stop at the surface of anything. When he was six years old, his father put him to work in the family printing shop and trained him to be a "printer's devil." Thus, he is the ideal person to help write this book.

Through his years, he has spent time writing magazine articles, compiling indices of newspapers, and working with computers — all the while enchanted with the possibilities of using newspapers to analyze the flow of the past in our mountain country. "Just who are you," I asked him one time. "*An imagineer*," he answered.

Preface
The Scholar And The Legend
The Research of Coleman A. Hatfield

FOLKS tell the tales of the feud between the Hatfields and the McCoys along the borderlines where Virginia is joined by West Virginia and Kentucky. Those who remember the feud speak of the men and women involved as though they were still flesh and blood, instead of characters in history. They tell about Devil Anse Hatfield and Randal McCoy, of Jim Vance and Cap Hatfield, of Johnse Hatfield and Roseanna McCoy as if they were every day acquaintances and friends or enemies.

Yet for all this, the deeper meaning of the feud has been obscure, for good and sufficient reasons. The last active feud participants died in the 1960's, closing a chapter of history. Those left living in the ensuing years have talked about the feud without first-hand knowledge. Though books have been written about the feud, few have had access to the hearts and minds of the people caught up in its drama.

By 1909 at the latest, however, the Hatfield family had produced a scholar and a gentleman who taught himself how to do accurate research. His name was Coleman Alderson Hatfield, the son of William Anderson (Cap) Hatfield and the eldest surviving grandson of the legendary Devil Anse Hatfield. He was a lawyer whose passion was for truth. His greatest attribute was a prodigious and "eidetic" memory, of the type many refer to as a "photographic memory." His great achievement in life was to record the recollections that were his cherished possessions, given to him by his father and his grandfather.

Through the years as the feudists passed away and as exaggerations sprouted like ramps — the wild onions (or leeks) of the feud country — Coleman A. Hatfield worked alone and later with the help of his children to preserve a painstakingly correct account of the events of the feud. At times he hired professional genealogists to help him find traces of the earliest Hatfields in America. At other times he dictated letters to anyone interested in writing about the feud. On one occasion he wrote an article to indicate to the general public the scope of the work that needed to be accomplished before an accurate history of the feud could be written.

That article found its way to print in the summer of 1952, when the City of Logan, West Virginia, Coleman A. Hatfield's home, celebrated the centennial of the year when its first mayor took office. A commemorative book was published for that celebration and Hatfield was asked to share his understandings of "the Hatfield pioneers." In that article, he wrote:

> Much has been written and many stories have been exaggerated regarding the conflict, which lasted during the '80's. There were approximately one hundred fifty men who participated at various times and places in the pitched battles along the border....
>
> Few are living who remember the clashes of galloping raiders across the border of seventy years ago. The Hatfields and McCoys alike, as well as their neighbors, whose ancestors had come into these rugged hills a hundred years before the feud days, have all come from the pioneer stock who pushed the frontier of civilization across the hills.[1]

That final sentence should be noted well. Coleman A. Hatfield was telling attentive readers that the tales of the Hatfields and McCoys go well beyond the simplistic image of the uncouth "hillbilly" of popular imagination. Hatfield was explaining that the feud was a complex network of events that proceeded from the frontier experience as that experience was fading into history.

Just why Coleman A. Hatfield never published his book is a matter of some question. Certainly his ingrained modesty played a role in that decision. So too did his quite reasonable concerns that his tale of the feud would be misunderstood in the glare of public opinion. A third reason for his decision was based upon his reluctance to make a spectacle of the feud, which he believed to have been a tragic misfortune for both families. In the introduction to his work, Hatfield wrote:

> For one who has had no experience in writing, the thought of relating the story of a mountain feud of three-quarters of a century ago is a monstrous undertaking. It also seems to be somewhat a violation of my family's privacy. Since my earliest childhood, the watchword of the household was secrecy, and airing the family troubles with strangers was frowned upon. On the other hand, I have been asked very often by those who know me to write an authentic account of the warfare in which my people were engaged during the last quarter of the nineteenth century. I therefore ask my readers to realize that two opposing forces, my inhibition and my belief that the world should know the true causes and conditions which spawned the Hatfield-McCoy Feud, are at work within me as I write this account.[2]

Coleman A. Hatfield also understood full well that he might be accused of presenting only the Hatfield side of the tragic contention between two families. Despite his admiration for Virgil Carrington Jones' classic work about the feud that was published in 1948, Hatfield believed knowledge of the surface facts of the feud was an inadequate basis for interpreting the conflict. In that light, Hatfield also wrote:

> The reader may also believe as he reads the lines which follow that the writer is biased in his thinking, since he is, after all, a Hatfield. I honestly believe, however, that the history of this feud has been told for the last two generations in a light more favorable to the McCoy family of Pike County, Kentucky, than to the Hatfields of Southern West Virginia. It is my sincere desire to tell the facts, to give credit where credit is due, and to place any blame where it belongs.
>
> It should be obvious that the responsibility for such a fratricidal quarrel cannot be laid at the door of one family alone. Each side must bear its responsibility and not expect the world to believe that this tragic event can be explained in terms of black and white, good and evil. I therefore make but one request: that the reader withhold his judgment and make no decisions for or against either side until he has read the last word. Then the feud will be seen merely as one of the incidents peculiar to the development of American civilization ... After all, it is a story which concerns people, some good, some bad, but most, like the rest of us, somewhere in between.[3]

Coleman A. Hatfield tried on at least one occasion to have his manuscript published, with unhappy results. He then put the work aside, leaving it in the care of his children as a record for future generations. He supplemented his written account of the feud with tape-recorded memories that were done with the help of his son, Coleman C. Hatfield. After Coleman A. Hatfield passed away in 1970, his son kept both collections safe in his homes in Chicago and in Stollings, a small residential community near Logan, West Virginia.

In October 1993, this writer asked Coleman C. Hatfield for permission to listen to the tape recordings and read any other works Coleman A. Hatfield had written about the feud. After discussions that lasted until March 1994, Coleman C. Hatfield asked if a new history of his family could be written that would put the feud in proper context and that would save other long-lost tales of the extended family for future generations. The present work is the result of those discussions.

As the work proceeded, Coleman and the writer agreed that a detailed biography of Anderson (Devil Anse) Hatfield would be a better product than another book that concentrated solely on the feud. We also agreed that such a work should be largely as Coleman A. Hatfield wrote it in his original manuscript, but with enough facts about the development of the Logan-Pike-Mingo County environs to show that Anse Hatfield's life was part of his time and place, not merely the activities of a savage feudist. This book was written with that hope in mind.

Yet the tale of the Hatfields is an American epic, endlessly fascinating, and the subject of much controversy and debate. Those who read this, including the still-thriving Hatfield and McCoy families, will find points where they disagree with the conclusions. This record is presented to the honest candor of the public, however, without apology, as an account of the research of a learned man into the role of his family in history.

Robert Y. Spence
April 2003

Chapter One
THE YOUNG DEVIL
The Early Life of Anse Hatfield

THERE are times when the autumn wind makes the red leaves swirl hectically around the base of the marble graveyard statue of Devil Anse Hatfield on Island Creek, reminding his descendants and their Appalachian kinsmen of a haunted past and awaking the memory of gunfire. Yet despite the legends of the feud between the Hatfields and the McCoys that raged along the border of West Virginia and Kentucky more than one hundred years ago, few have known much about the life of Anderson "Anse" Hatfield.

That knowledge comes as a shock to those who live among the rolling and beautiful woodlands that were Anse's home for more than eighty years. Scores of thriving mountaineers believe that he was the most genuine Appalachian of all — a huge, rugged, self-reliant, imposing figure who dominated his fellowmen and who fiercely protected their values. He was all that, a biographer admits. And he was more than that. In popular imagination, Anse Hatfield has become a symbol for all those who have lived along the watersheds of the Tug Fork and Guyandot Rivers. Thus it is important to separate the reality of his life from the mysteries of his legend.

The Birth of the Devil

His tale must begin at the beginning. Nancy Vance Hatfield, the mother of Anderson Hatfield, went into childbirth on September 9, 1839, at the log cabin home she shared with her husband, Ephraim Hatfield, on the Straight Fork of Mate Creek, a tributary of the Tug Fork of the Big Sandy River which marked the border of Western Virginia — today's West Virginia — and Kentucky.

Anse's birth was normal for that time and place. It is likely that Nancy Hatfield was attended by at least one midwife, known in popular usage as a "granny woman." Ansie, as the boy was also nicknamed, was the fifth child in Ephraim and Nancy's growing family, preceded by John in 1829, Valentine in 1834, Elizabeth in 1836, and Martha in 1838. During the following twenty years, Ephraim and Nancy would have six other children: Ellison in 1842, Elias in 1848, Emma in 1849, Biddie in 1850, and twins Smith and Patterson in 1854. The oldest boy, John, died in 1841, at age twelve.

The Lives of Ephraim and Nancy Hatfield

Ephraim and Nancy Hatfield were typical Appalachians. Anse's father was 27 the year his fifth child was born, and Nancy Hatfield was 26 years old. Though no photograph of Ephraim has survived, historians have saved ideas about his huge frame and general appearance. He was known as "Big Eph" during his lifetime, which lasted from 1812 until 1881. One descendant jokingly claims that he was at least eight feet tall and weighed six hundred pounds. The more prosaic truth is that he was a mere six-feet-four inches and weighed only 260 pounds. Ephraim was considered a giant of his day, the "bully" of Mate Creek, and other proud Appalachian men often tested him in wrestling matches. The tales told of Big Eph Hatfield were like those of Paul Bunyan or other American folk heroes. He was a widely respected figure in the Tug Valley.

Nancy Vance Hatfield was the moral and intellectual equal of her husband. Her life spanned the eighty-two years between 1813 and 1895. Nancy was thought to be a "woods colt," the illegitimate daughter of the Rev. John Ferrell and Elizabeth (Betsy) Vance, who once lived in the neighborhood of Abingdon, Virginia, and who later moved to the Tug Fork region. Nancy looked like a Vance. She was tall and strong with handsome facial features. She was hawk-faced with a high forehead, a jutting nose, and a squared-off chin. Nancy looked like the pioneer woman that she was. She could read and write and owned a few books on medicine, so she became a skilled midwife, in much demand by her neighbors. That practice, and the general hospitality that marked generations of Hatfields, helped her children build the network of friendships that became so important during the Hatfield and McCoy feud. It is of interest in that light that eight of Nancy's grandchildren became doctors.

Ephraim and Nancy were in the prime of life and were physically strong when Anse was born, thanks to the difficult work of keeping a farm along the Tug Fork. They were independent because it was the common practice for neighbors to hold a house-raising for a newly married young couple. When a log house was built in that fashion and a farm established, the newlyweds of the 1830s had no debts because mortgages were unknown. If a man and woman were active and responsible parents, they could raise a family with only normal hardships.

Though general statements about families are a complicated matter, it is clear that Ephraim and Nancy Vance were, in a curious fashion, both strict and lenient toward their children. The parents expected the youngsters to work but wanted them to be happy.

The Importance of the Land

A mountaineer family worked together as an economic unit. Anse Hatfield and his brothers and sisters had the usual responsibilities of Mate Creek children.

The sons plowed fields, chopped and sawed trees, and kept the family supplied with water. The daughters cooked and cleaned. When the work was finished there was time for other interests. The younger Hatfields played childhood games and explored their surroundings. Both sexes fished, and the boys hunted. In that way, the first experiences Anse Hatfield had concerned the land. The land along Mate Creek meant work because farming was the livelihood. The land also meant pleasure because in his free time Anse could explore and hunt.

Those who have not spent time wandering through the hills of the Allegheny Plateau do not understand what it means to live there. Though ravaged now by over a century of coal mining, the land is awe-inspiring. It is a shaggy region where the rivers have many branches and where the hills fold and buckle against one another.

Geologists say that this vast region once was the bed of an ancient sea. When the Allegheny Mountains lifted from the sea some two hundred million years ago, the plateau rose with it in an undulating manner, creating scores of synclines and anticlines. As the seawater drained, the earth was carved into narrow ridges and valleys that eroded into the dark-forested hills that Anse Hatfield knew in his youth. The land rose from the sea so gradually that the rivers formed at the same time and cut their general courses on their way to the Ohio River without leaving their paths.

In imagination it is easy to think what the land meant to young Anse Hatfield. Between the year of his birth and the year he went to war, the highlands were densely wooded. Theodore Roosevelt and other historians who have written of the land during the pioneer era have described it as vast and beautiful.

Because that era was still alive in Anse's youth, it is most likely that he saw the land the same way as his immediate ancestors — a place of mystery and wonder where a man could hunt bears and deer in woods where the trees formed a canopy overhead and where the underbrush grew thick and rank. Anse Hatfield wandered through that land, learning which streams branched out of each hill and how tributaries led to the rivers. His first source of pride was his knowledge of the hills and his skill as a hunter.

So it is that the first tales we have about the life of Anse Hatfield are the tales his grandson told about bear hunting. That grandson was Coleman Alderson Hatfield, the son of William Anderson (Cap) Hatfield, Anse's most able son. The tales of Anse as a mighty hunter moved Coleman A. Hatfield. In his mature years, Coleman wrote manuscripts about Anse's life as keepsakes for future generations of Hatfields. In one such manuscript, Coleman wrote about how the forests affected the development of Anse's character and personality:

> As you might expect, one who was born and reared in the mountains more than a century ago, when the forest furnished food for every form of life that lived among the virgin trees and mighty rocks, a boy was well equipped by his nature to meet

every condition of the wild life which surrounded him. This is true of Anse Hatfield, a man of the timberland, one who loved the deep recesses of the forest, the clear waters and the food supply, not only game, but also every form of edible fruit and nut that he encountered.

Young Anderson was the embodiment of all that the influences of the wilderness could make out of a race of men in two hundred years. Going back from the time of his birth, not many years before the middle of the 19th century, it easily can be seen from his boyhood experiences bear-hunting that he was equal to every condition which confronted him as part of the life of people of his time.[4]

Coleman A. Hatfield wrote that such experiences furnished deep insights into the character of Anse, who believed himself to be invincible. Until his final years, Anse always wanted to take the lead among those who followed him. He wanted to be first on a bear's trail, and he scoffed at those who grew tired easily. While others complained of the cold winters or hot summers, Anse seldom felt the effects of bad weather. "Why, you can pound snow down my backside all day, and I'll never get cold," he said.[5] Anse said that he could go without sleep night after night and never weary and that when he had a job to do, he never got hungry.

Anse Hatfield's First Bear Hunt

That tirelessness was one of Anse Hatfield's characteristics from the beginning of his life, as shown by the way he acted when he hunted his first bear. That happened in the fall of 1854, the year that Anse was fifteen years old. Anse had told his mother he was going out to hunt squirrels, taking a rifle and some powder and shot. By suppertime, Nancy Hatfield was getting anxious, telling Big Eph that she was afraid Anse might have been hurt in an accident. At different times, Coleman A. Hatfield heard the part of the tale directly from Nancy Hatfield and the rest of it from Anse himself. Coleman told the first part of the tale in a way that saved the conversation between Anse's parents.

> Ephraim said, "Why, Nancy, you're always gettin' scared. That boy's all right. He's fifteen years old and plenty able to take care of himself. Why, he can do a man's work now and he's as stout as a bear."
>
> "Speakin' of bears, Ephraim," I said, "do you think a bear might have jumped on him in the woods?"
>
> "Nancy, I be burned if you don't get the silliest ideas in your head. A bear never jumps on anybody unless you have him

cornered and he has to fight his way out, or unless he's been crippled by a shot and you get close to him. Why, if a bear even gets a glimpse of a man in the woods then he goes the other way. Besides, Ansie has hunted so much that he's a dead shot. No bear is goin' to get in speakin' distance of him. Why, that boy, I've seen him shoot a squirrel's eye out in the top of a tall hickory when I couldn't even see the squirrel before it fell. He's not goin' to let any bear slip up and jump on his back."

"You know," says I, "Ephraim, I just study about Ansie sometimes. He doesn't want to do anything but hunt and be in the woods, tree wildcats, and follow bear tracks. When he's got the powder and ball he brings in all the squirrels he can carry. Why, he's worse to hunt than you were when you killed the old panther back when we were first married, and when he gets on a varmint's trail he just won't quit. I think we're feeding Ansie too much bear meat. He's gettin' so strong and big and growin' like a bear. His back and shoulders are so much like a bear that he busts out of his buckskin jacket and, besides, he can run up the hill as fast as most boys can on the level and climb a tree like a squirrel. I just get so worried about Ansie for fear he will fall and get killed."

"Now, Nancy," says Ephraim. "There you go worryin' your head about something that has never happened and maybe never will. That boy's got to grow up with the mountains and learn to take care of himself just like his old pappy did, and you know how that was when I killed that limb-founded panther with a butcher knife that I had in my scabbard."

"Well, I'll say this, Eafie. He's more like you than any of the boys."[6]

Nothing was decided then. Anse was gone all night and the next day. Nancy was more troubled than ever about her missing son. When Anse was still gone late in the morning of the second day, Big Eph told his older son Valentine, who was called "Wall," to saddle a horse and ride with him to Ben's Creek, where Anse's uncles lived near each other. Eph thought Anse might have gone to one of his uncle's homes for breakfast. By that time, the whole family had become anxious about Anse and a search party of family and neighbors was organized. In the meantime, Anse had been busy. Coleman recalled how Anse told the tale:

Yes, sir, I remember it like yesterday, when I went huntin' that October day. My dogs, Old Fife and Drum and Old Rounder and the rest of the pack got a big spike-horn buck lined out. I got a glimpse of him as he went over the top of the ridge. The last I heard of the hell-fired dogs, they were goin' out of hearin', barkin' "skally-hoop! skally-hoop!" — just a singin' a tune after that deer. I fired one shot as it topped the ridge, but it was too far away, and I might have even creased it at that. But in runnin' after them dogs, I fell and upset my shot pouch and didn't notice 'till I was a mile on my way that I had lost my shot. There I was with my gun shot empty, bullets lost, and that spike buck a-leadin' every dog I had clean out of the country.

So I walked along the top of the ridge on Big Pigeon Mountain for maybe an hour or two and, what did I see about sixty yards down under the top of the mountain but a big four-year-old bear asleep in a sinkhole full of leaves. I stood for a minute so mad I could have chawed a hickory saplin' off at the roots. Just to think, the first chance I ever had by myself at a bear with a good gun and a horn full of powder and no bullets. The longer I stood, the madder I got.

I just set that old squirrel gun down beside of a black pine tree and I tore down that hill a-kickin' the stuffings out of that bear nearly before he got his eyes open. I kicked his back end down that hill about twenty steps to a chestnut-oak. He was so flabbergasted that he took right up that big tree, and he never stopped 'till he got up to the forks about thirty feet off the ground with me havin' nothing to fight him with but my fists and a good pair of stompin' boots.

But that was the worst bluffed bear I ever saw as he sot down in the forks of that big tree lookin' back at me as if he was tryin' to figure out where I come from and what I had agin him by kickin' him up that tree. Well sir, I just took off my huntin' shirt and I whipped the body of that tree, and I hollered and hallooed at that bear to keep him up the tree.

In about two hours my dogs had given up the deer chase and had backtracked themselves and circled and found my sign where I had topped the ridge, and they come right to me and set in to barkin' at the bear, and it just looked like that it didn't have any mind to come down and face me and that gang of dogs.

I stayed there all day and all night and all the next day. I wasn't hungry nary hate, but I was just about starved to death for water. Well sir, it must have been after midnight. It was late in October and most of the leaves were down, and the moon had got high up, when I looked out along the ridge on Pigeon Mountain and I saw a light. I knowed it was a pine torch from the way they were carryin' it, and I started hootin' like an owl and they answered me. They could hear my dogs barkin' then, and they come right on out to me, and it was Brother Wallie and Pete Brooks.

They asked me if I was hurt, and I said, "Hurt? — the devil! The only one that got hurt here is a four-year-old bear. I kicked his behind so hard with my boot that he took to a tree."

My poor little mother had sent me some grub — a big piece of venison — and I didn't eat it. I divided it among my dogs because I wanted to take care of them first. I was so tickled to tree my first bear that I could have done without grub for a week.

They wanted me to come home without the bear and I said, "I'm gonna stay here until I get that bear's hide."

Wallie sent Pete back home to get some bullets and to give the word that my dogs and me were safe and sound. Then here come Pap with a whole gang of neighbors, and they give me a gourd full of water, and I took the corncob stopper out of the neck and downed every drop of it.

When we come down the ridge, we was a-totin' that old bear on a pole with four men at each end. To cap it all, they let me fire the shot that brought him out of the forks of that chestnut-oak.

Pap said I was spoiled to bear-huntin' now, and Mother never anymore objected to lettin' me have all the bear meat I wanted 'cause she said, "Anybody that's been raised on bear meat will never give up to nothin' nor the trail they are followin' atter."[7]

Anse Hatfield's Nickname

There are interesting aspects of that tale that concern Anse Hatfield's famous nickname, "Devil Anse." There have been many stories about the way he acquired the name. Some have suggested that he killed a panther in his youth and Nancy Hatfield then said, "That boy's not afraid of the devil himself." Others claim that his foe, Randal McCoy, once said Anse was "six feet of devil and 180 pounds of hell." Another tale is that he defended a certain locality called "Devil's Backbone" during the War Between the States. Still others argue that he was more worldly than others of his neighborhood, particularly a cousin who was called Preacher Anse Hatfield, and so was named "the Devil's Anse" for that reason. Perhaps most of those tales contain a seed of truth and the famous nickname was the result of those experiences.

Yet one should note well that when Wall Hatfield and Pete Brooks found Anse with his first bear in a tree and asked if he was hurt, Anse replied with the surprised statement, "Hurt? — the devil!" At the very least, that indicates that Anse had already thought of himself as fit to face the devil by 1854, when he was fifteen years old. When that information is recalled in the context of Nancy Hatfield's concerns for Anse, rather than admiration for his fearlessness, one thinks that Devil Anse may have invented his own nickname.

That knowledge in turn brings on speculation about Anse's character. Those who knew him well often spoke of Anse's sense of humor. He was inclined to tease his family and other acquaintances. The element of deviltry was strong in him. Appalachian men of Anse's time were in the habit of testing one another in wrestling matches. Anse was the winner far more often than a loser and pinned many opponents. One great-grandson is fond of the tale that Anse would use his thick, coarse, reddish-brown beard to scratch an opponent's face after he pinned him, rather as a bear marks its prey after killing it. Though no one can argue successfully that Anse was a "devil may care" character, he may have had the idea "if a devil he was, a devil he would be," taking much delight in the nickname.

Others understood that aspect of Anse as well. His younger brothers, Smith and Patterson Hatfield, referred to Anse in a joking manner as the "boogerman." Coleman A. Hatfield recalled one of his great uncles saying that he needed to go to "the boogerman's house" for some forgotten article. When Anse died in January 1921, one of the Hatfield twins said later that spring that the copperheads and rattlesnakes were getting thick on Island Creek since the boogerman left the woods, leaving no one behind to control the snakes.

Another who felt the edge of Anse's humor was George Swain, who wrote a Logan County history. Anse was one of the dignitaries on a political platform about 1916 when Swain was the master of ceremonies. Swain, fearing that he might hurt Anse's feelings, or worse, offend Anse by using the devil nickname, referred to Hatfield as "Uncle Anse." Anse stepped to the lectern and said, "I want you folks to know my name is Devil Anse Hatfield." That may have been humor or Anse may have been warning Swain not to take him too lightly.[8]

However the nickname evolved, it fit the man. Anse was as large, as clownish, and as dangerous as a bear. Using his rather high-pitched, nasal voice, he told tall tales about himself, amusing those close to him, winning friends with his humor, and entertaining first acquaintances such as Theron C. Crawford of *The New York World.* "I don't belong to any church, unless it is the great church of the world," Anse told Crawford. "You might say it is the devil's church that I belong to," he added. The younger Hatfields broke up in a riot of laughter at Anse's comment.[9]

The Importance of Experience and Education

A third significant characteristic that was part of Anse's personality was his versatility, which had an effect on his later life when he fought in the Civil War, established his farm, raised his children, fought the feud, and enjoyed a peaceful old age. It was necessary for a farm boy to know how to handle various chores.

Besides his work chopping wood, plowing fields, and carrying water, Anse needed to handle livestock, particularly horses. Besides becoming a deadly marksman with a rifle, he also became a skilled rider, which was something that his fellow Appalachians admired.

Another matter that should be considered when evaluating Anse as a young man is the question of education. Records of education on the Tug Fork are scanty because the minutes of the Logan County Court that were kept before the Civil War were destroyed when the Union army burned the courthouse in 1862. Some general statements are possible. When Virginia's Literary Fund was established, the people of the Tug and the Guyandot established small schoolhouses where teachers instructed their students in the proverbial three R's. Such schools were kept during the winter months, after the crops had been harvested but before new seed was planted.

Schools of that type did not give youngsters like Anse anything like an adequate education by the standards of later days. Yet one who finished six years of school, who could read and write, and who could do basic arithmetic, could get along well enough in the rural life of Appalachia. It is a mistake to think that those who lacked formal education dwelt in a world of ignorance. The Appalachians of the time learned about life by living.

Anse seemed to fit that mold. It is true that he did not attend school many years. It is true that he did not learn to read or write. He did learn basic math, although only in a practical sense, such as figuring how many feet of lumber could be cut from a tree of a certain size. Another error is thinking that because Anse did not attend school on Mate Creek that he did not appreciate how life could be enhanced by education. Later in life, Anse was one of the supervisors of a schoolhouse on Mate Creek and was one of those who hired schoolteachers to conduct classes. Anse did his best to make education available to his children and grandchildren.

For all that, Anse's education was meager. One recalls Squire Boone — the father of legendary frontiersman Daniel Boone — making the comment about his famous son, "Let the girls do the reading and Dan'l will do the hunting." Anse Hatfield was the same type youngster. From the scanty available evidence, it seems that Ephraim and Nancy Hatfield would have liked for Anse to have a formal education, but also thought that if he learned to take care of himself Anse could lead a useful life.[10]

In addition to Anse's humor and practical knowledge, there were other aspects of his character that emerged before he became a character in history through his activities in the Civil War. For example, we know that he was "shifty" in the original Elizabethan-era meaning of the word. "Shifty" in that sense does not imply deviousness or unreliability. Rather, the word was used in Anse's era to denote someone who was the opposite of shiftless. Through his long life, Anse exhibited a willingness to take on new enterprises, especially those that might make money. He was "shifty" in the sense of being ambitious and looking for new opportunities.[11]

When one thinks about that point, it becomes important to know something about the economic nature of the Tug Fork, Levisa Fork, and Guyandot River areas between the 1820s and the 1850s. Historians and biographers should ask what those valleys were like during Anse's youth, particularly because many such writers have failed to understand that time and place. Such writers have lent credence to the popular misconception of "hillbillies." The very word is odious to many mountaineers, in part because it contributes to the common misunderstanding of the Appalachian region of the eastern United States early in the nineteenth century.

The Economic Life of the Hill Country

When the first Hatfields and their neighbors settled the Tug Fork, the United States had not yet developed the market economy that became the most notable economic feature of Andrew Jackson's America. Forces were at work, however, that would determine the industrial future of the nation. In the 1790s, a Philadelphian named Tench Coxe presented a paper to the organization that later became the American Philosophical Society. Coxe argued that anthracite coal was plentiful in northeastern Pennsylvania and could become the fuel of the future if the resource was given proper management.

Coxe was quite correct. Anthracite coal did become an important fuel and began replacing the charcoal used to smelt iron in Pennsylvania before the 1830s. When railroads became a practical matter after the 1820s, the anthracite field was developed quickly and, indeed, became a prime example of the products that formed the backbone of the market economy. With timber, which was still readily available in the eastern United States at the time, anthracite coal met the energy needs of early American industries.

That point should be kept in mind while thinking about the economic position of Appalachia in early America. The only two products that would find a market for Appalachians were timber and coal. Like other Americans, the people of the Tug wanted to benefit from the shift to the market economy. The rugged terrain hindered them, but they could see the possibilities in timber and coal.

In 1852, when Anse Hatfield was 13 years old, a young Philadelphian arrived in the Guyandot Valley to try to make a fortune in coal. His name was Thomas Dunn English, most famous now as a literary enemy of Edgar Allan Poe. English had the financial backing of New Yorkers who wanted to cash in on the popularity of cannel coal (a substance that burned as easily as a candle), a rather scarce form of nearly pure carbon that had been found in Virginia's Kanawha Valley and other localities.[12]

English moved to the seat of Logan County, then called Lawnsville and later renamed Aracoma at English's suggestion. English incorporated coal companies such as the Otetiani Cannel Coal Company and the Methcomah Cannel Coal Company, which at one time held coal leases that totaled 11,000 acres.[13] English's dreams of a coal empire failed, though historians do not know why.[14]

During the same decade, however, the Guyandotte Navigation Company moved into the region and acquired 330,000 acres of coal land in the areas of present day Logan and Lincoln counties. That New York-based firm dammed the Guyandot River between the towns of Barboursville and Chapmanville and shipped coal on barges during the twelve years between 1849 and 1861 before Civil War troop movements destroyed the operation.[15]

Among the many people who knew about those matters was George Rogers Clark Floyd, a pioneer of the Tug Fork section who later encouraged the development of railroads in the region. Floyd was the father of John B. Floyd, who was one of the Hatfields' most powerful political friends during the feud years. George R.C. Floyd was also the mentor of Henry D. Hatfield, who became West Virginia's governor after the election of 1912. Henry D. Hatfield was the son of Elias Hatfield and the double nephew of Anse Hatfield.[16]

One result of this economic activity is the impact it would have had on Anse Hatfield's life. By the time Anse was coming of age, young men were floating timber down the mountain streams to markets in Catlettsburg and Ironton at the mouth of the Big Sandy River on the Ohio River. Such young men heard news from their acquaintances at the river ports or heard of reports in the improving newspapers that were distributed along the Ohio River between Pittsburgh and Cincinnati.[17]

With that knowledge at hand, the popular image of the mountain-locked and ignorant "hillbilly" disappears. Anse and his contemporaries were Americans of their time. They were limited in formal education but were practical and aware and concerned about the direction of their lives. When the issues of slavery, states' rights, and the nation's future came to a boil in the 1860s, the young men of that time and place joined the armies along with the rest of the nation's young men.

The Towns Of Southwestern Virginia And Eastern Kentucky

Another aspect of Anse's early life is the nature of the communities and the county seats of his day. There were few towns of any importance along the Tug Fork. Welch did not exist in McDowell County until the arrival of the coal industry at the beginning of the twentieth century. Mingo County and Williamson were not created until the same time. Bluefield was a hamlet in Mercer County. Aracoma — later the city of Logan — affected Anse's life in a slight manner. Pikeville was the seat of Pike County in Kentucky and also would be important in Anse's life.

Aracoma developed from a geographic location known as "Islands of the Guyandot" to a village called Lawnsville, to a town named Aracoma during the lives of Big Eph and Devil Anse Hatfield. It was called "Islands of the Guyandot" until 1827, then became Lawnsville that year. It was renamed Aracoma in 1853 and became the City of Logan in 1907, the year Anse Hatfield was 68 years old.[18]

The first significant citizen of the place was a ginseng and fur merchant named Anthony Lawson. Lawson was born in Northumberland, England, about 1780 and emigrated to the United States about 1815 with his wife and four sons. He settled first at Alexandria, Virginia, but by the early 1820s, Lawson met Andrew Beirne, a merchant of Monroe County, Virginia — later West Virginia. Beirne, a dour man with thick lips, a hooked nose, a shrewd aspect, and a pock-marked face, persuaded Lawson to go to the wilds of the Guyandot River and open a trading post.[19]

Lawson arrived at the confluence of Island Creek and the Guyandot River in the early 1820s, just in time to witness the creation of Logan County from sections of Giles, Tazewell, Cabell, and Kanawha Counties in 1824. He became a member of the first Logan County Court and persuaded that body to locate the county seat conveniently near his general store.[20]

Before Lawson died in the town of Guyandotte at the river's mouth during a return trip from Philadelphia in 1846, he had seen his village grow into an interesting spot. W.H. Brockenbough, a visitor in the 1840s, described it as a village situated in a fertile bottom at a bend of the Guyandot River, surrounded by mountains abounding in coal and stone. Its features included a courthouse, a clerk's office, a jail, two taverns, two stores, a smithery, a shoe-maker's shop, and private homes. By the best estimate, there could not have been more than twenty buildings in the village.[21]

The community was once disturbed by the War Between the States. Though it is true that a devastating flood on the Guyandot River washed away the public buildings in the spring of 1861 and that the courthouse was burned during the war, the town of Aracoma after that flood and fire was much like the village of Lawnsville before the trouble began. It is a common theme in American history that the people try to return to normality after a war. In Appalachia then, that meant that the people went back to raising their crops and selling what they did not eat in market towns like Aracoma.

Yet the town was considered the focus of government during its days as a county seat in Virginia and during the early years of West Virginia's history. In that era, before the state court system was reorganized by the legislature in 1880, the most important branch of government was the county court, which combined fiscal and judicial duties. In its small brick courthouse, that court presumed to act as a government for nearly nine hundred square miles of surrounding mountain land.[22]

In modern America, local and state and national government is considered an active presence in the lives of its citizens. That was not the way of life in Logan County during the twenty years between the war and the feud. Instead, the county court was lucky if its three members could meet once a month. Circuit judges — who literally rode a circuit of three counties or more back then — were not in the county seat more than four weeks each year to hear important robbery or murder cases.[23]

Those facts explain a lot about the lives of the Hatfields. Families like the ones who lived on Mate Creek took care of their own affairs. There were, at most, half a dozen families living in range of each other. For the most part, they left each other alone, except when their children wanted to marry. Disputes that arose were settled on an individual basis. If there was serious trouble, a person of good reputation or authority, like Big Ephraim Hatfield, stepped in to take care of the matter. Government was remote in their lives.

Pikeville, Kentucky, the second seat of government that would be important in Anse's life, followed a course somewhat different than Lawnsville's, although the two towns had much in common by the time the war began. William Robert Leslie, an erstwhile hunting companion of Daniel Boone, was the first to leave his mark on Pike County, establishing his home on Johns Creek, a tributary of the Big Sandy River that flows through Pike County. The region of today's Pike County was part of Mason County when Kentucky became a state. The territory then became a part of Floyd County before Pike County was created by the Kentucky legislature in 1821.[24]

Three years later, in 1824, the same year Logan County was formed in Virginia, the town of Pikeville was established. The Kentucky legislature passed the act creating that town in the vicinity of Chloe Creek on December 1, 1823. There was a matter of some dispute about who owned the property. Pike County's latest historian wrote:

> The commissioners met on the day before Christmas 1823 and agreed on a site opposite the mouth of Lower Chloe on land owned by Elijah Adkins, who donated one acre of land to the county for the courthouse and jail to be built. Elijah Adkins was later awarded the first river ferry authorized by the court in 1825 across the river from the site of the courthouse in Pikeville.[25]

Like Lawnsville, Pikeville grew slowly. When the war began, it was a marketing crossroads surrounded by farms owned by the children of the Appalachian explorers and others who settled in the Sandy Valley. Such towns were unpretentious places, though "court days" and election days were lively times when the citizens would renew friendships and rivalries before returning to everyday farm chores.[26]

Anse Hatfield and His Family

Knowing such facts about Appalachia, historians can understand Anse Hatfield as a young man. He had a sense of responsibility, but he was a free spirit. He was shrewd and versatile. He was vigorous. He loved the outdoors. Anse had become a skillful marksman and a good horseman. He was a great deal like his father, Ephraim Hatfield. Anse knew about the growing market economy of the nation and understood that timbering was a way to make money. He was practical, though his education was limited.

Other questions remain, however, about Anse's youth. Those questions involve the way he saw himself as a member of the Hatfield family and the way he may have related to his ancestors. Altina L. Waller wrote in *Feud* that there might have been some conflict between Anse and Ephraim Hatfield.[27] Her evidence was that Ephraim Hatfield did not grant Anse his own land when the son came of age. That is not impossible. The two men seemed to have similar characteristics and could have been rivals.

Later Hatfields argue with that idea. Coleman C. Hatfield, Anse's great-grandson, states that the common Appalachian family pattern was for the older children to go out on their own rather early in life and win their place in the world, while the younger children remained closer to home and took care of the parents in their old age.[28] If that was true for the Hatfield children, Ephraim and Nancy may have felt Anse asserted his independence during the Civil War and was capable of taking care of himself.

Another significant point in that argument was that Ephraim Hatfield lived until 1881, when Anse was 42 years old. Nancy Hatfield did not die until 1895, when Anse was 56 years old. The parents may well have believed that their highly independent son did not need guidance after 1861. In either case, Anse was not one to let anyone make his decisions for him after the age of 15.

The Importance of Eph-of-All Hatfield

Even more important is the way Anse related to his great-grandfather, the first Ephraim Hatfield in Tug Fork history. That Ephraim Hatfield was one of the colorful and largely forgotten characters of the Appalachian pioneer era, and he may have been Anse Hatfield's first hero. He is known in family lore as "Eph-of-All," signifying that he was the common ancestor of later Hatfields. There are no known portraits of him, but the thought that he was a hefty and muscular man makes common sense.[29]

Eph-of-All's most notable achievement was his rescue of Anna Musick from a band of Shawnee Indians in the 1790s. That tale deserves full treatment and will receive it soon. For now, it is enough to know that it was one of the common stories that pioneer families told each other. Eph-of-All Hatfield passed away in

June 1855 at the age of 90. He was buried a few miles from the Mate Creek home of Big Eph Hatfield.

Anse, who was in his sixteenth year when his great-grandfather died, may have heard the tale of Eph-of-All's rescue of Anna Musick from the old man's own lips. If so, Anse may have had an idol to emulate. Eph-of-All was an able, independent, and heroic Appalachian who took care of his kin and neighbors and who cut a dashing figure in regional history. Anse may have believed the old man was what a hero should be — one who protected his own. More than that, Eph-of-All may have served as Anse's bridge into history, a particularly interesting American past that was two centuries old in 1839, which forms the background for this tale.

---

[1] Logan Centennial Booklet, "Hatfield Pioneers," Coleman A. Hatfield.
[2] Tales of the Feuding Hatfields, "Introduction," Coleman A. Hatfield.
[3] Tales of the Feuding Hatfields, "Introduction," Coleman A. Hatfield.
[4] Anse Hatfield, The Mighty Hunter, Coleman A. Hatfield.
[5] Anse Hatfield, The Mighty Hunter, Coleman A. Hatfield.
[6] Anse Hatfield, The Mighty Hunter, Coleman A. Hatfield.
[7] Anse Hatfield, The Mighty Hunter, Coleman A. Hatfield.
[8] Lest We Forget, George T. Swain.
[9] An American Vendetta, T.C. Crawford.
[10] Coleman C. Hatfield Interviews.
[11] Coleman C. Hatfield Interviews.
[12] Coleman C. Hatfield Interviews.
[13] "Otetiani" was the Iroquois Indian name for the individual known to many historians as "Red Jacket." Red Jacket was one nephew of Chief Logan, whose family was murdered in 1774, one of the precipitating incidents of Lord Dunmore's War fought in the Ohio River country that year.
[14] The Land of the Guyandot, Robert Y. Spence.
[15] The Land of the Guyandot, Robert Y. Spence.
[16] West Virginia: A Bicentennial History, John Alexander Williams.
[17] Coleman C. Hatfield Interviews.
[18] The Land of the Guyandot, Robert Y. Spence.
[19] History of Logan County, Henry Clay Ragland.
[20] History of Logan County, Henry Clay Ragland.
[21] New and Comprehensive Gazetteer of Virginia, Joseph Martin.
[22] The Transformation of the Tug and Guyandot Valleys, E.A. Cubby.
[23] The Logan Circuit Court, Cush C. Chambers.
[24] Pike County: A Very Different Place, William David Deskins.
[25] Pike County: A Very Different Place, William David Deskins.
[26] The Logan Circuit Court, Cush C. Chambers.
[27] Feud: Hatfields, McCoys, and Social Change in Appalachia 1860-1900, Altina L. Waller.
[28] Coleman C. Hatfield Interviews.
[29] Coleman C. Hatfield Interviews.

Chapter Two
ANCESTORS OF THE DEVIL
The Hatfields in American History

HEROIC Appalachia haunts the Hatfield family. They remember — those who dwell in the starlight of its history — the tales of the clan: from Eph-of-All Hatfield's rescue of a young woman who became his wife, to the family's removal to the Tug Fork after hearing a brother-in-law describing the wild game of the region, to Big Ephraim Hatfield killing a panther single-handed, though armed only with a hunting knife. To understand the Hatfields, one must know the wild romance of pioneer America.

There are stirring words in T.K. Whipple's book *Study Out The Land* that may be the most fitting way to begin telling about the family that fought North America's most famous feud. Whipple wrote that the starting point of American history was the pioneer experience and such history must echo the spirit of Francis Parkman and Frederick Jackson Turner.

"All America lies at the end of the wilderness road, and our past is not a dead past, but still lives in us," Whipple wrote. "Our forefathers had civilization inside themselves, the wild outside. We live in the civilization they created, but within us the wilderness still lingers. What they dreamed, we live, and what they lived, we dream."[1]

The Hatfields In Colonial Virginia

That tale began in Virginia, the mother of the South. The first Hatfield to locate his home in the colony of Virginia was Thomas Hatfield, who appeared along with others at the quarter session court at Jamestown on the ninth day of February 1626. That day Hatfield filed a petition asking permission to leave the barren land and a decayed house at a place named Pasbehayes and establish a new home on the Charles River.[2] Joseph Hatfield left the community and moved to Elizabeth City County, Virginia, where he leased land on October 31, 1633.[3]

The scanty records indicate that the descendants of Joseph Hatfield then followed the Wilderness Road from Richmond, Virginia, to the Allegheny plateau of southwest Virginia, eastern Kentucky, and eastern Tennessee, though the Hatfields stopped for a generation or two on the way. The records also show that William Hatfield made a will in Southampton County, Virginia, in 1755, and that Josiah Hatfield recorded his will in the same county in 1778.[4] The Hatfields of the feud era and afterwards believed that they descended from Thomas

Hatfield and that William and Josiah and Captain Andrew Hatfield were pioneer members of the clan.

Captain Andrew Hatfield first appears in the records in Botetourt County, Virginia, in 1770. Some years before 1770, Andrew moved with his family to what is now Giles County, Virginia, and settled on Big Stoney Creek, a tributary of the New River, where his family built the Hatfield Fort as an outpost to guard against Indian attacks.

Captain Thomas Burke was placed in charge of that fort before 1773, and Captain Andrew was a member of Burke's company who was at the battle of Point Pleasant, the climactic event of Lord Dunmore's War that was fought on October 10, 1774 — the last struggle of colonial North America or the first of the Revolution (choose your historian). When the American Revolution began, Andrew served in the Virginia militia and became a captain on November 6, 1781.[5]

The importance of that information is found in the fact that the Hatfield men had become able and self-reliant pioneer explorers and Indian fighters on the frontier before the American Revolution. Those men would play a significant role in creating the United States. Though the links between Captain Andrew Hatfield and Ephraim Hatfield have not been established to the satisfaction of genealogists, it was the belief of Ephraim's descendants that they were closely related to the militia captain. The research of Coleman A. Hatfield led him to think that connection was very close.

> Captain Andrew Hatfield had brothers Joseph, George, and Jeremiah, and probably others. Joseph was a revolutionary soldier and a member of the company of Captain William Campbell, who was a commanding officer at the battle of Kings Mountain.
>
> At the time of the Revolution this Joseph Hatfield was living in what is now Russell County, Virginia, and his brothers George and Jeremiah were living in what is now Smyth County, Virginia, they having acquired land there on December 6, 1774.
>
> These three brothers left Virginia and went to Campbell County, Tennessee, about 1795. Joseph Hatfield died on August 26, 1832, and his widow, Rachael, was granted a pension and bounty land in Campbell County for his services in the Revolutionary War.
>
> In support of her application for a pension, Rachael offered the testimony of neighbors, the Crabtrees, Musicks, and Smiths. Richard Crabtree testified, "Joseph Hatfield was considered the best spy and woodsman on the western frontier." The widow Rachael died on May 19, 1858, at the age of 105.[6]

The Ancestry of Ephraim Hatfield

At that point a mystery arises in the tale of the Hatfields who settled Tug Fork. Because Captain Andrew and Joseph Hatfield were considered frontier heroes, there is a great temptation to believe that Andrew and Joseph had a relative who became the father of Eph-of-All Hatfield about 1765. Others are not as certain the connection is that close. Historians and biographers can only note that the descendants of Eph-of-All Hatfield believed his ancestors moved down the Wilderness Road from Tidewater, Virginia; that the Hatfields were noted frontier warriors and explorers, and that Ephraim was a man of ability and fame as an Appalachian pioneer.[7]

Coleman A. Hatfield, who assembled the most careful research into the question, believed that Eph-of-All Hatfield's father was named John Hatfield. A lawyer as well as a gifted writer, Coleman searched the records of Virginia for forty years and reached a conclusion he believed was right, though he could not find documentary evidence that would meet the requirements of scholarly research or genealogical societies.

When Coleman began a history of his family in the 1940s, his starting point was the life of the first Ephraim Hatfield, whom he called "the settler." His tale proceeded smoothly, taking note of all the records he had studied:

> Ephraim Hatfield's history, so far as we know it, began in Russell County shortly after the close of the Revolutionary War. We find where Ephraim Hatfield and his wife, Mary, joined in a deed of conveyance to Ali Smith and Andrew Smith, as recorded in the county clerk's office of Russell County in the year 1786.
>
> Ephraim Hatfield's wife appears to have been named Mary. Her father was Ericus Smith. He had settled on a two hundred acre tract of land on Thompson's Creek, New Garden District, Russell County, in 1774. Ten years later, the Virginia House of Burgesses decreed that inasmuch as he had been a settler for ten years, that he had taken legal title to the land.
>
> In 1786, it appears by inference that Smith had died and his widow, Rachael Smith, and some of her family, conveyed the farm of two hundred acres to two of the sons. It appears further that she had a daughter, Rachael Smith, who had married Joseph Hatfield of Lee County, Virginia, as mentioned in the deed.
>
> Ephraim's father was John, according to my family history. It may be found among the court annals of Russell County that John Hatfield is mentioned in some two of three places, particularly where he received bounties for killing wolves. We have no record of John Hatfield ever having visited the Sandy River country or anywhere near the Kentucky and West Virginia border.[8]

The Importance of the Virginia Frontier

Whoever Eph-of-All's parents were, the child was born into a violent world. The era of American history that preceded Ephraim's birth is well-known. The vital developments were determined in large part by European history. In 1753, the final and most murderous war between France and England — rivals for possession of North America — began when young George Washington became embroiled in a gallant and foolhardy conflict with French troops near the spot where the Allegheny and Monongahela Rivers flow together to create the Ohio River.[9]

The seven years that followed saw the French and their Algonquian Indian allies driven to the wall by their English, American, and Iroquois foes. On September 13, 1759, England's General James Wolfe and the Marquis de Montcalm, the French defender of the citadel of Quebec, died within an hour of one another as control of North America passed to the English. Though the formal Treaty of Paris that ended the war was not signed by the European governments until 1763, the battle on the Plains of Abraham at Quebec assured that young Ephraim Hatfield would grow up in an age when free spirits would question English colonial policies.[10]

One of the most important decisions that followed the surrender of the French became part of the Treaty of Paris. That was the provision called the "Proclamation Line" that presumed to limit the acquisition of lands and the creation of new settlements further west than the crest of the Allegheny Mountains. The rather stiff legalistic language of the treaty may have been unknown to the parents of Ephraim Hatfield, but the intention was clear. The English government decided that no colonial governor could "grant warrants of survey or pass patents for any lands beyond the heads or sources of any of the rivers which fall into the Atlantic Ocean from the west or northwest...."[11]

Given the nature of American frontiersmen, England's government had as much chance of making that ruling binding as it did making the Ohio River's water flow east. The Hatfield family and thousands like them were hungry for both freedom and land, a fact known too well by the sachems and war leaders of the Shawnee nation.

On the eve of the battle of Point Pleasant, Shawnee leader Cornstalk stood before his assembled warriors with a piece of oak bark in his hands. Twisting the bark, Cornstalk told the Shawnees that they could have treated the white men in that manner at one time. The Englishmen had become so powerful in America, Cornstalk argued, that the Shawnees would be crushed if the Indians fought alone.[12]

Indeed, as early as 1756, the third year of the French and Indian War, the Shawnees were assaulted by the Virginia government in a way that prefigured the storm which would break out upon the Ohio River thirty years later. On February

18, 1756, Andrew Lewis led 340 men from Camp Frederick on the New River near Ingles Ferry to strike at the Shawnees' backdoor on the Ohio River.[13]

The "Sandy Creek Expedition," as this was named, was an ignominious failure. The Big Sandy River flooded that month and, when rations gave out, morale gave out with it. On March 15, the officers voted to disband the expedition someplace along the Tug Fork — which received its name from the fact the men had to boil the "tugs" or their leather straps for food. The men straggled home as the expedition ended in that unfortunate manner.[14]

The importance of the "Sandy Creek Expedition" is that it demonstrated to the Shawnees that the Allegheny Mountains were not a safe barrier to prevent the spread of the frontiersmen who were anxious to explore, hunt, and eventually possess the land west of the mountains. Before long, "the long hunters," Daniel Boone and young Simon Kenton would carry their Kentucky rifles into the region of the Big Sandy and Tug Fork. This knowledge sparked the Shawnee war of 1774 to 1814 that would end only when the Shawnee power was crushed after the death of Tecumseh in 1813. The Shawnees rightly feared that the frontiersmen would take the Ohio River Valley and environs from the tribe.

Tecumseh, whose father was killed in the battle at Point Pleasant in 1774, realized that all Indians of the eastern woodlands would lose their homes if they did not unite. He spent the remainder of his life organizing an Indian confederacy, which failed after unwise followers fought the Battle of Tippecanoe against William Henry Harrison in 1812.

In that rough world, a man was forced to handle firearms as well as farm tools. A good livelihood depended on hunting. A family's safety depended on a good rifle and accurate marksmanship. For that reason, the most dramatic tale of Eph-of-All Hatfield's was his rescue of Anna Musick from the hands of Shawnees in the summer of 1792.

The Rescue of Anna Musick

That summer, Ephraim Hatfield was typical of the pioneers of the Clinch and Holstein River Valleys. He had married Mary Smith, probably shortly before the year 1785. It seems the young couple had four children — Joseph, born in 1787; Aike, in 1788; Valentine, in 1789; and Bridgett, or Biddie, born about 1790. Aike died young in a hunting accident, as we shall see very soon. Mary Smith Hatfield died in late 1791 or early 1792. As a widower, Eph-of-All had his hands full taking care of his children and farming his land. Then in the summer of 1792, the Shawnees struck the settlement near Honaker, Virginia. Coleman A. Hatfield told the story:

> On August 12, 1792, David Musick lived on what was then the frontier on Thompson Creek, Russell County, Virginia. Early in the morning of that day his home was besieged by a

band of Shawnee Indians, their headquarters being the Scioto Valley far away in the Ohio Territory.

Two of the boys had gone out to gather wood for the fire when they discovered the savages skulking near, ready for a dash toward the cabin. The children returned quickly, and the father directed that the doors be barred while he undertook to load his flintlock gun.

As the Indians charged the house, Musick had difficulty with his rifle. As he held his weapon in place, his wife brought a bit of fire from the embers in an effort to ignite the powder in the firing pan on the breech of the old gun, but the fire failed, and Musick was critically wounded by an arrow from one of the redmen.

They immediately sprang upon him with their tomahawks, and he was murdered in the presence of the affrighted wife and children. His widow, Anna, and their five children were carried away by the Indians.[15]

The Shawnee band was not anxious to leave, perhaps indicating that the Musicks lived some considerable distance from any neighbors. The Indians had trouble catching one of the Musicks' horses, which was loose in the pasture. After surrounding the horse, they creased its nose with an arrow and brought it under control. The Shawnees then butchered a steer, made a bag out of the hide, filled the bag with choice beef, and set the oldest Musick boy on a horse to go back to the Ohio country. Coleman A. Hatfield wrote:

The oldest son, a bright boy of twelve years with his fine head of red hair, was looked upon by the Indians with favor, as they had dreams of adopting him into their tribe as a future chief. They ate the meat from the fresh-killed beef without cooking it and required the poor mother and her children to eat raw meat for their food.

The smallest child of the Musick family, a boy of five years, cried and refused to eat the uncooked meat. Whereupon one of the savages cruelly grasped the child and jammed his face against a rough tree, causing lacerations, which left lifelong scars on the boy's face.[16]

An old man of the surrounding area learned of the raid and ran a few miles for help. He was overcome with exhaustion and fright, and he dropped dead at the doorway, though he was able to murmur a few words about the fate of the Musick family. A rescue party set out to save the Musicks and, about nightfall, learned that the Indians and their captives were camped on an island near the present town of Haysi, Dickinson County, Virginia. Coleman A. Hatfield added:

The Musicks heard one English-speaking Indian say that they would camp on the island because, "No white man come here." However, the posse of frontiersmen discovered the camping party at daybreak on the following day.

The brave little widow, seeing her rescuers, grabbed her smallest child and dashed toward the white men. One Indian threw his tomahawk at her, barely missing the mother and child as they ran for safety. One of the Indians was killed by the white men, and the others fled into the forest.[17]

Thus it is that the tale of the Hatfields who settled along the Tug Fork began with high drama. The family history began with a man trying to find a good home for himself in a new world. As time passed, his descendants became noted men on the American frontier. As more time went by, one Hatfield saved a family from captivity and perhaps sudden death beneath a tomahawk or scalping knife. The Hatfields had entered history at that particular time and place. It is important to understand the circumstances when the family came to the land of the Tug Fork.

The Hatfields on the Tug Fork

Andrew Lewis' "Sandy Creek Expedition" of 1756 seems to have been the first time the Virginia frontiersmen explored the Tug Fork of the Big Sandy River. The stream was designated the border of Virginia and Kentucky in 1792 when surveyors were given instructions to mark the line at the largest river. The flood-prone Tug Fork was swollen that year and was chosen as the border because it was thought to be a larger stream than the Guyandot River.

Eph-of-All Hatfield seems to have become interested in the Tug Fork region after it was explored by a half-brother of his first wife, Mary Smith Hatfield. The half-brother was known as Tom Smith, who lives in history as one of the frontier mysteries. It was not uncommon for men wanted by the law to go to the backwoods of Virginia and Pennsylvania. The far-famed Simon Kenton did so after fighting William Leach near Hopewell, Virginia. Kenton fled, thinking that he had killed Leach. Coleman A. Hatfield thought Tom Smith had a similar experience and wrote about that episode.

> The story is that Tom Smith came from Virginia down into the Tug River country. With whom he traveled or migrated, I do not know. But he was supposed to have been a half-brother to Ephraim Hatfield's wife, or some relationship of that sort; he went back to Virginia and told them about the territory in the Tug River country, and the prospects of good hunting and of a

place to establish homes. It was by reason of Tom Smith's trip down in here that Ephraim later moved.

There is also a story that Tom Smith had had some trouble of some sort in Virginia and came in this country dodging the law. I would say that he came down here with other settlers who were out to find a home across the mountains in the territory which had been wrested from the Indians as a result of the peace that was made between the Shawnees and the others along about 1794.[18]

The Hatfields believed that Eph-of-All liked the land explored by his brother-in-law so much that he moved there soon after 1792, or maybe just before 1800. That point has been disputed. The Russell County, Virginia, tax records indicate Eph-of-All owned property there as late as 1820. He may, in fact, have followed his sons Valentine and Joseph to the Tug Fork area.

At that time there were seven children in the care of Ephraim and Anna: the five children of David Musick, along with Joseph and Valentine Hatfield. Bridgett, the daughter of Ephraim and Mary Hatfield, had died, and young Aike Hatfield had been killed in a hunting accident. The tale of Aike's death, as told by Coleman A. Hatfield is worth knowing.

> There is a story among the Hatfields that one Ericus Hatfield, who was called "Eric" or "Aike" accidentally stabbed himself in the thigh while undertaking to bleed a deer that he had wounded and was attempting to hold and pierce with his hunting knife. The story is told that he was found in the mountains where he had bled to death without being able to return to his home.
>
> This must have been sometime after the year 1813 because Ericus in the year 1813 lists himself in the tax books as having one tithe and no property. The record is silent soon after that time. We must conclude, therefore, that Ericus was born in 1788 and that he was the second son of Ephraim.[19]

If Coleman's information was correct, that means young Aike Hatfield died by cutting his femoral artery sometime in his 25th year. By that time, it is likely that the Ephraim, Anna, and their children were living on Tug Fork. Though exact knowledge is not available, it is possible to write with reasonable accuracy about the general conditions of the time when the Hatfields moved to Blackberry Creek. A view of that society is needed to understand the dramatic events that followed the Hatfields in their later history. Another manuscript written by Coleman A. Hatfield sheds light on those times.

> It has been explained that the unsettled territory which remained with Virginia and which comprised old Fincastle

County (not including Kentucky County) was settled through the encouragement of the Virginia Colony. Home seekers who lived in the new counties were encouraged to move westward in order to settle up the new portions of the country...as far west as the Ohio River and south of the Big Sandy.[20]

The Nature of Life on the Tug Fork

Apparently, Ephraim and Anna were caught up in this social movement, since they seem to have been among the first to live along Blackberry Creek. It is not known whether or not the young couple had neighbors. If they did, it is likely the Hatfields had help setting up their new home through the pleasant pioneer custom of a house-raising. If no one lived nearby, it is a tribute to their independence that they built their own house and established their farm. Coleman A. Hatfield wrote paragraphs that paid tribute to Ephraim and Anna's essential characteristic.

> It must be borne in mind that in many respects, the settlers of the hills are greatly different from others of the open country. It is true that many handicaps have impeded their progress through the years that have gone by, but their story is the history of the making of a race.
>
> Honesty has been one of their cardinal virtues. Whatever you may say about mountain people, you are bound to admit from anything you may know or find out about them that they have been men and women of integrity.
>
> Their work has been hard in maintaining their homes and loved ones. While they have had strength of body and brain, the opportunities for training have not been so great as those opportunities have presented themselves to the inhabitants of the open country both east and west which surrounds the hills.[21]

By writing those paragraphs, Coleman made a point that will be important later in this tale. The nature of the land limited the contact between the mountain families and others who saw government changing and developing around the Allegheny Plateau. The mountaineers were isolated physically, but were also on their own intellectually. That does not mean they lacked intelligence, but it does mean that their independence was rather more intense than other Americans of that age. Coleman also took note of that point.

> It may be well understood the difficulties of the early settlers in all that confronted them in their occupation of new territory of the unsettled counties. The organization of local government was slow in development. The judicial circuits embraced several

counties. There was the local government with a sheriff always as the guardian of law.

For many years in this new, growing area even the county sheriff often had no more than one deputy, and that was afforded only when the economy of the county could support an extra arm for the chief law enforcement officer. With the court sessions coming so far between in the sparsely populated counties, the judge rode horseback for miles to serve the various courts of his circuit.[22]

The nature of politics in that society is another important matter. Wary readers will understand that the records are extremely scanty. Yet it appears from the folk tradition that lasted long enough to be recorded by later Hatfields that the outlook of Thomas Jefferson held sway until about 1830 — that is, the Hatfields considered themselves American yeomen, sturdy farmers, and independent voters. After 1830, it appears that the outlook of Henry Clay of Kentucky largely replaced the Jeffersonian philosophy. By that time, the Hatfields and their neighbors were anxious for the internal improvements which characterized Clay's "American system." As the issue of human slavery began dominating the political scene after the Missouri Compromise of 1820, the Hatfields adopted the outlook of Jefferson Davis, that localities and states had the right of self-determination.[23]

The slavery issue is a rather dicey point in the history of the Hatfield family. It is probable that there was little love lost between mountaineers and African Americans. Though the Bible of the Dingess family and the census records of the hill counties of western Virginia and eastern Kentucky show the presence of slaves, the number of African Americans does not seem to be as large as in other sections of the south. One descendant of Eph-of-All Hatfield puts the matter succinctly, "We were too poor to own slaves."[24]

The work on the hillside farms was done mainly by the parents and the children of mountaineer families. It has been noted by highland historian Horace Kephart and others that work on a mountain farm aged people cruelly fast. The photographic record bears out that point. It was not uncommon for mountain men and women to have careworn and lined faces by their early forties. In some families, like the Hatfields, the lifespan was long. Many others, however, were in their graves long before they lived seventy years. Coleman A. Hatfield's record of the farming life was one of his most vivid recollections.

> In order to have the most successful season in planting vegetables and grain, it was often necessary to keep in touch with some old reliable almanac, which was consulted by every family at the proper season of the year.
>
> The hard freezes were usually over by the first of March and there was often a spell of sunshine and real balmy weather for a

few days during the latter part of February or early March. This caused a "thaw" which often resulted in the ice breaking up in the rivers and going out with the melting snow. Sometimes the breaking of the ice could be heard for a long distance where the melting snows came rushing down to lift the ice and break the great sheets which reached across the rivers.

The surface of the ground was cold until the spring thaw. The well-shaded earth was protected by the great spreading oaks and other virgin timber which kept the ice all winter. The first days of sunshine caused it to break loose.

During the dry spells of the first spring sunshine, mountain folk would plant their potatoes and were very careful to plant them deep in the ground at that time. It not only protected them from later freezing, but in case of cold snaps in the spring, there was no warmth to insure the crop from freezing.

At any rate, the dark of the moon was the seasonable time in which to plant the potatoes. If you did not do this, they would often grow up toward the top of the ground. The bright sunshine would dry them out, but they also did not have a sufficient amount of earth to produce the good crops, which no family dared be without.[25]

The staple crops of the mountain land were corn, potatoes, sorghum, beans, cucumbers, squash, and other vegetables. Families kept hogs, which were allowed to run loose with the other animals. Cattle were not unknown, but bear meat and venison were also staples. Work began at soon as it was daylight and continued until dark, but the families thrived because their food was nourishing.

It is of passing interest in that light that when T.C. Crawford visited the Hatfields during the feud years, Anse and Vicie Hatfield went to great trouble to prepare a meal of their favorite food: fried chicken, fried pork, corn, beans, and "all the fixings." Anse and Vicie were anxious that their guest enjoy his meal and doubtless thought they were treating him like one of their own children. Crawford, however, wrote that the food was revolting, much to the displeasure of later Hatfields.

By the time the Hatfield family reached Blackberry Creek, the Hatfields well understood how much care their crops needed. Later echoes of their folk wisdom demonstrate how much preparation they did and how well they understood the land that provided their livelihood:

> In the case of corn, it was planted rather deeply and in the dark of the moon if a dry season was anticipated, or if anything could be detected through signs of early drought, such as winds drying out the earth and lack of rain.

Planting in the dark of the moon was desirable to get the benefit of all the moisture which had been held in the earth during the winter season. Sometimes the texture of the soil and the degree of snowfall and rainfall would often determine for the planter just whether he should plant in the "light" or the "dark" of the moon.[26]

When the Hatfields settled on Blackberry Creek, their farming livelihood was subsistence farming. They lived much as their ancestors had in the dim medieval past. Because few writers gave much attention to that traditional lifestyle as the United States developed, it was left to local writers to tell what had happened. One such writer was Henry Clay Ragland, whose biography weaves its way in and out of this tale. Ragland moved to Logan County in 1874, nearly twenty years after the death of Eph-of-All. Yet because Ragland grew up on a Virginia farm, he was able to describe the traditional life in a moving way. In his *History of Logan County,* Ragland noted:

> The early settlers, while having come from every class of society, were fortunate in having among them no drones, who are so often dubbed "gentlemen." Their business was not to gather pearls and gold as adventurers, but to establish homes, and by industry add to the wealth of the state. There were no "gold refiners and perfumers," among them, but they were rather sturdy farmers, carpenters and laborers, used to the axe and the rifle, and perfectly at home in the wilderness. While the country was rough and mountainous, only about one-third of it being adapted to cultivation, yet the one-third was extremely fertile and generous and yielded an abundant supply for man and beast. The climate was genial, especially in the valleys where the mountains shut off the rude winter storms and assisted in summer in maintaining a current of fresh air.
>
> There was entire absence of the poisonous malaria, which so often prostrates new settlements, and of all the settlers, no one is named as having been a physician or in any way versed in the science of medicine. Simple herbs were used for all the ills to which the flesh is heir, while wounds and bruises were treated with the simplest remedies.
>
> Separated from the outside world, the people learned to be dependent upon their personal energies and their personal management for the necessities and comforts of life. Substantial log houses were erected and the land cleared around them, in which were planted patches of corn, cotton, and flax, while the cattle and flocks which were driven from the settlements in Virginia were kept in an enclosure near the residences in order to

protect them from the wild beasts which roamed at will in the mountains, or in the then uncleared valleys.

Each settler brought with him his trusty rifle, and the ammunition with which to load it was manufactured here. Sulphur and saltpeter were found in almost every cave, while charcoal was easily burned, out of which reliable powder was made, and lead for the bullets was plentiful in every neighborhood. Thus armed and equipped, the black bear, the deer, and the buffalo, which still roamed at large, furnished meat for the families, while their skins furnished shoes and a portion of the clothing for the men.

Waterpower was abundant and small mills were easily erected at which the corn was ground. Honey, which was plentiful, and the juice from the sugar tree, which was made into maple syrup or maple sugar, took the place of the product of cane, while the bark of the sassafras root, or the bark of spicewood or birch or wintergreen was a splendid substitute for coffee.

There were numerous salines, and water from which the best salt could be made was found at a depth not exceeding ten feet from the surface. In addition to the viands above mentioned, the river and creeks were full of fish, the mountains in their season brought forth an abundance of huckleberry, blackberries and sarvice, and taken altogether, the table of a Logan County home in the early days furnished a bill of fare which kings might envy.

Spinning wheels and looms were found in every household, and while the men cleared the fields, tilled the soil and hunted the wild game, the children hooked the fish in the clear streams or gathered the berries from the hills, and the women — God bless them — prepared the cotton, flax and wool and wove it into cloth. Nature furnished the dyestuffs to color the cloth thus wove in almost every hue that could be desired. The dyestuffs consisted of the bark of trees and shrubs, with the copperas which was easily found in the caves.

Canoes were the largest crafts that floated upon the river, and when the work of the season was over, a little fleet of them loaded with pelts and ginseng would be found flowing down the sparkling waters of the Guyandot and Tug to the settlements in the Ohio, where the cargo would be exchanged for coffee and household goods and probably a few yards of calico with which to clothe some favorite daughter and make her envied by all the belles of the neighborhood.

Shoes were undoubtedly purchased to take the place of ruder shoes or moccasins which were made of buckskin in the mountain settlements, and whose heel taps would be trained to keep pace to the enlivening strains of the "fiddle." While it is nowhere asserted as a fact, we are satisfied — there being no mention of stills in the mountains in any of the newspapers of the day — that a few gallons of something stronger that water would furnish a part of the return cargo, to be used in celebrating the festivities of the Christmastide and giving to the old folks a reminder of the happy days known in "Old Virginia" when they were young.[27]

Mary Bland Hurst, who wrote one of the first histories of Logan County, gave another description of life as it was lived by the early Hatfields and their neighbors. Taking note of the independence of the farms, she wrote:

The house, considered as only a temporary one, which the settler built was of logs. It was usually small, having one room and probably an attic. The logs were sometimes hewn, more frequently not. The doors and floors were of timbers flattened with an ax. Nails were not often used, and if used at all, they were such as were hammered into shape in a neighboring blacksmith shop. The spaces between the logs were closed with blocks of wood, or with stones, and with a plaster made of mud. Every article of furniture was homemade. The fireplaces were spacious, often capable of receiving logs five feet long. Stoves being unknown, cooking was done by the open fire. The crane, which was an iron hook fastened in the chimney, served for hanging the kettle. Lamps of the crudest kind only were in use. They consisted of a pan of grease with cotton string laid in for a wick. Candles, at first, were a luxury.[28]

This was destined to change. As noted earlier, the market economy began taking shape in the United States in the 1820s. This was one of the key developments of the age and was one of the factors that changed American politics from the classic Jeffersonian outlook to that of the "American system" of internal improvements.

Appalachia was one of the last regions to experience that change, though the development probably was finished by the time Eph-of-All and Anna were elderly people. Catlettsburg, Ironton, and Guyandotte on the Ohio River were established before the 1820s. Pushboats, which were rather stout wooden boats propelled by long poles, were moving up and down the Tug Fork, Levisa Fork, and Guyandot Rivers by the time Joseph and Valentine Hatfield came of age.

Another question that concerns the pioneer lifestyle of Logan County during the years Eph-of-All's children were growing up is the matter of land ownership. That question leads writers into the tangled web of the land laws of colonial

Virginia. Land titles would become vastly important in the later history of the region because the traditional lifestyle would end there during Anse Hatfield's lifetime. The way it ended involved land titles. Henry Clay Ragland wrote paragraphs on that subject that are as important to history as his thoughts on the frontier lifestyle:

> The Legislature of 1792, however, passed an act which retarded settlement and which still hangs like a dark cloud over the country, thwarting its prosperity and keeping the lands out of market. The act provides "that any person may acquire title to so much waste and unappropriated land lying within this Commonwealth as he shall desire to purchase on paying the consideration of two dollars for every hundred acres."
>
> Up to that time, the lands were held for those who had shown that they intended to make settlement upon them, and were restricted to surveys of not more than 4,000 acres. As soon as this act was passed, preparations were made by those who had sufficient means to cover the whole country with entries and surveys, and no one having the right to survey the lands unless he had passed an examination before the president and professors of William and Mary College, and certified by them as able to do the work.
>
> Surveyors were not easily obtained by the pioneers who had driven the Indians from the country, but were employed by those who were able to give them a large amount of work to do.[29]

Ragland added that the territory soon was taken up by the wealthy men who could afford to hire such surveyors. *The History of Logan County* lists the major grants and indicates the nature of the trouble that would arrive during Anse's life. For the present, it is enough to know that there were legal questions whether pioneers like Eph-of-All Hatfield owned their land, or whether they were, in effect, "squatters" who could be compelled to leave if someone had a superior title to the land.

That point seemed to matter very little when Eph-of-All and Anna Musick Hatfield moved to the Tug Fork region. No tales have survived of their removal or the way they journeyed to that section, but the time of their resettlement seems firmly fixed by Ragland's history:

> At what is still known as the Hatfield place on Horsepen, Valentine Hatfield of Washington County, Virginia, settled at quite an early day. He was the father of nine sons and three daughters, and from them have sprung many of the Hatfields of the Guyandot and Sandy Valleys. Joseph Hatfield, who has already been mentioned as the brother of Valentine Hat-

field...settled at what is now Matewan, at about the same time that his brother settled on Horsepen."[30]

Like nearly all historians, Ragland made occasional errors. Joseph Hatfield did not settle near present-day Matewan at first, but moved there later. It is not always safe to trust Ragland's genealogy of the Hatfields, although he may have been correct in thinking Joseph and Valentine Hatfield were the first of their family to settle on Tug Fork. Ragland's history can be trusted, however, to date the settlement of the Hatfields safely between 1792, when the Shawnee threat was over, and 1810, when many pioneer families were moving into the Sandy and Guyandot valleys.

Historian Otis K. Rice wrote a history of such individuals titled *The Allegheny Frontier: West Virginia Beginnings*, in which he described how pioneer Appalachia moved from the frontier period to a time of "settled rurality."[31] That is the best existing description of what happened as Eph-of-All Hatfield's children came of age. It is, however, a time that has been misunderstood. The poet Edgar Allan Poe once wrote of the Virginia backwoods as a place occupied by sinister mountain men who knew little of civilization. Readers are left to their own discretion to understand if that was social history or Poe's vivid imagination at work. Certainly Coleman A. Hatfield took exception to Poe's image:

> The casual reader who seldom hears anything from the hill people except what he sees in flaming headlines about the eruption of some ancient feud or that a mountaineer has bushwhacked his neighbor over a wild hog might be led to believe that little goes on in the hill country except feuding, fussing, and fighting.
>
> Little is told of the neighborliness and brotherly kindness of even the "meanest" of the feudists when, along about June, they grab their corn hoes and met at the home of a neighbor to work out the corn.[32]

Though no one should make the mistake of thinking that the Tug Fork and Guyandot section was an Appalachian "paradise lost" between 1820 and 1860, it is true that the spooky image described by Poe and others is questionable at best. The tales of the hundred or so families written about by Henry Clay Ragland seem to confirm the idea that Appalachian people tended their crops, minded their own affairs, but helped their neighbors when help was needed.

When there was a corn hoeing or some such chore, the neighbors pitched in, going from farm to farm until the crops were harvested. In the evenings, it was common for the women to quilt and gossip together in a time-honored fashion. Another commonplace aspect of Appalachian life was for youngsters to dance and play traditional tunes and ballads on banjos, guitars, and fiddles.[33]

The older folks remembered that if a preacher was handy on Sundays, the neighbors would gather for services, though such meetings were not as common as some would have liked. A tale survives that one young couple wanted to get married, but visiting preachers were scarce at the time and the courthouse was far away. They adopted the usual, if informal, custom of setting up their own home and waiting for a preacher to come by to make the arrangement more dignified. The young couple finally heard of a preacher coming down the stream on a raft. They waded out to the middle of the river to meet him and the preacher performed a hurried wedding service on his way past the man and his wife.[34] The spiritual aspect of mountaineer religious life was described by Mary Bland Hurst:

> Each man believed in the Bible, drew his opinions from what he believed the Bible to teach. He bowed to no creed, but studied the Bible for himself. He formed his opinion from what he conceived one or more texts to teach. Feeling thus, he knew he was right, and because he knew only a little of it, he was positive of his correctness, and very fond of arguing for his position. This argument was not generally a reasoning, but a "capping text with text."
>
> He believed in religious freedom, a freedom that entitled each to believe, teach, and practice what he willed without interference from any source whatsoever. This attitude led to the formation of many sects. They were ready to follow a leader who could express their ideas better than they could.[35]

Coleman C. Hatfield recalled that church services were unusual, except late in the spring each year when it became possible for itinerant preachers to move through the community, giving names to localities such as "Camp Creek," a branch of the Guyandot River. That custom was so pervasive in early Appalachia that a certain tree was named "sarvis" because it bloomed early, about the time preachers arrived to conduct their religious services.[36]

In the light of such realities, it was natural for men in early 19th century America to take their greatest pride from their self-sufficiency. That aspect of mountaineers lies at the heart of this tale. Before describing the dramatic events of Hatfield history, one should pay attention to the words of Coleman A. Hatfield:

> It will be easily understood that throughout this area in the many decades which have passed that the frontier people had learned from experience to look to the family leader as an advisor and to rely upon their common kinsmen as protectors and helpers in all matters where such protection or help was needed.

It might take the form of avenging wrongs either real or imaginary committed by a member of another clan, or it might be in the form of humanitarian aid and in helping and caring for the needy of the settlement in time of sickness or death....

The old family patriarch of that era might be easily misunderstood until we consider all that had entered into the making of the generation who, with their ancestors, had been marooned for a century in the mountain fastness, living under the primitive conditions of their earlier ancestry while all the world went by.

The sons and daughters of the earliest pioneers, the descendants of the Anglo-Saxon vanguard, while retaining their native ability and sturdiness of character and with an ever-ready potential for leaving, easily became adapted to new conditions as leaders in that era.[37]

The Tale of Abner Vance

In 1817, when an important second chapter of the Hatfield saga began, that independent outlook had taken root all through the vast region of southwestern Virginia. If a man's pride was at stake, he acted in his own best interest, the most effective way he could find. Thus when a man named Lewis Horton offended old Abner Vance, who was Anse Hatfield's great-grandfather, he acted in a way that left its imprint on future generations of the family. The tragedy and death of Abner Vance marks the first time in history that close relatives of the feuding Hatfields were caught in an event reported by a newspaper.

On July 27, 1819, the *Lynchburg Press* reported, "On Friday... Abner Vance was executed at Abingdon...for the murder of Lewis Horton. He addressed the spectators, about four thousand, for an hour and a half, with considerable ability and died with the most perfect composure and heroic fortitude. He accused some persons of giving false evidence against him and said that if he had obtained a fair trial, and nothing but truth had been sworn against him, he thought the penitentiary would have been the proper punishment for his offense."[38]

Behind such bare facts is a more tragic tale. Coleman A. Hatfield told that story in greater detail, indicating that though Vance was in the wrong, the circumstances should have permitted a more lenient sentence. Hatfield wrote:

> Abner Vance, about the year 1817, lived on Clinch River in Washington County, Virginia. The story is told that a young man who came from a well-to-do family had taken Vance's daughter, and they had gone away, supposedly to be married.
>
> They lived in Baltimore, where he attended school as a medical student, according to one version I have. Later, Horton brought this girl back and had an argument with her father. It

was found out that they had not married, but that he had been living with her as man and wife.

Vance became so incensed after this fellow threatened to kill him that he procured his old mountain rifle whereupon he fired on Horton as Horton crossed the Clinch River, and Horton fell into the river and was either killed by the shot or was drowned. Zeke Daniels, a colored man who was a slave, pulled him out of the river.

Vance left that section of the country soon after that and came into the Sandy River country, down in some part of Wayne County, West Virginia, where his son, Richard Vance, had settled. He stayed down there for two years. Then he was persuaded by some, and I think his son favored it, that he go back and stand trial and get it off his mind and off his shoulders.[39]

Later Hatfields claim that the circumstances were more brutal. They believe that Lewis Horton rode to Abner Vance's house with Elizabeth (Bettie) Vance in a condition of advanced pregnancy. There Horton said contemptuously, "Here's your heifer. You take care of her."[40] Given mountaineer pride and given Abner Vance's standing as a preacher around Abingdon, such treatment was intolerable. Coleman A. Hatfield wrote:

> Vance went back, and the Hortons, who were quite influential in that county, used their means to prosecute him. He was convicted and sentenced to hang. He was executed at Abingdon, Virginia, though it is said that a reprieve was sent by the governor of Virginia.
>
> The messenger came on horseback and the reprieve was intercepted just as he was entering the crowd at the hanging ground. He was held back and kept from delivering it to the officer in charge. So the trap was sprung before the reprieve got there. It was delivered soon afterward, but too late.
>
> It is said that Vance stood on his coffin and preached his funeral or conducted a service. His song that he wrote while he was in jail awaiting execution has come down to his descendants and many of them have retained it.[41]

One of those many descendants was Nancy Vance Hatfield, Anse's mother. Many years later, she told one of her grandsons that the governor's reprieve for Vance arrived immediately after the hanging and that camphor was held under Vance's nose to try to revive him, though the effort failed.[42] Vance's funeral song charged Daniel, Robert, and William Horton with swearing lies against Vance.

Vance also claimed that a juror named Elliott voted to execute Vance, even though Vance once saved Elliott's life.

Hatfields of a later day believed that Abner Vance had taken refuge with Eph-of-All Hatfield while he was running from the law. Though there is little proof of the matter, the argument claims that Vance came from the same general area as Eph-of-All and that Hatfield's grandson married Vance's granddaughter.[43]

That tale was embedded deeply in the Hatfield family consciousness. The lesson that they learned was that it is not safe to fall into the clutches of a government held by unfriendly hands.[44] Between 1839 and 1921, popular wisdom and entertainment centered upon family tales. During the years that Anse Hatfield was coming of age, it is more likely than not that he heard the tale many times how Abner Vance was hanged. It is reasonable to think that was a tale that Anse would have recalled whenever he had dealings with governments.[45]

The Youth of Big Eph Hatfield

As Abner Vance met his mournful fate, the family of Eph-of-All Hatfield continued to grow in numbers and populate the Tug Fork region. When the younger son, Valentine, came of age, he married Martha Weddington and the couple began raising their family.

Valentine and Martha's family was large, even by the standards of that time and place. Their first son, Aly Hatfield, was born in 1804. The other children were Joseph, born in 1806, Ephraim in 1812, Andrew in 1813, John in 1814, Virginia Jane in 1815, Thomas in 1818, Jacob in 1819, twins "Slater" James and Cecilia in 1824, Phoebe in 1828, and Valentine Jr. in 1831. Thus in 1819, when Abner Vance was hanged in Abingdon, Big Eph Hatfield was a strapping seven-year-old who soon would take his place in history. Coleman A. Hatfield, Ephraim's great-grandson, recalled the family history:

> Ephraim Hatfield, the grandson of the settler, Ephraim, was born on the Virginia side of the Tug River on April 11, 1812. He was the third son of Valentine (Wall) Hatfield and Martha Weddington Hatfield, who settled on a farm which was known as Lang Bottom. There, Valentine and Martha reared a large family of nine sons and three daughters.
>
> Ephraim married Nancy Vance on August 27, 1828. His wife was born May 2, 1813, the daughter of John Ferrell who migrated from Virginia. The mother was Bettie Vance. Apparently, from the dates given, this young pair married at an early age.
>
> Ephraim was sixteen and Nancy fifteen. It often happened in those days that young people were married at an early age. No doubt Ephraim, with his enormous physique, at sixteen appeared

to be older than his years. Nancy and Ephraim lived long and happy and both lived to see most of their children living to maturity.[46]

The Death of the Panther

Big Eph was a mighty hunter and brought home many deer and bears, according to Hatfield family lore. His great-grandson wrote that his most notable feat as a hunter was when Ephraim killed a panther with a hunting knife near a cave on Mud Lick Mountain, near the present site of Red Jacket, West Virginia.[47] That happened soon after Ephraim had returned from a trip to Saltville, Virginia, not long after Big Eph and Nancy had married. Coleman A. Hatfield wrote that tale many times, recalling it in great detail.

>It was about the year 1831 when Big Ephraim Hatfield had located his home on Mate Creek in Logan County, (West) Virginia. Aly, the oldest of Big Ephraim's brothers, took him to bring back a supply of salt from across the country for the winter.
>
>Upon their return, they found that a panther had screamed around the premises of Ephraim's cabin and that it had killed a steer of one of his neighbors not far away and had eaten out the animal's liver.
>
>Nancy Hatfield told the story of how she was all alone in their log cabin and that in the middle of the night she had heard the screams of the great cat and had seen it standing on a rail fence at the back of the premises. She added that little Mattie, the baby, was crying, but when the shrill screams of the "painter-cat" alarmed them, the little child hushed her crying.
>
>Nancy arose and put more wood on the dying embers at the fireplace and caused the smoke and blaze to flash up the chimney. She feared that the panther would spring upon the roof and come down the chimney. She also rolled logs of firewood against the door and put dry powder in the old mountain rifle which sat in the corner by the iron pot.[48]

Big Eph and Nancy's nearest neighbors were not close enough for her to risk going outside. So she waited through the night for Eph to return from Saltville with Aly. The panther kept up its unearthly screaming through the night, though Nancy's baby was silent, either from fear or because Nancy's calming influence reassured the child.

>On the next day, Ephraim and his brother returned with their supply of salt. A party of neighbors was summoned from up the

creek and down near the river, where the scattered homes of the settlers were located.

They started out on the trail of the panther and soon found where it had killed and eaten part of a pig which belonged to a herd of swine of one of the neighbors. They soon got the trail lined out; it led down the ridge past the Obie cliff and on toward the rocky promontories not far from the river some five miles away.

From time to time the big beast had been overtaken and a battle with the dogs had ensued. Each time the faithful animals were repulsed and the great cat went on his way. Some of the men broke down and cried when they came upon their dying dogs killed by the panther because in those early days of the mountains the settler found that the dog was his best friend to guard him and his loved ones day or night.

The men said to Ephraim, "That big cat has killed six of our dogs, and we have only two left. We are going to quit." Hearing this, the grim-faced Ephraim muttered as he closed his jaws that he was still going to follow that burned varmint and that if it killed his slow trailer dog, it would have to kill him first.[49]

Ephraim and John Murphy, his brother-in-law, went on alone. They had only two dogs left. One was called the wolf dog because its sire was thought to be a wolf, and it was noted for its speed. The other was a small and heavy-bodied slow trailer named "White Tip" because he had white hair on the breast, about his neck, and at the end of his tail. White Tip always stayed with Big Eph and went in front as a guide. The men were armed with only Murphy's flintlock rifle and Big Eph's hunting knife, which he carried in a scabbard at his side. They went to the top of a rocky ridge on Mud Lick Branch of Mate Creek. Coleman's account then claimed:

> Murphy turned over the edge of the point of the mountain and went around the front point to a cliff where he could see the other side of the ridge. The slow trailer dog went down around the rocks and came into Murphy's view on the other side.
>
> Just as it approached a deep cave below the main rock, the great beast sprang out on White Tip, and he was thrown on his back between some small trees which had fallen down the hillside below the mouth of the cave.
>
> Both the cat and its victim were visible to Big Ephraim who stood on top of the rock. He pushed the wolf dog down the declivity toward the panther and White Tip, and then followed down the side of the rocks, holding onto small bushes which grew between the ledges.

Before Ephraim reached the panther, Murphy fired a bullet which went through the top of the cat's neck. Ephraim rushed in with his drawn knife, standing close to one of the fallen trees, and plunged the big knife into the panther back of its left shoulder and on into its heart.

Ephraim wheeled, knowing that the beast would release the dog and chase him. As he ran back, he saw the knife shoot backward out of the panther's side. The panther's blood spewed out in the frosty air as it died, causing a cloud of steam to rise from the cat's dead body.[50]

Hatfield and Murphy threw the cat's body across the saddle of Murphy's mare and then found their way out of the mountain. The panther was so large that its front feet fell near the ground on one side of the saddle, and the tail dragged the ground on the other side. Eph carried White Tip in on his shoulders and laid him on a bearskin near the fire. The dog recovered, but it was never able to bark again because the panther had bitten through its larynx.

Big Eph Hatfield was just nineteen years old, but his local fame was established. From then until the end of his long life, Ephraim was known as "old panther killer." As his son Anse and the other children grew, the panther tale grew in their imaginations, and their parents became among the most respected folks on Mate Creek.

There were, of course, other tales of Big Eph's exploits. One tale was that he went hunting one hard winter with a man named Nash Tiller. The two men killed two bears, took out the insides, and hung them up for the night near their campfire. Big Eph carried the bears up the mountain, though sleet had fallen on top the snow, making the mountains unbearably slick.

At the crest, Big Eph said, "Now see here, Tiller. I've carried these bears up the hill, now it's up to you to get them down the hill." Nash turned one of the bears over on its back, with the feet sticking up in the air. He sat down on the bear holding its four legs and slid down the hill, crashing into a thicket and through the timber. Tiller became wedged in a tree so tight that Big Eph had to find another hunter to help chop the tree down so Tiller could get out.

Big Eph Hatfield and His Neighbors

As might be expected, Big Eph won a reputation as the strongest and best fighter on Mate Creek. Coleman A. Hatfield's manuscripts save something of that tradition and the way that Big Eph's reputation as one of the best men on that creek grew through the following years.

> It is said that Ephraim Hatfield was a peaceable man, never wanting any trouble and never resorting to anything but fair play in any altercation that he had with other people.

But on one occasion there were some boat hands who had come up from the river. Among them was Fighting Jim Prather, Bill Prather, Riley Sansom, Jim Ellison, and a number of others who had come for the purpose of seeing Fighting Jim Prather fight Ephraim Hatfield — they being the two most powerful men in the surrounding country.

Ephraim declined to fight and told them that he didn't want any trouble and wasn't wanting any contest of that kind. Jim Prather closed in on him and kept insisting on trouble. So Ephraim took a swing at him after he had been struck and landed a blow over Prather's heart.

Bill Prather, who became excited and thought his brother had been killed, ran in with a spikepole and struck Ephraim over the head with it. Big Eph threw up his arm. The blow broke one bone of his left arm and the rest of the blow landed on his head.

There was no other damage, except that Eph became so infuriated after they got him started fighting that he cleaned up every one of them, whipped them down on the ground and threw them over the fence.[51]

Another time, a man came from Kentucky to challenge Big Eph, saying he was the "bully" of that state, just as Hatfield was the bully of West Virginia. Big Eph declined to fight at first and offered the man some dinner. But when they had eaten, the Kentuckian wanted to wrestle to find out which was the better man. Big Eph threw him and then tossed him out in the road. When the Kentuckian came to, Eph asked him if he wanted any more trouble. "No," the challenger said. "Tell you what to do, Eph. You just throw my horse over to me, and I'll go away and leave you alone."[52]

During following years, the Hatfield family was changing with the times. In 1850, old Eph-of-All Hatfield turned eighty-five years old and was watching his great-grandchildren grow to maturity. The Hatfields tell that about that time he made a sentimental trip to his old home in Russell County, Virginia, to visit old friends and find out what had happened around his former home on Thompson's Creek. Eph-of-All took Big Eph and young Wall Hatfield with him as they rode south through the cool autumn, often traveling at night and sometimes stopping to rest during the day as they rode Indian fashion on the trail.

Eph-of-All died five years later, at the age of ninety. The pioneer era in Appalachia was passing by that time. Americans had discovered that they could own a vast continent that was developing in huge sections, from the Atlantic Ocean to the Appalachian Mountains, from those mountains to the Mississippi River, from the Pacific Coast back to the Rocky Mountains, and from those mountains back to the Mississippi River. Yet as that drama unfolded, there was a lurking danger that threatened to tear the nation in half.

The Background of a War

The nation's terrible flaw was the tragedy of slavery. In 1820, when Eph-of-All Hatfield was fifty-five years old, Valentine Hatfield was thirty-one, and Big Eph Hatfield was a lad of eight years, Missouri sought admission to the union. A furious debate erupted in the U.S. Congress. Missouri was admitted to the nation, but only after men fought for months to agree upon the Missouri Compromise that banned slavery above the new state's southern border.

The wise New Englander, John Quincy Adams, recognized at once that the issue was only a title page to the great tragic volume that he could read in the future. The equally wise, though aged, Thomas Jefferson wrote that slavery was a firebell in the night that could spell the doom of the American republic.

The issue was joined between north and south over which section would determine the future of the United States. It was a matter of pride as much as economics. It was an issue of politics as well as race relations. It was a question of lifestyle as well as ambition. As the years rolled along, the struggle remained close to the surface and often dominated American political life, despite the best efforts to settle the matter proposed by some of the finest statesmen the United States ever produced.

Many have written that the mountain sections of Virginia and Kentucky were little affected by what happened. The point could be argued either direction. Yet one certainty is that the mountaineers were aware of what was happening. In Logan County, in particular, men began forming militia units to hold regular drills. "Militia groups do not form without reason," Coleman C. Hatfield argued.[53] They are created, he said, because men feel there are issues at work that eventually will threaten their security, their livelihoods, and the fortunes of their families.

Since that was the point at hand, it seems that the Hatfields and their neighbors were actively worried about what the future would hold. The way they would face such an uncertain future depended very much on their strengths of character, the attributes they inherited from their forbearers, and the important ideas at work in their minds.

Anse Hatfield was no more immune from those subtle processes than any other man or woman has been. The tales that he heard as a young man influenced the development of his character and helped determine his fate, just as they did for his Uncle Jim Vance and Randal McCoy, and just as such forces would help determine the lives of his children.

Anse Hatfield was the product of the pioneer experience in the eastern mountains. He was the child of a family that had produced frontier leaders and militia captains. He was the inheritor of the traditions of Eph-of-All Hatfield who had gone out armed to rescue a woman from the Shawnee Indians. Anse was one who had learned from his parents the importance of self-sufficiency, that was the result of independent farming. He had learned that mountain men, who prized self-respect, took care of situations as they arose, such as the time Big Eph

Hatfield killed the panther to protect his family. He had learned to be as bold as Eph-of-All and as wary as the grandchildren of Abner Vance.

When those characteristics were added to the innate aspects that Anse was born with, it is much easier to understand him as a youngster before the War Between the States. His self-confidence was matched by his self-respect. His humor was matched by his practicality. His knowledge of the outdoors was matched by his appreciation of the role of heroes in history. What he lacked in book-learning, he knew about from life. The only question about his character was whether or not he could forge his abilities into effective leadership.

Such was Anse Hatfield's situation at the dawn of the 1860s. On April 11, 1861, the long-simmering tensions of American political life boiled over as South Carolina Confederates bombarded Fort Sumter and the Civil War began. Eight days later, Anse Hatfield married his sweetheart, Louvicey (often spelled Levicy or Louvisa) Chafin, and soon thereafter marched away to war with other young men of his generation.

---

[1] Study Out The Land, T.K. Whipple.
[2] Virginia Magazine of History, Volume 3.
[3] Virginia Magazine of History, Volume 2.
[4] Notes on the Hatfield Family, Coleman A. Hatfield.
[5] Notes on the Hatfield Family, Coleman A. Hatfield.
[6] Notes on the Hatfield Family, Coleman A. Hatfield.
[7] Coleman C. Hatfield Interviews.
[8] Begats Interview, Coleman A. Hatfield.
[9] Montcalm and Wolfe, Francis Parkman.
[10] The American Revolution, Bruce Lancaster.
[11] The Annals of America, Volume 2.
[12] Border Forays, Lyman C. Draper Papers.
[13] Ingles Ferry was named for the Ingles family. The most famous of that family was Mary Ingles, who was captured by Shawnee Indians, but later escaped. She has become the subject of many history articles and novels through the years.
[14] West Virginia: A History, Otis K. Rice.
[15] The Death of David Musick, Coleman A. Hatfield.
[16] The Death of David Musick, Coleman A. Hatfield.
[17] The Death of David Musick, Coleman A. Hatfield.
[18] Begats Interview, Coleman A. Hatfield. A "tithe" was the word used by the early state governments of the nation that signified when a young man "came of age," usually age 21, but often younger than that. A "white tithe" was considered an adult white male. A "black tithe" was usually a slave and counted as three-fifths the value of a "white tithe."
[19] Notes on the Hatfield Property, Coleman A. Hatfield. There is some dispute about the age of Aike Hatfield. Other historians believe that he was younger than the 25 years reported here, perhaps as young as 17 years.
[20] Westward Movement of the Mountain Settlers, Coleman A. Hatfield.
[21] Westward Movement of the Mountain Settlers, Coleman A. Hatfield.
[22] Men of the Wilderness, Coleman A. Hatfield.
[23] Coleman C. Hatfield Interviews.
[24] Coleman C. Hatfield Interviews.
[25] Signs Governing Planting in Agriculture, Coleman A. Hatfield.
[26] Signs Governing Planting in Agriculture, Coleman A. Hatfield.
[27] The History of Logan County, Henry Clay Ragland.
[28] Social History of Logan County, Mary B. Hurst.
[29] The History of Logan County, Henry Clay Ragland.
[30] The History of Logan County, Henry Clay Ragland.
[31] The Allegheny Frontier: West Virginia Beginnings, Otis K. Rice.
[32] Neighborly Corn Hoeing, Coleman A. Hatfield.
[33] Jennie Ellis Wilson Interview.
[34] Coleman C. Hatfield Interview.
[35] Social History of Logan County, Mary B. Hurst.
[36] Coleman C. Hatfield Interview.
[37] Men of the Wilderness, Coleman A. Hatfield.
[38] Lynchburg Press, July 27, 1819.
[39] Interview About Abner Vance, Coleman A. Hatfield.
[40] Coleman C. Hatfield Interviews.

[41] Coleman C. Hatfield Interviews.
[42] Glen Dye Interview.
[43] Coleman C. Hatfield Interviews.
[44] Coleman C. Hatfield Interviews.
[45] Coleman C. Hatfield Interviews.
[46] Ephraim and Nancy Hatfield, Coleman A. Hatfield.
[47] Ephraim and Nancy Hatfield, Coleman A. Hatfield.
[48] Big Ephraim and the Panther, Coleman A. Hatfield.
[49] Big Ephraim and the Panther, Coleman A. Hatfield.
[50] Big Ephraim and the Panther, Coleman A. Hatfield.
[51] Begats Interview, Coleman A. Hatfield.
[52] Begats Interview, Coleman A. Hatfield.
[53] Coleman C. Hatfield Interview.

Chapter Three
THE DEVIL IN THE FIGHTIN'
Anse Hatfield in the American Civil War

WHEN the Civil War exploded with a blinding flash of fire at Fort Sumter in April 1861, few young men of the Tug and Guyandot Valleys of western Virginia faced a brighter prospect than twenty-one-year-old Anderson Hatfield. He was young, strong, and able, known as one of the best marksmen and horsemen of his community. His father owned thousands of acres near Mate Creek.

When the war ended four years later, Anse had won fame, but he faced the prospect of living out his life in one of the poorest areas of a humiliated region of the nation. The tale of how the region was ruined economically by the war and the way that Anse Hatfield reacted to that reality and became one of the most notable figures in that history is a dramatic story of how a youngster's formidable character was caught up in the violence of his era.

His family remembered that Anse's character was largely composed of perseverance, self-reliance, and self-confidence.[1] These traits, coupled with the need to protect his own family, were the base for the decisions Anse made during the war years.

Anse Hatfield's Role in the Civil War

That history can be told in three sections, as Anse fought first with the Logan Wildcats, then with the 45th Battalion Virginia Infantry, and finally with his own partisan unit. When the war began, Anse had strong feelings about the issues though he marched from Logan County with the Logan Wildcats on June 3, 1861. It should be noted that highly respected regional historians deny that Anse was in the Wildcats, citing the Compiled Military Service Records in the National Archives in Washington that were begun in 1903 and finished in 1929. It is possible that Anse's records were not saved in that collection because he did not finish the war with that unit.

Yet, given Anse's nature, it is not likely he would have remained inactive during the first year of the war. The likelihood is that he fought with the Logan Wildcats through the Fort Donelson campaign, and then returned home in time for the conception of his first child, Johnson Hatfield, who was named for William Johnson McCoy, one of Louvicey Chafin Hatfield's brothers-in-law. Anse probably remained with the Wildcats until February 1862 and then joined the Virginia State Line in order to protect his own.

Between 1862 and February 1864, Anse fought with that military unit, which became part of the 45th Virginia Infantry Battalion. Then he left the Confederate Army when he was ordered to execute one of his uncles. Anse formed a guerilla unit that acted as a home guard force as an ally of William S. (Rebel Bill) Smith, one of the most notable raiders of the borderline during the war.

To understand Hatfield's decisions and the way his actions cemented his character, it is important to know how the explosive news from South Carolina affected the mountain region in the spring of 1861. Different individuals made their decisions about which side deserved their allegiance, but the politics of the borderline were a complicated matter and it is important to know how the history of the region influenced its young men. Coleman A. Hatfield shed light on that most interesting topic.

> West Virginia was created a state on June 20, 1863. However, the prevailing sentiment north of the border of Kentucky most favored the rebellion. This may be explained for various reasons.
>
> First, the extreme southern section of West Virginia — having once been part of Montgomery and Washington Counties, Virginia — was settled by pioneers, many of whom came from the eastern portion of the Montgomery and Washington areas. They followed the trails along the borders of their native counties as far as the limit of the Ohio River.
>
> Whereas, in the case of Kentucky, which had become a separate state in the very early years of the formation of our government, the Old Dominion (Virginia) had lost its influence on its independent mountaineers and those who had settled the bluegrass lands westward.
>
> In the early part of the Civil War, while Kentucky continued to maintain her neutrality, there were border clashes between bands of men loyal to their respective states all along the Virginia-Kentucky line from the most northeastern corner of the state, where the Tug Fork of the Sandy River divided it from the Old Dominion, westward toward the Big Sandy.[2]

Anse Hatfield at the Start of the War

In that charged atmosphere, it was inevitable that militia groups were formed and began training for warfare years before the actual conflict began. In central Logan County, such an organization was created in 1852 and held regular drills until the war began, whereupon it divided into two factions, the blue and the gray.[3] The county was as troubled by public events as any other region. When the storm broke out, at least three groups of men went into the Confederate Army.

The most famous, the eighty-odd members of the Logan Wildcats, became Company D of the 36th Virginia Infantry. A second unit, twice as large as the Wildcats, was mustered into the 34th Battalion Virginia Cavalry. The third became soldiers of the 45th Battalion Virginia Infantry, and Smith and Count's Battalions of Partisan Rangers. At least three hundred Logan County men fought for the Confederacy.

Such strong interest in military service did not arise without reason. Logan County people were quite aware of the issues surrounding joining, and there is no better evidence for that fact than the journalism of the day. A curious article was printed in *The Kanawha Valley Star*, which was written by one using the pen name "Southerner." That newspaper, one of the many that sprang to life in the mountain counties because of the state's right issues, told of the way Logan County joined the south.

"Southerner" wrote that the mountaineers gathered at Chapmanville on May 11, 1861, and raised the Stars and Bars stitched together by a Mrs. Chapman, who told her sons to volunteer in its defense. Ira H. McGinnis, A. C. Ferrell, James A. Nighbert, and other local men spoke to the crowd, telling them that the federal government under President Abraham Lincoln intended to free American Africans and enslave whites. In Southerner's view, this was a deep and damnable degradation of the proudest and freest people on earth that revolted local hearts, minds, souls, and bodies.

Within minutes, a full company called the "Chapmanville Rangers" was organized with Charles J. Stone, Hugh Toney, John R. Chapman, and William T. Butcher as officers. A homeguard unit was formed for men over age forty-five; then the ceremony ended with the crowd singing "Dixie" as the flag was raised, with the words "Liberty" on one side and "Union of the South" on the other. Two weeks later, a similar ceremony was held in Logan, where the Wildcat unit was created. The men rode away in wagons to Charleston, leaving central Logan County practically defenseless.

The manner in which Anse Hatfield made his decision at that time is remarkable. His mother recalled for one grandson that Anse's choice to fight for the south was based more on his intense personal pride than any other factor. Anse could very easily have chosen to fight for the Union, if it had not been for the rash actions of one William (General Bill) France (or Francis), who became another noted figure in the war along the border. Nancy Hatfield recalled:

> My boy, Ansie, was captain of all the soldiers from Beech to Mate. When the war was about to start, they were practicing being soldiers among the homeguards on the other side over in Kentucky, and Ansie and two other neighbor boys, Mose Chafin and Davie Mounts, went over to watch them march where General Bill France had men on Peter Creek.
>
> General Bill said our boys were spies. When Virginia seceded, General Bill said to Ansie, "Look at the shape your

state is in." He made one of his men fight Ansie, and my boy got the best of him. Then he set another man on Ansie, and my boy then downed the second man.

Then General Bill told his company to drive our boys back across the river into Virginia. They threw rocks at Ansie and Mose and Davie. They had to run to keep from being killed because General Bill had fifty men or more. This caused a whole lot of trouble because all of the boys on our side of the river were terribly mad at the way General Bill's soldiers had treated them.[4]

One of the men France chose to fight Anse was Asa Harmon McCoy, brother of Randal McCoy, Anse's future foe in the Hatfield and McCoy feud. There would be fatal consequences for France and Asa Harmon McCoy, as General Bill was shot by Anse later in the war, and McCoy was killed by Jim Wheeler Wilson and Jim Vance, Anse's uncle, in the closing days of the struggle.

Soon after the trouble in Kentucky, word reached Mate Creek that Logan County's second Confederate regiment was being organized at the county seat. The way Anse heard that news and his immediate reaction are missing pages of history. However, regional newspapers did save descriptions of the local traditions of that time, which also were firmly entrenched in the memories of the community's old-timers long after the war ended.

At Logan C.H., about one thousand persons assembled to participate in the ceremony of raising the Southern Confederacy flag. Amidst the greatest enthusiasm of the assembly, the singing of "Dixie," etc., this beautiful emblem of our second independence was run up to the top of the pole by the fair hands of four young ladies, where, gracefully spreading itself to the breeze, it displayed the three stripes and fourteen stars in a circle, with one big one in the center for Virginia.

Mr. J.G. Newman of Kanawha, Col. G.R. Floyd of Logan, and Capt. Ira J. McGinnis of Cabell in succession then delivered appropriate addresses.

Col. Floyd, though not used to public speaking, develops in these times much of the fire and force of a born orator. His voice is powerful and melodious, and his bearing is striking and manly.

The day after the flag-raising, the ladies in military style, commanded by Major Browning and escorted by the volunteer company and the home guard, marched to the courthouse and invited Mr. Newman to address them again.[5]

The young were especially moved by the ceremonies and left their recollections in personal writings that came to light only many years later. Cora Chambers, one such writer who saved the tale, wrote, "In early years our mother told us when the Wildcats were mustered out in June '61, she rode horseback and wore a hoop skirt. There was lots of excitement. Old Dad Brannon beat the drum, and I guess that was all the band they had. A deaf and dumb boy got excited and rolled down the stairs that were in the courthouse."[6]

Anse Hatfield in the Logan Wildcats

Anse Hatfield was caught up in the excitement and climbed on one of the wagons that rolled out of Logan, taking the men to Charleston, where they would be mustered into the regiment being organized by John McCausland, an erstwhile instructor at Virginia Military Institute who had been ordered by Robert E. Lee to begin training troops for the struggle.

McCausland was a remarkable man and would have been such in any age or nation. He is most often recalled today as the man who ordered Chambersburg burned in Pennsylvania in 1864. Yet he also was the man who organized the first Confederate regiments in southern West Virginia and led them in the struggle for control of the important Kanawha Valley and at Fort Donelson and in defense of the Shenandoah Valley in the final year of the war.

Michael J. Pauley, one of McCausland's biographers, wrote that the soldier was of Scot-Irish descent and was born in St. Louis, Missouri, on September 13, 1836, a son of John and Harriet Price McCausland. John McCausland's parents died within a few months of one another in 1843. The three McCausland children were cared for by their grandmother until her death in 1849, when the boys were taken to live with their widowed aunt, Jane Smith, at Henderson (West) Virginia, a small town near Point Pleasant, where the Kanawha joins the Ohio River.[7]

John grew into a tall and slender young man with light blue eyes that turned almost black when he became angry. He was educated first at Buffalo Academy about twenty-five miles from his home. He then continued his education at Virginia Military Institute in Lexington, Virginia, between August 2, 1853 and the spring of 1857. While there, McCausland came under the influence of his greatest mentor, Thomas J. (Stonewall) Jackson.

After graduating first in his class at VMI with training in engineering, John went to the University of Virginia for the equivalent of a modern graduate degree. After some months studying law in the office of Judge John W. Brockenbrough, McCausland began teaching mathematics and artillery tactics under the supervision of Stonewall Jackson.

In 1859, at age 23, McCausland was in a perfect position to become involved in the dramatic events that year when John Brown occupied Harpers Ferry in an explosive and heedless act that triggered the violence of the era. McCausland stood at Jackson's side at Charlestown, (West) Virginia, when Brown was taken to the trial that ended with his conviction and hanging.

Brown's action at Harpers Ferry did more than "frighten old Virginia 'til she trembled through and through," as the song *John Brown's Body* later claimed.

Brown's raid planted the seeds of what the United States would become after the war that took the lives of six hundred thousand young men.

Many in the south after Harpers Ferry believed that it was imperative to keep control of the federal government to prevent abolitionists from igniting slave rebellions. When Republican Abraham Lincoln was elected president the following year, those southerners thought they had no choice except to leave the union.

When Virginia joined the ranks of the seceding states on May 23, 1861, all Virginia's young military officers were forced to make their decision for or against the union. McCausland was one who fought for the south. On April 29, 1861, Robert E. Lee sent McCausland a letter ordering him to "proceed to the valley of the Kanawha and muster into the service of the state such volunteer companies...as may offer their services...take command of them and direct the military operations for the protection of that section of the country."[8]

McCausland acted promptly, taking regiments like the Logan Wildcats into the 36th Virginia Infantry. His first general order was printed in *The Kanawha Valley Star* on May 11, 1861. That order called for volunteer companies from Mason, Jackson, and Putnam Counties to meet at the Putnam County town of Buffalo. Units from Cabell, Wayne, and Logan Counties were to gather at Barboursville in Cabell County. Companies from Kanawha, Wyoming, Raleigh, Fayette, Nicholas, and Clay Counties were ordered to report to Charleston.[9] Some historians think Anse Hatfield was among that number and reported to Barboursville with the remainder of the Wildcats in early June 1861.

The Logan Wildcats in Western Virginia

As these events happened, Virginia's military authorities soon understood that McCausland needed help and commissioned Christopher Q. Tompkins of Gauley Bridge, (West) Virginia, as a colonel to take charge of operations.[10] It was a critical moment in part because the state of Ohio was mobilizing men to cross the great river and push into the Kanawha Valley. At the same time, the Ohio counties north of the Kanawha River were expressing open hostility to the south, and among them were individuals who wanted to create a new state loyal to the union.

Early in the summer of 1861, Henry A. Wise, the former governor of Virginia, had taken command of "Wise's Legion," which arrived in Charleston on June 26, 1861, when the clash with Ohio troops was just days away. Ohio's youthful commander, George B. McClelland, decided that his main objective was to secure control of the Baltimore and Ohio Railroad in northwestern Virginia for the Union. But he ordered General Jacob D. Cox to cross the Ohio River, and Wise, anticipating this threat, posted nine hundred men at present-day St. Albans, sixteen hundred men on the Elk River, Ripley, and Barboursville, and another thousand men scattered from the vicinity of Rich Mountain to Gauley Bridge.[11] On July 13, 1861, Confederates under Captain Albert J. Beckett and Lt. N.B. Bowyers, collided with General Cox's Union troops at Buffalo and were forced to retreat. Cox's men followed them, but on July 17, Union troops fought Confederates led by Colonel George S. Patton — grandfather of the famous World War II general of the same name.

The Battle of Scary Creek, as that encounter was called, was the skirmish where Anse Hatfield saw his first action, though some historians argue that the Logan Wildcats were not present. The Union troops retreated and McCausland's men, including Anse Hatfield, chased them to Pocatalico, where McCausland decided the Union men were too well defended to be attacked successfully.[12]

Thus Anse Hatfield's first battle for the South was the first struggle fought for control of the Kanawha Valley, and Hatfield's side won. Despite that victory, General Henry Wise ordered the Confederates to abandon Charleston. Just why he gave that order is something of a mystery. He may have felt the spot was indefensible, despite the fact that many younger soldiers of western Virginia were mountain men like Anse, perfectly capable of defending the hills around Charleston. In any event, the rebels fell back along the line of the Kanawha-James River Turnpike, burned the bridge near the mouth of Gauley, and camped at Bunger's Mill near Lewisburg on July 31, 1861.[13]

Some historians believe that General Wise's retreat from Charleston convinced General Robert E. Lee, the commanding officer of the section, that it was a mistake to leave Wise in charge of operations. On August 15, McCausland and his men were reassigned to General John B. Floyd's command. Floyd, a former governor of Virginia and former Secretary of War under President James Buchanan, was ordered to save western Virginia from Union control.

McCausland's men joined General Floyd's troops at Camp Gauley on August 25, 1861. On the next day, Floyd attacked the Union troops at Cross Lanes and routed the soldiers led by Union Colonel Erastus B. Tyler. McCausland's men — including Anse — were then ordered to garrison Summersville, which they did, and where they camped until September 8, 1861.[14]

On that day, McCausland learned that Brigadier General William S. Rosecrans was advancing with six thousand men from Sutton to the vicinity of Powell Mountain. Rosecrans' men were fired upon by snipers as they moved forward. If Anse Hatfield was among those present, it is more likely than not he was involved in that action.[15] McCausland urged Floyd to attack Rosecrans as the Union men moved down the southern side of the mountain, but Floyd ordered another retreat, and the Union army occupied Summersville on September 10.

The immediate result of that decision was the historic battle at Carnifax Ferry on September 12, 1861. Though a military draw, Carnifax Ferry became one of the worst defeats suffered by the Confederacy in western Virginia because General Floyd retreated from his position after the battle.

After the battle at Carnifax Ferry, the 36th Virginia Infantry remained under General John B. Floyd's command, even though General Lee took command of the section after Floyd's army was defeated in the Cheat Mountain campaign that followed the battle at Carnifax Ferry. Both armies spent time maneuvering for the better position late that summer, but in early October the Confederates learned that Union troops had fallen back from Big Sewell Mountain to Hawk's Nest.

General Floyd ordered his men to pursue them in the direction of Fayetteville and on to Cotton Hill. McCausland and other officers urged Floyd to attack there, but as Floyd hesitated waiting orders from Richmond, the Union soldiers under Colonel C.A. Devilliers attacked the Confederates and forced them to retreat to Loop Mountain.[16]

The rebels could not hold that position and so, retreated again from Loop Mountain to Pine Creek to Meadow Bluff, and then on to Dublin, where they arrived on December 9, 1861.[17] The 36th Virginia Infantry, which included Anse Hatfield and the Logan Wildcats, was heavily involved in that long retreat, serving as the rear guard.

McCausland biographer Michael Pauley wrote that the regiment destroyed some three hundred tents, as well as food, blankets, and clothing during that retreat.[18] Though it would be of interest to know if Anse Hatfield was involved in all that, there are no such records. It is thought that Anse soon was involved in the most dramatic and notable battle in the early days of the war in the West — the struggle for Fort Donelson.

The Logan Wildcats at Fort Donelson

Fort Donelson was the siege that opened the Union's way south through the Mississippi Valley. The consequences were staggering — eventually fatal — for the South. At Fort Donelson, General Ulysses Simpson Grant earned his nickname "Unconditional Surrender." It also was the place where Nathan Bedford Forrest made his dramatic escape and so could continue to harass the Union soldiers for the remainder of the war. Fort Donelson was the battle which led Anse Hatfield to leave his fellow soldiers of the Logan Wildcats and go to the 45th Virginia Infantry Battalion. Civil War historian J.L. Scott recorded the beginning of that tale:

> The move from Newbern to Bowling Green, Kentucky, showed how the railroads, or in this instance, the lack of railroads, affected the war effort. As the crow flies, Bowling Green is approximately 250 miles from Newbern, but to move an entire army required the railroads....
> It was around January 8, 1862, when the 36th Virginia Infantry arrived in Bowling Green and along with the remainder of General Floyd's Virginia troops joined the forces commanded by A.S. Johnston....[19]

Albert Sidney Johnston was the southern general most trusted by Confederate President Jefferson Davis at the beginning of the war. Johnston and Davis had been fellow cadets at the West Point Military Academy. Some southerners considered Johnston as the model soldier until his death at the battle of Shiloh in the spring of 1862.

In 1861, however, General Johnston's assignment was to protect Nashville, which could be used as a base for the defense of the Cumberland and Tennessee Rivers, both of which flowed to the heart of the South. The nature of the terrain put the South on the defense and the North on the offense. Fort Henry was built on the Tennessee River to guard Nashville, but the site was so poorly chosen that when the river flooded, gunboats could move easily within six hundred yards of the fort. That was Fort Henry's fatal flaw.

On February 6, 1862, General Grant moved fifteen thousand men against Fort Henry, aided by gunboats commanded by Commodore Andrew Foote. The Tennessee River was at flood stage, the gunboats had moved into position, and Commodore Foote's men pounded away at the fort until it surrendered, but not before defending General Lloyd Tilghman ordered most of his troops to retreat to Fort Donelson.[20]

Fort Donelson was a much tougher nut to crack. It was located on a bluff, which made it a difficult target for gunboats. When the gunboat assault failed, General Grant settled in for a siege, though the Union commander thought John B. Floyd was "no soldier," and that General Gideon Pillow was simply "conceited."[21] Generals Floyd and Pillow agreed that an escape route was needed, and Pillow led the men out of the fort behind the fierce Nathan Bedford Forrest. The assault was a success, and the escape route was open.

General Floyd, however, showing the indecision that plagued him, ordered the men to retreat back inside the fort, leaving only a thin line of defenders to guard the escape route. An infuriated Forrest told Floyd he did not intend to sit out the war in a federal prison and led his men back out across the Cumberland River to Nashville and safety.

Among those who created and then defended the escape route was the 36th Virginia Infantry under McCausland, who saw sixty of his men killed that day. Anse Hatfield was one of the Logan County men involved in that action and may have heard of General Grant's famous dictum that the fort faced the prospect of unconditional surrender.

McCausland refused to surrender with others under General Floyd's command and seized two steamboats to escape with about half his remaining men across the Cumberland River. The other surviving half of the 36th Infantry surrendered with General Floyd, whose actions sparked an investigation by a furious Confederate President Davis.[22]

Another important development that followed the disaster at Fort Donelson was that the 36th Infantry was reorganized. Anse Hatfield left the Wildcats then and later joined the Virginia State Line, which became one unit of the 45th Battalion Virginia Infantry. Thus in the following months of the war, Anse was involved in the defense of western Virginia, which still included the Tug Fork and Guyandot River Valleys.

Logan County as a Confederate Stronghold

To understand Anse Hatfield's decision to serve with the Virginia State Line and his later decision to form his own unit of home guards, it is important to know what was happening in Logan County while Anse was away from the Tug and Guyandot with the remainder of the Logan Wildcats. The early war years were not an especially good time for Logan County.

Late in her life, Sarah Justice McDonald recalled how Union troops behaved when they pillaged her family's home in Logan County. She told one of her grandchildren that the men took all their livestock and moveable goods, then took her Uncle Charles Justice out behind the barn and shot him dead as a Confederate sympathizer.[23]

Bitterness caused by such incidents lasted for decades in Logan County. Another typical memory told about Asa Harmon McCoy, who was shot dead near a cave near the later site of Matewan on the Kentucky border. Until very recently, no one ever knew who fired the shot that killed McCoy, but popular suspicion fell on Anse Hatfield and his uncle, Jim Vance. Many later traced the start of the feud of the 1880s to that Civil War incident.

Another tale that was told in Logan County in later years was that a man named Pryce Lewis came to the community at the start of the war, pretending to be a buyer of goods for the Confederate Army, but actually acting as a Union spy. He struck up an acquaintance with Reece Browning, who served as Lewis' guide around the community. Lewis later gave reports to the federal government about popular attitudes in the county, which may have led to the Union decision to burn the local courthouse when the town of Aracoma was occupied in 1862.

By far, the four most often repeated war stories from Logan County are the ones that told of the battle at Chapmanville Gap, the skirmish at Harts Creek, the fire at the courthouse, and the hanging of Henry Walker. Such tales can be told in that order, and they are all pertinent to the first three years of the war.

Logan County was left alone in 1864 and 1865, though it should always be remembered that much work fell on the shoulders of women like Sallie Smith Garrett, who later told historian Mary Hurst that she and others "raised pretty good crops."[24] Sallie Garrett was also one who remembered Chapmanville Gap, saying that some in the county believed the tale that the gap was haunted after the battle there in the summer of 1861.

Logan County got that first taste of war on September 25, 1861, according to a report of the Chapmanville Gap battle that was printed in *The Cincinnati Gazette* of October 1 that year. That report claimed that a Colonel Piatt led 550 men of the 34th Ohio Regiment into southwestern Virginia, accompanied by another 500 men who were a joint force of the First Kentucky Regiment under a Lieutenant Colonel Enyart and 200 volunteers.

The forces moved together until they reached Peytona, on the Cole River — later renamed the "Coal River" — where they separated, Col. Enyart going up the Cole River. Col. Enyart did not meet the rebels in force at any place, but his men did meet and ford swollen rivers and marched on short rations, and were anxious to meet with Virginia rebels.

Col. Enyart's command immediately proceeded to the Boone Courthouse and encamped that night one mile beyond. The next day, after proceeding some sixteen miles, they came up against the advance guard of the Confederates, consisting of cavalry, when a brisk fire was exchanged. The cavalry retreated.

Afterwards, the battalion was immediately put in order of battle. The advance guard of fifteen men was led forward by Adjt. Clarke, proceeding along the road. Scouts were sent out on either side of the road to meet and repulse sharpshooters of the rebels. The force proceeded about two miles, meeting the rebel pickets, exchanging shots with them incessantly, and driving them back with increased confusion at each charge.[25]

Like many news reports of the time, this does not give many details of the actual battle at the gap, but there is a letter which was written by a soldier of the 34th Ohio Regiment which does give such detail. It was printed in *The Cincinnati Commercial* on October 8, 1861.

> The Zouave 34th Regiment, have had a chance to show their mettle. This was on Wednesday, on Kanawha Gap, near Chapmanville, Va.
>
> After marching 42 miles, they came upon the enemy, who was behind breastworks, but could not stand our boys' steady fire, for they retreated in utter consternation, their Col. J.W. Davis of Greenbrier, Va., (but the traitor is a native of Portsmouth, Ohio) being mortally wounded.
>
> We killed 20, took three prisoners, a secesh flag twenty feet long with 15 stars, four horses, one wagon, ten rifles (one of which I claim), 12 muskets and commissary stores (very low).
>
> We lost three killed, nine wounded, one since died. The rout of the enemy was complete, although they had a brave and skillful commander and a strong position, with two days' information of our intentions. They fled the moment their commander fell.
>
> The fight lasted about ten minutes opposite the breastworks but a running fire was kept up previous to that by the bushwhackers and rebel cavalry for two hours.
>
> At every turn of the road over the mountains they would fire upon our advance men, wheel around to gallop away. This kind of fight was kept up till we suddenly came upon their breastworks, immediately in the line of our entire column.
>
> It was made on the side of a knoll, between two mountain sides, the road running between the mountains and knoll on our right, and a small ravine running between the knoll and the mountain on our left.

The wily rebel commander had adroitly cut down the brush on the right, placing a force of one hundred men on the mountaintop on our right, who raked our column from the front to the center. This was to draw our attention from their breastwork.

Our men naturally fired upon the rebels on their right, steadily advancing up the road until within twenty feet of the enemy's work, when the rebels suddenly opened fire from their right, left, and center.

The order from Col. Piatt and Lieut. Col. Toland to flank right and left was immediately responded to by the Zouaves with a hurrah, a Zouave yell, and a cry of "wood up" by Little Red, a dash by our boys upon the enemy's right, left, and center, a fire from the enemy's breastworks, above which about 300 rebel heads suddenly appeared, unknown by our men 'till that moment.

They sent a perfect storm of bullets over, under and into our men. A few moments more and our boys were inside the breastworks, chasing them over the mountains.... They left 29 dead behind.

We buried our three brave dead comrades that night, carried our wounded to the house wherein the rebel colonel lay mortally wounded, deserted by all his men but one. Our whole column finally marched into the little town of Chapmanville, formerly headquarters of the enemy, and camped for the night.

In my next letter I may describe our home march — or I should perhaps say homeward swim — for we were in the water two days and two nights, and only half a cracker to each man was given out by our commissary.[26]

Following that battle, a Camp Piatt was established in southwestern Virginia, most likely in Boone County. From there, another Union troop, led by a Colonel John C. Paxton of the 2nd Virginia Regiment Cavalry, began a scouting expedition in the remote Logan County area known as Harts Creek and wrote the following report about what happened:

...Left Camp Piatt with 140 men on the night of the 12th...crossed Coal River and made as far as Thompson's at the mouth of Spruce Fork of Little Coal 26 miles. On the 13th traveled 30 miles to Gunnoe's on Pond Fork of Little Coal. On the 14th marched to Wyoming Courthouse, a distance of 17 miles, arriving there at 12 noon. Meeting no rebels and hearing nothing from there, crossed over mountains down Huff's Creek to Guyandot River, a distance of 16 miles and halted for the night.

I sent Captain Davidson of Company E with 25 men up Guyandot River to ascertain if the report was true that 13 rebels were encamped at the house of a Mr. Christian six miles above.

On the way up he discovered a rebel mountain brigade on the opposite side of the river, passed them without being noticed, forded the river and got in their rear and succeeded in capturing five horses and equipment, a lieutenant and three privates. Four others took to the mountains and escaped in the darkness.

Their saddle bags contained some 400 rounds of ammunition, which with their guns were turned over to the home guards who accompanied the expedition....

On the 15th we marched up Buffalo Creek and across the mountains to Pond Fork, thence to camp on the 16th with the loss of but one horse abandoned from fatigue.[27]

Far more serious action, as far as Logan County was concerned, was the action of the Union troops under Colonel Edward Siber, who burned the courthouse in January 1862. That raid cost the county its first deed book, which was hidden on the "backbone" mountain above Hatfield Island and never recovered. Allie McDonald told the beginning of that tale in a history article she wrote in 1976:

> Emma Fillinger was a child living with her parents, John and Sarah (Sallie) Fillinger in what is now known as "old Henlawson" when the war broke out between the states. After the war, she married Harrison White, and they were my grandparents. She told her grandchildren many stories of the olden days, including some about the war years....
>
> During the winter of 1862, a rumor was spread abroad that a company of soldiers were roving the countryside and were stealing horses, cattle and anything they could lay hands on, and that they were headed for the Guyandot River Valley.
>
> The farmers in that vicinity decided to herd their farm animals together and drive them to a safer place. John Fillinger was one of the men designated to take the livestock to Crawley Creek, as it was in a more remote section. Several men — riding horses, carrying many of the possessions dear to their hearts, and driving the livestock — left one morning very early for Crawley Creek.
>
> Later that day Emma Fillinger, a child of ten, hearing a noise, ran to the window and looked out to see what was happening, then ran to her mother and told her that a crowd of men

dressed in blue with little blue caps were passing, and her mother hurriedly ran to see and told her that they were Union soldiers, and she had been afraid they might come while John was away, but thanked God that they were going on.

Just then they heard a shot and the next instant the soldiers were turning around and coming back. They came toward their home carrying one of their men. He had been shot from across the river. They were talking in loud, angry voices — speaking in German. The Fillinger family were Germans, and Mrs. Fillinger could understand them and talk to them.

They ordered her to take the children to the loft and stay there and not disturb them. Some of the children were ill with measles, and she was afraid to take them to the loft, but she was more afraid to disobey their orders. Taking some food and water with her little brood, she climbed the rough steps to the loft, trembling and groping her way.

There were beds in the loft, where her sons often slept, and some bedding, and she was able to keep them warm. They were terrified and feared for their lives all the while they stayed up there, which was from around noon one day until the afternoon of the next day, but it seemed like an eternity....

During the afternoon Emma motioned for her mother to come and see what they were doing. The mother saw that they were digging a grave and knew their wounded comrade had died, and was sorely troubled as to what their fate might be. However, in a short time, they buried the soldier and immediately left, leaving the house as they had found it, only very dirty. But they destroyed and burned homes all along as they traveled to Logan, where they almost destroyed the whole town, burning the courthouse....[28]

Edward Siber, commander of the Union troops, wrote his report on the matter that was included in the series of books of official war orders published by the United States Government long after the war. In his report, Siber told about the march of men under a Major Ankele from Chapmanville to Logan, adding they were fired on from nearly every house along the way. Siber then wrote the heart of his report:

By this fire was mortally wounded Captain Goecke of Company B, which exasperated the men of the regiment so much that a number of them threw themselves in the river and reached, by swimming, the opposite bank, destroyed the houses from where they had been fired at, took away some rifles and made some prisoners.

> Having received a report of these unexpected hostilities, I hastened with the companies from Turtle Creek to join those in the Guyandot Valley, which I reached on the morning of January 14. Marching with the whole detachment under my orders and on both banks of the Guyandot to Logan, I found this place completely evacuated by the whole male population, which, armed with rifles, had retreated to a steep mountain on the other side of the Guyandot, where at the same time appeared a number of horsemen and where had been assembled a number of bushwhackers.[29]

Siber related that he made the Logan County Courthouse his headquarters, but saw that the local Confederates were so unpredictable that the only resistance to his troops would be sniper fire. His men were attacked once, and a Corporal John Behm of Company C was killed, but the attack was driven back. A heavy rain began that night, making it more difficult for the Union troops to remain in the area. Siber then wrote:

> I ordered for the next morning at four o'clock the evacuation of the place, which under the circumstances could not be held without more sacrifice of life, and as the inhabitants of this town had acted with so much animosity and other buildings of this place had long ago been converted into barracks used as a principal point of refuge for rebel cavalry, I thought it to be my duty to deprive the enemy of such position, only valuable to him and useless to us, and ordered to set fire to these buildings before my departure.[30]

Siber mentioned that the main opposition he faced on his journey along the Guyandot River and his retreat from the area was the persistent gunfire from a unit centered at Chapmanville called the Black Striped Company. J.E. (Uncle Ned) Peck believed that the Black Striped Company was the troop that caused the Union soldiers to be so hostile and that George Doss had been the member of that company that fired the shot that killed Goecke.

Creation of the Virginia State Line

The panic caused by such incidents across all of southwestern Virginia led to the creation of the military unit known as the Virginia State Line and to partisan companies that worked in cooperation with the regular army. In the spring of 1862, following the disaster at Fort Donelson, General John B. Floyd was relieved of his command, but retained his popularity among the people of southwestern Virginia, who petitioned the state government to give Floyd a responsible position defending the region.

On May 15, 1862, the Virginia Confederate Legislature — of which Logan County's James Andrew Nighbert was a delegate — authorized the creation of the Virginia State Line, with the intention of recapturing the western part of the state, particularly the Kanawha Valley salines, and to guard the Virginia Tennessee Railroad, one of the lifelines of the South.[31] Floyd was given authority to enlist twenty thousand men who were not eligible for service under the Confederate Conscription Act of 1862.

John B. Floyd was the brother of George Rogers Clark Floyd, one of the most powerful friends of Big Eph Hatfield and his family. Anse Hatfield, who escaped the Fort Donelson battle and who was at loose ends during the following months, was drawn rather naturally to service under John B. Floyd, who was described as one of the most popular figures in Anse's section of Virginia.[32] Floyd's men were given the choice of enlisting for twelve months or three years and were to serve under the same terms as partisan rangers — that is, they were given rights to a share in all property taken from "the enemy," according to *The Southern Advocate* of September 4, 1862.[33] Virginia also authorized Floyd to form two regiments and agreed to supply their needs for the first few months. Civil War historian Jeffrey C. Weaver wrote:

> The 1st Virginia State Line was organized with 10 companies in the latter part of 1862, most of the men coming from Logan County, Virginia. Several members of this regiment were former members of the 36th Virginia Infantry. Lt. Col. Beckley and two captains of the 1st Virginia State Line had previously served in the 36th Virginia Infantry, as had Major James A. Nighbert.[34]

The First Regiment included Captain Green W. Taylor's cavalry company of Logan County, Captain Daniel Elkin's cavalry company from Tazewell and Boone Counties, Captain William Chafin's cavalry company of Wayne County, Captain William T. Butcher's cavalry company, Captain William A. Dempsey's cavalry company of Logan County, Captain George W. Hackworth's cavalry company from Cabell County, Captain John Rundell's company from Wayne County, Captain Benjamin H. Justice's company from Logan and Wyoming Counties, Captain John Buchanan's company from Logan and Cabell Counties, and Captain Robert Lawson's company from Logan County.[35]

Creation of the 45th Battalion Virginia Infantry

The Virginia State Line did not exist long as a regiment independent of the Confederate forces from Virginia. The regiment was disbanded by Virginia on March 31, 1863, since it had become rather undistinguished because of many poor decisions made by Floyd and other commanding officers. Many of the soldiers then joined the 45th Battalion Virginia Infantry under Lieutenant Colonel Henry M. Beckley, which was made part of the Confederate Army on December 10, 1863.

Weaver's history of that battalion claims that it took Henry Beckley nearly eight months to put the company together, but by May 7, 1863, it was ready for action. The date of Anse Hatfield's enlistment has not been recorded, but Weaver's roster shows that Ellison and Elias Hatfield joined the first week of May. It is quite possible that Anse accompanied his brothers as well as another, most surprising, soldier of the Confederate Army — their father, Big Eph Hatfield.[36]

The unit the Hatfields joined was John Buchanan's Company, which was reorganized from Company 1 of the 1st Virginia State Line. Its officers were well known in southwestern Virginia at the time and have lived on in history, as many later were involved in the famous feud. The list includes: Captain John Buchanan, 1st Lieutenant William S. Ferrell, 1st Lieutenant Anderson Hatfield, 2nd Lieutenant Ellison Hatfield, 3rd Lieutenant James Williamson, 1st Sergeant John C. Sansom, 1st Sergeant Andrew M. Toler, 2nd Sergeant Harrison Stafford, 3rd Sergeant John Davis, 1st Corporal Augustus Francisco, 2nd Corporal James Duty, 3rd Corporal William T. Patterson, 4th Corporal Obediah Blankenship, and Corporal J. Buchanan.[37]

That regiment soon received orders from Major General Samuel Jones of the Confederate Army's Department of Western Virginia to aid the defense of Saltville, Virginia, under Brigadier General John Stuart Williams. The Confederates remained in the general area guarding the salt mines vital to the Confederacy until July 1863, when events took place that deeply concerned Anse Hatfield and his fellow soldiers from western Virginia, as described by Jeffrey C. Weaver.

> In cooperation with Major General Ambrose E. Burnside's planned major thrust into the heart of the Confederate States, Brigadier General Julius White led a brigade from Beaver Creek, Floyd County, Kentucky, to Gladeville, Virginia in early July 1863. Part of the still organizing 45th Battalion scouted into Pike County in early July 1863 and skirmished with White's command on Pond Creek on July 6. U.S. Army Colonel Dan Cameron led detachments of the 39th Kentucky and 65th Illinois into the Tug River Valley to disperse Captain John Buchanan's Company (Company B, 45th Battalion Virginia Infantry)....[38]

White reported that his soldiers had killed five rebels and captured twenty, but Buchanan's mountaineers may have won the skirmish. A correspondent for *The Lynchburg Virginian* wrote an account that claimed the federals were led by "the notorious" Colonel John Dils, who, many years later, became one of the supporters of Randal McCoy during the feud years. Though historians and biographers should not speculate, one cannot help wondering if Anse Hatfield was one of the defenders of the Tug and if Dils recalled the skirmish in later years.

A few Confederates were captured, including the three Francisco brothers, Oscar, Patrick, and Samuel, who helped Anse Hatfield on many occasions during the feud. *The Ironton Register* added that the fighting took place across Tug Fork in Logan County and that the Union troops burned John Buchanan's Logan County home.

White's men then defeated Confederates at Gladeville, Virginia, and more Confederate reverses followed around Wytheville and along the Virginia Tennessee Railroad, though the rebels counterattacked and drove back Union troops led by Colonel John T. Toland, who were acting as auxiliaries of White's forces. The main action that involved units of the 45th Battalion that summer, however, were maneuvers to protect the salt mines of southwestern Virginia.

Anse Hatfield is not known to have participated in any major actions, though it is likely that he was with the men encamped in Logan County near the end of November in the fateful year of 1863. Hatfield family tradition claims that Anse was frustrated by his role away from the dramatic events reported from Pennsylvania in July 1863, when General Robert E. Lee's forces were crushed at Gettysburg. In the absence of any testimony from Anse, his family believes that the actions of the 45th Battalion affected Anse's thinking when he chose to organize his own guerrilla band in 1864. Jeffrey C. Weaver's history contains two paragraphs which indicate the general condition of that time.

> On December 10, 1863, Captain John S. Witcher of the 3rd West Virginia Cavalry reported capturing some members of the 45th Battalion Virginia Infantry and eight other Confederate units during a scout through Boone, Wayne, and Logan counties. Federal reports for this area and period indicate skirmishing with generic "bushwhackers" and do not specifically mention the 45th Battalion Virginia Infantry. It is difficult to determine which refer to Beckley's Battalion and which to other Confederate partisans operating in the area. Prudence dictated that Beckley move his men to safer quarters for the winter.
>
> The 45th Battalion Virginia Infantry returned to Camp Georgia by December 20. This move out of the Tug and Guyandot Valleys inspired several men to leave the battalion on December 15. Those who remained on duty spent Christmas and passed into the New Year on the outskirts of Jeffersonville in Tazewell County.[39]

Anse Hatfield's Withdrawal from Confederate Service

That information is a precise match of Hatfield family tradition recorded by Coleman A. Hatfield. From his accounts, it appears that Anse did not want to leave his homeland unprotected, especially since Union troops had burned the main town in his home county while he and fellow soldiers were absent fighting in eastern West Virginia and Tennessee. Anse had more personal reasons for leaving the army that December as well, and his grandson recorded his reasons.

> In the fall of 1863, General Beckley's army was encamped in east Tennessee.... Among his soldiers were Anse Toler and "Slater Jim" Hatfield, brothers-in-law from Wyoming County. Slater Jim also was Anse Hatfield's uncle.
>
> Beckley's army was poised for action, guarding Lee's backdoor, ready to join his forces in combating the Union Army as it was breaking through the Cumberlands in a determined effort to roll across the plains of Georgia to the sea. All leaves were cancelled; Beckley stated that no man could be spared at such a critical moment.
>
> A message came to Anse Toler that his wife, back in the hills, was at the point of death and not expected to live. Toler felt that he needed a friend to approach General Beckley at such a serious moment. No one in the outfit was better suited or more willing to request a favor for any of his men than Lieutenant Anderson Hatfield....[40]

A third man involved in this episode was named Jonathan Morgan, a son of David Morgan of Wyoming County.[41] Anse's appeal to Beckley and other officers was not successful. In keeping with the mountaineer tradition that a man's first allegiance was to his own people, Anse counseled Slater Jim and Anse Toler to go ahead with their plans to return home and that he would intercede on Slater Jim and Toler's behalf if there was any other trouble from the officers. Slater Jim and Anse Toler rode away, arriving at Toler's house in the nick of time, according to Coleman A. Hatfield's history.

> When Toler reached his wife's bedside, she opened her failing eyes and said, "I knowed God would bring you to me, Ansie, before I died. I couldn't bear to leave the children until you were here. I'm so glad that Jim came with you. Sister Rachel will be able to bear it much better, knowing that both of you were here when I went home to Jesus."
>
> The grief-stricken soldier stood by and watched his neighbors and kinsmen lay the body of his wife to rest. After telling the children goodbye for a while, Toler and Slater Jim mounted their horses to ride day and night until they came again to General Beckley's command.

The stern old Southerner speedily called a court martial and, after reviewing the circumstances, ordered Anderson Toler and James Hatfield to be shot at sunrise on the following day.

He called Lieutenant Anse Hatfield and directed him to execute the condemned men at daybreak on the following morning. The grim-faced young officer muttered as he strode out of the headquarters of General Beckley that if Toler and Slater Jim had to die that many more would bite the dust.

Just across the valley, Vincent Witcher, the Confederate raider of the black flag, was encamped with his army. Under his command was old Captain Jim Vance of Russell County, a maternal uncle to Anderson Hatfield.

A secret message was dispatched by Hatfield to Jim, the message being carried by Henry Mitchell to bring forty of his best horses, saddles, and bridles for the use of Hatfield in carrying out a detailed order of General Beckley.

It should be recalled that this was very much a family matter, in the view of the Hatfields. Not only was Jim Vance one of Anse's uncles, but also Henry Mitchell was married to Biddie Hatfield, who was Anse's younger sister. In Anse's opinion, he was acting in the best interests of his own family, which was more important to him than service in the Confederate Army.

As the dawn lifted over the Cumberlands on the following morning, forty soldiers were riding in a sweeping gallop northward up the Clinch River Valley through southwest Virginia.

At the front of this column rode Anse Toler and Slater Jim. Next behind, with his eyes never wavering from the condemned soldiers as he led the remainder of the speeding column, came Anse Hatfield, an intrepid, brown-bearded soldier leaving the lost cause, riding back to the new state that only a short time before had joined the Union.[42]

If the order to execute Slater Jim Hatfield and Anse Toler was not enough incentive for Anse Hatfield to leave the rebel army, there was a second episode near the end of 1863 that also convinced Anse his services were needed closer home than they were in the army camp. F.S. Harris of Nashville, Tennessee, wrote an article about Anse printed in the October 1900 edition of *Confederate Veteran* magazine that explained the other circumstances:

> Some time, I think, about 1863, a party of men such as always infest border territory went to (Anse's) house and, in a most brutal manner, turned his family out. Nor was this near all the indignities to which they were subjected. On hearing of it,

Capt. Hatfield secured leave of absence from the army, and promptly settled with the villains.[43]

Whatever the exact circumstances were, Anse was not a man to remain inactive very long when stirring events were happening. His 1863 reunion with his wife, Vicie, led to the birth of their second son, the famous William Anderson Hatfield, known to students of feud lore as "Cap," so named because his father was a partisan captain and the son was "the little captain."

Anse Hatfield's Home Guard Partisan Band

Anse soon realized that the Confederacy could not recover from the disaster at Gettysburg and in that changing scene, his best role was to continue protecting the Tug and Guyandot Valleys as best he could, with men acting independently of the Rebel Army but in general accord with the Confederate war aims. At about that time, the winter of 1864, Anse became acquainted with William S. (Rebel Bill) Smith of Wayne County, West Virginia. How the two met is not known, but the Hatfield family claims that Anse was independent and that he worked in cooperation with Smith's actions during the final sixteen months of the war.[44]

Jeffrey C. Weaver wrote that Smith joined Company K 8th Virginia Cavalry at the start of the war and remained with that unit until the summer of 1862. He then joined the Virginia State Line but soon created Company D, 2nd Battalion Kentucky Mounted Rifles. He resigned from that unit on January 24, 1864, and began his raids as the leader of an informal guerilla regiment.[45]

Rebel Bill Smith's exploits as the leader of raids and one of the defenders of Saltville, Virginia, have been well documented by Weaver and by Byron Morris, who wrote a series of articles about Smith for *The Wayne County News* in 1988. Regrettably, not as much good work has been done concerning Anse's activities, though Weaver notes that Hatfield was present during several of Smith's raids. Coleman A. Hatfield saved some record of that time:

> Devil Anse and Rebel Bill Smith participated with the southern forces at the battle of Scary Creek which historians mentioned in the campaigns of southern West Virginia.
>
> Upon one occasion, old foxy Rebel Bill and Devil Anse, hearing of a Yankee steamboat headed up the Ohio River, mounted round bee gums on cart wheels and painted them black to resemble cannons. When the steamboat hove into sight, they commanded it to stop or it would be blown to pieces. A force of men went on board and took what supplies were available.
>
> On another occasion, old sly Bill donned a union officer's uniform and boarded a Yankee steamboat which was loaded with 150 Negro laborers under the direction of union forces. The men were being sent up the river to King's Saltworks. During the

night, the steamboat "mysteriously" caught fire and burned while the supposed Yankee officer swam ashore and disappeared.[46]

Yet, for all his wile, Rebel Bill Smith did not earn Anse Hatfield's full respect. Anse's grandson wrote that about twenty years after the war, Anse was reminiscing about the war days around a mountain campfire with his feud boys. One asked if Rebel Bill stood up in the face of battle. Anse, with his characteristic sniff replied that, "He had seen Bill at the battle of Scary Creek just as they began firing, and Bill went over the riverbank to find shelter, and he went so fast you could have played marbles on his coattail."[47]

The Killing of General Bill France

The most famous Anse Hatfield war exploit that is well documented is the killing of Captain Bill France (sometimes called "Francis" and other times called "General France") which happened toward the end of the war. The death of France is of interest to historians because of its complexity and because that encounter links the names Anse Hatfield and Randal McCoy for the first time.

Most interestingly, the two men, both Confederates, were the team sent to kill France, whom they considered one of the worst menaces to the borderland midway through the war. Anse Hatfield and Randal McCoy were to serve as the "point men" in that affair. That meant they were to bear the joint responsibility for killing France. Their weapons were single shot rifles. Anse, the better marksman, was to take the first shot at France. If Anse's shot missed, Randal was to fire the second shot.

The precipitating cause for the mission was that France had offended one of the Confederate sympathizers of the neighborhood. France's men needed horses and took those that belonged to Mose Cline. One soldier shot Cline through the chest and he did not recover from the shot for many years. The horses were taken to Brushey Fork of John's Creek, but the rebels decided to retaliate and recapture the horses. Coleman A. Hatfield recorded the tale.

> During the fall of 1863, while many of the mountain men were guarding their own homes and helping friendly neighbors to do likewise, Harmon McCoy of Pike County was still under the leadership of General Bill France of the Pike homeguards that backed the Union, while Harmon's brother, Randolph McCoy of Pike County, was devoting his efforts toward assisting the southern cause.
>
> It was generally known that Devil Anse and General Bill would never be able to compromise their differences. During this time, Randolph McCoy, who was the senior of Devil Anse by several years, came with a band of followers and met with Anse.

A raiding party was organized and led by Devil Anse and guided into the territory by old Randolph.

This was a secret mission, in which Hatfield and McCoy led their followers to strategic positions within the territory where General Bill was returning from his main headquarters to his home on Peter Creek in Pike County.[48]

Coleman A. Hatfield wrote that the raiders advanced upon the headquarters of France and surrounded it in the early hours one morning. Randal McCoy suggested that Devil Anse take a position near a fallen tree where there was a good view of any movement France might make when daylight came. France left his cabin that morning and stepped to a side porch to relieve his bladder. He was called upon to surrender, but failed to respond to the order. An order to fire rang out, and Anse Hatfield shot France with a minie ball. France died soon after telling the rebels where to find the horses of Mose Cline that had been stolen by the Union men.

The consequences of the killing of France would follow Anse Hatfield and Randal McCoy to their graves. Though the incident did not lead directly to the infamous feud of the 1880s, the episodes were indirectly connected because of events later in the war and by the impact it had on the lives of Hatfield and McCoy. As Coleman A. Hatfield noted:

> The killing of France through the combined efforts of Randal McCoy and Devil Anse Hatfield and their followers aroused the homeguards of Kentucky and orders were sent out to take Devil Anse and any men known to have been connected with him on this raid.[49]

The Raid on Devil Anse Hatfield's Home

Captain John Coleman of Pike County, formerly one of Anse's friends, gathered forty armed men and crossed the Kentucky border into West Virginia one wintry night. Anse and a fellow soldier were resting in his log cabin at the time, but Vicie Hatfield experienced a flash of intuition, according to her grandson, and warned the men to get away.

> Vicie came in and said, "Ansie, you just got to get out and go to the hills. I know it is dark and snowy, but I just feel that something is going to happen."

Devil Anse and his companion then went to their cave retreat on the head of Straight Fork of Mate Creek. Soon, Captain Coleman and his forty horsemen came riding up the valley and surrounded Devil Anse's home.

Failing to find Anse, Captain Coleman called Vicie aside and said, "I have strict orders to bring Devil Anse to Kentucky, dead or alive. All I can tell you is he must keep out of the path of my men while we are searching for him in this state."[50]

Anse's fear of being caught off guard and captured by a government in the hands of unfriendly authorities haunted him to his dying day. That characteristic had been instilled in Anse during his youth by the old tales of Abner Vance's surrender to authorities to face charges of killing Lewis Horton.

That feeling was reinforced during the years of the Civil War and would reoccur often during the feud years. The same feeling would become part of Cap Hatfield's mind and would haunt him until his death. For two generations after the feud, such caution was a Hatfield characteristic and, if the oldest Hatfield male present in a room spoke the word "hush" in a commanding tone, the room would fall silent. Such authority figures were not trying to impose their will without any reason, but were seeking to guard the family.

The Killing of Asa Harmon McCoy

Captain Jim Coleman's words to Vicie Hatfield served to warn Devil Anse of even more than just that he was liable to be captured; the threat became more imminent toward the end of the war when the Hatfields and Anse's Uncle Jim Vance — Nancy Vance Hatfield's younger brother — learned that one of General Bill France's most loyal followers was seeking revenge for the killing of France. He was Asa Harmon McCoy. Coleman A. Hatfield again wrote the most detailed account of the events that followed.

> Word came from over on Peter Creek that they were coming to kill Anse, who was not able to turn a hand because he was sick with the flu. Anse sent for Uncle Jim Vance. Uncle Jim was always their mainstay, the one they leaned on.
> Uncle Jim always called Anse by the name "Anderson." So he said, "Anderson, if they don't get you tonight, they won't get you tomorrow night." And he made his word good.
> Harmon McCoy was supposed to be the triggerman for Bill France. Now mind you, Harmon McCoy was a brother to old Randal, but Harmon was a northern sympathizer though Randal was a rebel.
> Randal was on some raids with Anse during the war. This was twenty years before the feud broke out, but they saw through the same spectacles at that time.[51]

Jim Vance sent for Jim Wheeler Wilson, a fellow soldier in Vincent Witcher's Civil War regiment, and asked Wilson to help him protect Anse.

Vance and Wilson went to the forks of the river and crossed over. "They heard Uncle Jim's voice from the rocks as he forded the river," Coleman A. Hatfield wrote. "They knew he had a crooked mind."[52] The two gunmen suspected they could find a trace of Harmon McCoy in the snow that fell that night. Coleman A. Hatfield continued that tale:

> Jim Wheeler Wilson and Jim Vance watched the home of Harmon McCoy that night. They saw the back door of the house open, and the light shone out on the snow. And they saw Aunt Margaret (or Aunt Peggy), who was his wife.
>
> They took her backtrack as quickly as they could, and they followed her backtracks up a small creek 'till they came to a hollow. When they saw the tracks that went on up that hollow, they decided that was far enough and they would go on in daylight.[53]

Asa Harmon McCoy was encamped in the kind of place that mountaineers called a "rock house," a natural formation at the head of many Appalachian mountains. Such sites are hard to approach head-on and so are easily defended. Vance and Wilson, however, were skilled in the ways of the mountains. They went around the hillside and approached McCoy's rock cave from the back. The Hatfield tale claims:

> Vance and Wilson came stealthily down the hollow and they saw Harmon McCoy sitting on a log near a fire. They said that he had a grooved gun that he had for a long time. It was a cartridge gun, wasn't one of the guns like they had in the Civil War.
>
> He had a whole poke full of cartridges — so many that a man could have fired a gun for a week or two. They came down behind him before he saw them, and they had their guns on him. They disarmed him and started with him out of there.[54]

Vance and Wilson had bound Harmon McCoy with a rope. As they marched along with McCoy as a prisoner, the three men began arguing. Vance taunted McCoy with tales that McCoy had started a fight with Anse Hatfield just before the war. McCoy replied he had not bothered Hatfield, but clearly the three were tense and agitated. Any spark could have ignited a fire. In later years, Henry Mitchell, Anse Hatfield's brother-in-law, told Coleman A. Hatfield he had learned the story from Jim Vance.

> I heard Uncle Henry Mitchell tell this up at my father's house here. Uncle Henry was around then. He married Anse's youngest sister, Biddie.

Uncle Henry said Harmon McCoy denied that he intended to kill Anse to take revenge for Bill France. Vance disputed his word and said that he had been watching McCoy and knew he intended to kill Anse.

Uncle Henry said Wilson "flirted" his gun. That was the word he used. I always thought that meant he was playing like he was going to pull his gun from his holster. But Harmon McCoy tried to twist away and Wilson shot his brains out. This was twenty-five years before Vance's death.[55]

In the tenacious memories of the mountaineers, events linger. The killings of Bill France and Harmon McCoy could be — and often were — recalled long after the Civil War. With that knowledge, it is not hard to imagine what might have been at work in Randal McCoy's mind in 1882 and in later years: "One of them shot my brother during the war and now they've killed three of my sons."

Though Randal may not have realized the irony of the situation, he was one of the men sent to kill Bill France. If Devil Anse Hatfield's shot had missed, Randal may have killed France himself, thus becoming the Confederate who most offended Harmon McCoy. As the war memories lingered, however, the seed of trouble was planted.

---

[1] Blood Is Thicker Than Water, Coleman A. Hatfield.
[2] Warfare On The Borderline, Coleman A. Hatfield.
[3] The Logan Banner, November 3, 1936.
[4] Warfare On The Borderline, Coleman A. Hatfield.
[5] The Kanawha Valley Star, May 14, 1861.
[6] My Sketch Book, Cora Chambers.
[7] Unreconstructed Rebel: The Life of General John McCausland CSA, Michael J. Pauley. This account follows Pauley's biography closely, though this work is in debt to Tiger John: The Rebel Who Burned Chambersburg, by David L. Phillips.
[8] Official Records of the War of the Rebellion, Series I. Vol. VII.
[9] The Kanawha Valley Star, May 11, 1861.
[10] Tiger John: The Rebel Who Burned Chambersburg, David L. Phillips.
[11] Tiger John: The Rebel Who Burned Chambersburg, David L. Phillips.
[12] Unreconstructed Rebel, Michael J. Pauley.
[13] Unreconstructed Rebel, Michael J. Pauley.
[14] Tiger John: The Rebel Who Burned Chambersburg, David L. Phillips.
[15] Coleman C. Hatfield Interviews.
[16] Coleman C. Hatfield Interviews.
[17] Coleman C. Hatfield Interviews.
[18] Coleman C. Hatfield Interviews.
[19] 36th Virginia Infantry, J.L. Scott.
[20] 36th Virginia Infantry, J.L. Scott.
[21] The Civil War: An Illustrated History, Geoffrey C. Ward, Ken Burns, and Ric Burns.
[22] Unreconstructed Rebel, Michael J. Pauley.
[23] Anna Justice Spence Interview.
[24] Social History of Logan County, Mary B. Hurst.
[25] The Cincinnati Gazette, October 1, 1861.
[26] The Cincinnati Commercial, October 8, 1861.
[27] Official Records of the War of the Rebellion, Series I. Vol. VII.
[28] A Civil War Story, Allie McDonald.
[29] Official Records of the War of the Rebellion, Series I. Vol. VII.
[30] Official Records of the War of the Rebellion, Series I. Vol. VII.
[31] 45th Battalion Virginia Infantry, Jeffrey C. Weaver.
[32] 45th Battalion Virginia Infantry, Jeffrey C. Weaver.

[33] The Southern Advocate, September 4, 1862.
[34] 45th Battalion Virginia Infantry, Jeffrey C. Weaver.
[35] 45th Battalion Virginia Infantry, Jeffrey C. Weaver.
[36] 45th Battalion Virginia Infantry, Jeffrey C. Weaver.
[37] 45th Battalion Virginia Infantry, Jeffrey C. Weaver.
[38] 45th Battalion Virginia Infantry, Jeffrey C. Weaver.
[39] 45th Battalion Virginia Infantry, Jeffrey C. Weaver.
[40] Blood Is Thicker Than Water, Coleman A. Hatfield.
[41] Floyd Hatfield Letter To Coleman A. Hatfield, May 28, 1962.
[42] Blood Is Thicker Than Water, Coleman A. Hatfield.
[43] Confederate Veteran, October 1900.
[44] Coleman C. Hatfield Interview.
[45] 45th Battalion Virginia Infantry, Jeffrey C. Weaver.
[46] Warfare On The Borderline, Coleman A. Hatfield.
[47] Warfare On The Borderline, Coleman A. Hatfield.
[48] The Killing of General Bill France, Coleman A. Hatfield.
[49] The Killing of General Bill France, Coleman A. Hatfield.
[50] The Killing of General Bill France, Coleman A. Hatfield.
[51] The Tale of Jim Vance, Coleman A. Hatfield.
[52] The Tale of Jim Vance, Coleman A. Hatfield.
[53] The Tale of Jim Vance, Coleman A. Hatfield.
[54] The Killing of Harmon McCoy, Coleman A. Hatfield.
[55] Coleman A. Hatfield Interview.

Chapter Four
THE DEVIL IN HIS MOUNTAIN LAIR
Anse Hatfield and the Timbering Industry

AS ANSE Hatfield recovered from his illness in the spring of 1865, the Confederate government of the south collapsed as Robert E. Lee's army surrendered at Appomattox that April. By the time Anse was able to get around again at his home on Beech Creek, Logan County was facing its uncertain future as a rebel stronghold in a new state, whose leaders wanted to become part of the rich and growing industrial new America that came to life during the war years.

The way that Anse's Logan County and the remainder of southern West Virginia became part of industrial America is a fascinating history that has been sadly neglected by the nation's writers, though it is one of the most intriguing tales of the times. When Anse was born in 1839, the society of his region was still much like the Appalachian frontier, though the Indian threat was part of the past. By the time Anse died in 1921, Thomas A. Edison and Henry Ford and the other creators of the new society had done their work and the frontier had vanished forever.

In this changing scene, Anse played a role that would be of interest even if the feud with the McCoy family had never happened. He returned penniless from the war but became one of his area's significant timber merchants before ten years had passed. He had not taken part in politics before the war, but before 1875 Anse served as chairman of his district's school board and as a deputy sheriff. He was only an up-and-coming young man before the war. In the decade that followed he had become a community leader with hundreds of friends.

The way all this happened must be clear before anyone can understand the feud. Anse's essential character had been part of him since his childhood, had been strengthened by the tales of his family, and then had been fortified by his exploits in the war. That life experience made the self-confident young Hatfield more able to carve his own place in the world, rather than depending on his parents for a livelihood.

Anse Hatfield and the Postwar Economy

Historian Altina L. Waller wrote that Anse faced the same dilemma that confronted other residents of the Tug and Guyandot Valleys at the end of the war: a serious shortage of land brought on by overpopulation and the one inescapable fact that the Allegheny Plateau is a steep place. By the 1870s, Waller noted, homes and farms were being built at a rapid rate and flat land became precious and, therefore, more valuable. Anse's problem was simple: how could he feed his family and how could he acquire land to use for profitable ventures?

Anse's solution to the difficulty contained the seeds of future trouble. In 1872, Hatfield filed suit against Perry A. and Jacob Cline for cutting timber on his land. The suit was settled out-of-court in 1877 when the Cline brothers gave Anse the deed for five thousand acres of Tug Fork land the brothers had inherited from their father.[1] This gave Anse the first land that he could use for large scale timbering and seems to have secured his position as a fledging entrepreneur.

Anse then agreed to a contract to sell timber to a merchant named John Smith, who had a store at the mouth of Pond Creek. The two men disagreed on the terms of the contract, so Anse took Smith to court. The suit ended with another partial victory for Anse — the court awarded him $350 damages, though the legal expense was high, forcing Anse to mortgage his land to the timber firm of James Andrew Nighbert and S.S. Altizer.[2] Those two key victories of the 1870s gave Anse higher prestige, though some may have resented his success.

That history became the background that must be used to explain the feud. The tale of how timbering changed Logan County in general must wait for a time, however, because it is more important first to know why Anse became a timber merchant to support his family. Anse's role should be explained in terms of the type of man he became after the war, when he was twenty-six years old, and when his own children and his adopted son became more important in his life.

Anse Hatfield's Eldest Children

Cap's son, Coleman A. Hatfield, called Anse's first two children, Johnse and Cap, "the war babies". Though Coleman was referring to the fact that the two older Hatfield boys were born during the Civil War, there are other interpretations of that phrase. Johnse — named for William Johnson McCoy, who was Louvicey Chafin Hatfield's brother-in-law — had the legendary good looks of his clan. Though only one photograph exists to show what he looked like as a younger man, he is said to resemble his younger brother, Troy, who was killed during a liquor dispute in Fayette County in 1911.

Johnse had the temperament that often accompanies a handsome appearance. He was popular with women and had frequent love affairs, though perhaps the most famous of his escapades was the romance with Roseanna McCoy, the daughter of Randal McCoy. Writers have made much of that romance — perhaps too much when the deeper causes of the feud are considered. Some other members of the Hatfield family considered Johnse too "stuck on himself," too much inclined to become embroiled in trouble and too inclined to let others settle the trouble as best they could.

Such was the opinion of William Anderson (Cap) Hatfield, Johnse's younger brother, who often was the one appointed by Anse Hatfield to settle the trouble Johnse started. Cap, the other "war baby," was born in 1864. He received his famous nickname because his father was a Civil War partisan captain and the son was "the little captain." It is a most difficult matter to explain Cap's character quickly and easily. Though one should not place too much emphasis on appearance as an indication of a man's personality, a general comment does seem to help anyone who may try to understand Cap Hatfield.

Cap resembled the Chafin family — his mother's people — whereas his father Anse looked like the Vances; Johnse Hatfield was a throwback to John Ferrell, the father of Big Eph's wife, Nancy Vance Hatfield, and thus Johnse's great-grandfather. As a Chafin, Cap was tall and thick-bodied. He was dark-haired in his youth and went bald in his later years. In his younger days, Cap suffered an injury to his right eye, which cost him half his sight and made him appear cockeyed, a trait which Theron C. Crawford found unattractive and used as evidence of Cap's "evil" nature.[3]

Given the circumstances of Cap's youth, it is possible to feel more sympathetic with him than some journalists and other writers have felt in the past. Cap received the wound which eventually caused his death when he was a mere sixteen years old. The great feud with the McCoy family began when Cap was eighteen. Anse — who fancied himself a commanding general during the feud — sent Cap out to raid the McCoys and commit other frighteningly violent acts while remaining in the background. Such decisions embittered Cap, who carried the bitterness to his grave. Coleman A. Hatfield wrote the deepest and most charitable words about his father.

> He was a man of strange and mixed emotions. Cap could be hot and impetuous when stirred to anger, but cool and studious when he had time to forget his troubles and reflect on the better things of life.
>
> Cap grew up after the Civil War, subject to all the influences of those days. There were no well-established schools, and it was difficult for parents to find a suitable teacher. Even when they could, his services might last for only a few months during the year....
>
> Cap was dearly loved by his friends and was feared and hated by his enemies. He often expressed the thought that life had been unkind to him, and that he was a victim of the circumstances surrounding him as he grew to manhood.
>
> He was, without doubt, correct in this assumption. It took time, education, industrial development, and religious growth to shake off the influences which bound family life in the hills during the days following the disaster of the war.[4]

The Adoption of Dan Christian

Cap and Johnse were mere toddlers when the timbering industry began in the hills of Logan County. A large family was considered essential to a successful life in that time and place, and it would be a few years before the two older Hatfield boys were joined by younger brothers and sisters. In the meantime, about 1870, Anse Hatfield, showing both his practical and his kindly side, "took in" another young man named Dan Christian, who became something of an older brother to Johnse and Cap. Again, Coleman A. Hatfield explained those circumstances.

> There were no other children born in the family after Cap for another four years. Uncle Bob — Robert E. Hatfield — was not born until 1868. The two boys were only big enough to be around, just little scallywags, but they were not big enough to do anything.
> A train of wagons came along from Virginia and called for water. Grandfather had a good water well, so they stopped. The man in charge told Anse, "We have a boy here that's sick. He's going with us; he has no family back home but his grandmother where he came from, and he's sick. We've got to leave him here with you, if you can take care of him."
> Of course, that was right up Grandpap's alley, to take care of somebody, do some neighborly act, and be kind and so on. So he said, "Yes, have the boy come in."
> Danny made a good chore-boy. The family all liked him, and he was always just the same as one of the family. He grew up with them there, and later he married and settled on Thacker Creek and raised a large family.[5]

During Cap's later years, at the time of the Matewan shooting episode that followed the feud years, Dan Christian saved the lives of Cap and his stepson, young Joseph Glenn. That was a striking example of the way networks of friendship became important during that era of Appalachian history. In the meantime, Johnse and Cap were growing up, and Johnse led Cap into the first serious trouble the two experienced.

Johnse and Cap Hatfield's Christmas Eve Frolic

On Christmas Eve, 1880, Johnse told Cap that a frolic — a square dance — was going to be held that night at the home of a Maynard family that lived on Lick Creek. Johnse asked Cap to take care of feeding the Hatfield cattle, and then follow Johnse to the frolic, bringing a pistol with him. Others at the frolic were young men from Pigeon Creek, Turkey Creek, and Sulphur Creek, all tributaries of the Tug Fork. The Hatfield boys referred to the Pigeon Creek boys rather insultingly as "Pigeonites." Trouble began very soon.

> As the evening wore on and the square dancers were making their rounds, Johnse, feeling the "corn," threw his shoulder into one of the Pigeonites known as Dow Dempsey. An altercation immediately ensued. While Johnse talked, the tiger-like Dempsey felt for a two-bladed knife in his sleeve.
> Cap, who was always the silent guardian of Johnse, noticed the action. Stanley Vernatter and "Turkey Jack" Spaulding, two other Tug Fork allies, simultaneously drew their weapons, and Vernatter commanded Dow Dempsey in a determined voice to "stand to the rack."
> Dow Dempsey wheeled and disappeared through the rear door. As he did so, Harry Baisden tossed Dempsey a pistol. Dempsey then crept around the Maynard home until he reached the corner of the building where he saw Cap Hatfield leaning with his hand extended against one of the posts of the front porch.
> Dempsey fired, thinking he was shooting at Johnse Hatfield, but without being noticed by Cap Hatfield. The bullet entered near Hatfield's left kidney and tore through his lower abdominal cavity. The ball later was cut out by a doctor from beneath the skin on the front of Cap's abdomen.[6]

The Christmas Eve party broke up in a riot, and the youngsters scattered to their respective neighborhoods up and down the river. Word was sent to Anse Hatfield who lived eight miles from the Maynards. Anse rode down to the scene, bringing Dr. George Lawson.

Medical care at the time was primitive. There were no hospitals and, except for the amputation of limbs, surgery was unknown in the mountains. Victims of gunshots often were forced to recover as best they could. Such was the case with Cap Hatfield's wound that night.

Dr. Lawson told him that a portion of the descending colon had been cut away, and for some time Cap had trouble digesting food, as the corn he had eaten for supper that night spilled out of his wound, instead of passing into his intestines. Yet Cap told his family and friends he was determined to live. He did so as eventually the wound healed.

Dow Dempsey was killed later in another shooting episode by Charles Richardson, the police chief at Catlettsburg. The wound Dempsey inflicted on Cap eventually proved fatal, although he lived another fifty years, until the fall of 1930. An autopsy was performed, showing that cancer had formed around the scar that Cap carried for the rest of his life as a result of the fracas of 1880.[7]

Timbering in Logan County

Despite such troubles and unusual circumstances, the community into which Cap and Johnse Hatfield and Danny Christian was growing was more interested in the exciting news of the timber business than it was in occasion and random violence like the Christmas Eve shooting. The way Anse Hatfield became a timberman was more important in the tale of his life than his troubles about Johnse and Cap and such minor matters as the disputed ownership of a hog. Altina L. Waller's research into that question indicated that land ownership was Anse's central concern. Coleman A. Hatfield agreed with Waller's analysis, showing how his region reacted to the war as it recreated its economy.

> When the generals of the North and the South met on a memorial Sunday morning at Appomattox and ended the fratricidal struggle of four years duration, that meant that this nation would live and that a new day would be dawning, though we wonder if the historians of that time looked with optimism upon the scenes of destruction which had spread over the land.
>
> How long would it take to repair the losses and to recoup the damages which had been done to the nation and to its manhood? How did the war retard development of the education and religious enlightenment of the people across the hills and valleys?
>
> Instead of looking down upon a land of chaos and disappointment, the men of that day saw the opportunities of the nineteenth century. Seven years after the close of the Civil War, a great railroad had been built across the hill country from east to west and fittingly called the Chesapeake and Ohio because it opened the land from the waters of the Chesapeake Bay on the east to the great Ohio River on the west.[8]

Men such as Anse Hatfield's friend George R.C. Floyd visited the Summers County town of Hinton, where the Chesapeake and Ohio Railroad was built in West Virginia. Floyd, a brother of Civil War General John B. Floyd and one of the region's largest landowners, was impressed with what he saw. Floyd and others began telling their neighbors about regional possibilities. Thus to know men like Anse Hatfield is to know how Logan County and the surrounding region became a greatly different place during the final four decades of that century.

That is a history in which politics and economics are interlocked. Though there are many ways to tell the history, it is most useful to view that field through the lens of the key personalities: Anse, of course, but also William Dyke Garrett, John William Straton, James Andrew Nighbert, and Henry Clay Ragland. The respective biographies of those men let historians understand Logan County in terms of religion, politics, finance, and journalism. They all were significant in the life of Anse and in the history of their time and place.

Their collective biography began at the end of the war. In the summer of 1866, Logan County was controlled by a faction of Republicans led by three members of the county court that much later would be renamed the Logan County Commission. The three Republicans in charge of local matters that summer were Rhodes B. Perry, Milton A. Mullins, and Eli Trent. Their first meeting that left a surviving record was held in Paulina Cartwright's hotel on June 20, 1866.[9] Though little business was handled that day, later accounts indicated that the three commissioners tried to reestablish county finances by approving a tax rate of sixty-seven cents per hundred dollars land valuation.

The still-disenfranchised former Confederates who had returned home were furious. The state constitution in effect at the time kept the rebels from voting so they could neither approve nor disapprove the court's actions. It would be another six years before the Confederates were "reconstructed" by the Constitution of 1872, and they could do little to control the local government until then.

John William Straton — whose family had settled in Logan County about 1820, who had served the Confederacy by raising troops and leading them to battle, and who knew something about the law — took a lawsuit to court to see if he could vote. The West Virginia Supreme Court ruled against Straton, who was more furious than ever at the government as a direct result of the court case. If he could not vote, Straton reasoned, there were still avenues open through which he could make his displeasure felt.[10]

One such avenue was a "social" club, which in later years was named Camp Straton United Confederate Veterans. It is impossible to overstate how important Camp Straton was to the political organization of Logan County between 1872 and 1902. There have been writers who argue that the most significant political organization in Logan County's history was the Democratic regime headed by Sheriff Don Chafin that served the interests of coal operators between 1912 and 1956. The point can be argued. While Camp Straton held sway for thirty years, very little happened in Logan County that its leadership did not like. With Camp Straton as its organizing principle, the local Democratic Party stormed back into power in the election of 1874 and did not lose its grip for three decades.

Straton could not achieve that much power alone; he needed allies. He found them. His right-hand man was James Andrew Nighbert, who was an interesting study in the way personality affects history. Nighbert was tall and handsome with a Scot's finely-shaped head, and a distinguishing white beard that he sported in his later years. His attributes were as striking as his appearance. He was ambitious and canny, but he concealed his immense drive for wealth behind his kindly and genial manners.

Nighbert was born in Montgomery County, Virginia, on July 21, 1833, a son of George W. and Elizabeth Scaggs Nighbert, who moved to the Malden Saline in Kanawha County in 1837. The Nighbert family moved to a Logan County farm in 1844, but young James Andrew was educated at an academy in the Kanawha Valley town of St. Albans. As he matured, Nighbert worked as a salesman in the general store of Anthony Lawson — Logan County's first merchant — and later for Straton. In later years, Nighbert married Straton's daughter, Vicie, who had suffered through an unhappy first marriage.[11]

In 1861, Nighbert had "purchased the sheriffality," but when the Civil War began, he served the Confederacy first in the 36th Virginia Infantry, then in the Virginia State Line, and finally ended his war service as a member of the Virginia Legislature from 1863 to 1865. As in the case of many other Confederates, Nighbert's main concern at the end of the war was restoring his personal finances. Though he opened a new general store at Logan Courthouse with J.E. Robertson, and though he made money clarifying and selling Appalachian ginseng, Nighbert, with his canny head for business, was among the first to realize that most of the accessible wealth of Logan County was timber. Soon he was getting rich. Very soon he was setting an example for younger men like Anse Hatfield.

No one knows how Nighbert and Anse Hatfield became acquainted. One possibility is that Anse met Nighbert on one of Hatfield's trips to the courthouse to buy goods in the general stores. The two may have met on the day that Nighbert stood under an umbrella in the pouring rain to help men enlist in the Logan Wildcats when the war began. What is certain is that they were allies more often than not.

Feud historian Altina L. Waller wrote intelligently that Nighbert and his allies wanted to bring a modern Victorian-era capitalist economy to Logan County, and that Anse Hatfield and his family came to be seen by Nighbert and his allies as an obstacle to that goal. While the point is well-taken, there are arguments against it as well.

Nighbert and Hatfield were fellow soldiers, fellow Democrats, and fellow Logan Countians. The nature of Logan County's society is that alliances can and do change at the drop of a hat. Logan Countians will drop the hat themselves to make the changes possible. It is true that on the surface Nighbert and Hatfield appeared at cross-purposes on many occasions.

It is equally true, however, that there was a mutual underlying respect between Hatfield and Nighbert that was based on their common cause in the civil war, on the fact that both men often needed political allies and so were careful not to offend one another, and on the additional fact that the two men cooperated when they could and opposed each other when they were forced to do so.

Such arguments will come into play in this history when it is time to unravel the complex network of the feud. In the meantime, it is important to know that the alliance of Straton and Nighbert began changing the politics of Logan County, which was their first step in changing its economy. Anse Hatfield received benefits of the change, including the possibility of selling timber to Nighbert and others as new industry took root in the county.

While studying the way the new Logan County economy was created, the point should be recalled that transportation and communication are inseparably bound together in all ages and in all places. In Logan County in 1870, this meant that the people who lived on the rivers and their tributaries received information first and then it spread gradually. That also meant that those who traveled often learned information first and gave it to their friends first. In that meaningful way, William Dyke Garrett first became an important friend of Anse Hatfield.

Dyke Garrett served Logan County and the region so well in so many ways that he became one of the community's most revered citizens. He was the man who would baptize "the devil" toward the end of Hatfield's long life. Dyke founded the first "Campbellite" Church of Christ on Crooked Creek in the 1870s — long before journalist Theron C. Crawford wrote his account of the feud that claimed there were no churches in the region. Yet Dyke's most important original service to his home folks may have been spreading the news that timbering — a small concern before the war — had become an important new force along the Tug and Guyandot watersheds.

Dyke deserves an introduction for those reasons. Dyke Garrett was the son of John and Eliza Godby Garrett, born in 1841 on Big Creek, one of the three creeks on which the pioneers settled and later built the town of Chapmanville, at the heart of Logan County's northern section. Dyke Garrett was tall and slim and incredibly quick in his movements. He was a lover of woodlore and music, playing the fiddle with the best of the mountain musicians of his locality.

Dyke marched away to the Civil War when the conflict began. A doctor discovered he was deaf in one ear and ineligible for the military. He agreed to go with his troop as a chaplain — more for the excitement of the war than any deep religious conviction. Yet a shattering experience came upon him. Like Anse Hatfield, Dyke was asked to take part in the execution of young deserters. He agreed, but was conscience stricken as a result and began thinking seriously about religion. "God doesn't want us to live that way," Dyke once said, remembering his war experiences when he was ninety-seven years old.[12]

With such religious ideas in his head, Dyke returned to Logan County after the war and married his sweetheart, Sallie Smith. She began changing him for the better. Then one night, Dyke went with his fiddle to play at a square dance held in a school building on Big Creek. As he left the school, a lightning bolt struck the fiddle, knocking Dyke to the ground.[13] In Dyke's view, God got his attention. Some short time later, in the year 1868, Dyke was baptized by Alexander M. Lunsford. Despite his wife's protest, "Dyke, you couldn't preach. You couldn't convert anybody," Dyke began his evangelist's work and so traveled through all sections of Logan County.

Historians do not know if Dyke Garrett met Anse Hatfield before or during or after the war. The men were both consummate woodsmen and fellow bear hunters, and Anse was equally interested in the news that Dyke told about events in Logan County. That news included the fact that the first postwar "splash dam" had been built on Crawley Creek near Dyke's home to make it easier to take timber to market. That meant that there was money to be made cutting the trees and shipping them to markets like those in Guyandotte, Catlettsburg, Ironton, and Cincinnati. A way was open for Anse to feed his growing family.

Anse Hatfield's First Timbering Work

In the following years, Logan County's first fame was won as a source of timber, particularly the dense growth of nearly flawless trees that grew on its hills. Writers like Henry Clay Ragland, Logan County's first successful journalist, would sing the praises of its wood and coal so that a timber and mineral industry would begin the economic growth that ended the older way of life in the mountains.

For all those reasons, Anse Hatfield was typical of the mountaineers who turned to timbering after the war. Timbering was already an honored livelihood in the hills at the time. Logan County folks had been aware of the value of their woodland since the creation of the community. Before the war, some mountaineers had worked in the forests during the winter months getting log rafts ready for the spring tide on the rivers, when the rafts would be taken to sawmills on the Ohio River.

The timber taken to market then was considered some of the finest wood on earth by mountaineers like Anse. Mary B. Hurst, who wrote the first social history of Logan County, noted, "Trees in the area were poplar, buckeye, sugar maple, red maple, locust, cherry, sweet gum, dogwood, ash, elm, sycamore, butternut, black walnut, hickory, white oak, chestnut, beech, birch, pine, and spruce."[14] In short, the woods were varied. As the nation industrialized, it needed more lumber, and the Appalachian hills were a nearby source of that wood.

In the considered opinion of Edwin A. Cubby — who wrote a history of the Guyandot and Tug Valleys — timbering firms changed life in the region by linking the local economy to the national economy for the first time.[15] After timbering companies began operations in the region, there was more cash in circulation. County residents became more aware of the possibilities for a growing economy. Work became more dependent on the fortunes of national firms that operated in the region.

John F. Ferrell once recalled that the first lumber business of any importance in Logan County was started on Crawley Creek by Garrett and Runyon in 1876.[16] That Catlettsburg firm was the first to hire labor in the field, though they were followed very soon by Enoch Baker of Nova Scotia, who built the first splash dam on Crawley Creek. Those two were followed by the Yellow Poplar Lumber Company, which worked on Island Creek and Rich Creek, and then by James Omar Cole and Clinton Crane, who cut most of the prime timber sent to market from the Logan County hills.

Today's historians know much about Cole and Crane because the aged J.O. Cole gave an interview to *The Logan Democrat* in April 1915.[17] Cole told the newspaper that he had gone to California in 1850 to take part in the gold rush.

Though he did not find gold, he made money by selling goods to the forty-niners and returned to his home in Peru, Indiana, in 1869. Cole then joined forces with Clint Crane. The pair made money from various concerns and moved into southern West Virginia in 1879. During the forty years that followed, Cole and Crane made most of its money on timber, but also held title to vast seams of coal, from which their descendants — including songwriter Cole Porter — lived comfortably.

James A. Nighbert And Henry Clay Ragland

There were not many Appalachian citizens who became wealthy from timbering. One who did, however, was James A. Nighbert. The Logan County deed books show that Nighbert began buying timberland in the early 1870s and continued to do so until almost the end of his life in the late 1890s. He was shrewd enough to concentrate his holdings in one area, the Copperas Fork of Island Creek. After Nighbert died, his widow, Vicie Straton Nighbert, sold the thirty thousand acres they owned on Copperas Fork to the New England investors who created Island Creek Coal Company, the firm; that more than any other force, reshaped life on the Tug and Guyandot.

Nighbert was not a single-minded businessman. During the War Between the States, he had been a member of Virginia's Confederate Legislature. As he was busy buying coal and timberland after the war, he also resumed his political career, taking an active role in the senatorial district, serving as a member and president of the Logan County Court between 1880 and 1889, as a member of the town council, and attending national conventions of the Democratic Party.[18]

Such activities made Nighbert one of the most important men of his community, but he also realized that he was merely a large frog in a very small pond. If he were to become very rich, Nighbert thought, Logan County would have to grow. He needed a stronger voice to effect that change. A newspaper was the solution to his problem, and Nighbert lucked out because a journalist moved to the Logan Courthouse in the spring of 1874. His name was Henry Clay Ragland.

Ragland, a Confederate veteran, aspiring lawyer and journalist, soon became a valued citizen of the town and remained one until he died in May 1911. A native of Hadensville, Goochland County, Virginia, Ragland also was one of the most influential men who ever lived in Logan County. Through his newspaper, *The Logan County Banner*, Ragland acted as the spokesman for the new industrial era in the community.

Ragland was of Welsh descent and was born May 7, 1844, the fourth son of Hugh N. and Eliza Eades Ragland. The first thirty years of his life present an interesting study of a sickly child who grew up on a farm, but received a good "old field school" education, and learned the politics of the Whig Party of the United States before Virginia seceded from the union on his seventeenth birthday.

Ragland served as a horseman in Company B of the Fifth Virginia Cavalry and was captured by Union troops near Luray, Virginia, in 1864. He spent the remainder of the war in the Point Lookout Prison, where the food was scant and poor, but was released at the end of the struggle in better health than when he joined the army.

In 1869, Ragland was elected surveyor of his native county, but because former Confederates were not allowed to hold public office at the time, he became a schoolteacher. As such, he traveled around Virginia and the new state of West Virginia before arriving in Wayne County about 1870. There he "studied law" under H.K. Shumate. Studying law was a common American practice of working with an older member of bar associations. Ragland also learned something of the printing trade, and heard of the possibilities in Logan County. He was admitted to the Bar in the town of Aracoma in March 1874.[19]

Ragland's new hometown was not an impressive place then. Though information about it is hard to come by, there are two sources that can be trusted. One was printed in the report of a shooting that involved Urias Buskirk and Peter Morgan in *The Cincinnati Weekly Enquirer*. That newspaper stated:

> Logan Courthouse, the seat of the county of that name, hardly rises to the dignity of even a country village. It is located away among the hills of the Guyandot, completely isolated, and about sixty-five miles from the mouth of that stream, which empties into the Ohio near Huntington.
>
> Besides the courthouse, which is a primitive structure, a curious specimen of architecture and very unpretentious in its style, there are but few other houses in the place. These include the inevitable country store and the blacksmith shop, the dwellings being small rough log and plank buildings, quite comfortable, however, in their arrangements.[20]

The town was described by J.C. Elkins, who moved to town in 1877, just three years after Ragland arrived. Elkins' memories tell of a very small village of seventeen houses, nine business buildings and three public buildings. The homes were owned by A.J. Perry, Wes Dingess, R.J. Perry, John William Straton, Sarah Thompson, Andy Lee, Francis M. White, and Betty and Peggy Neace on Main Street; George Zirkles, H.S. White, John Buskirk, a Dr. Rickett, and John Chafin on Stratton Street; and Loop Justice, Scott Dejournette, and Dan Tucker on Dingess Street.

The business establishments were the Oakland Hotel that belonged to Louisa Buskirk, the Aaron Brewer Hotel, an unoccupied store, an empty frame building, and the J.A. Sidebottom Store on Main Street; the J.B. Buskirk Hotel, the G.M. Dingess saloon, the R.E. Lowe Saloon, and "The Big Store," that belonged to James A. Nighbert and J.B. Robertson on Stratton Street. The public buildings were the post office at the home of Francis M. White on Main Street, the courthouse, and the jail, set between Main Street and Stratton Street.[21]

Ragland soon found his place in that community. With his keen legal mind, his genial ways, and his sense of the way the town needed to develop, he made friends quickly. Soon after his arrival, he became the friend and then the legal adviser of James A. Nighbert, who was the town's most successful merchant and timber dealer. In the election of 1876, Ragland was elected to the state legislature and soon became chairman of the Logan County Democratic Executive Committee.[22] On January 9, 1878, he married Louisa Buskirk, the widow of Urias Buskirk, who had a hotel in town and who inherited her late husband's timber holdings. By 1880, Ragland was a well-respected citizen who had held several public offices.

During the last half of the 1870s, Straton, Nighbert, Garrett, and Ragland achieved many of their purposes. Straton's law license was reinstated by the West Virginia State Bar in 1873. He was then elected Logan County's clerk, a position he held for many years. Straton then secured the contract to rebuild the county courthouse, a project finished in 1875. His hold on the local Democratic organization became firmer. The existing courthouse records indicate — though they do not prove the point — that members of the House of Delegates and the State Senate owed much to the Straton-Nighbert-Ragland organization.

Ragland himself was elected to the House of Delegates in 1876. He does not seem to have played a remarkably prominent role in state politics. But during those years he became Nighbert's attorney-of-record and helped the timber merchant become a more powerful financial force in regional affairs. Ragland also began writing articles for such newspapers as *The Huntington Advertiser* and learned more about the journalists' trade so he would be ready to edit a newspaper when the time arrived.

Nighbert became a member of the Logan County Court after the election of 1880 and soon was elected its president. Though the county court was stripped of its judicial power by the West Virginia Legislature in 1880, it remained the most powerful governmental body on the local level, administering all civil, federal, state, and local laws that affected the county. The matters that concerned Straton, Nighbert, and Ragland demonstrate the power of Camp Straton United Confederate Veterans. Nearly all questions of finance, politics, and public opinion were in their hands. Other public officials, such as Squire Valentine (Wall) Hatfield — Anse Hatfield's older brother — were compelled to pay attention to the leaders of the veterans' organization and were often allied with those men.

Anse Hatfield's Political Position

Anse's political position is a matter that requires some explanation. Altina L. Waller's research indicates that Anse enjoyed much success in the 1870s.[23] Her evidence on that point is that Anse restored his family's economic standing, providing a good living for his sons, Dan Christian, and other allies. Waller wrote that during that decade, several of Anse's friends — Elliott Rutherford, Harrison Blair, and G.W. Taylor among them — were elected Logan County's sheriff in succession. Candidates for sheriff of the county at the time, and for many years thereafter, were considered the leaders of their political organizations.

Waller added that evidence of Anse's standing in the community is demonstrated by his role in the arrest and trial of Riley Sansom on charges of killing one "Negro Mose" in 1870. Sansom, it will be recalled, was the equal of Big Eph Hatfield in stature. Riley and Big Eph were friendly rivals for the legendary title of "best wrestler" on Mate Creek.

Hatfield family tradition adds that Sansom trusted Anse Hatfield and said he would surrender only to Anse.[24] Whatever the circumstances were, Anse was sworn in as deputy sheriff and brought Sansom to the courthouse. Sansom was tried there, but acquitted by Justice Evan Ferrell because he claimed "Negro Mose" was lurking in the mountains with plans of murdering former Confederates like Sansom himself and Anse Hatfield.[25] Anse testified on Sansom's behalf. Later Hatfields recall that the friendship was not impaired by Anse's role in Sansom's arrest.[26]

Yet it seems that Anse had his difficulties as well as his success in the local political and economic networks of the 1870s and 1880s. Waller reported that G.W. Taylor acted as a friend of Hatfield's on some occasions and as his determined enemy at other times.[27] In 1878, Taylor filed suit against Anse to collect a debt. Anse countersued, but lost the case and was ordered to pay Taylor. Waller dates Anse's decline in influence from that point, noting that between 1881 and 1890, Anse lost nineteen lawsuits and had other troubles with the courts.

In thinking about Anse's political position, it is a good idea to recall the nature of community life in Logan County during that era. Anse was never an entirely "modern" man, despite his timbering interests, his dealings with courts, and the changing economy of his home county. His network of friendships was based more on his personality than it was on economic concerns. The Hatfield family has warm memories of Anse as "a big, shaggy man," who would have wanted to be remembered as "the best bear hunter the world ever knew."[28]

The family recalls that he was jovial, with a keen sense of the ridiculous. They claim Anse was always ready to go hunting with anyone, that he enjoyed sitting around his fire telling tall tales, and that his friendships were based partly on the instincts he inherited from his mother Nancy, who spent long hours serving her neighbors as a midwife. In short, there were human characteristics in Anse Hatfield's nature that made him a good friend, if a bad enemy.

Devil Anse Hatfield's Sense of Humor and Tall Tales

None of this is designed to convince anyone that Anse was a saint. His appearance — with his huge frame and his wild man's beard — was cultivated to make one of his pastimes more interesting. Anse got a charge from scaring people silly.[29] That amused him. And it is one of the reasons that writers like Theron C. Crawford and John Spivak were able to convey the unreal impression that Anse was a barbaric mountain man. The fact should be recalled as well that Anse was notorious for kidding unsuspecting first acquaintances, as well as old friends. Coleman A. Hatfield told one such tale about Anse's humor.

> Big Fightin' Jim Prater had swung the axe among the logs and tree laps all day. There were stacks of firewood on each side of the path where he had worked at the base of a great mountain, the wind roaring in the trees all around.
>
> It was drawing near the close of the day, and darkness was gathering in the deep ravines of the hills. The clouds above were threatening, and the harbingers of a long dreary winter seemed to be lending voices everywhere. The dull roar in the heavy forest and even the snow on the ground seemed to hang on, awaiting more crystals to fall from overhead.
>
> Just as Jim was thinking of calling it a day, as he prepared to lay down his heavy axe, a low noise came from the dark ravine further up the mountain somewhere in the region of the big boulders, where the old hollow oaks stood reaching out their branches as if awaiting the falling of winter from the skies.
>
> Big Jim thought he heard a voice in a low bass tone calling down the defile of the mountain, as it brought forebodings which made a chill run down his spine and his hair stand on end. Something said, "Who are you?" The big woodchopper thought he was sure of the question which came ominously to his ears as he paused with axe half-lifted. Again he heard the voice saying, "Who are you?"
>
> Awe-stricken as he was, he was unable at first to determine within his mind whether it was a sound from the trees or from the old deserted house which stood up the valley to his right where, it was claimed, that the Indians of other days had slain a white settler with his wife and little ones.
>
> Soon again he heard the voice saying, "Who are you?" Then, fearing that it was some enemy mistaking him for a foe, and that the inquirer had "dropped a bead" on him, Big Jim straightened, trying to steady his jaw, and said to the voice, "This is Big...Big Fightin' Jim Prater!"
>
> At his back another voice broke loose from among the trees and said, "I har...har...hardly knew ye!" Big Jim, not having his old musket with him, immediately struck the blade of his axe in the end of a large backlog, as he wheeled and ran down the rocky road, believing that enemies had surrounded him and were trying

to assure themselves that they had the right man. It was, of course, Anse and his boys having some fun.[30]

Anse's own grandchildren were often his prey when he decided to tell scary stories — an ancient pastime in the hills before modern society closed in. Coleman A. Hatfield was in one such audience and saved one of Anse's tales in the old man's own style.

"Grandpa, tell us a haint tale," asked one of the half-dozen grandsons, as they sat around the hearth looking intently at the old man gazing at the burning backlog.

The old man spat into the embers and cleared his throat. "Well, I don't believe in haints, but I have had one or two things a-bothered me in my time."

"Tell us about it," everyone shouted.

"Well, it was this way. Back a long time ago, old Jasper McCoy was bushwhacked in time of the Civil War, and they never knowed who done it. Some said it was the homeguard or other Rebels. Anyway, we buried old Jasper in the graveyard at the forks of Bear Wallow Creek.

"Years later I was ridin' past the graveyard one night on my way home. The moon was up and shining full. Just as I was passing the big gateposts at the lower end of the graveyard I saw a boot in the road, and it made me think of old Jasper. He was a pegleg man and, of course, wore only one boot at the time.

"I might not of a-noticed it if that plague-taked boot hadn't been movin' along up the road just as if old Jasper was standin' in it on his good leg and intending to walk home with me!

"When my hoss saw the boot movin' he stopped and began to 'booger' at it. That made me think all the more that the old hoss was seein' things. Now, mind you, I wasn't scared myself, but the hoss seemed to be bothered. You know, if a hoss isn't moon-eyed, he can see better than a man.

"Purty soon the old hoss started walkin', and the boot started movin' again. I was just too contrary to put spurs to Old Tobe and ride out of there quick, so I got down to see where that golblamed boot was walkin' to. I picked it up and looked underneath, and there was a big toad frog as big as my fist that had crawled up in a hole in the bottom of the boot.

"The fall nights were gettin' cool, and that toad frog had got under the boot to keep warm. The limb-founded critter had got fastened with his head and forelegs inside the boot and his hind legs on the ground underneath. He was wedged in such a shape he couldn't back out, and the only thing he could do was push his hind legs against the dirt and go frontwards. That was what made the boot move up the road.

"It didn't scare me, but it made Old Tobe so scared that he shook all over and was still quiverin' when I turned him in the barn. Still, I ain't satisfied but what that old hoss didn't see old Jasper McCoy after all."[31]

Anse Hatfield, Frank James, and the Deer-Hunting Yarn

A character like Anse Hatfield — who saw himself as larger-than-life anyway — naturally attracts tales invented by other imaginative writers. A tale persists that Anse Hatfield and the outlaw Frank James crossed paths in 1875, when the James gang was accused of robbing the bank at Huntington. Coleman A. Hatfield denied that tale in no uncertain terms.

> This writer has read a fantastic story about Frank James passing through the mountains about the year 1875 and meeting with Anderson Hatfield. Certainly I, the eldest living grandson of the old feud leader, would have heard this years ago had it been true. My people would certainly have told the story of the bank robber from Clay County, Missouri, if this meeting ever took place. But no one who was even suspected of being Frank James ever passed the way of the Hatfields....
>
> It may be remarked here that some of the happenings of the feud days are exciting enough to bring bloodcurdling thrills to the screen viewers of today without mixing the feudists up with outlaws, train robbers, and bank artists who tormented peaceable citizens in the first decade following the Civil War.[32]

In his later years, after he had become famous, Anse, who loved to tell tall tales about himself, was interviewed by several journalists. Anse would have told the tale about Frank James, if it had been anywhere close to the truth. An example of the kind of tales Anse did tell about himself was saved by his grandson.

> "Well," said Grandfather Anse, "I'll never forget the time when I brought home four deer with one shot. I know that most folks won't believe what I say, but it's true.
>
> "We were huntin' in the mountains where there was a haul road where timber had been hauled down the slope. I was at the upper end watching for deer to cross. My brother had gone around the ridge to get in behind the deer where they were feeding. He was told to turn the dogs loose and halloo them back in my direction.

"So I took a stand and was watchin'. I heard the dogs yelping, coming nearer and nearer down the ridge and headed for a long hollow where they would cross. It wasn't long 'til I saw an old doe and another half-grown buck trot up into the haul road about a hundred yards down the slope.

"When they got into the open, they squatted to the ground resting. I fired and the bullet passed through both of their bodies. I hurried down to bleed them as we always do, and then I ripped them open to take out the entrails.

"Believe it or not, two living fawns which were ready to be born to the old doe raised up. There I had two little ones to take home and raise on the bottle. So with one bullet I brought home four deer."[33]

The Trial of the Two Sandy Shoats

Anse's mountaineer life, typified by such hunting tales, ghost (or "haint") yarns, and humorous encounters like the one with Jim Prater, would change forever during the decade after 1875. Timbering and the new economy would be the most powerful force in that alteration. His family believes to this day that Anse did not want the change to arrive the way it did.

Yet after 1880, the year that Johnse Hatfield was eighteen years old, events began taking place that would transform Anse from a young timberman, a mountain hunter, and a typical Loganite of his generation into a legend. That change began with a trial about the ownership of a hog and a love affair between two youngsters.

Anse Hatfield may well have wondered what the dispute about the hog had to do with him. That may seem surprising because so much ink has been spilled explaining how Anse's cousin Floyd Hatfield had a hog on his property, that Randal McCoy claimed the critter, and that McCoy became bitter when a justice-of-the-peace awarded the hog to Floyd Hatfield after a trial in which Bill Staton sided with the Hatfields against the McCoys. A few words of commonsense are needed. Though grudges were held for years in the hill country, a somewhat closer inspection of mountain life belies the puffed up romanticism written about the pig trial.

Genealogists have labored long and hard at their trade and have proven that it was a common occurrence for Hatfields and McCoys to marry each other, as well as other members of the some four hundred names reported in the census records of the region. The mountain genealogies are so tangled that it is difficult to know whether loyalty was stronger to the Hatfields or the McCoys. All historians can do is report, as accurately as possible, what individuals did in particular situations.

In that light, Floyd Hatfield and Bill Staton were closer relatives of Randal McCoy than they were of Anse Hatfield. Floyd Hatfield was the son of John Hatfield, who was one of the brothers of Big Eph Hatfield. Yet Floyd Hatfield was married to Esther Staton, the sister of Bill Staton. Some mountaineers think that she was named "Easter." The question has not been resolved.

Complicating this matter further, Esther or Easter Staton Hatfield also was a great-granddaughter of old William McCoy, the grandfather of Randal. Cap Hatfield's branch of Anse's family believes that Anse looked on the pig trial as more a falling out of McCoy kinfolk than anything that he needed to worry about.

What may have happened is that when the Hatfield and McCoy feud got the attention of journalists in the late 1880s, such writers looked back at everything that ever happened involving the families and wrote that those events were the underlying causes of the violence. It may be more sensible to think that the feud began only after Ellison Hatfield — Anse's brother — was mortally wounded by three of Randal McCoy's sons on the famous Election Day of August 1882.

Despite that, feud historians have been fascinated by the hog trial and that tale still finds its way to written and televised accounts of the troubles. Anse Hatfield may be partly responsible for that fact. In his later years, when journalists interviewed Anse on the point, "What started the feud?" Anse, perhaps to save himself time and trouble and in order to mislead people who were too curious, would answer, "It was about a pig."

Virgil Carrington Jones wrote in his book, *The Hatfields and the McCoys*, that the trouble about the hog began in the fall of 1873. Later feud historians such as Otis K. Rice, Altina L. Waller, G. Elliott Hatfield, and Truda Williams McCoy, have followed the general outline presented by Jones. Waller adds interesting speculation about the economic ties between Anse and Floyd Hatfield. Waller also wrote that the dispute between Floyd Hatfield and Randal McCoy was taken to court in 1878. Many such writers have claimed that the justice of the peace who heard the evidence was Preacher Anse Hatfield, a cousin of Devil Anse. Coleman A. Hatfield had a different tale to tell, claiming that Squire "Wall" Hatfield — Anse's older brother — was the original justice of the peace, though Wall soon disqualified himself from hearing the case.

Hatfield wrote that it was a common and sensible matter for the mountain folk to let their swine run loose in the woods to fend for themselves because the land had not yet been heavily timbered. Old timber, such as was common in Logan and Pike Counties of the 1870s, produces heavy mast, that is favored by pigs and bears.

Rather than using valuable flat land to grow corn for feed for animals, it made more sense to turn the animals loose after carefully "marking" their ears with well-recognized cuts to prove ownership. Some were not careful about cutting the pigs' ears and mistakes could and did happen, especially when one remembers that pigs will root for mast and damage their own ears doing so. Coleman A. Hatfield wrote:

It was sometimes difficult for the mountain folk to round up their "grunters" after they had fattened on the mast following the nutting season in the fall. Often the pigs would become wild when they were raised under the rock cliffs far back in the recesses and cliffs of the mountains. They would dash away like all other wild things at the approach of a human.

Randal McCoy lived on Blackberry Fork of Pond Creek in Kentucky. Floyd Hatfield, a cousin of Anse, lived on one of the creeks on the West Virginia side. Two well-grown Sandy shoats were said to have swum the river where they were caught up and placed in the hog pen of Floyd Hatfield. They had no markings in their ears, so it was impossible to tell who, if anyone, was the owner.

Randal McCoy came over and said, "Floyd Hatfield, you have put up two of my hogs." Whereupon Floyd replied, "Them's not your hogs — they've got no markings on their ears. They just come out of the woods, wild as rabbits, and I have a right to put my mark on them and keep them. And that is just what I'm about to do."

Randal replied, "If you mark them hogs and try to keep them, I'll just sue you." "Sue and be dimmed," said Floyd. "Them's my shoats now, and they ain't nothing you can do about it." Said Randal, "I'll sue you before Squire Wall Hatfield, and I know he'll do right." "I'll be there," retorted Floyd.[34]

Randal sought out Wall Hatfield and received a summons that was served on Floyd Hatfield, ordering Floyd to bring the two hogs with him to court. Another justice of the peace, named "Stafford," was chosen to hear the case, and about six witnesses appeared for each side. The evidence was contradictory, though there was no apparent deliberate lying on the part of any witnesses, according to Coleman A. Hatfield, who heard the tale from his father, Cap Hatfield. The Hatfield account added:

> Among those testifying was a big, two-fisted, strapping, swashbuckling young mountaineer named Billy Staton, who witnessed for his brother-in-law, Floyd Hatfield. It should be remembered that with all their educational disadvantages, there was the utmost respect for a man's oath "as a witness," and that the witnesses on both sides were endeavoring to tell the truth in their sworn testimony.
>
> Staton's reputation for physical prowess and his commanding demeanor on the witness stand was considered by the McCoys to have had a strong bearing in the determination of the

case for Hatfield, although this undoubtedly was far from the truth.

The McCoys and Staton glared at each other as they lined the two sides of the squire's log cabin court, while each took his turn in their efforts to delineate the facts which they believed necessary to win. Influenced by the heated testimony, Staton, while looking hard at the McCoys, declared that sandy-colored hogs were all that Floyd Hatfield would raise because "the pigs had to hide themselves in the sandbars of the river to keep the McCoys from catching them."

The court rapped for order as the opposing witnesses argued. Billy Staton shouted, "You McCoys shot my fishing poles in two where I had them set on the riverbank." "You're just a d___ed liar," shouted Paris McCoy. "Order! Order! Gentlemen, this is not a fishing trip," said the squire. "This is a lawsuit over a couple of Sandy Bar hogs, so everybody be quiet in my court."[35]

When the courtroom settled down, Stafford ruled that the absence of markings on the hogs' ears meant that Randal McCoy could not prove ownership. Stafford ordered the hogs returned to Floyd Hatfield and further ruled that Randal McCoy should pay the court costs, whereupon Hatfield commented, "That's what I've always heard — possession is nine parts of the law."

While Anse Hatfield was not involved in that case, its aftermath did become an important part of the feud that began in earnest in 1882. With the benefit of hindsight, conditions might have been better if Justice Stafford had shown some of Solomon's wisdom by giving Floyd Hatfield one hog and Randal McCoy the other, or, as a later Hatfield argued rather puckishly, if Floyd had barbecued the pork and invited Randal to supper.[36]

Ellison Hatfield and the Killing of Bill Staton

More serious trouble came later and reached its crisis on June 18, 1880, when Bill Staton was killed by Paris and "Squirrel Hunting" Sam McCoy, nephews of Randal McCoy.[37] Again, according to Coleman A. Hatfield's history:

> From the day of the hog trial forward, bad blood existed between Bill Staton and the McCoys. It was noised about that this was not the end of their troubles. In the spring of 1880, when Abe Phillips' corn was ready to hoe, Sam and Paris McCoy came over to the West Virginia side to take the job hoeing corn.
>
> They had worked one day, and then it became known to Bill Staton that Sam and Paris were on Bill's side of the river. The next day, these boys met in a bloody scene which had a profound bearing on the terrible feud.

When Phillips' corn was being hoed, Bill Staton came riding by his farm. Sam and Paris threw down their hoes, came out of the field and across the fence to the shade under a big oak, and there the tragedy took place.

Many who had heard or read of this tragedy no doubt have formed opinions as to who was the aggressor. Some say Staton went there for trouble. Of this, we are not sure. Whatever may be said, it should be remembered he was riding on the public highway and was killed on that highway.

Sam and Paris McCoy were arraigned in court at the next term, and it was then that Ellison Hatfield took a very active part in prosecuting the McCoy brothers. Ellison's reason was that Staton was a brother to Ellison's wife, as well as to the wives of Ellison's cousins, Floyd Hatfield and Ephraim Hatfield.

It should be remembered too that up to this time, Devil Anse Hatfield had taken no part in the trouble. His brother Ellison, however, attended the court trial and testified against Randal's nephews. From that day forward, the old clan leader, Randal McCoy, swore vengeance against Ellison Hatfield.[38]

The Romance of Johnse Hatfield and Roseanna McCoy

Two months after the killing of Bill Staton, Johnse Hatfield met Roseanna McCoy. Historians and other writers have written endlessly about the love between that young couple. Movie and television screenwriters have been equally fascinated, though few have taken the trouble to understand the mountain lifestyle. Some writers have dwelt on the twin themes of Victorian propriety and how this matched a mountaineer's "fierce pride" and "wounded honor."

The point is true enough that mountain folk are proud. That fact does not rule out the equally valid idea that mountaineers accepted love and sex as natural. The mountain folk seemed to be pleased that young people were attracted to one another and seemed to know that strong marriages could develop from relationships that began before a preacher was handy.

Virgil Carrington Jones wrote that when Johnse first saw Roseanna at the 1880 election, he "hatched a plot as old as Eve" and "stared with lustful anticipation at the bounteous curve of her bosom."[39] A bit later, Jones added that the mountaineers anticipated trouble from the love affair because "... Devil Anse did not want the blood of his arch enemy, Randal McCoy, mixed with that of his own."[40] Other writers have been equally inventive, concocting mountain dialect with a certain careless abandon, though there are no recorded interviews with Johnse or Roseanna to tell what they were thinking or feeling, or, for that matter, exactly how their love began.

In this light, Coleman A. Hatfield had pertinent arguments to make about Anse Hatfield's role in "breaking up" the budding romance between Johnse and

Roseanna. His essential argument was that Anse had little reason to feel any bitter animosity toward Randal McCoy, Roseanna, or his own son Johnse.

> Historians of the feud have pictured Anderson Hatfield as a stern father who objected to the marriage of his sons with any but those whom the old leader himself chose to be the spouses of his offspring. Nothing could be further from the truth.
>
> As a matter of fact, Johnse was married four times in his life, and his father never had anything to say about his marital contracts or agreements.
>
> In order that you may understand this, after the first blast from old father Randal, Roseanna together with Johnse came to the home of Devil Anse and were aggrieved to know that Randal had taken such a belligerent attitude toward young Hatfield. After it became known that McCoy so violently opposed the marriage of his daughter to Johnse, she returned home, but was driven away and found that her father made it so unhappy for her that she could not stay with her people.[41]

Just why this was so is an open question. The most likely argument is that the prison sentences served by Paris and Sam McCoy became a lingering wound in the mind of Randal McCoy. The memory of the Civil War death of his brother may have haunted McCoy. But there were as many reasons for him to be the friend of Anse Hatfield as there were for the two to dislike one another. Coleman A. Hatfield also wrote on that point.

> Our historians have failed in another delineation of the love affair. They picture old Randal as an ancient and violent enemy of Anderson Hatfield, as if this had lasted for many years.
>
> It has already been related in another place that Randal and Anse fought and bushwhacked together on the same side during the war, and that while neither man directly contributed to the downfall of Randal's brother Harmon, yet he was murdered by Jim Wheeler Wilson with the assistance of Jim Vance, the uncle of Anse Hatfield.
>
> If family relationships had anything to do with it, there would have been a more kindly relationship between the sons and daughters of Randal and Anderson than there would have been between the sons and daughters of Harmon McCoy and Anse. Yet we find that Nancy McCoy, the daughter of Harmon McCoy, was the first wife of Johnse Hatfield.[42]

Whatever the circumstances were, Roseanna McCoy and Johnse Hatfield were not wed, though Roseanna gave birth to their daughter, Sarah Elizabeth

McCoy, in the spring of 1881.[43] The baby lived only a few months and died of measles later that year. Roseanna lived until 1888 but then died — some claim of a broken heart, because Randal would not forgive her for loving Johnse. Truda Williams McCoy, who wrote the book most sympathetic to her family, claimed that Randal's attitude contributed to Roseanna's passing and that Johnse Hatfield was conscience-stricken as a result of her death.[44] Coleman A. Hatfield agreed with that idea. Johnse, in the meantime, was attracted to Nancy McCoy and that couple married on May 14, 1881.[45]

The Changes in Pikeville

As these private matters troubled the Hatfields and McCoys, the new economy began taking firmer hold of Logan County, West Virginia, and Pike County, Kentucky. The Yellow Poplar Lumber Company moved into Pike County in August 1881, paying about a dollar and a half per tree, according to William David Deskins, Pike County's most recent historian.[46] That account added that the rise in the timber business was followed by the construction of locks and dams on Big Sandy River, which made the economy stronger and helped the local tax base become somewhat larger. The economic changes were accompanied by a rise in population — America's first recorded postwar "baby boom," which was a national phenomenon.

The improving economy and lifestyle allowed Pikeville to build a new courthouse, which was finished by the end of March 1888, according to *The Ironton Register*.[47] The new courthouse was followed by the establishment of the Pikeville Collegiate Institute, which later grew into Pikeville College. By the turn of the century, Pikeville and Pike County were as prepared as Logan County was for the arrival of the coal-based economy.

Yet before the region was touted as the coalfield of the nation, it received its first national attention from Joseph Pulitzer's newspaper, *The New York World*, whose reporters learned about the beginning of the Hatfield-McCoy feud from the pages of *The Louisville Courier-Journal*. Such attention came in the wake of the murder of Ellison Hatfield, the true beginning of the troubles and the most shocking event that changed Anse Hatfield's life forever.

---

[1] Feud: Hatfields, McCoys and Social Change in Appalachia: 1860-1900, Altina L. L. Waller.
[2] Feud: Hatfields, McCoys and Social Change in Appalachia 1860-1900, Altina L. L. Waller.
[3] An American Vendetta, Theron C. Crawford.
[4] The War Baby, Coleman A. Hatfield.
[5] Interview With Coleman A. Hatfield, Coleman C. Hatfield.
[6] The Christmas Eve Fracas, Coleman A. Hatfield.
[7] Coleman C. Hatfield Interviews.
[8] Industrial and Educational Development, Coleman A. Hatfield.
[9] Logan County Court Records, June 20, 1866.
[10] Conversation with Mary (Molly) McDonald Justice. This history must contain a terrible lapse of historical correctness to indicate what was going on in Logan County in 1866 and following years. There are no sources that a historian is bound to respect. My source for this is a conversation I had with Mary McDonald Justice — my aged grandmother — about 1965. Her

uncle was Astynax McDonald, the lieutenant of the 36th Virginia Infantry Company D (the Logan Wildcats) in the final years of the Civil War. Styn McDonald, as he was known, was a close personal friend of John William Straton and became the president of Camp Straton United Confederate Veterans after Straton himself died in 1902. Uncle Styn, who lived on until 1911, told my grandmother the story and she told it to me, adding a very creditable "rebel yell" that she also learned from Uncle Styn.

[11] The Logan County Banner, December 22, 1898.
[12] The Logan Banner, April 5, 1937.
[13] Frankie Whitman Interview.
[14] Social History of Logan County, Mary B. Hurst.
[15] Transformation of the Tug and Guyandot Valleys, Edwin A. Cubby.
[16] Logan Centennial Booklet.
[17] The Logan Democrat, April 29, 1915.
[18] The Logan County Banner, December 22, 1898.
[19] Logan Circuit Court Records Memoranda Book A.
[20] The Cincinnati Weekly Enquirer, August 26, 1874.
[21] The Logan Banner, July 24, 1937.
[22] The Logan Democrat, June 29, 1911.
[23] Feud: Hatfields, McCoys, and Social Change in Appalachia 1860-1900, Altina L. Waller.
[24] Coleman C. Hatfield Interviews.
[25] Feud: Hatfields, McCoys and Social Change in Appalachia 1860-1900, Altina L. Waller.
[26] Coleman C. Hatfield Interviews.
[27] Feud: Hatfields, McCoys and Social Change in Appalachia 1860-1900, Altina L. Waller.
[28] Coleman C. Hatfield Interviews.
[29] Coleman C. Hatfield Interviews.
[30] The Hoot Owl Story, Coleman A. Hatfield
[31] The Haint Tale, Coleman A. Hatfield.
[32] The Truth About Frank James, Coleman A. Hatfield.
[33] Four Deer With One Bullet, Coleman A. Hatfield.
[34] Argument Over Two Sandy Shoats, Coleman A. Hatfield.
[35] Argument Over Two Sandy Shoats, Coleman A. Hatfield.
[36] Coleman C. Hatfield Interviews.
[37] Feud: Hatfields, McCoys and Social Change in Appalachia 1860-1900, Altina L. Waller.
[38] Argument Over Two Sandy Shoats, Coleman A. Hatfield. Readers should note that the Ephraim Hatfield mentioned in this passage was not Devil Anse Hatfield's father, but another cousin of Anse.
[39] The Hatfields and the McCoys, Virgil Carrington Jones.
[40] The Hatfields and the McCoys, Virgil Carrington Jones.
[41] Death of Roseanna McCoy, Coleman A. Hatfield.
[42] Death of Roseanna McCoy, Coleman A. Hatfield.
[43] The McCoys: Their Story, Truda Williams McCoy.
[44] The McCoys: Their Story, Truda Williams McCoy.
[45] Feud: Hatfields, McCoys and Social Change in Appalachia 1860-1900, Altina L. Waller.
[46] Pike County: A Very Different Place, William David Deskins.
[47] The Ironton Register, March 29, 1888. Cited in Pike County: A Very Different Place, William David Deskins.

Chapter Five
THE RAGE OF THE DEVIL
The Beginning of the Hatfield and McCoy Feud

ELLISON Hatfield — Anse's younger brother — lay dying on the afternoon of August 9, 1882, with twenty-seven knife and gunshot wounds inflicted by Tolbert, Pharmer, and Randal McCoy Jr., the sons of old Randal McCoy.[1] Ellison was a handsome man and a well-respected citizen of the Tug Fork Valley. He died that day.

That night, someone took the McCoy brothers across the Tug where they bound them to pawpaw bushes and shot them dead. Anse Hatfield was never convicted of murdering the McCoys, but popular suspicion fell upon him. In Anse's region during his time, suspicion was enough to start a feud.

The next morning, searchers who included Randal's son, Jim McCoy, found the trio. Tolbert McCoy's hand was over his forehead, as if to ward off bullets. Pharmer had fallen and was swinging by the ropes that held him to the pawpaw bushes. Randal Jr. was kneeling with the top of his head blown away.[2] America's most famous feud had begun.

The eight years that followed were the most terrible time imaginable for the two families. Nancy Hatfield, the wife of Cap Hatfield, once was quoted saying, "It was a horrible nightmare to me. Sometimes for months Cap never spent a night in our house. He and Devil Anse, with others, slept in the nearby woods to guard our homes against surprise attacks...."[3] Anse himself was quoted saying he was sorry the troubles began. Even Randal McCoy, the man who suffered most from the violence, said he and Anse Hatfield once had been friends and Randal only wanted the killing stopped.[4]

Hundreds of pages have been written to explain why the feud happened. Many paragraphs have been used to explain how the grudges from the Civil War, the sorrows of Roseanna McCoy, and the alleged theft of a hog built into the anger that led to the feud. The "isolation" of the two families has been cited as one reason for the violence. Justified criticisms of the inadequate nature of Appalachian courts have been voiced. The simple truth is that the feud does not reflect mountaineer character, which was and is peaceful in most instances.

Coleman A. Hatfield wrote that his family always believed that the trouble began when Bill Staton was killed by "Squirrel Hunting" Sam McCoy and Paris McCoy. Ellison Hatfield had been a witness against the McCoy brothers in the trial that followed. The Hatfields thought that the McCoys held a grudge after that trial and were seeking a way to retaliate against Ellison Hatfield.[5]

By the end of the feud in 1890, both families were sick to death of the violence. It has been conceded that Hatfields and McCoys were repelled by the memory of that time. One local historian stated that several men warned him never to ask Cap Hatfield about the feud — that Hatfield resented such questions in his later years.[6]

The Death of Ellison Hatfield

If one were to pick a moment when the feud began, however, that would be the week of August 5, 1882, when a famous election was held near the home of Preacher Anse Hatfield on Blackberry Creek, which flows into Tug Fork on the Kentucky side of that stream.[7] Coleman A. Hatfield wrote his account of the dispute that began that day between Ellison Hatfield and the three McCoy brothers.

> The fifth day of August 1882, which was Saturday, was Election Day in Kentucky and the time when Randal McCoy had sworn vengeance against Ellison Hatfield because Ellison had testified against McCoy's two nephews, Sam and Paris, who were tried on charges of killing Bill Staton on the West Virginia side. Ellison Hatfield's testimony had made him a marked man, as far as the McCoys were concerned.
>
> That was in the spring of 1882. In August, Ellison, Elias, and perhaps Wall Hatfield had gone over into McCoy territory in Pike County. It was said that Randal prompted his boys to go to the election, and he went with them. They drank some whiskey that Randal gave them at his home, and they claimed they saw Ellison's tracks in the road and swore they would cut the tracks in the dirt to show their enmity toward Ellison.
>
> The McCoys mounted their horses and headed for the election grounds. They dashed up in single file, bravado fashion, shouting at the crowd of men who were on the grounds. Ellison was wearing a big rush hat that somebody had made for him, and he took off his hat and waved it as he said in a jesting manner to the McCoys, "Come on, boys, this is hay for your horses!"
>
> Tolbert McCoy, a handsome man with a beard like General Winfield Scott Hancock of Civil War fame, led the charge at Ellison as the McCoy boys sprang from their saddles. Tolbert yelled, "Ellison Hatfield, I'm h___ on earth!" Ellison replied, "You are a s___ hog."[8]
>
> Tolbert began swinging his knife and stabbing Ellison about the breast and cutting him across the arms, while Floyd and young Randal came in from other sides as their brother Pharmer (Dick) McCoy shot Ellison in the back.

It was said that Randal had a piece of an old fence rail that he aimed to come up and strike Ellison with when he was down, but that bystanders prevented Randal from striking Ellison.

Dick McCoy broke to run for the woods in the meantime. Elias Hatfield took after him and shot a pistol empty, but overtook Dick in the woods. Elias pointed his empty pistol at Dick and told him he was going to kill him if he did not surrender. It was also said that another one of Randal's boys had participated, although they didn't get ahold of him.[9]

Other feud historians have added details to that account, claiming that the trouble began when Tolbert McCoy demanded a sum of $1.75 or $2 from "Bad 'Lias" Hatfield, the cousin of Preacher Anse Hatfield and thus, the cousin of Devil Anse. Those writers claim that when Tolbert was rebuffed by Bad 'Lias, Tolbert turned his rage on Ellison Hatfield, who tried to defuse the anger with his joke about his hat being hay for the horses. Coleman A. Hatfield's tale, however, indicates that men of the McCoy family planned to pay back their grudge for Ellison's role in the trial of "Squirrel Hunting" Sam and Paris McCoy.

Another point of interest is Truda Williams McCoy's version of the Election Day events. She wrote that Tolbert pulled a knife only after the fight with Ellison began, and then the other McCoys boys joined their brother. She also wrote that Anse, who intended to dominate the Pike County election by buying votes and passing out whiskey, appeared on the scene, pulled a pistol and fired pointblank at Pharmer McCoy's head. The pistol misfired. "Devil Anse looked at Pharmer with deadly hate, and he spoke in a deadly voice: 'The Lord shore must a-been with ye; I never took better aim at a buck in my life,'" she wrote.[10]

If that actually happened, it escaped the attention of Coleman A. Hatfield and other feud historians. Those writers all indicated that Anse was not present, but that word of the assault on Ellison was sent to Anse's home on Beech Creek, twelve miles away on the West Virginia side of the Tug Fork. Ellison was taken to Anderson Ferrell's home about four o'clock that afternoon. His mother, Nancy Vance Hatfield, and his wife, Sarah Staton Hatfield, soon came to the cabin to nurse Ellison. At about the same time, Preacher Anse Hatfield — still a justice of the peace — ordered constables Tolbert Hatfield and Joseph Hatfield (and some claim Matthew Hatfield) to take the McCoy brothers to the jail in Pikeville for safekeeping and to face assault charges.

That party started for Pikeville, but stopped at the home of Floyd McCoy for food. One of the constables in charge of the McCoys decided to spent the night at John Hatfield's house, further up Blackberry Creek.[11] That proved to be a mistake because Anse Hatfield arrived there the following morning with a band of followers and took charge of the McCoy brothers. At that point, the sequence of events became most interesting.

Paul McAllister, one of the students of Tug Fork history and lore who lived and worked in Matewan, West Virginia, argues that of all the decisions made during the feud era, the strangest was Anse Hatfield's actions after he heard Ellison had been assaulted and wounded. McAllister believes that Anse reverted to his status as the captain of a partisan band during the Civil War and acted accordingly in August 1882. That is a compelling argument.[12] Yet historians must wonder if there were other ideas at work in Anse's mind and if other men present influenced his thinking.

Anse Hatfield's Ideas of Justice

When one thinks about Anse Hatfield, one should always recall that he was never an entirely modern man. The pioneer era of Appalachia, which may be dated roughly from 1753 until 1839, was always present in his mind. Frontier justice could be a rough matter and, indeed, one could argue that the shooting of the McCoy brothers on the bank of the Tug was a final lethal explosion of such frontier justice before a modern era court system was established in original Logan County, which included the Tug Valley.

Another idea at work in Anse's mind on the night of August 9, 1882, may have been that his great-grandfather, old Abner Vance, had trusted his life to a court and had been hanged, justly or unjustly. Anse may well have believed that there may have been no justice for the West Virginia Hatfields in the Kentucky courts. While that does not mean that Anse was justified if he killed the McCoy brothers, Anse may have thought that was reason enough to make certain the McCoys would not be freed.

A third idea that Anse may have acted upon was the idea of the regulator. In frontier North Carolina there was at least once instance of early Americans superseding legal authorities by claiming that English common law allowed citizens to act for their own best interests in cases of authorities failing their responsibilities. That tradition dated back to English common law, which included the idea of "hue and cry," allowing citizens to apprehend suspected felons when no constituted officers of the law were readily available.

The Role of Charlie Carpenter

Another man present when the McCoy brothers mortally wounded Ellison Hatfield was one Charles C. Carpenter, whose origins have remained a mystery. Carpenter taught school in a one-room building on the West Virginia side of the Tug and had indeed been hired by a school committee that included Anse Hatfield. Anse naturally thought that Carpenter was a learned man and respected the way an educated man should behave in a particular circumstance. On the night of August 9, 1882, Carpenter had a decided influence on the course of events that blackened the Hatfield name in the minds of many who have written about the feud. Coleman A. Hatfield again explained those circumstances.

Mob rule hardly ever gets out-of-hand over any situation without some leader who sparks the movement and without whom the unorganized, unthinking, potentially dangerous destructive force would never be released or get underway.

Among the mountain folk, who had been erstwhile neighbors and who had grown up in the hills and knew common problems, even their petty differences were resolved by their solemn regard for the law — and this though there were imperfections in the administration of the law because of travel barriers, slow communication, lack of schools and religious institutions, all of which otherwise accompany a well-organized society.

Then appeared on the border Charles C. Carpenter. Nobody seemed to know whence he came and only a few hints were ever learned of his past. For all his exceptional breadth of learning and ability, however, at heart he seemed to be a bad man. He told his boys in 1882 that he had been shot at least once every year since the Civil War and that he usually carried a pistol, though he was a schoolteacher.[13]

Hatfield wrote that though Carpenter had earned his reputation as a learned man through his months of school teaching, he was the man who encouraged Anse Hatfield to act as the leader of a band of regulators and to execute the McCoy brothers. Carpenter "drew up" a set of proposed laws that was approved by Anse and his fellow "regulators." Anse kept the papers for many years, perhaps intending to use them as his justification if he ever was tried for the murder of the McCoy brothers. Coleman A. Hatfield also saved the "regulations" as written by Carpenter.

Inasmuch as the people along the border of our two states have been greatly shocked and grieved by the commission of a foul and bloody crime perpetrated upon Ellison Hatfield, one of our worthy citizens, who has been a loving father, a kind and generous neighbor, respected by all who knew him, and, who has now been struck down by the hands of McCoy assassins, whom we now have in charge.

And whereas it is the pleasure of all who have met in this presence to consider putting down such heinous crimes and stamping out such foul and blood-thirsty deeds of violence lately committed along the shore of our two states.

Now, wherefore, be it resolved that there shall be summary action to put an end to murder and violence and that we hereby agree to stand together in all that we do for the protection of ourselves and other citizens of this territory, and that the guilty be punished according to their deeds, an eye for an eye and a tooth for a tooth, and that all other things which be just and proper be done for the good of our community.[14]

After writing that grim message, Carpenter delivered it to the crowd that had gathered around the house where Ellison Hatfield suffered. That scene, according to the Hatfield account, was lurid:

> By the red glare of the flickering pine torches Charles C. Carpenter harangued the crowd of approximately thirty young men and boys gathered around to hear the reading of his resolutions.
>
> He told of having served four years in the Civil War, that he had traveled since that time in the far west, in the Rocky Mountains and southward, and that he had served on vigilante committees where there had been outlawry and outrages committed against citizens such as in the locality. He assured his listeners that all of this was perfectly legal where it was voted upon by "peaceful" citizens for the best interests of the country and that there was no one among them whom objected.[15]

A formal vote was taken. Carpenter's "resolutions" were approved, and the gunfire exploded along the Tug Fork later that rain-soaked night. Randal McCoy, who had gone to Pikeville to round up a posse to save his sons, did not arrive in time and learned about the death of his sons late in the morning of August 10, 1882. There were few, then or now, who were not in sympathy with a father losing his children so violently. Interestingly, Coleman A. Hatfield is not known to have written an account of the killing of the McCoy brothers.[16]

Despite the shock and grief Randal felt, the people of the Tug did not erupt with the retribution that romantic novelists have portrayed as a mountaineer characteristic. Instead of organizing an army to take revenge, Randal went to the circuit court which served Pike County. There he sought indictments for the men whom he believed had killed his sons. Judge George N. Brown called a sixteen-member grand jury that indicted the Hatfield partisans.

The list of men indicted included Anse, Cap, Johnse, Wall, and Elias Hatfield; Charles Carpenter; Joe Murphy; Dock, Plyant, and Sam Mahon; Selkirk and LD. McCoy; Tom Chambers; Lark and Andy Varney; Dan and John Whitt; Alex Messer; and Elijah Mounts. The court records show only that those men were not found inside the borders of Pike County by the end of February 1883.[17]

Carpenter eventually escaped any consequences of his actions. Soon after the McCoy boys were murdered, he gathered some of his followers and fled to Tennessee, where it was believed he remained sometime near the town of Sweetwater. A quarter century later, one Jess (Redbrush) Browning and others moved to the southwestern part of the state of Washington. One day, an older man with a long beard streaked with white and red walked up to Browning and said, "Do you remember me? I am Charles C. Carpenter, who knew you when you were in your teens. You went to school to me on Mate Creek during the eighties."

Browning later returned east and nothing else was learned about Carpenter's fate. Yet Coleman A. Hatfield quoted Dr. Elliott Rutherford — for whom one of Anse Hatfield's sons was named — saying the feud would never have happened, had it not been for "that bull-eyed Charlie Carpenter" and his absurd "resolutions."[18]

Reactions of the Hatfields

The Hatfield family was devastated by the killing of Ellison and later came to regard the killing of the McCoy brothers with bitter shame. Some eighty years after the famous month of August 1882, Coleman A. Hatfield wrote an account of the death of Ellison Hatfield that saved his family's attitude toward that violence. The facts should be recalled in that light, but also with the knowledge that Coleman A. Hatfield received his information from Anse and Cap Hatfield, and that Cap was eighteen years old when the feud began. Coleman A.'s first thoughts were about Ellison Hatfield.

> In the sad story of the killing of Big Ellison Hatfield of the borderline country, a typical mountaineer and father of five children with a sixth posthumous babe born a few months later, it should be recalled that his widow was left to do the best she could in rearing their offspring.
>
> Sarah Hatfield did not marry again, but managed to rear all of her children, who grew to strong manhood and womanhood and who became good citizens and parents in the community where they resided.
>
> One of Sarah's grandsons became a successful lawyer, another a physician, and all contributed their share to the friendly neighborliness of all who knew them in the countryside around and about. But these children grew up without the companionship, the love, and the fatherly care of the big-hearted neighbor and worthy citizen such as Ellison was known to be. These facts often have been forgotten by those who have written about the violence of the feud.[19]

Coleman A. Hatfield also understood that both families had lashed out at one another without taking the law into consideration. He admitted that mountaineers of the time did not trust the law as much as they should have, although, as writer Altina L. Waller noted, there was much more evidence that the mountaineers turned to the law to settle their troubles than other writers have indicated.

Coleman A. Hatfield's words on that matter should become part of the body of knowledge about the feud.

> Readers of the feud stories may be reminded here that they have heard many tales which seem to favor the unfortunate trio of Randal McCoy's sons who were cruelly murdered on the ninth day of August 1882 following the death of Ellison Hatfield....
> What was done to them was not the American way. At least, we would like to think that most judicial determinations carry with them more of the fruits of justice that what may often happen in a wild country, even of our mountainous section, four score years ago in a spot forty miles from any courthouse and perhaps a hundred miles from the place where a judge of competent jurisdiction could be found to try such a case.[20]

The Smouldering Fires

Nearly everyone who has written about the Hatfield and McCoy feud has had to deal with the fact that very little happened between February 1883 and January 1887. The list of writers includes the scholarly Altina L. Waller, who noted that the first part of the feud ended with the shooting of the McCoy brothers. That list also includes the careful Otis K. Rice, who wrote a chapter titled "The Smouldering Fires" in his book *The Hatfields and the McCoys*. And, most surprisingly, the writers' list includes Theron C. Crawford, a writer for *The New York World*, who wrote one of the first journalistic accounts of the troubles and who was most bitterly critical of Logan County and the Hatfield family. Some of Crawford's words about the aftermath of the killing of the McCoy brothers are worth remembering in that light:

> This very decided act of retaliation upon the part of the Hatfields for a time subdued the McCoys. For five years there was nothing more than the ordinary neighborhood quarrelling. Murders which were committed during those years in brawls, bar room rows, election fights, and disputes which grew out of trials at court, were incidental killings which had no relation to the great feud.[21]

The Era of the Feuds

Otis K. Rice's illuminating book written in 1982 is also most helpful for readers trying to understand the events of the central years of the 1880s. Rice wrote that the feud that involved Anse Hatfield and Randal McCoy was a manifestation of the "widespread troubles" of eastern Kentucky during that era.

Such troubles included violence that Rice characterized as "almost unrestrained lawlessness" in eastern Kentucky, including incidents in Lawrence, Boyd, and Carter Counties and other violence in Breathitt County. Another feud, which Rice described as characteristic of the times, was the French-Eversole War of Perry County, Kentucky. In Rowan County, the Tolliver-Martin-Logan vendetta dwarfed the Hatfield and McCoy feud. There were so many election fights in eastern Kentucky during that time that *The Louisville Courier-Journal* included roundup reports of such troubles.[22]

Even Coleman A. Hatfield, who began his detailed studies of that era in 1909 or soon thereafter, believed that the Hatfield and McCoy feud was only one episode in a wider field of study. Hatfield wrote that while the Hatfield and McCoy feud was a latter day reaction to the forces that spawned the pioneer era of the Cumberland Plateau, it also was characteristic of its time. On that subject, he wrote:

> Many would believe that the Hatfield-McCoy feud is the only vendetta of its kind which has occurred, and the fiery headlines of newspapers throughout the last quarter of the 19th century might lead readers to believe that the characters who have enacted this tragedy are the fiercest and most heartless men of all time. And yet we are told that many such vendettas have occurred throughout the southern Appalachian highlands before law and order reached into the mountain fastnesses.
>
> Would not a question arise in your mind as to the basic causes which prompted men to engage in the fratricidal destruction throughout the Cumberlands and Southern Alleghenies? Around the border of Kentucky and through the hills there was the Howard-Baker feud, the Frenches and the Eversoles, the Holbrooks and the Underwoods, the Hills and Evans, to say nothing of the Tollivers and Martins, along with many other conflicts of varying duration.
>
> So the headline hunters go in desperate effort to alarm the reading world with their bloodthirsty stories. Even the dead are slandered in the tales of immorality which are pictured as having occurred.... Hospitable neighbors who are family leaders and patriarchs are pictured as bloodthirsty outlaws ready and willing to commit any act within the category of crime.[23]

Otis K. Rice made the point that Anse Hatfield's role in the early feud years was at its most intense on the night of August 9-10, 1882, when his temper exploded when Ellison Hatfield died. After that, Anse seemed to have sought a return to normal life. Randal McCoy, understandably, was embittered by the death of his three sons and sought the counsel of Perry Cline to bring the Hatfields to justice, as McCoy defined the concept.[24]

The Character of Randal McCoy

At that point, the essential character of Randal McCoy becomes most important to the tale of the feud. Historians seek fairness, avoiding diatribes. Perhaps the fairest way to approach that subject is to quote Truda Williams McCoy first, since she was the writer most in sympathy with the McCoy family. She made her point when she wrote about the pig trial — that Randal was a proud man, much too proud to let offenses go unanswered.

> He had a standard of right and wrong — a code which he lived by. He believed in God and the Devil. No man in his right mind could doubt the Devil — not after he had lived as close to the Hatfields as he had. Sure, he was religious in his way, but not to the point where he would let a d___ Hatfield walk all over him and take it lying down. God didn't expect that of a man — not of a McCoy anyway.[25]

If that is an accurate view of Randal McCoy's nature, it is most surprising that he did not launch an armed assault on the Hatfields upon learning of the death of his sons. Truda Williams McCoy argues that Sarah (Sally) McCoy, Randal's wife, who begged Anse Hatfield to spare the boys, was prostrated by the murder, took to her bed, and pleaded with Randal not to use violence for revenge. Her thoughts on that matter were based on her religious nature, according to the McCoy historian.[26]

Otis K. Rice and Altina L. Waller took a dimmer view of Randal McCoy's character. Rice wrote that McCoy combined "a morose nature with a tendency to talk about his troubles with all who would listen."[27] Waller agrees in essence with Rice, adding that this tendency made Randal more unpopular than he would have been otherwise. She wrote that McCoy's part was taken by Perry Cline and others only after it became apparent that the sweeping changes affecting the valleys of the Tug, the Guyandot, and the Big Sandy could benefit themselves.

Fears of the Hatfields

The events of the central years of the feud convinced the Hatfields that they were not safe in any circumstances. That conviction, in turn, sparked a new round of violence that turned the Hatfield and McCoy anger into a genuine feud. In simple terms, after 1886 the Hatfields were on the defense while the McCoys were on the offense. That meant that even other Hatfields, who had not been deeply involved in the feud, were at risk alongside Anse and his immediate family.

Elias Hatfield, Anse's brother, reentered the tale at that point. Elias, who was fond of being called "Good 'Lias," had been a fortunate man until 1886. He had been present at the famous election of August 1882 and had helped arrest one of the McCoy brothers involved in the fracas. Few students of the feud believe that Elias was one of the killers of the McCoy brothers. On the surface, Elias appeared out of harm's way.

Elias Hatfield did not feel very safe, in the opinion of Cap Hatfield's branch of the family. Those voices claim that Elias, though he enjoyed a seemingly impeccable reputation, had a nature much like Randal McCoy's. They state Elias was nervous and fidgety, apt to see enemies behind every bush. They add that Elias was fearful of being ambushed and that he needed the protection of younger Hatfields, whom he called "Anse's hellhounds."[28]

In the spring of 1887, Elias told Anse that he was concerned that the McCoys were watching his house, waiting for the chance to catch Elias off guard and shoot him. Elias' evidence was that he found a forked branch on a hill overlooking his Tug Fork home. The branch was the right height for a man to rest a gun and draw a bead at the house. "Something'll have to be did about it," Elias said to Anse, according to Cap's faction.[29]

Nevertheless, the opening years of the feud seem to have come to an end with three lesser episodes, which are yet important in the events that followed. First was the marriage of Johnse Hatfield to Nancy McCoy, who would leave him later and marry Frank Phillips. Phillips would, of course, play a most fateful role in bringing the feud to an end. The second episode was the assault on the Bill Daniel's home that was led by Cap Hatfield. Third was the killing of Jeff McCoy, also at the hands of Cap Hatfield and another gunman.

Roseanna McCoy and the Marriage of Johnse Hatfield

Though the tales can be told in any order, the marriage of Johnse Hatfield and Nancy McCoy seems to be the earliest episode of the three. The relationship between the couple has been dated to early 1881 by Virgil Carrington Jones, among others.[30] No one seems to know why Johnse "broke up" with Roseanna McCoy, his earlier lover. Certainly he had reasons for remaining loyal to Roseanna, but Hatfields long have known that Johnse was fickle.

Sometime in the year 1885 Johnse was out late one evening when he was surprised by a group of McCoys led by Randal's oldest son, Jim McCoy. Johnse was arrested on the trumped-up charge of carrying a concealed weapon, a charge which greatly amuses later Hatfields because nearly all men went armed in the hill country at that time.[31] Roseanna rode to the Hatfield home and warned Anse about Johnse being in danger. Anse and his boys rode to rescue Johnse, though it is an entertaining fiction that the Hatfields made the McCoys beg for mercy.[32]

Romantic writers have again made much of Roseanna's actions to rescue Johnse. Theron C. Crawford led the pack writing about that aspect of the feud. His book, *An American Vendetta*, includes an illustration of Roseanna supposedly riding in a breakneck fashion down a precipice to warn Anse of the danger. The episode probably was not that dramatic, but it does add a touching moment to the violent history of the feud.

Romance reared its head again when Virgil Carrington Jones wrote about the way Anse and other Hatfields reacted to Johnse's relationship with Nancy McCoy, who has been described as willful and passionate. Nancy was the daughter of Asa Harmon McCoy, who had been killed at the end of the War Between the States. Anse Hatfield was accused of being the killer of Randal McCoy's brother. Jones wrote that Randal McCoy was again outraged that one of his nieces had married a Hatfield and that the Hatfields again rejoiced at "outwitting" a foe. Jones then wrote:

> On the Hatfield side, the rejoicing was loud and sincere at first; then it slowly took on a rancid tinge. For, as the months went by, it gradually was realized that Johnse, the bold, domineering, and unrepulsed lover, was becoming the most henpecked husband along the Tug. His days as an active member of the clan were numbered and reduced. Nancy had taken the powder out of his gun. Devil Anse, once proud of the ways of his son with women, now chided him sourly and, behind his back, stamped the ground in disgust.
>
> After a time, a more serious complaint was directed at Johnse's marriage. The Hatfields suddenly realized that someone in their clan was spying for the enemy. It was evident that the McCoys knew too much about Hatfield plans and actions for their knowledge to be laid to coincidence. More and more, as the Hatfields sought the leak, the finger of suspicion pointed toward the women and finally settled on Nancy, who must still have the welfare of her own family at heart. But before any guilt could be uncovered, the finger of suspicion jabbed in another spot.[33]

The Assault on the Daniels Women

Nancy McCoy Hatfield, as she was known by that time, had a sister named Mary, who was married to Bill Daniels. The Daniels lived on the Kentucky side of Tug Fork, but Nancy and Mary, who were talkative, visited often. The Hatfields also suspected that Nancy and Mary were tracking movements of the Hatfields and passing such information along to the McCoys, detectives, and legal authorities in Kentucky. The Hatfields sought to stop the flow of information from that source.

Accordingly, one night in 1886, a band of men led by Tom Wallace and Cap Hatfield broke into the Daniels home and whipped the two women with a cow's tail, warning them to quit gossiping about the troubles of the two families and passing information to the Kentuckians. Hatfield and Wallace took turns holding Daniels at bay while they whipped the two women.[34]

Truda Williams McCoy's account of that event varies in some detail from the writings of Rice and Waller. She identified the two women as Mary Daniels and her mother-in-law. That account claims Mary Daniels fought back against Hatfield and Wallace, but was knocked unconscious. Bill Daniels was absent, she wrote. Her book adds that Nancy McCoy Hatfield confronted Johnse Hatfield about the violence, told Johnse she knew who the raiders were, and swore that she would shoot Cap Hatfield if she saw him again, with or without proof of Cap's involvement in the beating.[35]

The Killing of Jeff McCoy

The death of Jeff McCoy followed in short order. Jeff was a son of Asa Harmon McCoy and a brother of Nancy McCoy Hatfield. In the autumn of 1886, Jeff killed one Fred Wolford in Pike County. He then fled to West Virginia and learned of the beating of his sisters at the home of Bill Daniels. With the help of Josiah Hurley, McCoy sought to arrest Tom Wallace, but failed to do so, and only succeeded in infuriating Cap Hatfield. Hatfield obtained warrants for the arrest of McCoy and Hurley, but McCoy attempted to escape but was arrested by Hatfield and Wallace. McCoy jumped into the Tug to swim to safety on the Kentucky side. When he reached the shore a fatal shot hit him. It is not certain if Hatfield or Wallace fired that shot.[36]

Anse Hatfield intervened at that point to try to stop further trouble or bloodshed. That was a curious decision for a man accused so often as being the arch-plotting "devil" of the feud era. On December 26, 1886, Anse sent a letter that had been written by Cap's wife, Nancy Smith Hatfield, to Perry Cline in Pikeville. Addressing Cline as "friend Perry," Anse wrote that neither Bill Daniels nor any of the McCoys was in any danger from the Hatfields. Anse wrote that he only wanted the trouble to end and promised Cline he would do anything in his power to make that possible.[37]

Anse's letter was of no use. Some historians have written that his peace initiative failed because of the hot tempers of other feudists, such as his Uncle Jim Vance and his son, Cap. On the McCoy side, those writers argue, Randal McCoy, Perry Cline, and Asa Harmon (Bud) McCoy (son of the Civil War victim) guaranteed that there would be more violence. Not unexpectedly, Cap's son, Coleman A. Hatfield, wrote that Cap's actions were misguided and deplorable, even for the twenty-two-year-old man that Cap was at that time. He added that Cap was afraid that the talkative Nancy and Mary would stir up further trouble and that Cap's actions were meant to bring events under some control. If so, that was a serious misjudgment because word of the violence inevitably circulated through the hills and provoked a new round of trouble.

There was an odd aftermath to the killing of Jeff McCoy. Tom Wallace was arrested and placed in the Pike County jail at Pikeville, though Cap Hatfield escaped arrest. One morning the jailer, whose name was Maynard, brought breakfast to Wallace and Charlie Mitchell, who was Wallace's companion in many escapades. One of the prisoners grabbed the large coffee pot and struck Maynard, who was peg-legged. Wallace and Mitchell escaped on the road to West Virginia, and swam across the Tug to safety.[38]

Yet the somewhat connected events of 1886 had another consequence that was vastly more serious. Between 1882 and 1886, it seemed that there was no "feud" in the sense that there was a vendetta in the eastern Kentucky meaning of the word, as in Rowan and Breathitt and other counties. Until journalists began trying to piece together the tale of the Hatfields and McCoys, the semi-comic episode of the pig trial and the failed romance of Johnse Hatfield and Roseanna McCoy appeared to be events without consequence. The serious trouble was the killing of Ellison Hatfield and the vengeful killing of Tolbert McCoy and his brothers.

The Role of the Detectives

Other plots preyed on the minds of the Hatfields as well. To understand what the family was thinking in the central years of that decade, it is important to know something about detectives or bounty hunters who were roaming the hills of the region and how concerned the Hatfields had become of being taken by surprise.

Coleman C. Hatfield argues that America's fascination with detectives is rooted in the murky ideas at work in many minds at the time of the Civil War. Hatfield claims that slave owners of that earlier time had become fearful of slave insurrections and sought better information of plots as they were being hatched. In fairness, that was true from the other side as well, because northerners and abolitionists were afraid that southerners were plotting for control of the federal government and meant personal harm as well[39]

That mentality led to the formation of the Pinkerton Agency just before the War Between the States. Though its efforts to protect President-elect Abraham Lincoln on his journey from Illinois to Washington, D.C., were somewhat comical and produced much ridicule in the South, and though Pinkerton spying efforts were laughable during the war, the romance of the private detective took hold of public imagination and, with the help of motion pictures and television, that tradition has never died.

The "bounty hunter" aspect of the detectives was something that became a danger to the Hatfields. Historians should be careful to remember the difference between "bounty hunting" and respectable detective work. In a later time, "detectives" became police officers who investigated crimes. "Bounty hunters" were those who sought to arrest suspects by any means possible.

To many young men of the 1880s, detective work and bounty hunting were exciting occupations, much as playing professional sports or being a jet pilot became at a later time. In the middle years of that decade, there were many episodes that involved the Hatfields and McCoys and bounty hunters — some humorous, some grim, and a few somewhere in between.

Aunt Lou Ragland and the Detective

One tale told by Coleman A. Hatfield explained how Louisa Goins Ragland, the wife of *The Logan County Banner* editor Henry Clay Ragland, helped foil one bounty hunter who wanted to apprehend Anse or his sons.

> Mrs. Henry Clay Ragland — "Aunt Lou," as she was familiarly called — was one of the grand old women of the '80s, loved and respected by rich and poor alike, an outspoken and loyal friend to the Hatfields.
>
> She related that Bill Baldwin, a young detective from Virginia, said to her, "Mrs. Ragland, I have never seen Cap and Johnse, two of the Hatfield brothers, and I would give five years of my life to get a shot at either of them at sixty yards, off-hand, and furthermore, I could collect more than a thousand dollars for either. I would make it worthwhile if you could give me information which would help in capturing them."
>
> "Look here, young man," she answered. "You may be a slick city detective, but you've no business fooling around here looking for any of the Hatfields. They are my friends and you needn't think there is anybody around in this place that's going to betray those boys, for all the money the Kentucky governor offered for them. You might as well get gone, for if you talk that way around here you might wind up getting the doctor to pick a few slugs of lead from under your hide."[40]

Old Dan, The Sleuth Tramp

One of the most persistent detectives who tracked the Hatfields during that time was Dan Cunningham, who became one of the subjects of "pulp fiction" tales between the 1880s and the 1920s. Cunningham and scores of other detectives invested many hours trying to get a bead on Anse and his family, with only marginal success.

During that time, another detective called "Old Dan, the sleuth tramp," whose family name has escaped history, bedeviled the Hatfields, though he should not be confused with Dan Cunningham, whom the Hatfields knew on sight. "Old Dan" appeared on the Logan County scene during the middle years of the feud, according to Coleman A. Hatfield.

> One of the most notorious of the so-called detectives was a man called "Old Dan." He first made friends with the McCoys and convinced Randal that if McCoy would furnish a few hundred dollars, certain Hatfields could be delivered into McCoy's hands.
>
> By the same token, "Old Dan" went to Anse and collected several hundred dollars. He convinced the Hatfields that he would deliver the McCoys into West Virginia. In the game of playing both sides against the middle, "Old Dan" and other men did capture Big John Dotson, a McCoy ally, and brought him to the courthouse in Logan County.[41]

Logan County's courthouse records do not indicate that anyone named John Dotson was tried in the circuit court, though the records of the 1880s are abysmal. The record of a case could be lost very easily, as a long search for other information about the Hatfields and the McCoys proves.

Coleman A. Hatfield wrote that "Old Dan" and two nephews met a sad fate in later years, when they were accused of murdering and robbing an elderly minister. Legal papers were served on the detective, but "Old Dan" escaped in the woods. In the meantime, however, "Old Dan" made much trouble on the borderline, according to the Hatfield records:

> One time "Old Dan" and eight others ambushed the Hatfields in the head of a creek where they took a position at a cliff near a line of beech trees. It was there that Bad Dick Evans accidentally discharged his rifle, the bullet penetrating his foot. Then all nine of the detectives ran away over the mountain.
>
> Anse and his men obtained warrants for the arrest of the would-be kidnappers. Since there were no charges against the Hatfields in their own state, the detectives had no legal warrants and were not accompanied by any West Virginia law officer.
>
> The detectives were pursued in turn and picked up, one by one, and brought to Logan Courthouse. A raiding party led by Cap Hatfield followed Bad Dick Evans into Wayne County, where he was arrested.[42]

After learning the fate of Evans and others, "Old Dan" crossed the Tug Fork to escape the Hatfields. Cap Hatfield told the others it would be easy to follow the detective's tracks because it was "as long as a boat paddle," according to Coleman A. Hatfield, who added:

"Old Dan" was followed to the home of Ralph Steele across the Kentucky border at the mouth of Beech Creek, where the detective was lodging for the night. The Hatfields, armed with kidnapping warrants, surrounded the house after dark and pushed the front door open.

"Old Dan" was sitting by a warm fire with a pepper-box pistol hanging on the wall above his head. Cap remarked, "Dan, I'd thought you would have had that artillery handy." Dan replied, "There's a time and place for all things." Cap said, "Dan, I'd be powerful insulted if you shot me with a cheap gun like that."

The Hatfields started across the mountains with "Old Dan" on the forty-mile trip to Logan Courthouse. Early the next morning, the Hatfields got two long ropes from a pushboat captain and one said, "Now, see here, Dan, we're just going to fasten your hands behind your back with these ropes. It might be possible we would need to stop along the way and maybe let you swing from an old apple tree."[43]

The trip to Logan County took two days, perhaps in part because Cap Hatfield occasionally gave "Old Dan" a "good kick in his hip pocket" until Cap tired of the game. When the party reached Anse Hatfield's home, Hatfield asked "Old Dan" where he got the authority to bother the family. "Old Dan" produced warrants, but Cap Hatfield said the documents were bogus. "Old Dan" called Cap a liar. Cap pulled a pistol and would have shot "Old Dan" if Anse had not thrown a hand in front of the pistol hammer, suffering a badly cut thumb as he did so.

Eventually, "Old Dan" was turned over to Logan County Sheriff Ed Peck, but, again, there is no record of any official action against him. The Hatfields believed that "Old Dan" left the area soon after that ignominious episode or, at least, they never had any further trouble from "Old Dan." The story of "Old Dan," however, was a humorous sidelight to the history of the feud, as was another of Coleman A. Hatfield's tales, one that told about an encounter with a scarecrow.

The Real McCoy Scarecrow

The fears that plagued the Hatfields during that time were very serious in most instances, but the tale of the scarecrow was an exception to that rule. In Coleman A. Hatfield's manuscript collection, the scarecrow incident was another lighter moment for the feudists.

As the various members of the feuding families worked during the spring and summer seasons clearing land, plowing and planting corn and other crops, there was a cessation of hostilities because the enemies had other things to do to take care of their families, such as raising hogs and cattle and selling a few rafts of timber which were floated down the rivers during the freshet season.

One summer it was brought to the attention of Anse that his son Cap was in considerable danger from shots that were being fired from across the river while Cap and his hired hands were working his corn. They had not been able to see anyone, but would often hear a shot from the south side of the river.

While Cap and Billy Johnson, the hired man, were working in the field one morning before daylight, Anse and a companion went into the mountains on the Kentucky side of the river in an effort to find out where the shots were coming from and whether they were intended for any member of his clan.

On the Kentucky shore south of the river there was a large cornfield which was cultivated each year by a family named Daniels. As the two investigators crept low against the ground, hidden by the underbrush, they detected that an occasional shot was coming from a scarecrow which had been erected in the cornfield.

There they found mounted on top of a large snag from a broken tree the effigy of a man dressed in a shirt with outstretched arms and trousers and an old hat on top of his head. This was an excellent scarecrow, but there was something else — from the bottom portion of the effigy came the shots which were aimed across the river.

Anse and his companion began firing at the scarecrow as the dawn broke over the hills. Suddenly they saw someone jump away from the brush which half covered the rear portion of the scarecrow. They knew then that someone on the Kentucky side had taken advantage of what apparently seemed to be a purely innocent scarecrow to shoot across the river.

As Anse and his companion crept nearer, crawling through the bushes, the occupant of the effigy ran into the deep woods. Anse remarked to his companion, "That ain't no scarecrow, that's a real McCoy."

After that, Cap kept on the alert on his side of the river so that none of the mountain rifles could reach him as he went up and down the field between the cornrows.[44]

Bad John Wright

A much more serious episode is connected with the history of those years as well. That was the tale that involved Bad John Wright, another detective who made life difficult for Anse Hatfield and his family during the 1880s. Coleman A. Hatfield told that tale:

> Bad John Wright of Elkhorn River, in Letcher County, Kentucky, once set out with a party of ten men to seek financial rewards by capturing the Hatfields. Bad John had no "blood" interest in the feud, but it was his practice to go out to neighboring states and bring back those who allegedly had broken the law.
>
> On one occasion, Bad John Wright, with his men, crawled up to the top of a point on Pounding Mill Branch, a tributary of the Tug Fork that flowed between Peter Creek and Blackberry Creek on the Kentucky side.
>
> It was John's intention to gather as many Hatfields as possible in his grasp and to take them back to his private graveyard, where, it was said, he had an assortment of victims which lay sleeping on the Kentucky hillside.
>
> It was common to see Bad John riding homeward from some mission across the Kentucky mountains with his long handlebar moustache, his broad-brimmed, peaked-top hat, his long rifle balanced across his saddle horn, and perhaps two horses following in tandem, each with a silent victim balanced across a saddle.
>
> The Hatfields learned later that on that occasion, Bad John was watching them from his hill above Pound Mill Creek with a spyglass in his hands, the only telescope in the Kentucky hills, so far as anyone knew.
>
> Bad John watched the Hatfields some time, then remarked to his followers there were too many armed Hatfields to take at that time, even if they were caught by surprise. That was a good joke for the Hatfields, when they found out about it weeks later.[45]

The Defense of the Guyandot Riverbank

Because of such episodes, the Hatfields felt themselves under siege as 1886 grew to a close. That was true despite the fact that the family enjoyed considerable political protection from West Virginia politicians like State Senator John B. Floyd and Governor E. Willis (Windy) Wilson, for whom one of Anse's sons was named in later years.

The Hatfields had a considerable number of powerful friends in and around Logan Courthouse. Though James A. Nighbert has been described as a foe of Anse's family because of economic differences, a closer inspection of the local power structure makes it clear that Nighbert was more a friend than an enemy.

On one occasion, Nighbert let Anse and his followers "hide out" in a remote section of Logan County that Nighbert owned on Dingess Run Creek, that later was called Fort Branch. At another time, Nighbert served as one protector of the Hatfields in a remarkably chilling episode saved by Coleman A. Hatfield.

One day Anse and other Hatfields came to the courthouse where they were conferring with Colonel George R.C. Floyd, an elderly citizen who had served with his brother, General John B. Floyd, in the Southern Army during the Civil War.

Soon a horseman was seen riding at full speed down the creek on the other side of the river. The rider crossed the river at the old ford and rode into the center of town shouting, "The McCoys are coming! The McCoys are coming! Everyone look out!"

Soon the town was in a furor of excitement. Anse hurried immediately to Sheriff Ed Peck, and they called in Colonel Floyd, who took command at the request of the sheriff. The old army officer wanted the men available to arm themselves, and then ordered Major James A. Nighbert to deploy the force along the north side of the river behind sawlogs and standing trees.

By the time Floyd's men were in position, the town's people spied a caravan of ten covered wagons headed north toward the courthouse. Soon the word spread throughout the area that the Kentuckians were coming, and that it appeared they were using the covered wagons to conceal their identity, and that the wagons were loaded with armed men.

Floyd called for a double-barreled gun as he marched up and down, giving orders to the men not to fire until he gave the command.

Just then, two noncombatants from Boone County who were in town, and who were without arms, started to run for the mountains back of Logan. The old colonel angrily demanded that they stop or he would fire. He said, "Stand your ground! Every man here must fight if need be or at least help out in this situation. If my brother, General Floyd, and I had seen such cowardice from men like you in time of the war, they would have been shot at sunrise."

Sheriff Ed Peck dispatched a half-dozen men, who dashed through the river on horseback to meet the advancing enemy.

The wagon train was commanded to stand still 'til it could be searched.

It was discovered that the wagons contained only migratory settlers of peaceful men, women, and children, who had been traveling for days across the rugged terrain from North Carolina in an effort to reach the Ohio River Valley, where they were to settle in Indiana and westward.

They were given safe conduct through Logan and sent on their way, no doubt rejoicing that they had come through the lines of the feudists and safely crossed the warpath of the Hatfields and McCoys.[46]

With dangers like that in mind, the Hatfields turned to politics to make their position safer. During the final three years of the feud, this involved the governments of West Virginia and Kentucky. It also helps to know the roles played by Perry A. Cline, Frank Phillips, and even the federal courts in the years that followed.

---

[1] The Hatfields and the McCoys, Virgil Carrington Jones. In The McCoys: Their Story, Truda Williams McCoy argues that the third McCoy boy involved in the assault was Bill McCoy, the fifteen-year-old brother of Randal McCoy Jr., who was then seventeen. She wrote that the two looked so much alike that even close friends often could not tell them apart. The Hatfields blamed Randal Jr. and most feud historians agree that Randal Jr. was the assailant.
[2] The Hatfield-McCoy Feud Reader, Shirley Donnelly.
[3] A True Mountain Queen, Howard B. Lee.
[4] The Land of the Guyandot, Robert Y. Spence.
[5] Coleman C. Hatfield Interviews.
[6] Sigfus Olafson Interview.
[7] Even the exact date of the famous Kentucky election that week has been disputed. Coleman A. Hatfield wrote the election was held on Saturday, August 5, 1882. Other sources claim the voting took place on Monday, August 7, 1882.
[8] The Death of Ellison Hatfield, Coleman A. Hatfield. Coleman A. Hatfield adds a note for the sake of clarity at that point. "It should be explained here that the poorer disreputable scavenger swine subsisted on that grain which fell with the dung behind the ox team as they drew the rafting logs along the timber haul road toward the river. Such animals were held with little respect as compared with the fat porkers that fed in the chestnut flats on the higher elevation of the mountain."
[9] Coleman A. Hatfield Interview, Coleman C. Hatfield.
[10] The McCoys: Their Story, Truda Williams McCoy.
[11] Feud: Hatfields, McCoys and Social Change in Appalachia 1860-1900, Altina L. Waller.
[12] Conversation with Paul McAllister, Robert Y. Spence.
[13] Charles C. Carpenter, Coleman A. Hatfield.
[14] Charles C. Carpenter, Coleman A. Hatfield.
[15] Charles C. Carpenter, Coleman A. Hatfield.
[16] Coleman C. Hatfield's opinion on this question is that the Hatfields of his father's generation shunned such matters, labeling them "jailhouse" or "graveyard" talk. The Hatfield thought that such discussions were not only dangerous but somewhat disreputable.
[17] The Hatfields and the McCoys, Virgil Carrington Jones.
[18] Charles C. Carpenter, Coleman A. Hatfield.
[19] The Death of Ellison Hatfield, Coleman A. Hatfield.
[20] The Death of Ellison Hatfield, Coleman A. Hatfield.
[21] An American Vendetta, Theron C. Crawford.
[22] The Hatfields and the McCoys, Otis K. Rice.
[23] Mountain-Made Men, Coleman A. Hatfield.
[24] The Hatfields and the McCoys, Otis K. Rice.
[25] The McCoys: Their Story, Truda Williams McCoy.
[26] The McCoys: Their Story, Truda Williams McCoy.
[27] The Hatfields and the McCoys, Otis K. Rice.
[28] Coleman C. Hatfield Interviews.
[29] Coleman C. Hatfield Interviews.
[30] The Hatfields and the McCoys, Virgil Carrington Jones.

[31] Coleman C. Hatfield Interviews.
[32] Coleman C. Hatfield Interviews.
[33] The Hatfields and the McCoys, Virgil Carrington Jones.
[34] The Hatfields and the McCoys, Otis K. Rice.
[35] The McCoys: Their Story, Truda Williams McCoy.
[36] The Hatfields and the McCoys, Otis K. Rice.
[37] Anse Hatfield Letter to Perry A. Cline. This has been cited often in feud histories. Copies of the original hand-written letter have been saved by the Hatfield family, probably as proof that Anse was not the arch schemer of legend.
[38] Charlie Mitchell and Tom Wallace, Coleman A. Hatfield.
[39] Coleman C. Hatfield Interviews.
[40] Aunt Lou Ragland and the Detective, Coleman A. Hatfield.
[41] Old Dan, The Sleuth Tramp, Coleman A. Hatfield.
[42] Old Dan, The Sleuth Tramp, Coleman A. Hatfield.
[43] Old Dan, The Sleuth Tramp, Coleman A. Hatfield.
[44] A Scarecrow -- The Real McCoy, Coleman A. Hatfield.
[45] Bad John Wright, Coleman A. Hatfield.
[46] Invasion by the McCoys, Coleman A. Hatfield.

Chapter Six
THE DEVIL BEDEVILED
The Hatfield and McCoy Feud Roils Up

IN THE REMARKABLE year 1888, Anse Hatfield became forty-nine years old. The notorious feud was at its most intense. Anse was seeking a way out of the troubles so he could go ahead with the ordinary business of living a mountaineer's life. Yet his family was under siege, and it was becoming a difficult matter to make peace with the McCoys, particularly with younger men reaching maturity who sought revenge for past wrongs.

That was the year before Coleman A. Hatfield was born on Grapevine Creek, on the West Virginia side of Tug Fork. That was the year that the route of the Norfolk and Western Railroad was surveyed through the region. It was the year that Cap Hatfield became twenty-four-years-old, already a marked man because of his role in killing the McCoy brothers in 1882, beating the Daniels women, and killing Jeff McCoy in 1886.

The Role of Perry A. Cline

At that moment, Perry A. Cline played his most significant part in the feud, according to Altina L. Waller. Cline, who resented the loss of his five thousand acres to Anse Hatfield in an 1877 lawsuit, was among those who sought revenge against the Hatfields. In the company of J. Lee Ferguson and Frank Phillips, with the backing of Pike County political and economic powers Tobias Wagner and John R. Dils, Cline approached Kentucky Governor Simon Bolivar Buckner in hopes of bringing the Hatfields "to justice."[1]

In Waller's opinion, this was the development that changed the feud forever from a (more or less) private dispute among mountaineers to a significant event in the transformation of the Logan-Mingo-Pike region, from an economic backwater to an important area in the changing economy of the United States. She wrote that the importance of the feud lies in its symbolic effect as the older rural traditions of the region passed into history. In that light, she wrote that Anse Hatfield, who in the 1870s and early 1880s seemed like an advocate for a new economic era based on timbering, was likewise transformed into a representative of the older mountaineer traditions.[2]

If Waller's thoughts are correct, the nature of the events of the middle phase of the feud become vastly more interesting. Those events included the roles of Simon B. Buckner of Kentucky and E. Willis Wilson of West Virginia, both in the feud and in changing economic conditions. Other events of that time are the roles of Perry Cline, Frank Phillips, and Theron C. Crawford. Another important theme is the contention of the two states over possible trials of the feud participants.

A point that will become important to this tale soon is how the changing nature of the American economy in the 1880s and 1890s changed the hill country south of the Ohio River. In the meantime, it is more important to know first the roles of Cline and Phillips in the feud year 1888 and how Theron C. Crawford of *The New York World* first brought the attention of the outside world to the dramatic events of the early 1880s in Logan and Pike Counties.

Altina L. Waller agreed with Coleman A. Hatfield when he wrote that the feud was "renewed" by Perry A. Cline's thirst for revenge, after Cline lost his five thousand acres to Anse Hatfield late in the 1870's. Hatfield's writings suggest that Cline was politically ambitious as well as having a desire to take part in the changing economy of the region, though he also took note of Randal McCoy's activities in that year.

> During the political campaign of 1887 old Uncle Randal McCoy continued his usual agitation keeping alive the smoldering feud fires in Kentucky. His brother-in-law, Perry A. Cline, was the prosecuting attorney of Pike County.
>
> Cline was a long-haired, bewhiskered, gaunt man whose ill-fitting clothes made him appear more ancient than his years. He had "read" law in the "chimney corner" at night and had been admitted to practice after a year's study in the office of an active attorney.
>
> This kind of legal training was all that was required in those days. Sometimes vociferous practitioners of Cline's type stated to the unlearned jurors that as an attorney he had never "rubbed his back against a college hall." This was sometimes accepted as a meritorious advantage with his listeners and perhaps this met their approval.
>
> One could stride down the old log courtrooms with puncheon floors and rough-hewn benches and stand before the judge and jury, wearing a homespun shirt with unkempt beard and hair waving in unison with the motion of one's arms and flowing coat, talking long and loud of law and justice and about what jurors should consider in fairness to the state and to the prisoner before they brought in a verdict of murder in the first degree. Such was the "law" in the hills of those days.[3]

Other feud historians have had kinder opinions of Perry A. Cline. Waller wrote that Cline's network of personal contacts led to his rise in Pikeville. After 1874, Cline was appointed deputy sheriff and in 1878 was elected sheriff. That was an important position because sheriffs were paid fees by the counties for all their services. Cline took advantage of the post to acquire his first wealth. By 1884, Cline was in a strong political position and ran for the legislature, where he became a member of the faction that backed Simon B. Buckner for governor in 1887. In that way, Cline maneuvered into a position to strike back at Anse Hatfield and strengthen his own political faction in Pike County with hopes of becoming richer as the coal and timber boom took hold there.[4]

The natural connection between Randal McCoy and Perry Cline was their kinship through marriage, though that does little to explain Cline's indifference to McCoy in the aftermath of the killing of Ellison Hatfield and Randal's three sons in 1882. Coleman A. Hatfield suggested that McCoy contacted Cline in 1887, rather than Cline contacting McCoy. However the alliance was formed, it meant trouble for Anse Hatfield. Coleman A. Hatfield wrote:

> The eccentric Randal McCoy determined that he would employ his best efforts through his brother-in-law to secure the arrest of Anse Hatfield and many of the feudists on the charges which had been brought against them after the Election Day fight in 1882.
>
> New efforts were made by Perry A. Cline, who besieged Governor Buckner to secure the extradition of Hatfields from West Virginia to Kentucky. Application was made through the Kentucky chief executive to Emanuel Willis Wilson, the red-mustached governor of the mountain state.
>
> Proper papers were placed in the hands of Frank Phillips, deputy sheriff of Pike County, who was designated as the officer to take charge of the Hatfields when they were taken to Kentucky.[5]

The Role of Frank Phillips

Frank Phillips' rise to fame was typical of young mountaineers in eastern Kentucky during his era. He was twenty-five-years-old in 1887, the same age as Johnse Hatfield. Kentucky Adjutant General Sam E. Hill gave an accurate description of Phillips, describing him as "a handsome little fellow, with piercing black eyes, ruddy cheeks, and a pleasant expression, but a mighty unpleasant man to project with."[6]

Like Perry Cline, Phillips became a ward of John Dils after Phillips' father was killed in the Civil War.[7] It is likely that Phillips and Cline met that way, and it is more likely that Cline was the man who suggested to Governor Buckner that Phillips could settle accounts with the Hatfields.[8] That judgment proved correct because it was Phillips, perhaps exceeding his legal authority, who led the raids into West Virginia that resulted in the death of Jim Vance, the battle of Grapevine Creek, and the kidnapping of Hatfields by Kentucky authorities. Those were the dramatic events that ended the feud between 1888 and 1890.

Anse Hatfield's Attempt to End the Feud

In the meantime, according to the Hatfield family records, Anse Hatfield was becoming concerned how the political tides of Kentucky could harm his family. Anse reacted with a two-pronged offensive of his own. One part of Anse's offense involved his own lawyer and his West Virginia political connections. The other prong of Anse's offense involved public relations, as he agreed to an interview by *New York World* reporter Theron C. Crawford. Coleman A. Hatfield had interesting words to write about Anse's use of the courts and politics.

> It appears that near the close of 1887, one Johnson Hatfield, not the son of the feudist but a native of Pike County who owned a hotel in Logan and had business relations there, had been requested by his distant kinsman, Anse Hatfield, to consult with Andrew J. Auxier, a well-known Kentucky attorney who represented the Hatfields and who at one time was judge of the court in Pike County.
>
> A meeting was arranged between Andrew J. Auxier and Johnson Hatfield on one side, and Perry A. Cline and James York on the other side. Sometime prior to December 10, 1887, York, Auxier, Hatfield and Cline met at the Pikeville Courthouse and agreed that further efforts to extradite Hatfields to Kentucky would cease, provided that the sum of $225 would be paid by the Hatfields to Cline for expenses which Cline had incurred thus far in the matter of securing the extradition papers.
>
> Upon his return to Logan, Johnson Hatfield made an affidavit before John A. Sheppard, in which Johnson Hatfield stated that he was acquainted with the persons named in the Pike County indictments who were charged with killing the McCoy brothers in 1882. Johnson Hatfield further stated that in a private conversation at Pikeville Courthouse with Cline, York and Auxier that Cline agreed to settle the troubles between the Hatfields and McCoys for $225.
>
> When this news trickled back to the capitals of the two states, the two state governors were incensed over such an agreement. The payment of the sum by Anse Hatfield through his representatives was never denied by Cline.[9]

If Randal McCoy heard of this exchange, his reaction was not recorded by any of the feud historians. If he had, it is likely to think he would have seen Cline's actions as a betrayal of McCoy's trust. One reaction that was recorded by the Hatfield's historian was that of Governors Simon B. Buckner and E. Willis Wilson, as Coleman A. Hatfield wrote:

The public well understood the fiery blast which was released by Governor Simon Bolivar Bucker of Kentucky on the last day of December 1887, when he addressed the General Assembly of the Bluegrass State and referred to the fact that public officials of certain counties were either "unwilling or incapable of performing the duties of their offices."

It can be well understood how those familiar with the tense situation which had existed over the matter of extradition of the Hatfields and which now came suddenly to an end with nothing done toward the prosecution of the vendetta of the West Virginia and Kentucky mountains.

After the apparent failure of any extradition of the Hatfields to Kentucky, Governor E. Willis Wilson sent word to Anderson Hatfield that he wanted no more bloodshed on West Virginia soil and no crimes committed by its citizens.[10]

In his exchange of letters with Governor Buckner and Perry A. Cline, Governor Wilson made his point clear. He was suspicious of Cline because of the Johnson Hatfield affidavit and because of many letters and petitions supporting the Hatfields that arrived at his office. The Hatfields had acted as his allies when Wilson ran for governor in 1884. At the very least, Wilson wanted to make sure the Hatfields were treated as fairly as the McCoys, a fact underlined later when Anse Hatfield named his son in honor of Governor Wilson.

Yet, Governor Buckner's year-end message in 1887 was interpreted by some as a warning for Hatfields to stay out of Kentucky because that state's officials intended to see that the law was enforced. That warning and the continued presence of men Coleman A. Hatfield termed "card-carrying detectives" put the Hatfields in a worse defensive position as the year 1887 ended. With that knowledge in mind, it was natural enough for Anse Hatfield to seek an end to the feud by turning his attention to better publicity for the Hatfields. At that moment, Theron C. Crawford appeared on the troubled scene.

The Role of Theron C. Crawford

Theron C. Crawford's account of the feud is of interest for two reasons. His was the first published account of the troubles other than articles in *The Louisville Courier-Journal* and other area newspapers. Crawford's work was done in New York City, then and now the information capital of the nation, thus receiving more attention than other accounts. Crawford's work, accompanied as it was with sketches by a penman named Graves, also set the image of the mountaineer in popular imagination.

The drawing of Anse Hatfield that is found on the back of this book's dust jacket became the model for a thousand drawings of mountain men: a wide-brimmed hat, trousers tucked into high boots, a rough shirt and jacket, a long beard and mustache, a cartridge belt, and rifle held ready at the side. Down through the years there were cruel caricatures that used those elements, nearly all intended to show that mountaineers were an American abnormality. Crawford's words fit those drawings.

Crawford's trip was suggested by an unnamed "English friend" who mentioned that American life lacked dramatic features and that the feud was a proper subject to remedy that shortcoming. It is more likely than not that Crawford read the accounts of the feud in *The Louisville Courier-Journal*, since that newspaper's owner, Henry Watterson, and Crawford's boss, Joseph Pulitzer of *The New York World*, were close friends. Armed with that background information, it seems that Crawford knew the article he wanted to write before he arrived in Charleston, West Virginia, sometime in October 1888.

Crawford admitted he dictated his story in three hours while he was still exhausted from his journey, having lost fifteen pounds during the ten days he was away from New York. "I have been away in Murderland for nearly ten days," he wrote. "No one, unless he has had the actual experience of a visit to the region made notorious by the Hatfield-McCoy feud would believe that there is in this country such a barbarous, uncivilized, and wholly savage region."[11]

Crawford's contact in Charleston, West Virginia, was John B. Floyd, the son of George R.C. Floyd and the nephew and namesake of General John B. Floyd of Civil War fame. It is not known how Crawford and the younger Floyd met, but Floyd was then the Assistant Secretary of State for Governor E. Willis Wilson. John B. Floyd may have thought that the Hatfields needed good publicity to help them through the dangers.

Crawford described Floyd as "an honest, courageous, and fearless man," who had the "absolute confidence of all the people of this region." He wrote that Floyd was sympathetic with the Hatfields and advised Crawford that the best way to meet Anse Hatfield was to go straight to him without asking permission beforehand.[12]

Be that as it may, Crawford was not impressed with Logan County, claiming it was an isolated region with no railroads, telegraphs, school buildings, or churches. The reporter believed that the feud events were isolated incidents, but then wrote that they were "an incident in a series of cold-blooded murders which are almost without parallel in the history of the country." The feud, he wrote, was a family quarrel that led to the "usurpation" of the law and the "downright violation" of the court system.[13]

Crawford met Floyd in Charleston, which Crawford judged a primitive city where men were admired for killing those who offended them and where an African-American man had been killed by a Ruffner Hotel night clerk for merely trying to return to his duties at the hotel after dark. Crawford wrote that Logan Courthouse was a two-day ride from the nearest railroad station over "roads" that followed the creek beds. "Days and weeks will pass without any more word coming from Logan Courthouse to the outer world than could be gotten out from Central Africa," he noted.[14]

Once in Logan Courthouse, Crawford was equally appalled by conditions in town. He wrote that it was a place where there were frequent brawls and where court days were the only amusements of Logan County folk. Crawford wrote that they came to town only to drink "the vilest liquor known to the trade" and that the place was one where "the intellectual grade is so low physical prowess counts for everything." The people disputed with one another about trivial matters and "a blow is nearly always followed by the drawing of a knife or a revolver."[15] Crawford also wrote a detailed description of the layout of Logan Courthouse.

> Logan Courthouse during a session of the court presents a picture which is a duplicate of all court sessions throughout the petty towns of this benighted region. The place is about as large as Piketown and is very similar in character.
>
> There is a little, long, straggling street of frame houses, small shops and stores, coming down to a square brick courthouse building, to which is attached the jail. The people come to court not because they have any business there, but to simply meet their friends and to go on a spree.
>
> You will see, up and down the street, people exchanging gossip, sitting down in the sun telling stories, or making preparations for the glorious fun of getting drunk in the afternoon. They are always very friendly in the morning, and quarrelsome in the afternoon, but they all unite in one thing — in a cordial suspicion and hatred of all strangers. The stranger who walks during the latter part of the day through one of these court towns, when everybody is well fired-up with liquor, simply places himself in the way of insult and a quarrel.[16]

Crawford wrote many paragraphs in that style, describing the men as hopelessly violent and apt to fight a close friend over next to nothing. He wrote that the women in town were revolting. And he wrote that anyone who arrived at Logan Courthouse who was not a native or a "drummer" — the slang for a salesman of that era — was suspected of being a detective. At another point in his screed, Crawford claimed he had not had eaten a morsel of wholesome food for nearly ten days and that his experiences taught him that he "had reached the limit of my ability to live the life of a mountaineer."[17]

The way that Crawford wrote his tale is as interesting as his description of the community. Floyd and Crawford arrived in Logan Courthouse on one weekend that October. On Sunday, Floyd took Crawford to see Elias Hatfield, Anse's brother who had moved to town. Elias Hatfield made a strong impression on the reporter, who described Elias as a tall, deep-chested man with a powerful frame. Elias also impressed Crawford with his "English" good looks, but

Crawford wrote that there had been threats against the life of Henry D. Hatfield, who was Elias' oldest son. *The World's* writer noted that if anyone harmed Henry D. Hatfield, Elias would take quick revenge.[18]

Crawford and Floyd stayed in Logan Courthouse that Monday and Tuesday, but on Tuesday night Henry D. Hatfield traveled the fifteen miles to Anse's home to tell his uncle that Floyd and Crawford were on their way to see Anse. The next morning, the travelers hired a guide and set out horseback up Main Island Creek. Crawford could not bear the company of the guide, whom he termed "stupid." They fired the guide and went ahead in a wagon.[19]

Upon reaching Anse's "lair," they found Elias Hatfield and French Ellis waiting for them. Ellis called Anse Hatfield out of his field, and Crawford recorded the impression he had of Anse, which is one of the earliest physical descriptions of the feudist that has survived. Crawford wrote:

> Anse Hatfield came right over the field to us. He received us with boisterous hospitality. It was deeply interesting to witness the ardor and enthusiasm of the man in receiving friends whom he knew didn't "want him."
>
> Anse Hatfield is said by those who knew Stonewall Jackson to bear a marked resemblance of this noted Confederate General. He has a powerful frame and is broad-shouldered and deep-chested, but with that curve to his shoulders that goes with all the mountain types that I have seen in this neighborhood.
>
> He wore a brown coat, blue shirt, and blue jean trousers tucked into high boots. He had a Colt revolver in the holster under his coat, and he carried a Winchester rifle in his right hand. This man is always spoken of in this neighborhood as industrious, and though awkward in look, he is intelligent and well informed.
>
> Anse, although a man of fifty years of age, has not a gray line in the brown of his thick hair, mustache, and beard. He has a pair of gray eyes set under the deepest of bushy eyebrows. His nose has such an enormous hook as to suggest the lines of a Turkish scimitar.
>
> He wore a black hat, faded by long exposure to the weather, pulled down over a deeply-lined forehead. He piloted us up to his house and showed us in with marked courtesy and ease. As we entered the house, I noticed, beyond, two or three able-bodied men, armed with Winchester rifles, patrolling.[20]

Crawford judged Anse's home as small and primitive and made much of the fact that John B. Floyd had caught Cap Hatfield by surprise. Crawford spilled much ink in his article denouncing Cap Hatfield at every occasion, obviously thinking Cap was the worst of his family and perhaps the worst man in the

Logan-Pike County region. Yet Crawford seemed to like Anse and spent as much time praising the older man as he did blaming Anse for the feud troubles:

> Anse Hatfield is a jovial old pirate. You can sit and talk with him, and perhaps enjoy for a time his conversation. He is bright and ready, with a good store of information. As a hunter, he is the most skillful horseman in this region.[21]

For historians, the most valuable section of Crawford's work was his extended interview with Anse Hatfield, which was saved in the reporter's memory during the Wednesday afternoon, evening, and Thursday morning that Crawford and Floyd spent at Anse's home. That was the first time any reporter had interviewed the feudist.[22] Hatfield gave Crawford an account of the events of the feud, which formed an important section of *An American Vendetta*, but the questions that followed were equally interesting.

Crawford first asked Hatfield if he had killed the three McCoy brothers in August 1882. Anse replied he had not been present and did not know who was responsible for burning the McCoy house in 1888. Anse added, however, "No man who were there would tell anyone if he was." Crawford did not ask other questions on that point.

The reporter then said to Anse, "Mr. Hatfield, I want to ask you about your ideas about killing. There is no one in this community who has ever charged you with having killed anyone for the pleasure of it?"

Anse said, "No, I don't believe they have. I'm not that sort of a man."

Crawford replied, "But if they were to kill any member of your family in fair fight, what would you do?" Anse replied, "Well, I reckon I should get away with them just about as soon as I could." The reporter said, "That is your idea, then?" Anse answered the question, "Yes, sir. Any man that wants to try it, he'll find out."

Crawford asked, "Now, what would you do if any detective came here and tried to take you?"

Anse smiled and slowly replied, "Well, now, I don't propose to be bothered anymore. I have been out hiding in the brush. I have been kept away from my wife and babies many and many a time. I do not like to be kept away from my babies. I want this row settled now. It has gone on long enough. I intend to stay at my house, where I am, for the present. If the governor sends a proper requisition here for me in proper form, why, I wouldn't kill the man who brought it out."

Crawford asked, "What would you do? Would you surrender?" Anse said, "No, indeed, I wouldn't. I might possibly go out into the woods. I have been out there many a time, and I reckon nobody can catch me in these mountains. I simply will not be taken." The reporter asked, "How many men have you constantly on guard?" Anse said, "Nine men."

At that point, the conversation moved away from the feud as Anse invited Crawford inside for supper. Crawford described Louvicey Hatfield as a stern-faced little woman with black eyes and black hair who stood by the fire and beamed open hospitality upon the guests while handing them their food. Crawford wrote:

> There was the regular corn pone, fried pork, snow-white butter, sweet potatoes, sliced tomatoes, and the hard beans of the mountains. It was a dinner for a hearty and extremely hungry man, but not much to tempt a fastidious appetite. It was served with such hospitality that one was forced to eat heartily, as the host from time to time showed burning anxiety to see his guests take hold and eat something.[23]

When supper ended, the Hatfield women modestly retired to the bedrooms, leaving the men sitting in a semicircle around the fire. The women seemed unhappy that Crawford, Floyd, and other visitors had disturbed the normal household routine. The conversation turned again to the theme of violence. Crawford was interested in why so few deaths had happened, and Anse had an answer for the reporter.

> I will tell you. The human varmint is the most curious and most cunningest varmint there is. When he goes into a fight, he turns his body sidewise, so that there is presented for the bullet only four inches of lifespace and even at that he doesn't hold up fair and square. He just keeps dodging and frisking about and so when the bullets come along they don't find him. That is the only way that I can account for it.[24]

Hatfield swore again that he would protect his family, but also repeated his earlier statement that he wanted the trouble settled. Cap Hatfield agreed, saying, "If this thing can only be settled, why, we would be willing to lay down our accoutrements and munitions of war."[25] That was a most unusual statement for a man Crawford called "the most advanced type of human murderer" the reporter had seen.[26]

Crawford then asked Anse if he was a religious man. Anse replied, "I belong to no church, unless you say that I belong to the one great church of the world. If you like, you can say it is the devil's church that I belong to."[27] That statement has been included in nearly every account of the feud yet written. One wonders what Anse meant. Clearly, he was joking, as he and his family roared with laughter. Some have thought there was a serious intent, that Anse was telling Crawford that he was drawn to the evil side of life. It may be more sensible to take it as a face-value joke. The remark did cause Crawford to wonder about Anse's basic character, in words often neglected by feud historians.

Anse Hatfield spoke of his virtues. He said that he never told any lies. His neighbors have verified this. He tells no lies about himself. When he says that he does not know about certain killings, it is because he has taken great pains not to know. He scrupulously pays his debts. He is hospitable to people in his class ...

But the special virtue claimed by Anse Hatfield for himself was this: He said, "People have given me a reputation of being fond of killing people. Now, I am not a quarrelsome man. All that I want is to be let alone. If I was a killer and disposed to be revengeful, there is many a man that I could have picked off from the brush if I felt so inclined when I lived on Tug River.

"Why, sir, I have been a hunter and a trapper for years. I have tracked many a bear and deer over this country. I know every foot of it. I have been out in the woods for days and weeks at a time. I have got many a dry, rocky nook in the mountains where no man living could find me.

"But don't you suppose in those days, when they were hunting me down Tug River way, that I had plenty of opportunities when I was under snug cover to pick off every day some one of the men who were after me?

"But I didn't do it, simply because none of them had as yet done anything to me. The fact that they were trying to was nothing."[28]

Crawford wrote that Anse Hatfield was very much interested in the object of his visit to the feud country. John B. Floyd told Hatfield that Crawford was very anxious to have the feud settled and that was the real reason for Crawford's trip to the hills. Crawford wrote, in a rather disparaging way, that Anse did not seem aware of what newspapers were and that he imagined New York would be very much like a more distant section of the hill country.

Yet in the next sentence, Crawford revealed that Anse was quite aware of ways to make money. The reporter offered the feudist the chance to go with him to New York, dressed in mountain fashion for exhibits, and that Crawford would pay him $500 per week. This, Crawford claimed, made Anse stare at him with wide-open eyes in amazement.

Anse was equal to the occasion. "Well, now, see here," he said. "I want to make a bargain with you. When this here Hatfield-McCoy feud is settled, I want to come down to New York, and if you will get me that there engagement, why, I'll give you half I get out of it. But there is no use of talking about it now. Them there varmints of the officers of the law would not like any better chance than to catch me outside of these here mountain lines, and there is not enough money anywhere to tempt me to put myself within their reach."[29]

A final point that Crawford made about Anse Hatfield suggests that he came away from the interview with considerable respect for the feudist, even though Crawford's account of the time and place is a mixed bag of expected perceptions and genuine admiration for some of the realities of the feud country. Crawford wrote:

> There is some apparent justification for the acts of such an outlaw as Anse Hatfield. He is an energetic, soldierly man who served all through the Confederacy and who learned in that war his first disregard for the taking of life. When he returned to this community, he found it just as he left it.
>
> The law officers are officers in mere name. It would not have been possible for him at the time of the killing of his brother, Ellison Hatfield, to have obtained any punishment for the three McCoys who set upon him and cut him 'til he fell, mortally wounded.
>
> So taking that view, it is not hard to understand how Anse Hatfield organized a band of executioners to punish the three men who, without reason and spurred on by the rage of a petty quarrel over the most trivial of subjects, attacked and killed a man whose sole fault was that he was trying to make peace and to prevent the quarrel from reaching serious consequences.[30]

Despite his reluctant admiration for Anse Hatfield, Crawford's basic contention that Logan County was "Murderland" did not change. His final thought on the community was that it was the most backward and cruelest place he had ever seen. He wrote a summary of that view at the conclusion of one of his earlier chapters.

> The great missionary societies which are devoting so many sums to the establishment of missions abroad could well afford to turn their attention towards this outlaw land, where murder reigns supreme, where the rule of man of might is absolute, and where justice and the common comforts of modern civilization are absolutely unknown.[31]

In short, Crawford thought Logan County could be redeemed only by the creation of the modern American society that was being constructed around the economy that took shape following the Civil War. James A. Nighbert and Henry Clay Ragland and their allies could not have agreed with Crawford any more.

Appalachia's Role in the Changing United States

It was no accident that *The New York World* was the first national newspaper to take notice of the feud, nor was it happenstance that the popular image of the "hillbilly" was fixed by Grave's illustrations that accompanied Crawford's article. *An American Vendetta* was one of the most typical "new journalism" articles created by the *World*, which was owned by Joseph Pulitzer. During the 1880s and into the 1890s, Pulitzer was doing as much to transform the nature of journalism as the first John D. Rockefeller of Standard Oil Company was changing ideas about light and energy, or banker J.P. Morgan was changing ideas about high finance, or Andrew Carnegie was changing the realities of steel-making.

Pulitzer was, in short, the giant of journalism in his day. He was a driven, highly ambitious, six-foot-four nervous wreck whose goal was to create the best newspaper in the world. W.A. Swanberg, one of Pulitzer's biographers, wrote that if the journalist had enjoyed good health, he would have created a worldwide news empire that may have influenced life long into the twentieth century.

With his ambitions, Pulitzer reflected the changing nature of American life in his time, as well as boosting newspaper circulation with the now-accepted use of "sensations," scandals and pseudo-science. The blot on Pulitzer's record is that he helped William Randolph Hearst create a public attitude that led to the Spanish-American War of 1898. Despite that grave error, it is possible to read the pages of the *World* as one way of understanding how the United States became a vastly different place between 1882 and 1921, or from the beginning of the Hatfield and McCoy feud to the end of Anse Hatfield's life.

However, the most important way to understand that time is to become aware of the way forces gathered that changed Hatfield's West Virginia. This is a most complicated matter. If a writer wanted to be absurd, he or she could trace the beginning of the industrial age back to the prehistorical discovery of fire.

Yet the year 1859 is a convenient place to begin the tale of how Hatfield's West Virginia changed because that was the year that Edwin Drake drilled the nation's first modern oil well near the town of Titusville on the Allegheny River in western Pennsylvania, an event which forever changed American ideas about energy and, in time, would give the coal industry a competitor that eventually broke the hold of coal over the United States.

Those who like photographic imagery can purchase a symbol of that moment. In the museum at Titusville there is a photograph that shows Drake in his 1850s finery and a top hat standing beside his well alongside another gentleman dressed in dark trousers and coat with a white shirt, a bow tie, and low-crowned hat.

The second man was William Smith, familiarly called "Billy," who did the actual drilling of Drake's well. Smith learned that technique while he worked drilling salt wells in West Virginia's Kanawha Valley for the Ruffner family. Thus it is with a delightful irony that one can write about how West Virginia became part of the modern industrial era. Smith was the West Virginia worker that helped make that change possible.

Wary readers may be wondering what that development had to do with the life of Anse Hatfield. The importance is that the oil industry was the first of the modern American corporations that did so much to change the nation from a rural country that had regions where the pioneer era lingered to one where no one, even Anse Hatfield, was immune from the industrial age.

With that irony in mind, one can detect a shortcoming among West Virginia historiographers. Few have written about how ideally located the state is for a study of the industrial age in the eastern United States. With its eastern border running parallel to the Shenandoah Valley, the Tug Fork marking the boundary of the coalfields of West Virginia, Virginia, and Kentucky in the south, and the Ohio River uniting the markets of the Midwest with the oil, steel, and coal concerns of the north, the state is the perfect geographic expression of the way modern America was created.

State promoters since the time of J.H. Diss Debar have been quick to point out West Virginia's convenient location for the benefit of industrialists. Yet if the industrialists agreed with Diss Debar and other promoters, the state government reacted slowly to the changing scene of the 1870s. That point has a direct bearing on Anse Hatfield's life because he was more akin politically to the succession of "bourbon" governors than he was to the "progressive" state leaders.[32] Anse lost much of his power with statehouse officials after 1888, which was one more reason why he was so anxious "to get this row settled."

As one thinks about the way the industrial age changed West Virginia, it is possible to find that thematic writing does not help very much because efforts were so varied. River improvements, timbering, railroad construction, and coal mining may indeed have led the state's way to industry, but there were significant developments in the concerns of petroleum, natural gas, glass, stone, clay, chemicals, iron and steel, textiles, manufacturing, and (later) electricity that also had an impact on the state. Infernally complicating any effort to tell the tale are the equally important concerns about politics and corporate structure that make that era a historian's worst nightmare.[33]

Chronology is more useful. Although timber, rivers, and coal were important to West Virginia before the Civil War, the change of the state and the start of its industrial era seems to have been signaled first by the petroleum business, which took root in West Virginia in 1859, the same year that William Smith drilled the well for Edwin Drake in Pennsylvania. State historians call that enterprise the Rathbone Well, located on Burning Springs Run in Wirt County, on land owned by John Valleau Rathbone and leased to Samuel D. Karnes of Pittsburgh.

By July 1859, the Rathbone well was producing about one hundred barrels a day, and the Burning Springs area soon resembled such Pennsylvania towns as Titusville and Pithole, the most famous of America's "oil boom" towns northwest of Pittsburgh. Before long, the state's oilfields were caught up in the corporate battle for control of that resource, thus taking West Virginia directly into the battles that would be fought by the industrialists.

From Burning Springs, the petroleum industry grew rapidly to the Little Kanawha and Eureka fields of Wirt, Wood, and Pleasants counties. More oil wells were drilled along the Ohio River in the region of Volcano and St. Marys, and by the 1890s, there were oil wells around Sistersville and in Wetzel, Doddridge, Harrison, and Pleasants counties. After 1900, Lewis County and the region around Mannington became more important.[34]

The Rathbone well and similar operations might have faded into the obscure footnotes of history, had there not been consequences. The wealth generated by that area set northern West Virginia on a course to become part of the richer and more powerful age that was emerging. In 1869, ten years after the Rathbone well was drilled, Michael Late Benedum was born in Bridgeport. Known to one biographer as "the great wildcatter," Benedum came of age during the oil boom of northern West Virginia and became that region's most notable spokesman for industry as his career grew from West Virginia to the American Southwest and on to Central America and Eastern Europe.[35]

There was another consequence as well. With its new wealth shaping the new age, northern West Virginia became somewhat estranged from southern West Virginia, a social condition which persists. Viewing itself as a more progressive and richer section of the state, northern West Virginia wanted to be as far removed as possible from episodes like the Hatfield and McCoy feud. When politicians from that region moved into the statehouse in the late 1880s, that attitude became another factor in the Hatfields' estrangement from state government.

Yet there were important developments in the southern part of West Virginia that would be equally interesting and equally important milestones of the new age. In November 1869, Collis Porter Huntington announced he had purchased control of the Virginia Central and the Covington and Ohio Railroads, forming the new Chesapeake and Ohio Railroad.

Fired by ambitions to have a national railroad, Huntington pushed the C&O to Hinton in West Virginia's Summers County and then down the New River to its confluence with the Kanawha River, and on through the Teays Valley to join the Ohio River in 1873. There — dissatisfied with the town of Guyandotte, perhaps because its police officer gave him a ticket for leaving his horse unhitched — Huntington founded a new city he named in his own honor.[36]

As the C&O was being built, and by the time the city of Huntington was chartered, there had been other developments in the state that would be important to the new industries and the new politics. In 1871, the year an amendment to the state constitution returned voting rights to all male citizens, Henry Gassaway Davis was elected to the United States Senate, the first West Virginia Democrat to win that office.

It is not likely Davis would have won that office, which became so important to his later career, if Davis had not had the support of Democrats from the southern part of the state. Davis' election to the Senate was a significant moment because, like the discovery of oil on Burning Springs and the construction of the C&O, Davis' rise to power was a hallmark of the new age.

Davis was a rough-hewn man, born in 1823, who learned railroading by working at that trade. Among his favorite sayings was, "Charity ought to begin and stay at home."[37] Comparisons with Henry Ford of Model T automobile fame are almost inevitable. The two shared the attributes of being hard-headed businessmen first who made the most of their opportunities in transportation.

West Virginia historians Charles H. Ambler and Festus P. Summers wrote that Davis was born in Baltimore, Maryland, on November 16, 1823. He served as brakeman and conductor on the Baltimore and Ohio Railroad, and then became station agent for that line in Piedmont, West Virginia. When the Civil War began, Davis and his brothers opened a general store, and Davis himself learned his first political lessons when he won contracts to supply the Union Army with goods. By 1871, he had become an important businessman and politician in the Upper Potomac Valley. In 1868, Davis was elected to the Senate of West Virginia, and three years later was elected to the U.S. Senate.[38]

Davis' interest in politics had been awakened by attempts by the U.S. Congress to modify the Morrill Tariff Act, which became law during the Civil War. As an early West Virginia coal operator, Davis sought to protect and then expand the tariff on that mineral. His efforts to do so are a complicated history, which does not need to be examined in detail at this point. The significance of Davis' role in West Virginia history is that he acted in cooperation with Stephen B. Elkins, who was his son-in-law, and with Johnson N. Camden and Nathan B. Scott to influence both political parties between 1871 and 1913.

In the considered judgment of John Alexander Williams, those four men were as responsible for the political development of West Virginia as the men who had gathered in Wheeling in 1861 to form a new state from the original western counties of Virginia. Williams argued that those four men set the pattern of using West Virginia's natural resources and its political structure to serve their own interests and the interests of other larger industrials such as the creators of the Standard Oil Trust. In doing this, he also wrote, the four used local leaders who served as political and economic middlemen during the emerging industrial age.[39]

The statewide pattern first created from the ambitions of Davis, Elkins, Camden, and Scott eventually was copied in all sections of the state and in all business concerns. Seen in this light, the Nighbert and Straton "ring," like the Dils faction in Pike County, Kentucky, was a mirror image of the main political and economic force of the time. The C&O Railroad served the same role in the history of southern West Virginia as Davis and Elkins' West Virginia Central and Pittsburgh Railway Company did in the northern and central parts of the state.

Earlier in this history, the importance of the Norfolk and Western Railroad was mentioned as the greatest economic event of southern West Virginia during the years of Anse Hatfield. That line was joined by a third railroad company after the turn of the twentieth century. The late-coming railroad was named the Virginian and was the brainchild of Henry H. Rogers, one of the creators of the great Standard Oil Trust. When that triad of railroads — the C&O, N&W, and Virginian — coiled around the southern coalfield region from Mercer County to Cabell County, the shape of the society that Anse Hatfield had known so well would become entirely new.

The Hatfields in the Age of Industry

To understand changes in West Virginia, it is interesting and perhaps useful to put matters in an individual perspective. Awareness of the timeline helps. Anse Hatfield was born in 1839. Coleman A. Hatfield, the grandson who did the most in his family to save the feud tales, died in 1970. That was a period of 131 years. Anse Hatfield was born in a time and place where one did well to cross the ridges on foot. His grandson lived to see men walking on the moon.

It was a time that will be seen as the stuff of legend by future generations. Men and women who lived in America between those years saw transportation change from horses and wagons to railroads to automobiles to airplanes to spaceships. They saw communication change from word-of-mouth to newspapers to radio to television to the first computers. It is little wonder that Anse, Cap, and Coleman Hatfield were all so different from each other.

Explaining the relationship between Anse and Cap Hatfield is not an easy matter. They shared some characteristics, but were very different in other ways. Nearly all witnesses have testified that Anse Hatfield was at peace with himself, except when dangers threatened. At those times, his ability with a rifle and his keen sense of how to behave in particular circumstances came into play.

Cap's temperament was similar in that way. Yet Anse seemed to have the ability to relax more than Cap did, and Anse had a more playful sense of humor. The Hatfields have saved minor tales of Anse as a bear hunter to illustrate that point. When he had killed and skinned a bear, Anse would throw the bearskin around his shoulders and scare the daylights out his younger children and grandchildren.

Cap, on the other hand, was a more brooding man. There were good reasons. Theron C. Crawford — who despised Cap — wrote that Cap was the most watchful of the clan, expressing real surprise when John B. Floyd walked into the Hatfield house and caught Cap resting. There were terrible responsibilities placed on Cap's shoulders when he was a very young man. In 1888, for example, when the feud began reaching its climax, Cap was 24 years old. His son, Coleman A. Hatfield, remembered later that Cap seemed haunted by the experiences of his youth.

In popular lore, Cap has been remembered much as Crawford described him, as a low murderer and skulking villain who was fond of killing from ambush. Quite understandably, the McCoy family has remembered Cap the same way that Crawford did, often citing the 1888 New Year's Day raid on the McCoy cabin as evidence of Cap's evil nature, also believing that Cap was the man who fired the shot that killed Allifair McCoy. Without excusing the violence of the feud, and admitting that Cap could be a violent and deadly man, later Hatfields have tried to explain his character in its full context. Coleman C. Hatfield argued:

> My father believed his father was a hunted man most of his life. Cap was extremely wary. It did not take much to make him suspicious to the point of being paranoid. My father seldom talked of some of Cap's decisions and actions, calling that "jailhouse talk" or even "graveyard talk." My father stressed the point in our conversations that there were warrants out for Cap's arrest until his death in 1930.
>
> Despite that, my father always felt that Cap would have valued education and thought that education would have made him a kinder man, if Cap had had the chance to grow up in a more refined country. Cap was denied that chance because he was born when and where he grew up, which was still largely a frontier region.
>
> There is even some evidence that Cap longed for a more peaceful life. In his later years, after he studied the law, Cap began collecting books. It was the mark of a learned man during his lifetime to be able to speak well in a public setting and in an impromptu manner. Cap was fond of the oratory of Robert Ingersoll and memorized some of Ingersoll's speeches, such as his famous comment while standing at the tombstone of Napoleon.
>
> I am not making these points to prove that Cap was an angel; but a large part of the responsibility for Cap's reputation must be attributed to Anse Hatfield. Cap was extremely loyal to his father, but Anse was in the habit of seeing himself as an army general, sending junior "officers" like Cap out to take care of the trouble.
>
> Cap went to his grave bitter about those facts. Some who have written about the feud have argued that Anse left instructions behind that Cap could not be buried in the family plot at Sarah Ann where you can find Anse's statue. The opposite is true. Cap did not want to be buried with Anse.
>
> Before leaving the subject, there is another point that should be considered. In the final year of my uncle Willis Hatfield's life, I had a conversation with him. He told me then, in a very solemn voice, that the whole Hatfield family would have been killed if Cap had not been present to protect them and warn them of dangers. That is another side of Cap that Hatfields always will remember.[40]

The Nature of the Industrial America

Another factor to consider when thinking about the feud is what was going on elsewhere in the nation. Historians who have studied the era from 1884 to 1894 in the greatest depth have identified four major themes and one sidelight which are useful in analyzing the society of the feud region, as well as the rest of the United States.

Those themes include the rise of technology in the nation's cities, the growing rifts between the government and working people, the passing of the frontier as a social force in North America, and the way industry was concentrating wealth in the hands of the few as opposed to the many. (The sidelight was the reaction to the aesthetic sense of "the gilded age" that gave birth to the nationalistic tradition in art.)[41]

Such themes can be studied in any order. Yet to understand the Hatfield family, it may be a good idea to look first at the passing of the frontier, because that was the time of Anse Hatfield's youth. Wise words about that theme were written for *The Annals of America*. Those ideas echoed the sentiments of Frederick Jackson Turner's thoughts on that subject.

> By 1890 there was no more frontier; with a few small exceptions the country was permanently settled. What remained to be done was the difficult and sometimes dangerous task of holding and developing what had been gained. The obstacles to this development were many, and the Indian had the misfortune to be counted among them; he succumbed more quickly than did the land to the white man's progress.[42]

"The Wild West," which was soon to be made a pageant by Buffalo Bill Cody and to be immortalized by countless "dime novels," makes an intellectually interesting counterpart to the tale of the Hatfield family. That, at least, is the way later Hatfields have thought of that matter, according to Coleman C. Hatfield:

> There is another point I wish to stress. During the lifetimes of Anse and Cap Hatfield, southern West Virginia was not typical of the eastern United States. The Cumberland, which is the name some geologists have given to this region, is some of the wildest and roughest terrain east of the Mississippi River. Others have made the point that the frontier "lingered" here, by which I think they mean that attitudes and folkways of the 1790s lived on here a hundred years after New York City had changed.
>
> Let me give you an illustration of what that means. The famous "Wild West" lawman, Wyatt Earp, was born in 1848,

which was the same year that Elias Hatfield was born as one of Anse's younger brothers.

Now if the feud had been fought out west of the Mississippi, say in New Mexico, today it would be thought of the same way as the Earp's famous confrontation with the Clantons at the OK Corral. Instead, because the feud was fought east of the great river, the Hatfields and McCoys have been abused in popular mythology more than either family deserved.[43]

A properly skeptical reader will ask at this point what kept southern West Virginia from developing as quickly as the rest of the eastern part of the nation. A lot of ink could be used trying to answer that question. But there are some speculations based on the second theme in one volume of *The Annals of America*, the theme of the changing technology in the cities of the United States during the ten years after 1884.

That book argues that rural America still dominated the nation's demographics, but by 1884 the cities had become the centers and sources of American life. Changing technology gave the cities the energy to grow, thus giving the nation the goods, the money, and the setting for expansion.

Elevated railroads, cable cars, good post offices, public gardens, better shipping, hotels and inns, all contributed to improving life in the cities. At the end of a collection of photographs about conditions in the south printed in *The Annals of America*, there is the world-famous likeness of Anse Hatfield and his family, reprinted to show the marked contrast between the south in that era and developments in other sections of the nation.

There were no cities in southern West Virginia in 1888. There would be no cities in the region until about 1920. Therefore there were no internal dynamics that could create the wealth that would foster improvements. Such ideas should lead writers and readers straight back to the old problems of the Cumberland, the difficulties of transportation and communication.

Theron C. Crawford wrote in 1888 that the by-ways of southern West Virginia were roads in name only, that they were creek beds that often forced travelers to ford rivers, just as the Cumberland explorers had done a hundred years before Crawford's time. Lacking roads, there was limited movement of goods. Lacking goods, there was little awareness of a better way of living. Lacking awareness of better forms of living, there was little need for communication. Lacking communication, there was little understanding of the Cumberland region.

There is a great illustration of this point that also reflects the slow pace of changes in the hills before the turn of the century. In 1886, the year that Jeff McCoy was killed and the year that Elias Hatfield began warning Anse that the Hatfields were still under the gun, the inventive Ottmar Mergenthaler sold his first working linotype machine to *The New York Tribune*.

That point may seem very far removed from the feud country, as indeed it was. Yet the linotype was the greatest breakthrough in printing technology since the time of Johann Gutenberg in the 1450s. It made communication of ideas such as Theron C. Crawford's much more accessible and easier to circulate.

The first linotype in Logan County did not arrive until 1911, a full twenty-five years after *The New York Tribune* bought a Mergenthaler machine, and, coincidentally, the year that Dyke Garrett finally persuaded the aging Anse Hatfield that he better make peace with God while he still had the time. Given those facts of communication, it should surprise no one to learn that the Hatfields and the McCoys did not get a chance to answer the accusations brought against them by Crawford and others.

When one recalls the undeveloped nature of society in Logan and Pike counties, it is easy to see how the impressive power of the society of the United States overwhelmed southern West Virginia and eastern Kentucky when it arrived, seemingly overnight on a train, during the 1890s. Yet it remains to be seen how the government of West Virginia, which had taken shape between 1865 and 1888, reacted to the changes and how it acted when faced with conditions of the feud.

The Government of West Virginia in the 1880s

Charles H. Ambler and Festus P. Summers called that government "the bourbon democracy" and dated it between 1872 and 1897 — or between Anse Hatfield's earliest recorded interest in timbering and the aftermath of a shooting that involved Cap Hatfield in Matewan in 1896. The historians wrote that state politics was controlled during that quarter century by the Democrats, who stormed to power on the strength of the unpopularity that had overtaken the men who created the state between 1861 and 1865.[44]

Otis K. Rice has identified the leaders of that government as Governors Henry Mason Mathews, Jacob Beeson Jackson, E. Willis Wilson, and William Alexander MacCorkle, aided by such figures as John Kenna and Charles Faulkner. They were generally opposed to the "ring" composed of Henry G. Davis, Nathan B. Scott, J.H. Camden, and Stephen B. Elkins, who in turn promoted Aretus Brooks Fleming, who served a term as governor.[45]

Ambler and Summers wrote that the state government was weak, though it was generally in the hands of the governor, who was aided by an auditor, treasurer, attorney general, superintendent of schools, and secretary of state. During the 1880s, the state government was strengthened by the creation of a state board of health in 1881, a mine inspector's team in 1883, and a labor commissioner in 1889.[46]

Mathews' administration was plagued by an inadequate tax base brought on by delinquent tax collections and by a labor disturbance when railroad workers began a violent strike in 1877. Though he encouraged internal improvements,

Mathews lost much popularity in 1877 when he authorized a state militia to control the railroad workers.[47]

Mathews was followed by Jackson, whose most important battle was tax reform aimed at correcting abuses by the Baltimore and Ohio and Chesapeake and Ohio Railroads. Local opposition to Jackson's orders defeated his plans and perhaps led to the election of E. Willis Wilson in 1884. Wilson owed his election to his attacks on the railroads and monopolies, though his reforms were defeated in turn by opposition in the state legislature.[48]

The election of 1888 was a most curious matter even in West Virginia. Republican Nathan Goff Jr. ran against Democrat A. Brooks Fleming, but Fleming challenged the election results and asked the legislature to decide the issue. State Senate President Robert S. Carr sought to be named governor in the meantime, but Governor E. Willis Wilson claimed it was his duty to maintain state government until the dispute was resolved.[49] Anse Hatfield may have sighed with relief when he thought about state government between 1888 and 1890.

The two other governors of the "bourbon democracy," Fleming and MacCorkle, were hamstrung by political disputes. During Fleming's term, the Republicans were bitter because they believed Democrats stole the election. While MacCorkle was governor, the Republican-controlled legislature refused to enact his recommendations, leaving state government virtually ineffective during that time.[50]

The upshot of all this, as far as the Hatfields were concerned, was that West Virginia's government did not act against them. E. Willis Wilson was a friend who owed the Hatfields a debt for supporting him for governor in 1884. Thus he refused to grant Kentucky Governor Simon B. Buckner's request to extradite the Hatfields. This gave the Hatfields safety between 1885 and 1890, when Wilson turned over the reins of state government to Fleming.

Fleming was not as sympathetic to the Hatfields as Wilson had been and did not prevent Frank Phillips and other McCoy allies from seizing Hatfields when the Kentuckians could do so. By the time MacCorkle became governor, Anse Hatfield had retreated to Main Island Creek. The later troubles experienced by Cap Hatfield can be considered dangers independent of the feud years, and MacCorkle was not involved in the settlement of the troubles.

Logan County Politics in the 1880s

The Logan County political scene is much more difficult to understand because there are no surviving county newspapers before the spring of 1889. Altina L. Waller wrote that Anse Hatfield fell into political disfavor after 1880 and did not win any other disputes before the Logan County Court after that year.[51] On the surface, this would argue that Logan County Court President James A. Nighbert was fighting the Hatfields.

But — as we have noticed previously — Nighbert and his "ring" were not Anse Hatfield's hostile enemies on all occasions. Hatfield family tradition claims that Anse was as popular a man with his fellow Logan Countians in the 1880s as he had been earlier in his life. Though the McCoys might dispute that point, Anse does not seem to have been as unpopular as some feud historians have written, if the words of Coleman C. Hatfield are accurate:

> My father told me that before T.C. Crawford's book was read to him in 1889, Anse was largely indifferent to what anyone thought of him. Except when he felt threatened, Anse was a rather clownish man. It was one of his favorite "pranks" to scare the h___ out of people, and he enjoyed playing the "devil."
>
> When my grandmother, Nancy Smith Hatfield, Cap's wife, read Crawford's book to him, Anse became angry at first and then sought to change the way people thought of him. That was the reason you hear so many stories that date back to his older years about how kindly he could be.
>
> Of course, my family believes that Anse, Cap, and the others were never social outcasts. There are many stories that have gone unnoticed about Anse or Cap quietly approaching a neighbor's house in the dead of night and asking permission to stay on their premises.
>
> My father told me many times that one or both of them would knock on a neighbor's door and say quietly, "This is Anse," or "This is Cap." They would say, "Don't strike a light. I want to stay in your field out of sight tonight if that's all right with you." And the neighbors would tell them to go ahead.
>
> There was another side to it as well. Anse and Cap were admired as political thinkers and many also owed debts to them because of their kindness or the kindness of Big Eph and Nancy Vance Hatfield. They would turn to the Hatfields for advice on some matters. That gave the family a wide network of friends.[52]

Even after Henry Clay Ragland began publishing *The Logan County Banner* in the spring of 1889, the local newspaper did not contain diatribes against the Hatfields that one would expect from journalism of the day, if the Nighbert and Ragland faction was as opposed to Anse as some histories suggest.

Ragland was not a man to keep his mouth shut about much of anything. His opinions are clearly on record about everything from prize fights, which he detested, to the Spanish-American War, which he likewise detested. The careful work of Edwin A. Cubby in *The Transformation of the Tug and Guyandot Valleys* does not directly address the topic of Ragland's attitude toward the Hatfields, though Ragland's political philosophy on other matters is stated clearly in Cubby's work.

Cubby wrote that Ragland's politics were a guide to the thinking of the common man of Logan County in the 1890s. If so, the Logan County common man of that time was a complicated individual. In the political and economic sense, George R.C. Floyd, for instance, called Ragland a "tomtit," a bird that could peck equally well when its tail was turned uphill as it could turned downhill.[53]

Ragland was a fiery Democrat and a dedicated populist of the type that fought for the agrarian protestors of the 1890s. He was a supporter of William Jennings Bryan, the Democrat furthest to the political left in that decade. When Bryan ran for president the first time in 1896, Ragland dropped out of his own race for Logan County prosecutor so he could devote all his time to Bryan's campaign, which Ragland believed was the greatest crusade of all time.[54]

Given all this, it is most surprising to find that the result of Ragland's lifework was the triumph of the "money powers" that he spent so much of his life fighting. Ragland disliked concentrated capital as much as he admired the agrarians. He warned Logan Countians constantly about the dangers of falling into the traps of financiers like Henry C. King of the Morris-Swan land dispute.

Ragland, however, could not achieve his highest ambitions to change Logan County into a coal-producing section without the help of the developers and financiers that he hated. The journalist wrote endlessly about the importance of bringing a railroad to Logan County and rejoiced when Collis P. Huntington's Chesapeake and Ohio Railroad became interested in the faltering Guyan Valley Railroad in the late 1890s.

If Ragland had political sympathies one way or another, it would seem that he would have been a natural ally of Anse Hatfield, if Hatfield was the defender of traditional values in the Cumberland. Yet there were as few words in Ragland's newspaper defending Anse as there were denouncing the Hatfields.

The problem is how to reach a conclusion about Anse's position in Logan County between 1888 and 1890. The scales do not move emphatically one way or the other. What is known is that Anse was a former Confederate soldier with much personal popularity among his fellow Logan County citizens. It also is known that the feud generated bad publicity for Logan County and that the Nighbert and Ragland allies wanted favorable publicity so they could change the local economy for the better as they saw matters.

The Eve of the Raid on Randal McCoy's Home

Historians know that the leaders of the state government were in unanimous opposition to violence, but they knew enough about political reality to avoid offending their allies. The state government was so weak at the time that attempts to change local politics were unsuccessful, at best, and disastrous, at worst.

What seems to have happened is that Governor E. Willis Wilson turned to his Assistant Secretary of State, who was John B. Floyd, and asked Floyd to go down to the feud country and settle the trouble. Floyd, who became the titular head of his family in 1880, went to see Anse and asked him to stop the feud however he could.

Anse then sought to win Perry A. Cline's assistance, though Cline was willing to "talk out of both sides of his mouth." When the feud came to its worst crisis between 1888 and 1890, Cline seems to have supported Frank Phillips, as Phillips took direct action against the Hatfields, leading to the arrest and surrender of the Hatfields and the famous trials in Pikeville in 1890.

When Anse's attempts to end the feud by peaceful means failed in 1887, and when a surviving brother warned him of imminent danger, Anse turned to his well-remembered Civil War tactic of a preemptive strike at the heart of his perceived enemy and sent a small band of raiders to attack Randal McCoy's home on January 1, 1888.

When that raid only produced another public relations disaster, Anse retreated to Main Island Creek, where he fortified himself and swore to spend the rest of his life peacefully, if only his family was left alone. The details of that history tell of the end of the feud.

---

[1] Feud: Hatfields, McCoys and Social Change in Appalachia 1860-1900, Altina L. Waller.
[2] Feud: Hatfields, McCoys and Social Change in Appalachia 1860-1900, Altina L. Waller.
[3] Renewal of the Feud in 1887, Coleman A. Hatfield.
[4] Feud: Hatfields, McCoys and Social Change in Appalachia 1860-1900, Altina L. Waller.
[5] Renewal of the Feud in 1887, Coleman A. Hatfield.
[6] The Louisville Courier-Journal, February 7, 1888. This was cited in The Hatfields and the McCoys, Otis K. Rice.
[7] Feud: Hatfields, McCoys and Social Change in Appalachia 1860-1900, Altina L. Waller.
[8] Renewal of the Feud in 1887, Coleman A. Hatfield.
[9] Renewal of the Feud in 1887, Coleman A. Hatfield.
[10] Renewal of the Feud in 1887, Coleman A. Hatfield.
[11] An American Vendetta, Theron C. Crawford.
[12] An American Vendetta, Theron C. Crawford.
[13] An American Vendetta, Theron C. Crawford.
[14] An American Vendetta, Theron C. Crawford.
[15] An American Vendetta, Theron C. Crawford.
[16] An American Vendetta, Theron C. Crawford.
[17] An American Vendetta, Theron C. Crawford.
[18] An American Vendetta, Theron C. Crawford.
[19] An American Vendetta, Theron C. Crawford.
[20] An American Vendetta, Theron C. Crawford. I have taken the liberty here of changing Crawford's spelling "Ance" to the proper "Anse." Crawford's longer paragraphs have been broken into smaller ones in this account as well.
[21] An American Vendetta, Theron C. Crawford.
[22] In the 1975 television program that starred Jack Palance as Anse Hatfield, there was a misleading rendition of Crawford's famous interview. Crawford was shown asking "Ance" if he agreed with the description that the feudist was "six feet of devil and 180 pounds of hell." Palance as Hatfield gave "Crawford" a sharp look without a direct answer.
[23] An American Vendetta, Theron C. Crawford. Some things, including Hatfield family hospitality, do not change. A New Yorker might not like the food, but mountaineers do.
[24] An American Vendetta, Theron C. Crawford.
[25] An American Vendetta, Theron C. Crawford.
[26] An American Vendetta, Theron C. Crawford.
[27] An American Vendetta, Theron C. Crawford.
[28] An American Vendetta, Theron C. Crawford. Crawford quoted Anse using "authentic" mountain dialect, which I have changed into more conventional English. In the 1950s, when men and women of Anse's time were living, I listened to them tell tales by the hours. Though at times they would "mangle" a verb form or use some rather old-fashioned language, their conversation seemed to mirror the language used in the King James Version of the Bible. It did not sound like the more colorful, "invented" dialect that some writers have used in feud histories. By this, I do not mean that they often spoke of the grand themes in the King James Bible, but that the conversation had a similar quality of sentence structure and word usage. I am aware some may disagree with this point. Such disagreements are valued because they make discussions interesting.
[29] An American Vendetta, Theron C. Crawford.
[30] An American Vendetta, Theron C. Crawford.
[31] An American Vendetta, Theron C. Crawford.

[32] A word of explanation is needed here because West Virginia politics were a complicated matter long before the election of 1960, which focused national attention on that question. "Bourbons" were, essentially, politicians who came upon the scene in the wake of the Civil War. While they were never opposed to making money for themselves, or seeing West Virginia make money, they sought popularity by adopting the speech-making skills and gladhandsmanship of politicians who held offices before the war. The thought leads one naturally to think the "bourbons" might as well be called "good old boys," the phrase that is indispensable to understanding attitudes in the American South. Anyone trying to understand that point is advised to read W.J. Cash's book, The Mind of the South. The "progressive" West Virginia political figures, on the other hand, were those more openly in alliance with J.H. Camden, Henry G. Davis, Stephen B. Elkins and other industrialists. When control of the statehouse passed from the "bourbon" leader E. Willis Wilson to the "progressive" Aretus Brooks Fleming, the Hatfields suffered. Yet one should remember that "bourbons" and "progressives" infested both the Democratic and the Republican parties and that West Virginians will make ad hoc political alliances with anyone who serves their ends. Other state historians argued there were two other factions at work during the era: the "redeemers" and the "agrarians," both of whom had elements in common with the "bourbons" and "progressives." It was a complicated matter. Coleman C. Hatfield has pertinent words about how complicated state politics can be: "I don't know anything about politics. I have lived only in Chicago and West Virginia."

[33] This is impossible without predecessors. Thanks are due to Otis K. Rice for West Virginia: A History, John Alexander Williams for West Virginia: A Bicentennial History, and West Virginia USA by Jerry Wayne Ash, Straton L. Douthat, Bill Kuykendall, and Harry Seawell.

[34] West Virginia: A History, Otis K. Rice.

[35] West Virginia: A History, Otis K. Rice.

[36] The Semicentennial History of West Virginia, James M. Callahan. Collis P. Huntington was, of course, a more important figure in American history than this brief sketch would suggest. Born in Harwinton, Connecticut, on October 22, 1821, Huntington became a traveling salesman in 1837 and later joined the gold rush to California in 1849. He became well-to-do as the owner of a hardware store in Sacramento and joined others who created the Central Pacific Railroad in 1861. That was the line that became part of the first transcontinental railroad. In 1870, Huntington helped create the Southern Pacific Railroad and became one of the most influential developers of his era before he died on August 13, 1900. Biographical information from The New Grolier Multimedia Encyclopedia.

[37] West Virginia and the Captains of Industry, John Alexander Williams.

[38] West Virginia: The Mountain State, Charles H. Ambler and Festus P. Summers.

[39] West Virginia and the Captains of Industry, John Alexander Williams.

[40] Coleman C. Hatfield Interviews.

[41] The Annals of America, Volume 11.

[42] The Annals of America, Volume 11.

[43] Coleman C. Hatfield Interviews.

[44] West Virginia: The Mountain State, Charles H. Ambler and Festus P. Summers.

[45] West Virginia: A History, Otis K. Rice.

[46] West Virginia: The Mountain State, Charles H. Ambler and Festus P. Summers.

[47] West Virginia: The Mountain State, Charles H. Ambler and Festus P. Summers.

[48] West Virginia: The Mountain State, Charles H. Ambler and Festus P. Summers.

[49] West Virginia: A History, Otis K. Rice.

[50] West Virginia: The Mountain State, Charles H. Ambler and Festus P. Summers.

[51] Feud: Hatfields, McCoys and Social Change in Appalachia 1860-1900, Altina L. Waller.

[52] Coleman C. Hatfield Interviews.

[53] West Virginia: A Bicentennial History, John Alexander Williams.

[54] Transformation of the Tug and Guyandot Valleys, Edwin A. Cubby.

Chapter Seven
THE HELLFIRE OF THE DEVIL
Anderson Hatfield and the End of the Feud

ONE HUNDRED years after the Hatfield and McCoy feud ended, the two families who lived in the hills of the Cumberland began trying to explain to the world what had happened in the terrible decade of the 1880s. "We no longer fight with each other," one Hatfield said. "Our fight today is against misrepresentation and against lies."[1]

That thought was in the mind of Coleman C. Hatfield when he began talking about the night of January 1, 1888, when one of the worst episodes of the feud — if not the most tragic encounter — began, when the Hatfields decided to raid the home of Randal McCoy. Coleman C. Hatfield's thoughts centered on the mind and motives of his great-grandfather, Devil Anse Hatfield.

> It is natural, I suppose, that I should think so much about Anse while trying to put the feud in a historical context. Most historians have judged rightly that he and Randal McCoy were the two dominant figures in the feud. All of us today have to understand what they were thinking before we can create accurate history.
>
> After 1882, Anse was haunted by the thought that he or his loved ones would be taken across the borderline to Kentucky, where they would face a hostile government. No doubt Randal McCoy and his allies thought this was "bringing the Hatfields to justice." But Anse thought he and his loved ones would not receive justice, but would be met with mere vengeance.
>
> Historians must always remember that the fate that Abner Vance met in 1819 at the hands of the Horton family in Abingdon was always present in Anse's mind between 1883 and 1888. He did not have much trust in government anyway, and the thought of being captured by an unjust government chilled him.
>
> Those who have depicted Anse as a man itching to destroy his enemies are mistaken, in my best judgment, though I am a Hatfield and must see things from my family's perspective. It seems to me, nevertheless, that Anse was a hunted man in 1888 and acted with thoughts of self-preservation in mind.[2]

The Role of Jim Vance

If such thoughts were in Anse Hatfield's mind, it is reasonable to think that he turned to his Uncle Jim Vance for advice. Vance, who was 12 years older than Anse, has been described accurately as one of the most wary of the feudists, and his role in the events of 1888 is one of the most crucial points of the entire tale of the feud. Vance's background as the vigilant, active, and most suspicious of the Hatfields is a matter which must be clear before the tale can be told. Coleman A. Hatfield, who wrote a manuscript about Vance's life, understood the importance of the old man's nature in the final years of the violence.

> One of the leaders of the Hatfield clan was Bad Jim Vance. He was the maternal uncle of Anse Hatfield and was born in the year 1827 among the Clinch River hills in Russell County, Virginia. Old Bad Jim in his earlier years had traveled by steamboat down the Tennessee River to the Missouri country, where he sojourned for a time, then returned up the Ohio and back to his native Virginia. His roving, rambling disposition had made him a rough and ready adversary in personal quarrels with his enemies.
>
> He was a six-footer, bewhiskered and muscular, and was afflicted with lateral nystagmus, which, in time of impending combat when men face each other with hands moving toward the holster, old Jim never backed down. His rolling eyes made his enemies quail in his presence, and the motion of his hand was faster than any other known in the Virginia hill country.
>
> At the outbreak of the Civil War, Bad Jim was fully acquainted with the impending strife between the North and South over slavery. At the age of 34, he enlisted as a soldier of the Confederate Army under General Vincent Witcher. Like Quantrell's men of Missouri, they carried the black flag and took no prisoners as they dashed up and down the great Shenandoah Valley, as well as through the mountain passes of western Virginia and Kentucky, down to the Tennessee River.
>
> The black flag carried by Witcher's men struck horror into the hearts of all who saw this rushing cavalcade of hard-faced, hard-hipped, rough-riding band, with their belted pistols and hanging rifles, as they rode heedlessly on their missions of terror, pillage, and bloodshed.
>
> The nature of Witcher's responsibility to the Confederacy required him to send squads of his soldiers in various directions to accomplish the nefarious act of stealing the best horses which could be found. No soldier of this dreaded band of marauders was more trusted by the old general of the black banner than Bad

Jim Vance because no one "knew his horses" or the best places to plunder as well as Vance.

Bad Jim found a ready welcome at the tables and firesides of his many relatives and sometimes aided in the avenging of supposed wrongs against his kinsmen, paying back many grudges nursed by them.[3]

Coleman A. Hatfield wrote that during the four tragic years of the War Between the States, trouble that may have been based upon Vance's role in the taking of horses for the Confederacy arose between Vance and Wilburn Lockhart, who was one of Vance's cousins who lived in Russell County, Virginia. Lockhart was allied with Harmon Artrip and Jim Nichols; the Lockhart faction and the Vance faction voiced threats against each other. Such were the conditions when Vance returned to Russell County in April 1865. Coleman A. Hatfield continued his tale.

At that time, Captain Jim Vance was about thirty-nine years of age. In the prime of his manhood, the bewhiskered ex-guerilla strode about his work wearing a new .41 caliber Colt pistol, a formidable weapon for that day, which he had named "Kate Witcher" in honor of the wife of his wartime chieftain.

One day Captain Jim plowed a field, which he expected to plant with corn as soon as it was ready. This was discovered by his enemies. The next morning his wife, Mary, was out doing the milking and looked down the valley at the partially plowed field.

She saw three men behind the new rail fence surrounding the field near the timber. They seemed to be busily placing long strips of bark or other pieces of wood between the rails of the fence as a protective screen to hide themselves. She went back to the house to warn Jim as quickly as possible without being seen by the assailants.

Captain Jim immediately rode roundabout to the home of his Uncle Dick Ferrell, where he found his right-hand men, Jim Wheeler Wilson and Henry Mitchell, both of whom had been soldiers with Vance under the command of General Witcher.

That trio took the long way around to reach the place where the three enemies were concealed behind the fence. Vance and his companions came stealthily down through the sparse woodland until they reached a point not far from the fence where they could see their foes concealed in firing position.

Vance fired a deathshot at Harmon Artrip, while Wilson shot Lockhart's arm off. Jim Nichols started to run back down to the river seeking safety. Henry Mitchell, who was armed with a cap and ball pistol, pursued him. Mitchell snapped his pistol at

Nichols, but the old pistol would not fire. Mitchell then took hold of Nichols and ordered Nichols to surrender.

In the aftermath of this episode, Vance did not think it was safe for him to remain in Russell County waiting the reaction from the friends of Artrip and the others. Vance immediately saddled his horse and rode away to the mountain fastness of the Kentucky and Virginia borderline, where he found safety among his kinsmen.

Later, Old Jim established a country store on Thacker Creek, where he was able to obtain merchandise from the pushboats which traversed the Tug Fork of Sandy River down to the terminus of the steamboat traffic. He soon engaged in the business of rafting and floating choice timber down to the Ohio, where his rafting crews brought back goods and supplies on the pushboats for Vance's store. That was the nature of Captain Jim Vance's life before the feud began.[4]

Coleman A. Hatfield's research also shed light on Jim Vance's role in the first years of the feud, a subject which has not yet received much attention from mountain land historians. Given Vance's nature, it would seem likely that he would have been one of the ringleaders in the kidnapping of the three McCoy brothers who stabbed and shot Ellison Hatfield. That was not the case, as Coleman A. Hatfield noted in his manuscript:

> Doubtless it may seem strange to you that with all Bad Jim's predisposition for taking up the cudgel and wading into battle for his kinsfolk, that he did not participate in avenging the death of Ellison Hatfield after the election fight of August 1882.
>
> There had been some ill-feeling between Bad Jim and his nephew, Elias Hatfield, in a dispute over certain timberland, so that when the original trouble occurred in 1882, the differences of the two men had not been settled. It was not until six years later, just at the close of the year 1887, that Bad Jim's friendship with Elias Hatfield had been settled and the ties of blood relation bound them again.[5]

The Role of Elias Hatfield

Earlier in this history there was an explanation about how Elias Hatfield had become concerned that the McCoys and their Kentucky allies were planning to kidnap him or his son, Henry Drury Hatfield. That fact, added to Anse Hatfield's similar concerns and Jim Vance's suspicious nature, became one element in the fuel that exploded on the night of January 1, 1888. Another element in that witch's brew was Anse Hatfield's desire to end the feud once and for all. Those seemed to be the points Coleman A. Hatfield stressed in his writings.

Just previous to the end of the year 1887, Elias Hatfield, brother of Anse, had sold his property at the mouth of Mitchell's Branch on Mate Creek, not far from the present mining community of Red Jacket, West Virginia. Elias had moved to a farm down the river, just below the mouth of Mate Creek.

He had become suspicious that someone was watching his house from the Kentucky hills with the intention of ambushing him when the opportune time arrived.

Investigation by his friends proved that the "lookout" had been prepared on the Kentucky mountainside and brush placed around that point to conceal the would-be killer. A staunch bush had been trimmed, leaving the forks of the young sapling clearly visible and there were signs that a gun had rested upon the forks.

From this point, the Hatfield house, barn, and other buildings could be easily seen. Elias' suspicion was that this ambuscade was the work of the McCoys who lived back across the mountain on the Blackberry Fork of Pond Creek. It was well known that Calvin McCoy had lately become the owner of a new .38 caliber Winchester rifle, the most deadly weapon in the hills at that time.[6]

The Hatfield Meeting on Christmas Day 1887

Thus on Christmas Day 1887, the Hatfields gathered at the home of Captain Jim Vance on Thacker Creek, where Anse and Elias Hatfield and Jim Vance met with several nephews, cousins, and other kinsmen to talk about a way to end the threat. Coleman A. Hatfield saved a memorable description of that meeting.

It was one of those unusually sunshiny days of the winter when most of the men sat outside in the log yard. The dread silence was broken by Elias Hatfield, whose judgment in matters of importance often was considered the last word in many decisions made for the welfare of the kinsmen.

Elias naturally considered his personal welfare the all-important matter at hand, and he expected to map the strategy and give orders for others to carry out. Elias related his story to all the men as he set his foot up on a log of firewood. He made the remark that an attack on Randal McCoy's home would "have to be did" in order to forestall the impending danger which was about to befall him.

> Elias said he was sure the McCoys were watching his house, and unless Randal McCoy was destroyed, "your old uncle would be the next to fall in the war," which Randal had sworn to carry on until all Hatfields were destroyed.
>
> He said to many of his nephews and to the older men, "Your old uncle's health will not admit him going to help make the raid on the McCoys, and you will have to bear the brunt of whatever might happen."[7]

Anse Hatfield did not think it was a good plan to attack the McCoys and felt that they should forget the whole matter, in Coleman A. Hatfield's opinion. Anse added that the evidence of the supposed ambuscade on the Kentucky hillside might have been for a hunter who prepared a "rest" from which he could fire at squirrels, turkeys, or some other game. But Elias insisted on the attack and that "Anse's hellhounds" were the men who should assault the McCoy home.[8]

Coleman A. Hatfield then wrote that Jim Vance intervened in the discussion in a decisive manner. Though Vance was then sixty years old — some twenty years older than Elias — he sprang to his feet and said he would lead the men to attack the McCoys and "put a stop to the devilish schemes of old Randal."[9] Despite Vance's words, Coleman A. Hatfield also wrote that his faction of the Hatfields always believed the feud would have ended early in 1888, if it had not been for Elias' actions.

> Here it should be remembered that though the feud had broken out in 1882 when Ellison Hatfield was cut to death and the three McCoy brothers were slain, nothing of serious moment had occurred between the two clans since that time except the legal battles, offers of reward, and the annoyance caused by "detectives."
>
> But now a time had come when Elias Hatfield, one of the family's leaders, was insisting that a new trouble should begin. No one should forget that Elias was the man who induced Ellison Hatfield to go over and help their kinsman on the fatal Election Day in August 1882, or that Elias was the one who showed the most interest in that election, or that Elias was the one who captured Dick McCoy after the assault on Ellison. In that way, Elias became the main agitator who rekindled the smoldering feud fires.[10]

As usual, there are other opinions. Truda Williams McCoy, who received most of her information from interviews with her kinfolk, argued that Anse Hatfield was the man who ordered the assault with the vow, "Randal will have to die."[11] Coleman A. Hatfield wrote that after the Christmas Day meeting, the Hatfields waited six more days before approaching Randal's house. The group included Jim Vance, Charlie Mitchell (alias Charlie Gillipsie), Johnse Hatfield, Cap Hatfield, Tom Mitchell, and Ellison Mounts. All were 25 years old or younger except Vance. Robert Lee Hatfield started out with the band, but turned back, perhaps because his mother pleaded with him to do so.[12]

Coleman A. Hatfield wrote that Anse drew upon his Civil War experiences as the raid was planned. Anse believed that action later called "a peremptory strike" was needed, just as it was when he and Randal McCoy killed General Bill France during the War Between the States. This meant that secrecy was needed, which limited the number of men who were sent.

The Raid on the McCoy Home

The raiders traveled on foot between Mate Creek and Blackberry Fork of Pond Creek and approached the McCoy home on two nights, December 31, 1887, and January 1, 1888. This fact has escaped history until the present. Coleman A. Hatfield wrote at least two accounts of the raid and supplemented his writing with tape-recorded interviews with his son made in the 1950s and 1960s. This history draws upon his most vivid rendition.

> The first night they went there, they were on the hillside around Randal McCoy's home. It was a cold, frosty night. There was a rail fence around the edge of the hill above the house. Someone leaned against the fence, or fell against it, and the whole fence, panel after panel, just slid down the hill. They suspected that their presence was known so they did not go through with it that night. They returned the next night with the intention of kidnapping Randal McCoy
>
> Jim Vance went up to the door of McCoy's house that second night and shouted, "Stir us up a light!" They heard Calvin McCoy throw a cartridge into the chamber of his .38 caliber Winchester rifle. Jim Vance jumped aside from the door and the bullet shot right through the door a split-second after he jumped aside. If he had not stepped when he did, he would have been killed right there on the spot.
>
> Old Jim had a shotgun in his hand, an old muzzle-loader, and as he jumped out of the way he shot it up through the porch shed, where the McCoys had all kinds of oxbows and pig yokes and homemade twists of tobacco and a bag of cotton there.
>
> This bag of cotton caught on fire when the shot hit it. Just then, Tom Mitchell climbed up the side of the house and got on the porch roof in the back where there were windows. Randal McCoy grabbed a shotgun and fired at Mitchell and shot three fingers off Mitchell's right hand — the middle finger, the ring finger, and the little finger.

Another shot was fired by one of the McCoys inside the cabin that hit Ellison Mounts in the arm. They told me it was a diagonal shot, and I believe it broke one bone in his arm. Part of that shot hit Johnse in the back, and those were all the wounds that the Hatfields suffered that night.

They could hear Calvin and his father talking. Cal said, "Pap, I'm going first!" He said, "They'll kill me, but let me go first, and you get away." I don't remember if they said Randal protested his choice there or not, but anyway, Cal dashed out of the house with his .38 rifle ready, and he went toward the stable or the corncrib.

Randal broke out of the back of the house as Calvin covered him. Randal was wearing only his nightclothes, or at least he was thinly clad, and they said he hid in stacks of wheat that night. As Calvin ran for cover to shoot back at the Hatfields, he was shot in the back of the head and fell on his rifle with its lock pulled back. His brains and blood ran down inside the front of the lock of the gun.

Just then, Allifair McCoy ran out of the house with some water to try to put the fire out. Her water ran out so she went back for a churn or pail of milk. Allifair was a grown daughter, but she was crippled in one leg. I'm not sure what caused that, probably infantile paralysis, but she was crippled in one leg.

It is my understanding that there was no intention to kill the women. But when Allifair dashed out with that milk, Ellison Mounts, thinking it was a man, shot her. There has been talk that Cap fired the shot, but Ellison Mounts confessed on the scaffold when he was hanged at Pikeville in 1890.

The shots that wounded the Hatfield party, Randal McCoy's escape to the wheat stacks, and the killing of Calvin and Allifair McCoy all happened in less than a minute after Jim Vance jumped out of the way of the shot that came out of the McCoy house and fired the shot that started the fire.

By the time Allifair fell dead, Jim and Johnse had rallied and began piling kindling against the house to start a second fire. Sarah McCoy came out of the house, and Jim Vance or maybe another clubbed her with a gun. She fell to the ground, and they left her there, where she pulled a mattress or featherbed out of the house and lay on it, covering herself the best she could.[13]

Reactions to the Raid

Coleman A. Hatfield's research did not include information about Anse Hatfield's reaction to the raid or whether or not the Hatfields knew that there would be any retaliation. He wrote that the Hatfields did learn that Randal McCoy placed his slain children and his suffering wife in a wagon the next morning and took them down Pond Creek to Pikeville, where he met with Perry A. Cline to see if the Hatfields could be arrested.[14] Coleman C. Hatfield did have thoughts about Anse's reaction.

> Anse knew that the Hatfields might be able to end the feud if Randal McCoy was killed because Anse thought that Randal was the source of the continuing trouble. He was alarmed when he found out that Uncle Jim Vance and the others had failed.
>
> I do not think he knew that the retaliation would come as quick and as hard as it did. Anse knew that others could inflame popular opinion against him, but he did not know that the West Virginia government would stand aside from the matter, as it did when Frank Phillips led his men to Grapevine Creek.[15]

When Theron C. Crawford of *The New York World* interviewed Anse later that year, he did not question Hatfield about the assault on McCoy's house, or at least Crawford did not record any such conversation in *An American Vendetta*. It was left to later Hatfields to reflect on the meaning of the cabin raid, which Coleman A. Hatfield expressed in his collection of manuscripts.

> It is terrible to reveal this story because my sympathies were so fixed and molded early in my life that I am biased in favor of my clan, be they right or wrong.
>
> In later years, Hatfields have been known to visit the family graveyard overlooking the old homeplace of the McCoys and to kneel upon the earth and shed tears for their one-time enemies who lost their lives in that terrible family conflict.
>
> But all the tears that may be shed and all the heartache which may be endured will not bring back those who suffered and died on both sides of the borderline. It will not bring back poor, lame Allifair McCoy, the innocent daughter of the old clan leader, who was giving the last efforts of her life to the service of her loved ones when she was shot down. The shock of the death of Allifair was lamented by the Hatfields, as well as the grief-stricken McCoy relatives. There was no intention by either side to wage war against women and children.[16]

Though the Hatfields did not intend to harm Allifair or Sarah McCoy, the raid on Randal McCoy's house was a disaster. The full power of the changing American and Appalachian society crashed on Anse Hatfield's head. Journalists from *The Wheeling Intelligencer, The Louisville Courier-Journal, The Cincinnati*

Enquirer, and, later, *The New York World* pounced on the story, successfully — if not accurately — portraying Anse as the devil incarnate.

Perry A. Cline saw another chance to wreck vengeance on Anse and renewed his contacts with Kentucky politicians seeking to bring the hill counties under better control. A wave of revulsion swept through Pikeville and all of Pike County, and at last gave Randal McCoy the public sympathy he needed to fight the Hatfields. Detectives swarmed into Logan County seeking to capture Hatfields and collect reward money. Most importantly, Frank Phillips was reinvigorated and began drawing armed men to his side to act as "deputies" and to invade Logan County.

The immediate result was the killing of Jim Vance.

The Killing of Jim Vance

On January 10, 1888, Frank Phillips led thirty-eight men across the Tug Fork to kill or capture the Hatfields. Among the band were Harmon (Bud) McCoy, Lark McCoy, and John C. McCoy, three of the sons of old Asa Harmon McCoy who was killed near the end of the Civil War. The armed men went up Thacker Creek to its head and then crossed Pigeon Creek. Coleman A. Hatfield wrote his account of the events that followed.

> On top of Thacker Creek Mountain, old Captain Jim Vance and young Cap Hatfield had left the main body of the Hatfields in the encampment at the headwaters of Big Muncey Creek. Old Jim had left Anse in charge of their camp and took Cap with him toward Thacker Creek for a short visit to Vance's home.
>
> They had killed some squirrels along the way. Jim's wife, Aunt Mary Vance, had joined them on Pigeon Creek, carrying the dressed squirrels in a large wooden bucket as she went down Thacker Mountain on the south side to see what was ahead. She came running back up the hill and shouted to Jim, "Old man, I see them coming." Jim asked how many McCoys there were, and Mary replied, "It looked like there must be thirty."
>
> As the Kentucky men rode single-file up the narrow defile of Thacker Creek, old Captain Jim called, "Cap, let's charge 'em. I'm going to sell out this day." The two ran down the mountain about seventy yards and took positions behind the oak and locust trees which stood near the pathway, and then opened fire on the McCoys.
>
> Bud McCoy, Harmon's son, was thrown from his horse by the force of a bullet, which creased the side of his head. The McCoys dismounted and began firing as their horses stampeded. Some followed the horses while others charged up the mountain on foot.[17]

Jim Vance ordered his wife to run as fast as she could back to the Hatfield camp for reenforcements. She had not been gone more than a minute when a shot struck Jim, incapacitating his right arm and leaving him defenseless. Coleman A. Hatfield wrote:

> Old Jim shouted, "Cap, get back to the top of the hill. I'm shot for death. Tell Anse and the boys to be ready." Cap retreated as ordered by Captain Jim, and it was found later that twenty-seven bullets had hit the tree Cap was using for cover.
> Frank Phillips rushed up and placed a gun against Old Jim's head and fired the shot that killed Vance. Vance had dropped his Winchester rifle, but was holding a .41 caliber Colt when he died with a death grip on the trigger. If he had been able to fight back, he surely would have killed Phillips with that pistol.
> Bud McCoy and Lark McCoy stood on each side of Old Jim's body as they shook hands. Bud said, "This is the man that killed our daddy in the time of the war." The two waded in Jim's blood and dipped a corner of a handkerchief in blood-feud revenge.[18]

With Jim Vance dead, Cap Hatfield left the top of Thacker Mountain with the McCoys in hot pursuit. He stopped long enough to put his boot heels in the forks of a dogwood to jerk the boots from his feet so his footprints could not be easily discovered. Armed with his rifle and pistol, he ran to the home of Floyd Hatfield on Mate Creek and asked to ride Floyd's yellow horse "Claybanks" to the Hatfield camp.

Cap quickly threw the saddle on the horse's back and clinched the girth, though he did not wait for the bridle to be found. He headed to the mountain above Beech Creek, guiding the horse with his rifle barrel, and galloped down Grapevine Fork of Beech to the home of his Uncle Wall Hatfield as dark was falling.

When Cap reached Wall Hatfield's house, he found no one was home. He then ascended the left fork of Beech Creek to the home of Joe and Betty Simpkins, who were his aunt and uncle. The two gave Cap another pair of shoes, and he then rode on to the gap of the mountain between Beech Creek and Mate Creek. By that time it was too dark to see clearly and the mountain gap was a strategic place where an enemy could be lurking. Coleman A. Hatfield wrote:

> Having dismounted, and now leading his horse, Cap thought he saw the white shirt of a McCoy crouching in the fence corner along the path at the top of the hill. The enemy's rifle seemed to be pointing outward from his shoulder. Without calling out, Cap fired at the white spot. A groan answered his shot and a kicking,

moving object rolled into the roadway. It proved to be one of Bill Canady's white-faced steers with long horns reaching out like a McCoy with a deadly rifle ready to fire.[19]

In the meantime, the McCoys had lost Cap's trail at the top of Thacker Mountain and rode back to Pike County. Yet the death of Jim Vance seemed give new heart to the McCoys, who believed the Hatfields were in full retreat.

The Surrender of Wall Hatfield

During the ten days that followed the killing of Jim Vance, Frank Phillips led many raids into Logan County, whose public officials sought protection from the state government, which was still under Governor E. Willis Wilson. During the raids, Phillips captured Andy Varney, L.D. McCoy (a son of Selkirk McCoy, then considered one of Randal McCoy's enemies), Tom Chambers, Moses Christian, and the three Mahon brothers, Sam, Dock, and Plyant.[20] Dock and Plyant Mahon were two sons-in-law of Wall Hatfield. Another, most surprising development, was the surrender of Wall Hatfield himself, whose story was written by Coleman A. Hatfield.

> In 1888, Frank Phillips and other leaders of the McCoy clan contacted Squire Wall under a flag of truce at his retreat known as the "Devil's Backbone," at the forks of Beech Creek in West Virginia. Phillips induced Hatfield to surrender to the Kentucky authorities, stating that he would be allowed to come back home and that all differences between him and the Kentucky authorities could be "fixed up."
> Wall was allowed to come home under the provision that he contact Devil Anse and his brother, Elias Hatfield, which Wall did in the deep forest on the headwaters of Island Creek, where the three brothers consulted for some two or three hours.
> They stood beside an oak tree in the heavy forest and, as they conversed, Squire Wall, with a large jackknife, was busily engaged in cutting three deep grooves diagonally across the tree. Younger men discovered those tree marks later and suggested that they represented the three brothers who were left as leaders of their clan following the death of the fourth brother, Ellison Hatfield.
> It was learned later that Squire Wall told his brothers that Phillips promised they would be exonerated and allowed to come back home if they crossed the river into Kentucky. Anse and Elias refused to believe the word of Frank Phillips and Randal McCoy and did not take Wall's advice.[21]

About one week after Wall Hatfield conferred with Anse and Elias and then returned to Kentucky, where he was arrested and placed in the Pikeville jail, Logan County officials acted in defense of their authority. The Logan Circuit Court issued warrants for the arrest of the McCoys and ordered Constable John Thompson to patrol the land along Tug Fork.[22]

The Role of Governor E. Willis Wilson in 1888

West Virginia Governor E. Willis Wilson learned of the orders of the Logan Circuit Court and again intervened in an effort to end the feud, sending a personal representative to investigate the troubles.[23] Coleman A. Hatfield wrote:

> Shortly thereafter, William F. Floyd, son of Colonel Floyd of Logan County, was sent by Governor Emanuel Willis Wilson to investigate rumors of the feud and to report to him.
> Floyd left the courthouse at Logan with seven men, one of whom was Harry Thompson, a constable. They rode across the mountains southward in an attempt to locate Anse Hatfield on the state border forty miles away.
> They found that Anse and his men had barricaded themselves on Grapevine Creek in clear view of the Kentucky hills. Rumor had it that the McCoys were assembling in large numbers.
> For days, the friends of the Hatfields had watched the Kentucky side of the river along Peter Creek, Barren She Creek, Pound Mill Creek, and Blackberry Creek, it not being known along which tributary the advance would be made, even though it was claimed that armed men had been seen on Barren She Creek.[24]

At about the same time, the brothers John and Wes Mounts, who were Hatfield allies, went to Pikeville, where they saw Sheriff Dick Murphy and Prosecuting Attorney Perry A. Cline organizing another force of mounted raiders and giving them instructions how to proceed against the Hatfields. Cline and Murphy also gave the raiders saddlebags loaded with dynamite in expectation that the Hatfields would be barricaded and they would need to blow up the fortification. The Mounts brothers ran thirty-five miles through the mountain gaps to bring that news to Anse and his men.

The Mounts brothers and the Floyd party arrived back in Logan County at the same time, during the third week of January 1888. On January 19, Floyd and his party rode to Anse's home at the mouth of Thacker Creek, where they found Louvicey Hatfield home alone.

Louvicey, who did not know the Floyds very well, failed to recognize William F. Floyd. Thinking that the band might have been McCoy allies, she told them that she did not know where Anse was. The Floyd party, however, soon found Anse and his men at their fortified point on Grapevine Creek, not long before the McCoys arrived in force as the only pitched battle of the feud began in earnest.

The Battle of Grapevine Creek

Coleman A. Hatfield's description of that battle is chilling, even at a time distance of more than a century after the event and more than fifty years since Hatfield wrote his history. He wrote:

> Shortly before William F. Floyd and his men arrived at Anse's headquarters, the Hatfield women sent two girls to report that a large number of armed men had been seen on Peter Creek, on the Kentucky side of the river. "General Bill" Floyd, as he was known by the Hatfields, called Anse and his men out from behind their barricade, and they conferred in an open field.
>
> The McCoy raiders, who had been concealed on the Kentucky side, had seen the riders traveling down the river in the direction of Grapevine Creek. Big Jim McCoy and Frank Phillips led thirty-two Kentuckians in pursuit of Floyd's men, but before the McCoys reached the mouth of Grapevine Creek, they met two young girls returning home after warning Anse about the danger.
>
> Frank Phillips demanded to know who the men were that rode up Grapevine Creek and who it was firing shots on that creek. When the McCoys did not receive a satisfactory answer, David Straton (a bounty hunter and a son of old Major John William Straton), who was guiding the McCoy raiders, took a rope from his saddle and threw it over a sycamore limb, threatening to loop one end of the rope around the neck of one of the girls if she refused to give them information.
>
> Big Jim McCoy stopped Straton, and the girls were released. The band then dashed up Grapevine Creek until they came in sight of the Hatfields, who were lined up in battle formation.[25]

In that way, the governor's representative and Logan County public officials were caught in circumstances that made it appear they were backing the Hatfields. That is a point that has been widely misunderstood by journalists who have written about the feud, terming the conflict a civil disturbance between two states. That was an understandable error because the conflict was serious enough, as Coleman A. Hatfield described it.

The Hatfields fired the first volley while the McCoys wheeled their horses and rode out of sight up above the mouth of the creek. They tied their horses among the pawpaw bushes and other small trees that grew along the stream bank.

Just then another contingent of the Hatfields, who were squirrel hunting back in the mountains and separated from the main body, came in behind the horses and began to fire, causing the horses to stampede down the river past the mouth of Grapevine Creek.

Devil Anse, viewing the whole scene from higher ground, detected a flanking movement by Frank Phillips, who was trying to crawl up the channel of Grapevine Creek with a squad of six men, in an effort to surround the Hatfields.

Anse called his men back and told them he had seen a hundred horses go down the river past the mouth of the creek. He ordered the men to cross the lower point of Grapevine Creek in order to separate the McCoys from their horses.

Most of the McCoys, knowing the danger of being separated from their horses, broke from their positions and pursued the stampeding animals. Their quick action following the horses foiled an ambush planned by Anse and his men across the lower point of Grapevine. The Hatfields went across the wooded area to cut off the McCoys and had almost reached the river road before the McCoys passed down the river chasing their horses.[26]

When Frank Phillips saw Anse and his followers crossing Grapevine Creek, Phillips and his men charged the house of Cap Hatfield a short distance away. One of the men helping guard the house was Billy Dempsey, one of William Floyd's party who had been wounded when the gunfire began, and who thought his best role after he was shot was to guard the women and children as best he could.[27] Phillips and his men got to Cap's house, where there was another chilling scene, according to Coleman A. Hatfield.

Billy Dempsey, who was mortally wounded, was also near Cap's house. As he lay bleeding, he called for water. Eskie Smith ran to him with a gourd full of water. One of Phillip's men fired at her, and the bullet struck a large floor puncheon leaning against a picket fence.

As Phillips and his men moved through the yard, they found Billy Dempsey in a fodder pen with an arterial wound in his thigh. Phillips asked his name and he replied, "Billy Dempsey." Phillips said, "I'll demp ye," lowered his rifle and shot out Dempsey's brains.[28]

In the meantime, there were other actions on other fronts of the battle. Robert Lee Hatfield shot Harmon (Bud) McCoy in the shoulder. McCoy mounted his horse, crossed back over the Tug Fork, and rode toward Peter Creek. Another McCoy kinsman saw the bloody sleeve of the shirt and called out, "Are you hurt bad, Bud?" Bud McCoy replied, "No, not bad, only my gun shoulder. It'll be well in a few weeks, and I'll be up and at them again. I'm sure glad the bullet didn't hit me in the dynamite pouch. That might have blowed my horse out from under me!"[29]

The Hatfield Purchase of Twenty-Five Rifles

One of the intriguing questions connected with the battle on Grapevine Creek is simply, who won anything? Truda Williams McCoy argued it was a victory for the McCoys, who returned to Pikeville with tales that the Hatfields acted cowardly.[30] Altina L. Waller in *Feud* appeared to agree with the McCoy account.[31] In the light of history, however, it seems that the encounter was a draw, although Billy Dempsey paid with his life. No one named Hatfield or McCoy was killed or captured and the battle of Grapevine Creek did not settle the feud. There was a little-known consequence. The Hatfields decided they needed better arms. Coleman A. Hatfield told that tale.

> At the Grapevine Creek fight, Anse, Cap, and a few other of the Hatfields were armed with .45 caliber one-shot cartridge Spencer rifles. The remainder of the Hatfield side had only cap-lock squirrel rifles and such other muzzle-loading weapons as had been handed down from the Civil War. Winchester repeating rifles were used by many McCoys who obtained them from the riverboats that came up the Levisa Fork to Pikeville.
>
> Following this encounter, the Hatfields met in council and decided that they must have bigger and better weapons to prevent the McCoys from crossing the river from Kentucky with their big, fast-firing cartridge guns. This experience at Grapevine demonstrated the fact that the slow muzzle-loaders and one-shot rifles were no match for the guns which carried a whole handful of cartridges in the magazine.
>
> Cap said, "Pap, if we get the biggest and best guns that we can buy, it's the only way to keep Old Randal and Frank Phillips from crossing the river on us. If we don't out-match them in artillery, they've already got us bested. Right now, they've got no respect for us."
>
> Anse said, "All right, Cappie, your wife knows how to write the letter, and you know where to get the guns. So you send to the place and get us some new guns."

The Hatfields immediately ordered twenty-five Winchester repeating rifles from Springfield, Massachusetts, with ten thousand rounds of ammunition. The guns were shipped to Brownstown (later renamed Marmet — a Kanawha County town), which was the nearest railroad station.

One day late in October 1888, Anse received notice that the guns had arrived. He said, "Now, Son Cappie, I want you and Elias Simpkins to take the wagon and horses and go after our artillery." The two men set out on the journey, which required approximately one week crossing the rugged mountains where the road was no wider than a bridle path in some places.

The Hatfields found out later that Nancy Hatfield, Cap's wife, had made a mistake, leaving one zero off the cartridge order so the family received only one thousand rounds instead of ten thousand. But Anse said, "That's no trouble at all. We can get plenty of cartridges from the pushboats when they come up the river. I would have gotten these guns brought up the Big Sandy, but Jim McCoy and his men might have captured the pushboat and turned our own guns on us after they had already been paid for."

It should be explained that the Hatfields were concerned about Jim McCoy because he was the most-respected leader of his family.

When the two "gun-toting" weary wagon drivers returned with their boxes filled with new octagon barreled rifles, there were no more raids from either side of the river. To all intents and purposes, the battle of Grapevine Creek ended the feud.[32]

The Role of James A. Nighbert in 1888

There was, nevertheless, another consequence to the battle of Grapevine Creek that deserves attention. That was the effect that the battle had on Anse Hatfield's mind. Anse's constant concern was that his sons or other allies might be taken across Tug Fork. In the summer and fall of 1888, he began thinking that it might be the wisest decision to move away from Tug Fork, to a section easier to defend, and where he had stronger allies. Anse's most literate grandson again explained how the feudist drew on his old friendship with James A. Nighbert.

From the beginning of the feud and throughout the decade of the 1880s, Anse Hatfield often went to Logan on court days, elections, and other occasions, meeting with many of his old friends of Civil War days.

In a conversation with James Nighbert, Anse, anticipating trouble with the McCoys, said, "Major Nighbert, I've got to have some place for a camp for my men, and I am wondering if you can help me out."

The major replied, "Anse, I know of no better place for you to camp during this fall weather than on Dingess Run. I will furnish you with a place where there is fine water and plenty of wood for cooking, and, besides, there's good squirrels and 'coons if you want to hunt them."

"How about bears," Anse said. "Fine," replied Nighbert. There's bears in the hills a little further back, and there's no end to the wild turkeys." The Hatfields remained in that hollow through the summer, and the place was renamed Fort Branch because the family had taken refuge there.

As the weather grew colder late in the fall, Major Nighbert sent Sheriff Ed Peck to tell Anse that his old friend, William Wallace McDonald, had invited him to camp at Rock House on Guyan River.

A natural rock fort stood in the middle of a heavy forest of virgin timber where Anse could stand off an army if need be. Besides, that place offered protection from the cold winter. Anse readily accepted the invitation and camped in the rock house during one of the terribly cold winters of the eighties.[33]

Anse Hatfield's Purchase of Land on Main Island Creek

One point of that tale is that Anse always had ready allies. There were men in the hills as well who were willing to deal with Anse, even if they had no particular part in the feud. One such friend was Lewis (Old Hawk) Steele, who made a deal with Anse that set him free of the troubles that beset him on the Tug Fork. Steele, an old friend of the Hatfields, was the subject of another manuscript by Coleman A. Hatfield.

> In the latter days of the feud, the Hatfields withdrew from the border and bought lands from a settlement of the Steele family who lived across the watershed from the state border on Tug Fork. The Steeles were prepared to move to other parts of the country. The Hatfield interest was centered around Lewis Steele, a bachelor member of one branch of his family.
>
> "Old Hawk," as he liked to be called, was a soldier of fortune, a rolling stone who visited his kindred at rare intervals. He was a picturesque figure with his flowing hair and long beard. Although he had a fine set of teeth, there was a slight cleft in his upper lip which might make young boys think they were about to be bitten by a grizzly bear, particularly when Old Hawk

was excitedly relating some hair-raising stories of the wild west.[34]

The Steeles were one of the pioneering families of the Main Island Creek section of Logan County. Old Hawk owned some five thousand acres of that region, including the site of the later community of Sarah Ann. In 1890, during one of Steele's rare visits to Logan County, Anse Hatfield contacted Steele and asked if Hawk would sell the Hatfields his land. Steele was agreeable and asked in payment a percentage of the timber profits that Anse thought he could make from a lumber operation.

That proved one of the shrewdest of Anse's many deals. Sale of the virgin timber paid off Hatfield's debt to Steele. Then, about the turn of the century, furniture companies became interested in using Appalachian hardwood for their products. "Burl," the stumps left behind from the first timbering, provided ideal wood for furniture, so Anse made a second profit from the land.[35]

Long years after the events of that time passed into history, the poet Paul Curry Steele wrote a fine narrative poem titled *Anse On Island Creek*, which portrayed the feudist as a man who finally had made peace with the world at large. That was another of Anse's most intelligent decisions because the immediate result of the battle of Grapevine Creek was the series of legal maneuvers that involved Kentucky, West Virginia, and eventually the federal courts as a more serious attempt was made to end the troubles.

Legal Maneuvers of the Two States

On January 9, 1888, Kentucky Governor Simon B. Buckner wrote West Virginia Governor E. Willis Wilson that he had received reports about the attack on the McCoy home and requested that the Hatfields named in the 1882 indictments be extradited to Kentucky. Governor Wilson replied that he had learned of the battle of Grapevine Creek and the killing of Billy Dempsey and expressed the hope that the two state chief executives could act together to settle the matter.[36]

While Governor Wilson's message was not a flat refusal of Governor Buckner's request, historians have concluded that Governor Wilson was acting in defense of the Hatfields and claiming that there was wrong on both sides. As the Kentucky Senate debated a measure to strengthen that state's National Guard, and as both states ordered their National Guard units to be prepared to defend the borders, Governor Buckner named Kentucky Adjutant General Sam E. Hill to confer with William F. Floyd to see what could be done about the matter.[37]

Governor Wilson replaced Floyd with Colonel W.H. Mahan, who was better suited to handle quasi-military matters than Floyd. Mahan reported to Governor Wilson that his investigation of the feud convinced him that the Hatfields were now law-abiding citizens who had no intention of making any trouble in Kentucky, but who did not trust the Kentucky government for fair treatment.

Governor Buckner then wrote another letter to Governor Wilson, defending the actions of Frank Phillips and asking again that the Hatfields be extradited to Kentucky. That letter convinced Governor Wilson that there was no point in further personal correspondence with Buckner. Governor Wilson ordered W.H. Mahan to seek the release of the nine Hatfields captured by Phillips, but when Mahan was unsuccessful, Governor Wilson hired Huntington lawyer Eustace Gibson to take the matter to the United States District Court in Louisville and seek a writ of habeas corpus so the Hatfields could be returned to West Virginia.

On February 8, 1888, the case went to the United States District Court before Judge John Watson Barr, with Gibson representing West Virginia and former Kentucky Governor J. Proctor Knott representing his state. The two attorneys presented their respective arguments to that court on February 10, and Judge Barr ruled that the Hatfields should be released from the Pikeville jail to the custody of his court.

On February 25 and 27, 1888, the habeas corpus case came before Judge Barr in the U.S. District Court. By that time, Governor Wilson and his aides had joined Eustace Gibson in defense of the Hatfields. On March 3, Judge Barr ruled that he did not have jurisdiction over the matter because the dispute involved two states. The judge ruled that only the United States Supreme Court had the right to rule in the case.

The attorneys for the Hatfields appealed the matter, and Judge Barr then ruled the case should go through the proper channel, to the United States Circuit Court of Judge Howell E. Jackson. On April 5, 1888, that court took up the case, and Judge Jackson granted the appeal to the United States Supreme Court.

On April 23, 1888, the U.S. Supreme Court heard the case, known by that time as *Plyant Mahon, appellant, v. Abner Justice, jailer of Pike County, Ky.* The court ruled that the Hatfields would have to stand trial in Kentucky, despite some disagreement about whether or not the original arrests of the Hatfields were legal.

Years later, after he had been trained as a lawyer, Coleman A. Hatfield wrote his family's opinion on the Supreme Court decision. "The court decided that the question was immaterial as to how the state takes possession of a prisoner. The effect of the court's opinion was that even by subterfuge and false promise the circuit court, once having jurisdiction of the prisoners, then has the right to try them."[38]

The Trial of the Hatfields

In August 1889, the Hatfield defendants went on trial for killing the McCoy brothers in 1882. By then, Ellison Mounts, the "woods colt" son of Ellison Hatfield, confessed that he had witnessed the killing of the McCoy brothers in August 1882. He said that Charles Carpenter had tied the youngsters to the pawpaw bushes and that the men who shot the McCoys were Anse, Johnse, Cap, and

Bill Tom Hatfield, Charles Carpenter, Alex Messer, and Tom Chambers. He also told the court that Cap Hatfield described how Jeff McCoy had been killed.

Wall Hatfield was tried separately from Alex Messer, Dock Mahon, and Plyant Mahon. Though Wall Hatfield steadily denied that he had anything to do with killing the McCoy brothers in 1882, the upshot of the trials was that all the defendants were convicted and sentenced to life imprisonment.

"Squire Wall Hatfield, not having participated in any overt act against the McCoy brothers who had slain Ellison Hatfield, was so despondent that he died two weeks after being taken to the penitentiary of the Commonwealth of Kentucky," Coleman A. Hatfield wrote. "All the other prisoners served sufficient time to justify their release by the parole authorities of Kentucky. Most of them served upwards of twelve years each before being released."[39]

On August 24, 1888, the Pike County Circuit Court also indicted the Hatfields for the murder of Allifair McCoy on January 1, 1888. The list of men indicted included Cap, Johnse, Robert, and Elliott Hatfield, Ellison Mounts, French Ellis, Charles Gillespie, and Tom Chambers. Only Ellison Mounts was then being held by the court. In due time, Mounts was convicted of murder. His appeal was rejected, and he was sentenced to hang in Pikeville on December 3, 1888.

The Hanging of Ellison Mounts

More than one year was spent appealing the case against Ellison Mounts. In October 1889, a reporter for *The Wheeling Intelligencer* interviewed Mounts, who was quoted saying he did not blame the McCoys because the Hatfields had made him take part in the 1888 raid. Nevertheless, Mounts was hanged at Pikeville on February 18, 1890.

A famous photograph exists, preserved by the Pike County Historical Society. That likeness shows Pike County authorities to the left, three seated and two standing, all but one bare-headed. Mounts is shown kneeling in the center of the photograph, with his head bowed, touching the railing of his scaffold. A preacher is kneeling beside Mounts, probably praying for him, while an official of the law stands to the right.

The Federal Court Story of Anse Hatfield

With the execution of Mounts, the Hatfield-McCoy feud passed into history. Though the tale of Anse Hatfield's life would continue another thirty-one years, there was never again any violence between the two families, though it is true that Johnse and Cap Hatfield, in particular, would have troubles of their own. The fact also is true that Anse Hatfield would have more dealings with the law, including one famous episode before Judge John J. Jackson in the U.S. District Court in Charleston, West Virginia.

The tale that Anse Hatfield was called into federal court on charges of selling liquor illegally was an episode that stands in stark contrast to other events of the time, including the grim accounts of the raid on the McCoy cabin, the killing of Jim Vance, the battle on Grapevine Creek, the dealings with the governments of West Virginia and Kentucky, the trials of the Hatfield partisans, and the hanging of Ellison Mounts.

There were two charges that mountaineers were eternally guilty of during that era. One was "carrying a concealed weapon." The other was "illegal distilling." Given the common culture of the Cumberland region, both charges were laughable because all men were armed and nearly everybody made or kept some liquor.

The charges were useful to detectives and others, however, because they were good excuses to get a man off his home ground and, in the hopes of the detectives, getting a man into the clutches of the law. Thus was the background of the federal court tale, as related by Coleman A. Hatfield, who placed the blame on Dave Straton, previously seen in this history as one of the fighters at Grapevine Creek.

> Dave Straton, a West Virginia native, had marital ties in Kentucky, where he often visited his wife's people and came in contact with McCoy sympathizers. He was looked upon by the Hatfields as one to be watched, although his father, Major John William Straton, had served in the war with Anse Hatfield.
>
> Dave visited the home of Anse on Tug Fork, under the pretext of selling Anse some merchandise which had been brought up on a pushboat from down the river. Among other things, Anse bought six bridles and saddles. In exchange, Dave took some calves, which were loaded on the boat on the return trip to the market.
>
> During the transaction, Anse gave Dave a drink of brandy from a gallon jug. After the trade was over, Dave insisted on buying what remained of the brandy. Anse said, "Dave, I ain't selling it. I got this from a boat runner down the river, and it's not for sale, but I'll give you whatever you want of it."
>
> Dave said, "I ain't got anything to put it in, so I'll have to take the whole jug. You can get some more." This was intended to get "evidence" against Anse so he could be hauled into an unfriendly court.[40]

Dave Straton then took his evidence to Dan Cunningham, one of the notorious detectives of the time and place. Cunningham insisted that Straton go with him to Charleston to appear before a federal grand jury that Cunningham hoped would indict Anse Hatfield for selling liquor without a license.

The indictment was brought against Anse in due order, and United States Marshall William (Bill) White was sent by the federal court on the eighty-five mile trip to Anse's home on Island Creek. Not too surprisingly, the Hatfields heard that a court officer was headed their way. Not only was there no liquor to be found at the Hatfield place, but Marshall White also learned that no one on Island Creek ever heard of anybody making liquor. When White got to Anse's house, his purpose was well known, according to Anse's grandson.

> Just before the fast-riding officer reached Anse's gate, he was met by more than a half dozen barking, growling bear dogs with their bristles standing up as they barred the way of the approaching rider.
>
> A young woman came to the gate and said, "Begone! Begone! What will you have, stranger?" The officer replied, "I want to see Anderson Hatfield. I have a warrant for him from the United States Court at Charleston."
>
> Feigning caution for his safety, Hatfield's daughter said, "Wait a minute, mister. Don't get off your horse just now. You might get dog-bit. Wait 'till I get back." She called to the dogs, "Down, Rattler. Get away, Rough!"
>
> She rushed to the house and Anse appeared on his front porch, dressed in hunting shirt, homemade breeches, and high-topped boots, with his long hair curling up at his shoulders.[41]

The officer told Anse that he was charged with selling a gallon of brandy to Straton the previous summer. Anse told White to go inside for food, and that one of the Hatfield boys would take care of the officer's horse while they were eating. When they had finished, Anse told White what he knew about Dave Straton and the liquor.

> "Dave Straton has been trapping for me and my men for the past three years," Anse said. "We ain't never done anything to Dave, and we're not going to. He's from our side of the river and I was with his old daddy, Major Straton, when he fit through the war.
>
> "But Dave is tricky and instead of keeping our old family friendship, he wants to tell others what he knows about us and try to lead them into our territory.
>
> "I ain't never sold Dave Straton no brandy and nobody else. We were at the pushboat on the river, and he sold me some saddles and bridles for our hosses, and I bought some other things from him and sold him some calves and cow hides.
>
> "After the trade was over we took a drink of brandy together, and he begged me to let him have the rest. I wouldn't sell it to

him. The trade was already over, and he just fell on that idea to make it look like he had bought liquor from me in the trade.

"It's all a plan to get me away from my home so they can capture me with the lowdown gang of detectives which have gathered in from everywhere. They're all a bunch of outlaws, and I know that you will protect me and see that no advantage is taken when I go to court."[42]

Marshall White told Anse that his trial would be on the docket in three weeks, but that if Anse promised to be in Charleston then, he could stay at home until called to court. During the three weeks before the trial, Anse sent friends and neighbors out to watch the gaps and passes in the hills, despite advice from friends like Harve Duty, who cautioned Anse not to go to Charleston. Anse left for Charleston when the time was right, according to his grandson.

Anse, with seventeen followers — all armed except himself — set out on the march across the mountains toward the West Virginia capital. Their course took them down Turtle Creek and Spruce River, across Big Coal River, and over Drawdy Mountain.

It was mild fall weather, and they camped and cooked by the fires where they rested at night. They shot squirrels and pheasants as they went along. After three days and nights, early in the morning of the fourth day they came out of the woods on the south bank of the Kanawha River opposite Charleston, where the ferry would take them across the river.

Curious crowds began to gather immediately on the other side of the Kanawha River, wondering who the bewhiskered, long-haired mountaineer was who led the retinue of armed followers.[43]

When Anse and his band arrived at the courthouse, they asked for White, who told them that the trial would begin in about an hour. When the case was called, Anse told his story to the court, just as he had to White. The prosecutor then told the judge that he thought the case should be dismissed because he learned that the charge was a ruse to get Anse out of Logan County where he could be kidnapped. Judge Jackson, in the meantime, had heard similar information. According to Coleman A. Hatfield's tale:

The venerable jurist rapped for order and said, "Upon the recommendation of the district attorney, the court hereby dismisses this indictment and the prisoner is discharged from further custody. Mr. Marshall, I want you to give Anderson

Hatfield all the protection that is necessary and to see that he has safe conduct back to his home in Logan County."

Anse arose and faced the court as he spoke. "Thank ye, Judge. I don't need any more help. All I want is to get across the river and back to the timber." Needless to say, it wasn't long 'till Anse did "get back to the timber." That phrase explained more of his life than could be written in volumes.[44]

In that context, "returning to the timber" meant that Anse Hatfield, the consummate woodsman that he was, had returned to the land that he knew best. Though warrants for his arrest remained in force until Anse died in 1921, he was left at peace in his home on Main Island Creek. In his later years, Anse became one of the most picturesque and colorful characters of southern West Virginia. With the federal court episode finished, the feud was past, though Anse's older sons soon would face other troubles.

---

[1] Coleman C. Hatfield Interviews.
[2] Coleman C. Hatfield Interviews.
[3] Captain Jim Vance, Coleman A. Hatfield.
[4] Captain Jim Vance, Coleman A. Hatfield.
[5] Captain Jim Vance, Coleman A. Hatfield.
[6] The Raid On The McCoys, Coleman A. Hatfield.
[7] The Raid On The McCoys, Coleman A. Hatfield. The word "admit" instead of "permit" became a strong memory for Coleman A. Hatfield and his faction of the family.
[8] The Raid On The McCoys, Coleman A. Hatfield.
[9] The Raid On The McCoys, Coleman A. Hatfield.
[10] The Raid On The McCoys, Coleman A. Hatfield.
[11] The McCoys: Their Story, Truda Williams McCoy.
[12] The Raid On The McCoys, Coleman A. Hatfield.
[13] The Raid On The McCoys, Coleman A. Hatfield.
[14] Interview With Coleman A. Hatfield, Coleman C. Hatfield.
[15] Coleman C. Hatfield Interviews.
[16] The Raid On The McCoys, Coleman A. Hatfield.
[17] The Killing of Old Captain Jim Vance, Coleman A. Hatfield.
[18] The Killing of Old Captain Jim Vance, Coleman A. Hatfield.
[19] The Killing of Old Captain Jim Vance, Coleman A. Hatfield.
[20] Feud: Hatfields, McCoys and Social Change in Appalachia 1860-1900, Altina L. Waller.
[21] Squire Wall Hatfield, Coleman A. Hatfield.
[22] Feud: Hatfields, McCoys and Social Change in Appalachia, Altina L. Waller.
[23] The Battle of Grapevine Creek, Coleman A. Hatfield. A note may be needed about the names of those creeks. "Pound Mill Creek" was named for the "pounding mills" that mountaineers used to have their corn ground for meal. "Barren She" meant a she bear that had not given birth to its young. "Peter Creek" was named for an individual. "Blackberry Creek" for the blackberry vines that grew thick at that spot.
[24] The Battle of Grapevine Creek, Coleman A. Hatfield.
[25] The Battle of Grapevine Creek, Coleman A. Hatfield.
[26] The Battle of Grapevine Creek, Coleman A. Hatfield.
[27] The Battle of Grapevine Creek, Coleman A. Hatfield. This Billy Dempsey was a cousin of Jack Dempsey, the famous heavyweight boxing champion of the 1920s.
[28] The Battle of Grapevine Creek, Coleman A. Hatfield.
[29] The Battle of Grapevine Creek, Coleman A. Hatfield.
[30] The McCoys: Their Story, Truda Williams McCoy.
[31] Feud: Hatfields, McCoys and Social Change in Appalachia 1860-1900, Altina L. Waller.
[32] Ten Thousand Cartridges, Coleman A. Hatfield.
[33] Anse Hatfield and Major Nighbert, Coleman A. Hatfield.
[34] Old Hawk Steele, Coleman A. Hatfield.
[35] Coleman C. Hatfield Interviews.
[36] The Hatfields and the McCoys, Otis K. Rice.
[37] The Hatfields and the McCoys, Otis K. Rice.

[38] Squire Wall Hatfield, Coleman A. Hatfield.
[39] Squire Wall Hatfield, Coleman A. Hatfield.
[40] The Federal Court Story, Coleman A. Hatfield. Hatfield had other relevant thoughts about Dave Straton. "The two families — Hatfields and Stratons — were friendly, except that Dave was regarded by some as being tricky, which proved to be true later at the battle of Grapevine Creek, where he was in the lead guiding the McCoys through into the Hatfield territory."
[41] The Federal Court Story, Coleman A. Hatfield.
[42] The Federal Court Story, Coleman A. Hatfield.
[43] The Federal Court Story, Coleman A. Hatfield.
[44] The Federal Court Story, Coleman A. Hatfield.

THIS PHOTO may be Anderson (Devil Anse) Hatfield, who would have been about 35 or 40 years old when this photograph was taken by an unknown photographer. The well-worn likeness was found in the personal photo album collected by his wife, Louvicey (Vicey) Chafin Hatfield. By that time, Devil Anse was a successful farmer and timberman and was unknown to the world at large. — Coleman C. Hatfield Collection

THE LOGAN COUNTY COURTHOUSE was this unpretentious structure that was built in 1875 and torn down in 1905. The three-member county court met in the building and presumed to govern 900 square miles of rugged hill country. — Robert Spence Collection

ANSE AND HIS FAMOUS UNCLE JIM VANCE posed for a photographer before a hunting trip in this likeness, also made by an unknown photographer. Shown left to right are Ellison Mounts, Anse Hatfield, Jim Vance, and a man named Borden, who arranged for the photography session. — West Virginia Archives

THIS PHOTOGRAPH of Anse Hatfield, made when he was about 60 years old, is considered by many the best portrait of the feudist. It was made in Charleston, West Virginia, by the Gravely-Moore studio. — Coleman C. Hatfield Collection / West Virginia Archives

RANDAL MCCOY IN HIS PRIME was the determined but tragic enemy of Devil Anse Hatfield. Some believed he described Hatfield as "six feet of devil and 180 pounds of hell." He had good reasons for thinking so because five of his children lost their lives to the feud. — Robert Spence Collection

NANCY VANCE HATFIELD — Anse's mother — is shown here in her later years, holding a toddler — probably a grandchild or great-grandchild. A pioneer woman and hill country midwife, Nancy worried constantly about Anse's well being. — Coleman C. Hatfield Collection.

JOHNSE HATFIELD was the start of much trouble for the Hatfield family.
— Coleman C. Hatfield Collection

ROSEANNA MCCOY is shown in this photograph when she was about 20 years old. Loved but then abandoned by Johnse Hatfield, Roseanna gave birth to their daughter, the short-lived Sarah. — Coleman C. Hatfield Collection

COLEMAN A. HATFIELD was a respected attorney by the time this picture was taken; he had already started compiling the Hatfield history. — Coleman C. Hatfield Collection

HENRY CLAY RAGLAND did more than any other single individual to change Logan County from a land of farmers and timbermen to a community of coal miners and coal operators. Lawyer and journalist, Ragland asserted his influence from his arrival in Logan in 1874 until his death in the spring of 1911. — Robert Spence Collection

ELLISON (COTTONTOP) MOUNTS was the wood's colt son of Ellison Hatfield. One of the most tragic figures in the feud, Mounts was the only man executed by the Commonweath of Kentucky in 1890. He confessed from the scaffold that he had fired the shot that killed Allifair McCoy in the 1888 raid on the McCoy home. — Coleman C. Hatfield Collection

ANSE HATFIELD posed for an artist named Henry Craven in 1911, when this likeness was made. A caption printed with the portrait in Life Magazine claimed Anse was "rich and religious" when the portrait was made. — West Virginia Archives

THE TOWN OF ARACOMA - later the City of Logan - was a small village in 1890 when this photograph was taken. The courthouse is in the center of the town, but there were not yet any churches when Theron C. Crawford visited the place in October 1888. — Robert Spence Collection

PIKEVILLE IN KENTUCKY is shown in this likeness, also made by an unknown photographer. Pikeville was as well known to Randal McCoy and his family as the place where their allies lived and worked. — Courtesy of Altina Waller

ASA HARMON MCCOY was one of the men who killed Jim Vance. — West Virginia Archives

WILDCAT FLAG — This photograph was taken of the well-worn Wildcat flag, which is now on display at the West Virginia Cultural Center, in Charleston, WV. — Photo by Martha Sparks

YKE AND SALLIE SMITH GARRETT, above, posed for this formal photograph when Dyke was about 70 years old. It was Dyke's proudest achievement to have baptized Anse Hatfield, telling a young friend that he had baptized the devil. — Coleman C. Hatfield Collection

At right, Dyke is photographed preaching the good news of salvation.

— On Display at the First Christian Church, Logan, WV.

HENRY D. HATFIELD became the most distinguished family member after the feud ended. He was a doctor, a member of the McDowell County Court, a state senator, the governor, and a U.S. senator. — West Virginia Archives

THE DEVIL TURNED TO STONE shows the graveyard statue of the feud leader. Made of Italian marble, the statue lists the names of the thirteen children of Anse and Louvicey Hatfield. It is the only object in Logan County mentioned on the National Register of Historic Sites. — Photo Courtesy of Raamie Barker

A MORE PEACEFUL HATFIELD FAMILY can be seen in this likeness, made long after the feud was over. Anse and Louvicey are in the front row with young Alie Hatfield. An unknown woman is left in the back row, standing beside Tennis, Joe, Willis, and Elizabeth Hatfield. — Coleman C. Hatfield Collection

CAMP STRATON UNITED CONFEDERATE VETERANS members gathered for this photograph at a meeting near Chapmanville in 1901. The UCV chapter ran Logan County politically for forty years. William Dyke Garrett is center in the first full row. Henry Clay Ragland is in the second row — behind the second man on Dyke Garrett's right — or the left as one looks at the photograph. — Robert Spence Collection

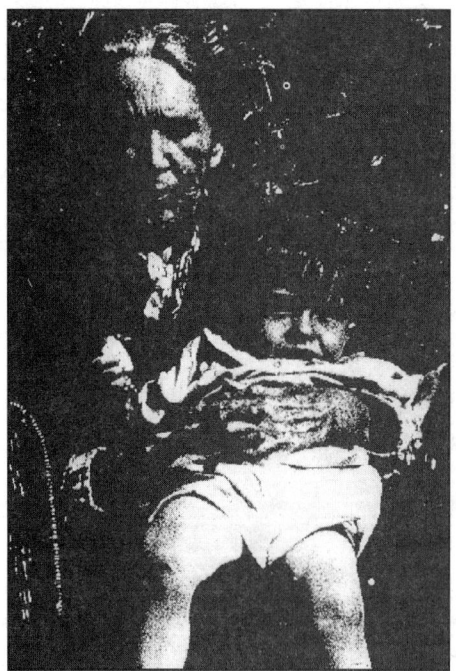

THIS TATTERED AND DISCOLORED PHOTO is of LOUVICEY CHAFIN HATFIELD who is holding Coleman C. Hatfield. — Coleman C. Hatfield Collection

THE "BOOGERMAN" POSES for the camera at his home. Anse is an elderly man by the time this snapshot is taken, and is well known throughout the country. — Coleman C. Hatfield Collection

FRANK PHILLIPS led the posse after the Hatfields and was involved in killing Jim Vance and fighting the battle of Grapevine Creek. — West Virginia Archives

TOM WALLACE was Cap Hatfield's companion in the beating of the Daniels women, one of the most horrific episodes of the feud. He was thought to have been killed in 1890, but it was later discovered he fathered one son in 1921. — Coleman C. Hatfield Collection

THIS STUDIO PHOTOGRAPH of Anse Hatfield is a mystery. No one knows when it was taken or by whom the photograph was made. He appears about 75 years old and had adopted an obviously more formal style of dressing.

CAP HATFIELD was Devil Anse Hatfield's most capable but most dangerous son. He later studied law and became a deputy and a security guard; he was both feared and respected by many citizens in the Logan and Mingo County region of West Virginia. — Coleman C. Hatfield collection

CAP GLENN, an aged Cap Hatfield, holding a pet fox, and Stewart Glenn pose for a photo. — Coleman C. Hatfield collection

CAP HATFIELD SITS and thinks about the past at the rocky "panther site" on the mountain side. The son of Anse was approximately fifty-five years old and a county deputy at the time this photograph was taken. — Coleman C. Hatfield Collection

DEVIL ANSE was often described as an excellent horseman and hunter. He maintained a special bond with "horse-flesh" and the Appalachian Mountains throughout his life. As Coleman C. Hatfield recalls, the horse's name was Fred. — West Virginia Archives

ANSE HATFIELD WAS IN HIS FINAL YEARS, at left, when this photograph was taken by an unknown photographer about the year 1920. Though careworn with time, Anse seems to have lost little of his personality and still enjoyed "devilin'" those close to him. — West Virginia Archives

ANSE WATCHES OVER THE HATFIELD CEMETERY near the lazy community of Sarah Ann. His statue, arrived and was erected in 1921, where it proudly stands today. — Coleman C. Hatfield Collection

TWO OF ANSE HATFIELD'S SISTERS, Emma and Biddie Hatfield are shown here. — Coleman C. Hatfield Collection

DEVIL'S PET BEAR plays with two unknown visitors at the Hatfield home. — West Virginia Archives

ANSE HATFIELD'S HOME on Main Island Creek in Logan County. — Coleman C. Hatfield Collection

CITIZENS GATHER at the Devil Anse home at Island Creek to mourn the passing of the family patriarch. — West Virginia Archives

ANSE HATFIELD'S FAMILY gathered for the solemn occasion of his funeral in January 1921. Anse can be seen lying in his open coffin with immediate family members in the first row in this likeness, made by an unknown photographer. — West Virginia Archives

THE ORIGIN OF THIS WORN PHOTOGRAPH is unknown, but it may have been made about 1914, when Anse was about 75 years old. The likeness may have been a promotional "still" made for a movie or a filmstrip about the feud, perhaps in cooperation with Emmett Datlon.

COLEMAN A. HATFIELD - the devil's historian - was in a peaceful mood when this photograph was taken on the Tug Fork near War Eagle about 1910. — Coleman C. Hatfield Collection

A YOUNG JOE HATFIELD, behind the driver's seat, poses for this snapshot in his early twentieth-century jalopy. — Coleman C. Hatfield Collection

JAMES (SLATER JIM) HATFIELD was the uncle of Anse Hatfield that a Civil War officer ordered Anse to shoot because he briefly deserted the Confederate army. This prompted Anse to leave the army at the end of 1863, according to Coleman A. Hatfield's account of the matter. Slater Jim is shown in this photograph with Rachel Toler. — Coleman C. Hatfield Collection

DEVIL ANSE HATIFIELD made up his mind to make peace with God and was baptized by William Dyke Garrett in the waters of Main Island Creek near his home at Sarah Ann in October 1911. Keen observers have noted that Anse (extreme right, second row) had his pistol in his pocket. — West Virginia Archives

Ellison Hatfield
Courtesy of West Virginia Archives

Louvicey Hatfield casts a stern gaze from her front yard.
Courtesy of Coleman C. Hatfield Collection

ANSE HATFIELD'S FAMILY might have changed out of their work clothes if they had known how famous this photograph would become. The family was living on Beech Fork of Tug River when this likeness was made about 1888. That's tragic Shepherd Hatfield standing seventh in the back row. His brother Coleman A. is just to his right, holding a pistol at a relatively unthreatening angle. Cap Hatfield is shown extreme right with the rifle in the second row. Nancy "Nan" Smith Hatfield is beside him. Anse and Louvicey are second and third from the left in the middle row. — West Virginia Archives

Allen and Willis Hatfield
Photo taken in the 1970s
— Coleman C. Hatfield Collection

Left to right, Dr. R. Mark Hatfield, Dr. Arabel E. Hatfield, and father, Dr. Coleman C. Hatfield
— Coleman C. Hatfield Collection

ANSE HATFIELD POSES with the Loyal Order Of Moose Lodge, Number 902, in Logan, WV. Devil Anse is standing in the front row, the third man on the left. — Courtesy of Coleman C. Hatfield Collection.

CAP HATFIELD STANDS IN THE CENTER of this group of Logan County deputies. Cap was a man not to be reckoned with and considered himself well-suited for law enforcement. — Courtesy of Coleman C. Hatfield Collection.

IN SPITE OF THE GLARE OF THE LENS, this rare photograph depicts the funeral service of Louvicey Hatfield, Devil Anse' beloved wife. Her coffin leans forward for the photograph, which was a custom of the times. She is surrounded by flowers, family and neighbors. — West Virginia Archives

WILLIS HATFIELD allows an unknown photographer to snap this picture in 1970. Willis was 82 years old. — West Virginia Archives

YOUNG COLEMAN A. HATFIELD takes aim with his trusty .45 caliber pistol. The grandson of Devil Anse, it is said that he was also a careful and gifted shootist. — Coleman C. Hatfield Collection

A YOUNG WILLIS HATFIELD was an able-bodied deputy in the mountainous region of Logan County. He often worked with and for several of his brothers who were also law enforcement officers. — West Virginia Archives

Chapter Eight
THE CHILDREN OF THE DEVIL
The Younger Hatfields Come of Age

CAP HATFIELD was a marked man after the raid on the home of Randal McCoy on January 1, 1888, the death of Uncle Jim Vance on Thacker Mountain that followed the raid, and the battle of Grapevine Creek ten days after Vance was killed. Cap's reputation made that fact inevitable, but another aspect of the feud was that Anse Hatfield's withdrawal from a vulnerable position left Cap more open to his enemies than he might have been.

The twenty years that followed Anse's decision to move to Main Island Creek in 1890 were the worst years of Cap's life. His reputation as the roughest and most dangerous man in the Logan-Pike-Mingo region kept Cap at bay, surrounded by McCoys and other foes on every side. Cap became more morose, more beset by the devils set free by the feud.

One of the little-known considerations was that Cap found himself facing difficulties feeding his family because his enemies kept him from maintaining a farm. His second son, Shepherd Hatfield, born in 1891, died from malnutrition in 1898, as much a victim of the family troubles as any of the McCoy children killed by gunfire during the feud.[1]

Cap eventually solved his difficulties in a most imaginative way, which was another fact that argues against the shallow view of Cap as a mindless killer. In about 1908, he escaped from his Logan County home and heritage by taking a six-month law course in Tennessee. While such training would be inadequate for a lawyer by the standards of today, the law course served its purpose. Cap had been taught to read by his remarkable wife, Nancy Smith Hatfield, and began to enjoy reading as a useful hobby. His growing awareness of a larger world and his training in the law gave Cap the means to become a more respectable man.[2]

In following years, Cap became a law officer in Logan County, and then opened a law office with his son, Coleman A. Hatfield, who then was joined by Cap's granddaughter, the equally remarkable Aileen Hatfield. While those facts do not suggest that Cap Hatfield had become an angel, they do lead one to think that Cap, the so-called outlaw feudist of the 1880s, had become part of the power structure that transformed life in the Logan-Mingo-Pike area between 1890 and 1910.[3]

During the same years that Cap was changing from a feudist to a Logan County deputy sheriff, his older brother, Johnse Hatfield, became a more mature man as well. The point is well taken that Johnse went to his reward without losing his fondness for the company of women.[4] Yet in the years after the feud,

Johnse was sent to state prison after being kidnapped by Humphrey (Doc) Ellis in another meaningless quarrel. His time spent in prison sobered the fun-loving Johnse, who won parole by saving the life of the prison warden.

Another important theme in the growing respectability of the Hatfield clan was the life-story of Henry Drury Hatfield, the son of Elias Hatfield, who was Anse Hatfield's younger brother. Henry D. was arguably the most successful Hatfield of the 1890 to 1910 era and afterwards. Elias had moved to Logan Courthouse to escape violence on the Tug Fork. As Elias's son, Henry D. grew up in the Logan County seat of government and became aware of the attractive possibilities of professional life and politics.

Henry D. was as close to Anse Hatfield as any son, because Anse had married Louvicey Chafin and Elias Hatfield had married her sister, Elizabeth Chafin. Both were daughters of Nathan Chafin. Thus Henry D. became Cap Hatfield's double first cousin, a relationship which, genetically speaking, was closer than a whole brother.

Henry D. studied medicine at the University of Louisville, Kentucky, became a doctor, joined Dr. Sidney B. Lawson in establishing the Hatfield-Lawson Hospital on a hill across the Guyandot River from Logan Courthouse, and later built another hospital in Welch, the seat of McDowell County. In 1908, Henry D. was elected to the state senate and in 1912 was elected governor of West Virginia, the youngest ever, at age 37. One of his daughters would marry the president of United States Steel Corporation.

Thus the Hatfields, whom Theron C. Crawford described as killers and outlaws during the era of the feud, became accepted participants in the political, economic, and social changes that swept the United States during the "progressive era." Such facts argue that the Hatfields were becoming more significant during Anse's lifetime and that the next generation of the family would fulfill the promise of their American heritage. It is the task here to show how the lives of Cap, Johnse, and Henry D. Hatfield began that subtle development.

Cap and Nancy Smith Hatfield

Cap Hatfield was in his eighteenth year in 1882 when he met Joseph and Nancy Elizabeth (Smith) Glenn after that young couple moved to the Mate Creek area about that year. Nancy was fated to suffer a harsh life, but bore herself so bravely that the late Howard B. Lee, author of West Virginia histories, called her "a mountain queen."[5]

Nancy was the daughter of L.P. Smith of Wayne County, and was born September 10, 1866. Her parents moved to Mate Creek sometime before 1880. That year, at age 14, she married Joseph M. Glenn, who was a southerner from Georgia and a rising young timber merchant and part owner of a general store. Though it is not known why the young couple remained on Mate Creek, they were living in that vicinity before the feud began in earnest with the death of Ellison Hatfield in August 1882.

Joseph Glenn had become the business partner of one William Smith, whose background is not known, though it is clear that he was no direct relation of Nancy Glenn. William Smith and Joseph Glenn sharply disagreed about some unknown business concern and became enemies. During the week of September 7, 1882, Glenn was shot dead from ambush on Mate Creek.[6] The assassin never was arrested, but Cap Hatfield's descendants believe to this day that Smith fired the shot.[7]

Despite Smith's motives, some writers, including Virgil Carrington Jones, tried to pin the murder on Cap Hatfield, implying, if not stating, that Cap had fallen in love with Nancy and took a chance murdering her husband. Jones recorded his account in the second footnote of chapter nine in his book *The Hatfields and the McCoys*, citing Thomas C. Whited as his source. In that light, Jones wrote:

> T.C. Whited remembers when a young fellow named Joe Glenn came to Logan. Later, the newcomer went on toward the Tug and, still later, it was told about the streets that he had married a daughter of L.P. Smith, over near the mouth of Grapevine Creek, after a brief courtship. The thing about the marriage that made news was that the bride was Cap Hatfield's sweetheart, who had taken on a husband at a time when Cap was hiding out to avoid arrest in connection with the feud. But it was a matrimony of short duration. Shortly afterward, Glenn was found dead beside the road, his body riddled with bullets. It was never known who killed him. Cap and the widow were married shortly afterward.[8]

The implication of this is apparent. Jones thought that Cap Hatfield had slain Glenn in order to marry Nancy. The charge is untrue. Nancy and Cap were first cousins, but were not married until more than one year after the death of Glenn. Though it is possible that the eighteen-year-old Cap had fired some of the shots that killed the three sons of Randal McCoy four weeks before Joseph Glenn was killed, Cap was not the "hardened killer" of legend in 1882. Coleman C. Hatfield recorded a more reliable account of those events:

> Joseph Glenn had gone to the barn of his Mate Creek farm that morning to get a hoe to begin taking in his crop of corn. Nancy remained in the house cleaning up the breakfast dishes. A few minutes after Glenn went to the barn, Nancy heard two shots fired from some location across the Tug Fork in Kentucky.
> She ran out to the yard and found Joe dying. She said he had been troubled for some weeks, fearing that he would be sued by

Smith. Her immediate thought was that Smith shot Glenn instead of taking his chances in court.

Joe died a few minutes after Nancy found him. Cap and Johnse Hatfield lived a short distance away and came running to see if Joe and Nancy were in danger. Anse and Louvicey Hatfield followed their sons to the Glenn's farm and did what they could to comfort Nancy.

One of the most unfortunate facts about the feud is that everyone in the Hatfield family has been slandered by fiction writers through the years. You may or may not have a high opinion of Cap Hatfield, but it takes a very small mind to accuse a 15-year-old woman of marrying her husband's killer. Nancy Hatfield did no such thing.[9]

As a point of fact, Cap and Nancy Hatfield did not wed until October 10, 1883, more than a year after the death of Joseph Glenn. Scandal mongering should not be accepted as history. Nancy, in the meantime, faced the same prospect that other women of that era confronted when their husbands died young. That was the prospect of the poor house, which terrified such women. Nancy's marriage to Cap was nothing out of the ordinary, and her decision to marry Cap was undoubtedly one of the luckiest events of his life.

Nancy Hatfield was her second husband's match in many ways. Though both grew up in a time and place where violence was common enough, and though it never was an easy matter to keep a farm and raise children in the hill country, Cap and Nancy managed to live a life decent enough to allow their children to become citizens of a much better world.

Hatfield family lore claims that Nancy Hatfield was a better shot than Cap and was better than him riding a horse.[10] Howard B. Lee added that Nancy gave Cap her own hunger for knowledge and shared with him the learning she had acquired in school in Wayne County. Lee wrote:

> Cap had a brilliant mind, and he set about to improve it. He and Nancy Elizabeth bought and read many books on history and biography, and they also subscribed for and read a number of the leading magazines of their day. In time they built up a small library of good books, which they read and studied along with their children.[11]

In a more practical vein, Nancy was as strong a character as Cap, as able to take care of herself and their children. Though the point the Hatfields make about Nancy being a better shot than Cap is a rather minor issue, and a rather amusing one at that, it also is a tribute to the independence of mountain women and deserves its note in history. Coleman C. Hatfield recalled:

One afternoon when Cap and Nancy were living on Island Creek, the women were busy getting supper ready while Cap and Coleman A. and the other men were out taking target practice and bragging about their skills to one another.

A "shikepoke" flew over. That's a small blue heron, though I have heard some people use the word to refer to other smaller wading birds. The men blasted away at the bird, and they all missed. The women came running out to see what in sam hill was going on. When they found out about it, Nancy picked up a rifle and killed the shikepoke with one shot. Cap was a little embarassed, but proud of his wife.[12]

Nancy would need her strong character in the years that followed. Though she once admitted that Cap was "not a very good risk as a husband" in 1883, she was loyal to him. He was equally unfortunate because he was forced to flee to Colorado in the wake of the troubles that came after the McCoy brothers were killed in August 1882.

Henry Clay Ragland's Role In Logan County

As Cap and Nancy Hatfield struggled to maintain a family, the new economic era took shape in Logan and Pike Counties. The tale is interesting, but complex, and its touchstone was made of land ownership, communication, finance, and transportation.

The events of that transformation did not proceed smoothly. There were starts and stops. The pace was irregular because at times it looked as though the new era would sweep everything before it, and at other times it looked like the traditional life of the hill country would continue unchanged indefinitely.

A first act was the creation of *The Logan County Banner* in March 1889, while the Hatfields and McCoys were still coming to terms with the raid on the McCoy home, the death of Jim Vance, and the battle on Grapevine Creek. While it cannot be argued that the creation of the newspaper was a direct result of the feud, that act was an indirect action and an attempt to improve Logan County's reputation.

The newspaper was a brainchild of five men: Henry Clay Ragland, James Andrew Nighbert, Hugh Caperton Avis, H.K. Shumate and Urias Beckley Buskirk. Ragland became its editor, but each investor put up $200, and a printing press, type, and other newspaper supplies were floated up the Guyandot River from Huntington so *The Banner* could begin operations.

The appearance of the newspaper was not impressive at first glance. The standard practice of that day in that place was to order "patent outsides" from newspaper companies in cities like Chicago. The "patent outsides" were single broadsheets with patent medicine advertisements, horrible poetry, and adventure or romance yarns on tabloid pages one and four. It was the responsibility of the local journalists to fill pages two and three.

This Ragland did with fine abandon. The "inside" pages of a typical *Banner* of the 1890s included notes about the Logan County folk who were in the county seat during the week, updates of business adventures, and surprisingly excellent editorials, nearly all aimed at convincing the larger world that the county was a coalfield waiting to be exploited.

In his fourth edition, Ragland stated his goal. "The newspaper will be devoted to the best interests of the people of Logan County; to the improvement of the education and morals of its people; and to the development of its great material resources."[13] The editor was true to his word. During the fourteen years that followed, Ragland campaigned tirelessly for the matters he thought were in the county's best interest.

Those matters can be grouped into four general considerations. First, Ragland sought to attract a railroad to Logan County. On at least eight separate occasions, Ragland thought success was in his grasp. Though the Chesapeake and Ohio Railroad did not begin its Guyan Valley Extension until the year 1900, when Ragland was close to retirement, an argument could be made that the editor's propaganda on that subject was most successful.

Second, Ragland sought to improve the county and Logan Courthouse by convincing his fellow citizens that practical measures to make the community cleaner, more law-abiding, more religious, and more in touch with the larger world would be in their own best interests. That concern was also a success. In the 1890s, Ragland convinced his fellow citizens to reorganize their town government and rewrite their laws. He also convinced Loganites to take measures for better sanitation, build churches and support them, and build a better school system.

Ragland's third great concern was to protect what he saw as the autonomy of local citizens, chiefly by supporting the Democratic Party, but also by resisting "the money power," which Ragland saw as the great daemon of his age. His most notable effort in that direction was his campaign against Henry C. King, who sought to claim title to the half million acres of southern West Virginia once owned by Robert Morris and later by James Swan just after the American Revolution.

The so-called "King Case" was a highly complicated matter with a surprisingly simple conclusion. King brought suit for that land in 1893. The matter was in the courts for thirty years. In 1910, the United States Supreme Court ruled against King, who received only a few strips of land that had never been taxed by either Virginia or West Virginia. Yet the odd conclusion of the case was that many private landowners sold their property, convinced that they would lose the case and that only larger concerns like coal and timber firms had the resources to fight King. In that sense, Ragland's third great effort was a failure.

Ragland's fourth concern was the establishment of a local coal economy. Though the event happened after Ragland retired from *The Banner* in the fall of 1902, that was his greatest triumph. Beginning in January 1890, Ragland wrote editorial after editorial that claimed Logan County was the greatest coalfield in the eastern United States. North of Coal River and south of Tug Fork, Ragland wrote, there was a marked decrease in the quality of Appalachian coal. The county needed only "the talismanic rod" of capital to be converted into "living beauty."

Ragland's greatest ally in that campaign was Nighbert. Nighbert purchased nearly 30,000 acres of land on Copperas Fork of Island Creek between 1870 and 1895. After Nighbert died without making a will in December 1898, the title to his land was taken by his widow, Vicie Straton Nighbert, the daughter of old Major John William Straton, Anse Hatfield's Civil War ally. In 1903, Vicie Nighbert sold the land for $600,000 to Boston and Cleveland investors who then created Island Creek Coal Company.

Though Vicie Nighbert was well-heeled for the rest of her life, the land purchase was one of the great steals of American industrial history. For their $20 per acre and stock in their company, the creators of Island Creek Coal extracted a vast fortune which fueled the expansion of their firm into all of southern West Virginia and eastern Kentucky, and then on into other coal-producing regions of the world. By the time Island Creek was sold to Armand Hammer's Occidental Petroleum Company in 1969, it had become a titan of the world's coal industry.

The result of the changes that followed in the wake of Ragland's campaign was that the hill country life known so well to Anse Hatfield vanished. By 1910, the regional newspapers were reporting the almost daily growth of the coal and railroad economy. Cap and Johnse Hatfield, and then the younger members of their family, Joe, Tennis, Coleman A., Willis, Henry D. Hatfield, and Joe M. Glenn (son of Nancy Glenn Hatfield), would be forced to cope with a new society as best they could.

The Gunfire At Matewan

By the time the election of 1896 came around, Logan County and the surrounding region had changed in many ways, and the Hatfield family was becoming a much different group of individuals. Another force that brought about those changes in the Hatfield men and women was the changing nature of the Logan-Mingo-Pike region. Cap Hatfield's son, Coleman A. Hatfield, described the general economic and political conditions of that time.

> About the middle of the decade, which closed the last century, there was great activity along the borderline between Kentucky and West Virginia. The great Pocahontas coalfield was being developed at the Virginia-West Virginia border. The coalfield towns of Bluefield, Welch, and Williamson, along with

many other mining communities, was beginning to grow and to develop.

In 1895, the southern half of Logan County was carved into the 55th county of West Virginia, and became known as Mingo, in honor of the tribe of which Logan, the warlike Indian chieftain, was master.

Men rushed into the rapidly developing area, seeking wealth and business advancement. Other types and characters followed. All kinds could be found in these overnight industrial towns.... While the feuds and wars of the mountain men were giving way to other activities, there still remained the smoldering fires of feuds, which often flared up.[14]

During this unsettled time, Cap Hatfield lost faith in the Democratic Party and became a Republican. Though Cap himself never explained his reasons for leaving the political organization that had been so important to Anse Hatfield, Cap's descendants believed that he had strong motives for the change.

First, Logan County had been tied to national economic trends by the changing nature of the timbering industry. In an earlier time, local timbering had been a rather self-directed operation. Timbering was a part-time occupation, much smaller in scope than organized timbering. Men went into the woods, cut their own timber, and sent it to the markets in Guyandotte, West Virginia, Catlettsburg, Kentucky, and Cincinnati, Ohio — one raft at a time. This gave such men direct control of their own lives and their own money.

By the early 1890s, more organized corporations and business organizations had moved into southern West Virginia and eastern Kentucky. The giant Cole and Crane organization, the influential W.M. Ritter Company, and the Yellow Poplar Lumber Company all had an effect on the economic life of the region. For the first time, when the national economy was weak, Logan County's men and women suffered with the rest of the nation. Coleman A. Hatfield recalled strong memories of that time that were related to the economy, but which had an influence on the politics of that time and place.

> When Dad (Cap Hatfield) was thirty-two years of age, we had moved over to Matewan from the head of Island Creek. That was in the spring of 1895, along about March. We lived one winter there, and Dad built a house. A sawmill had come in on Mate Creek up there.
>
> In 1892, Grover Cleveland was elected president for the second time and served until 1896, when William McKinley came in. I was seven years old in February of '96. I remember the events of that summer very, very well.
>
> They were sawmilling up on Mate Creek. They were hauling wagons up and down the creek there and loading cars of lumber

down at the mouth of the creek, five miles down from where we lived.

There was a big effort at that time to reorganize the politics of the state of West Virginia, and West Virginia went Republican for the first time in its history. Dad got to attending meetings up there at this sawmill camp and got to talking with people. And he became a Republican.[15]

Cap Hatfield's economic distress was compounded because the events of the feud and his reputation as the "bad man of the hills" kept him from following steady work. Yet his grandson once said that Cap was becoming more aware of politics, because his entire region was feeling the effects of the national depression that began in 1893.

I do not believe that Cap would have changed parties so dramatically if he had not believed that the Republicans could do more than the Democrats to restore prosperity to the nation and to his region.

Loyalty to the Democrats was strong in the Hatfield family and that was a loyalty that dated back to the time of the Civil War. Cap thought that the Democrats had failed the country, and that he was feeling the edge of the lost prosperity.

But we also have to remember that Cap's decision to become a Republican was not popular. Ragland, over here in Logan with *The Banner*, was the spokesman for the Democratic Party in the entire seventh senatorial district of West Virginia, and was an old friend of the Hatfields.

In some ways, Cap's decision to break away from the Democrats was both an indication of his alienation from Anse and a statement to the world that he intended to make his own independent decisions, not remaining an extension of his father or other Hatfields.[16]

A second powerful reason that Cap Hatfield became a Republican was the creation of Mingo County. There long had been serious tensions between the Guyandot Valley and the Tug Fork Valley because the economic and political life of the southwestern bend of West Virginia had been dominated by politicians and businessmen of Logan Courthouse before the creation of Mingo County. Naturally, the men and women of the Tug Fork felt that their ambitions were hampered by the courthouse faction.

As soon as Mingo County was created by the West Virginia Legislature, a political battle for control of the new county began. The Republicans moved aggressively to direct the fortunes of Mingo County. It is likely that Cap Hatfield believed that his best chance to remain politically powerful in the new county meant changing his party allegiance. This soon became common knowledge, for reasons later outlined by Cap's son.

> In 1896 there was considerable political activity among the border counties along the state line between West Virginia and Kentucky. Many who had followed the political paths of their ancestors since the days of Thomas Jefferson and Alexander Hamilton were often found to change their political affiliations.
> In the national campaign of 1896, this change, and the strife that accompanies such changes, was notable in the industrial areas in the border counties. Men from the outside who had come into this region were making their political influence felt in the organization of the county governments. There was an especially urgent rush to organize the new county of Mingo.[17]

Despite the emergence of the new age in the hill country, men still felt many of the same passions that they felt during the older time and acted on the same motives that had governed their conduct in past times. Coleman A. Hatfield saw this from the perspective of the small boy that he was that dramatic summer. In his latter years, he realized the deeper meaning of the choices Cap Hatfield made that summer and the meaning of the fires that still burned.

> In some instances, during this time of violent political activity, old grudges of former years flared up and bloodshed often resulted between men who had not formerly been aligned against one another as family feudists. Still, the pattern of the old feud days was often followed.
> My father carried his gun everywhere he went. He had come out of the feud over there and had been a feudist since 1882. They had fights and battles over there, and he was a man who just didn't back down from anybody.[18]

There was another man around the town of Matewan then who also had the reputation of being tougher, braver, more able, and more explosive than many of his contemporaries. He had the reputation of being the "bully" of Matewan. That man was John E. Rutherford, a son of old Dr. Elliott Rutherford, who once had been a friend of Anse Hatfield before bad feeling arose between the two families. Anse had, in fact, named one of his sons after Dr. Rutherford.

The trouble began when Dr. Elliott Rutherford got in a shootout with John Chafin, a first cousin of Louvicey Chafin Hatfield, Anse's wife and Cap's mother. In that encounter, John Chafin was shot in the spine and was crippled for life, walking with an unsteady wobble. Resentment lingered. There was further bad blood between John Rutherford and the Hatfields because the Rutherfords believed Cap Hatfield shot up John Rutherford's house some months before the election of 1896. Coleman A. Hatfield recalled:

> There was a saloon in Pike County, just across from Matewan. On this occasion, John Rutherford said to a crowd of Democratic workers and fellows, "Cap Hatfield has been making quite a stir. If he comes down here and votes the Republican ticket, let's put him over in Kentucky."
>
> Readers should remember that the old feud charges and indictments were still in effect then. "Putting a Hatfield over into Kentucky" meant turning him over to the legal authorities there, where it was possible he would be hanged.
>
> So that was the old gag, the old saw, to put a Hatfield across the river in Kentucky. Many Hatfields lived in dread of that and lived with their rifles. But Greenway Hatfield, Cap's own double cousin, said, "No — you'd better kill him if you're going to do anything, because if you start anything, he'll hurt some of you."[19]

Such were the circumstances when Cap Hatfield arrived at the Matewan poll on November 3, 1896. Elections along the borderline had not changed appreciably since 1882. Men still crowded around the polls, some drinking, some arguing, and others just watching the show. Yet there would be violence that day to match the troubles of August 1882, when Ellison Hatfield was mortally wounded by the McCoy brothers. Coleman A. Hatfield recalled:

> On this particular day, it was a whole lot like any other election, with fellows going around and speaking to this one and that one as they rode in. And Dad was mingling and mixing around with them. He'd gone there with a fellow named Marion Kennedy.
>
> They had an old Model 1873 Winchester rifle and a double-barreled shotgun that Dad had bought for Joe Glenn to shoot squirrels and learn to hunt. Joe claimed the shotgun and carried it mostly. Dad stuck to his old rifle, which was the best they had in those days.[20]

As Cap walked onto the election grounds, he passed the store owned by Dr. Elliott Rutherford, where John Rutherford and others kept their whiskey that day. Bliss Rutherford, John's older brother, tried to start trouble with Hatfield. "Cap," he said, "I'm surprised you're down here today. I can smell the nigger on you."[21] John Rutherford then joined his brother, according to Coleman A. Hatfield's recollection.

> John Rutherford came around chucking a handful of .38 caliber short shells. He dropped one and said to Dad, "Pick that up. I might have to kill some man today."
>
> To the old man, you know, that was an insult that burned him just like fire. He was trying to hold onto his temper, and he said, "John, there's no glory in killing a man. I wouldn't want to hurt anybody, and I wouldn't want to see you hurt anybody. We best let bygones be bygones."[22]

That seemingly stopped the trouble for a while. Toward evening, though, Cap Hatfield kept his promise to vote the Republican ticket, despite the jokes and other comments that his old friends made during the day. After he voted, Marion Kennedy walked up to Cap, put his arm around Hatfield's shoulders, and said, "Cap, let's go get some supper." At that moment, all hell broke loose:

> John Rutherford walked up behind Dad and shouted, "Look here, Cap Hatfield, look here!" Rutherford fired his shotgun twice at Dad. One shot cut the skin off the top of Dad's left ear, and the other shot blistered him across the base of his neck.
>
> In times of excitement, Dad was an awfully quick man. He shot Rutherford along on his right side just as Rutherford pulled another pistol from a holster and began firing again.
>
> By that time, there were five men shooting at Dad. They were Reece Halsey, Ed Hopson, Elliott Rutherford, Lewis Rutherford, and John Rutherford.[23]

The election grounds exploded. From the steps of the poll, an election official named Henderson Chambers shouted, "Pour it to him, Johnny! Pour it to him!" At that instant, a bullet hit Chambers and killed him. Later some on the scene said young Joe Glenn fired that shot, but Glenn denied the charge.[24]

Also at that moment, Cap Hatfield grabbed the double-barreled shotgun from Glenn, just as another bullet hit that weapon. The bullet shattered on the shotgun and the lead fragments imbedded in Cap's hand, leaving his knuckles scarred for the rest of his life. If that bullet had not hit the shotgun, it would have killed Cap Hatfield.

Joe Glenn ran to Cap shouting, "Pa, let's get away from here! They'll kill you!" Cap and Joe wheeled and ran down through an alley in the direction of the railroad tracks and the Mingo County road that led out of Matewan. As they ran, they passed a policeman. Cap ran on one side of the officer and Joe ran on his other side. Joe shouted to the officer, "Now, you tell those g__d__ men we're the stuff!"[25]

After Cap and Joe escaped through the alley, they ran over to the county road, turned, and went up Tug Fork to the mouth of Mate Creek. They were followed by Ed Rutherford, Reece Halsey, and the younger Elliott Rutherford, who pursued them to a railroad trestle that was built above the road. Elliott Rutherford shot two pistols empty, as Cap Hatfield crouched under an abutment and Joe Glenn ran another seventy-five yards up the creek. Rutherford was practically shooting down at Cap's head at the time, meaning it was some time before Cap could escape and join Joe.

As Cap left the trestle, he fired again at Halsey. The shot hit Halsey in the foot, slicing off two or three toes. Elliott Rutherford was busy reloading his gun, but he then began shooting from the top of the trestle. At least two shots from Rutherford's gun hit the ground between Joe Glenn's feet. Cap ran toward Glenn as Glenn fired one shot from the Winchester that went over Rutherford's head.

Rutherford crouched down to take better aim at Hatfield and Glenn. Cap then seized the rifle from Glenn and fired a second shot through Rutherford's heart. Then Cap said to Joe, "Let's take to the woods." The pair turned and crossed the dry bed of Mate Creek and went up through the bushes and on up the side of the steep hill. When they got to the top of that ridge, they rested, listening to the commotion in Matewan, according to Coleman A. Hatfield.

> The drunken men were swearing, and they heard women crying in the great excitement. They heard dogs barking. They rested for a while, because they had a clear view of everywhere. From that woodland, they could see out but no one could find their position. In a little while they went up Mate Creek ridge. The first thing Dad said to Joe Glenn was, "We'll go to Dan Christian's home."[26]

The two stayed in the woods all that day. The next night, they went down into the ravines where it was difficult to travel. Cap told Joe that he could not see well, so Joe led him to Christian's house, where they arrived on the second night after the shooting. They slept in the attic, and Christian's daughters brought them their first meal in two days. In later years, Joe Glenn said it was the best meal he ever had. In that way, Anse Hatfield's charity to Dan Christian many years before was repaid with interest.[27]

The unlucky skirmish at Matewan brought the Hatfields more unwelcome attention. In Logan Courthouse, Henry Clay Ragland wrote bitter words about Cap Hatfield in the pages of his newspaper. Ragland argued that such violence made it more difficult for the region to create an industrial economy. Ragland also seemed to argue that regional violence would end when the coal economy was established. Such claims were unlikely, as later events proved.

Cap Hatfield's Escape from the Williamson Jail

As Cap Hatfield and Joe Glenn remained at Dan Christian's home, men on horseback began riding up the creeks of the vicinity, looking for the pair. About twenty to twenty-five men, led by Reece Chambers and Bill Bevins, raided Cap's house and demanded to know if he was there. Nancy and her children knew nothing about the trouble. The party then went to Main Island Creek, where they learned nothing more at Anse Hatfield's house than they had learned at Cap's place.

In the meantime, Dan Christian hid Cap and Joe Glenn in a wagon and took them to the mouth of Thacker Creek, where they reached the N&W railroad tracks. The fast train stopped there that night about midnight, and Cap and Joe hid in the baggage car. The train went through Matewan at sixty miles an hour and did not stop until it arrived in Huntington, where Hatfield and Glenn surrendered to the sheriff, who let them stay at the Arlington Hotel.

The following morning, a detective named Jim Clark, who was a trusted friend of Cap's, arrived in Huntington, accompanied by Dan Christian. Clark told Cap he would have to stand trial, which was heard by the judge of the Mingo Circuit Court some months later. There is an interesting twist to the story of Cap and Joe's murder trial, which was saved in one of Coleman A. Hatfield's manuscripts.

> When Cap stood his trial, eleven of the jury were in favor of acquitting him because he had been attacked and fired upon first. It was proved that all he did was in self-defense and that the attacks were made by several men who were the aggressors, and began the fight by firing upon him.
>
> There was one old man on the jury who argued that so many men had been killed that he thought the verdict ought to be manslaughter. The other jurors did not want to report they were a "hung jury," so they brought in the verdict of involuntary manslaughter, which carried a light jail sentence. Joe was sent to the reform school at Pruntytown, but Dad went to jail in Williamson.
>
> Now Dad was always a suspicious man, and he heard in some fashion that he would be handed over to the state of Kentucky on the old feud charges because the warrants were still in effect. So after he stayed in jail three months, he decided to escape, which he did on the 30th day of July 1897.[28]

Shortly before the end of that month, Nancy Hatfield visited Cap in jail. He told her to sell some of his land around the mouth of Mate Creek to the newly-created Red Jacket Coal Company. During the same visit, she brought him a drill to bore a hole in the wall of the jail. The land was worth a fortune, but the Hatfields sold it for $500 to finance Cap's escape from jail. Nancy put the money in a basket with clothes and a .44 caliber pistol and waited for Cap the night he escaped along the road below Williamson.

In the meantime, Cap drilled through the wall and ran through Williamson that night. He met Nancy on the road, they said their goodbyes, and he escaped up the side of the mountain, dodging the rattlesnakes that had coiled there. He stayed the following night at George F. Browning's house, because Browning was his cousin, and then went on his way up Rich Creek. Coleman A. Hatfield wrote:

> On Rich Creek, Cap met an old friend named Mounts who agreed to ride in front of Cap to warn him if there was trouble ahead. They agreed Mounts would shoot into the timber like he was shooting at a squirrel as a warning if there was trouble ahead.
>
> Cap and Mounts came upon another acquaintance, who said, "Have you heard the tales?" Mounts said, "What is it, Ike?" "Why," Ike said, "Cap Hatfield broke Williamson jail the other night." Mounts answered, "Oh, it must not be so, Ike." Ike said, "Yes, I'll be darned if he didn't. He just tore it all to hell and throwed himself out the window."
>
> Mounts and Cap then went on, and Cap made his way out of danger, arriving at Anse's home on Beech Creek. From there, he and his two brothers, Troy and Elias went to Williams River in Webster County. Cap stayed in the Yew Pine Mountains there, where in some places it was forty miles from one house to another.[29]

Cap Hatfield In Colorado

Nothing much is known about Cap's days in the Williams River country, but some months after the escape, the Hatfield brothers returned to Main Island Creek, where Cap's wife and children were living near the rest of the family. Troy and Elias Hatfield, then fifteen and seventeen years old, respectively, got in more trouble during a dispute with Dave Kenney, with whom they worked on a timbering job. Cap was indicted again on charges of killing Kenney, but on October 28, 1898, a Logan Grand Jury cleared him of the charge.

In the end, the grand jury's action did not help that much, because charges were filed against Troy and Elias, who thought it was best to escape from the law and go west to Oklahoma. Cap, feeling somewhat responsible for his brothers, agreed to guide them to that state and, again, Cap's family was without a provider for many months. It was during that time that Cap's son, young Shepherd Hatfield, died of malnutrition, one of the saddest casualties of the family troubles.

In the meantime, Cap went with his brothers to Oklahoma first, and then thought it best that he move even further west, to the unsettled country of Colorado. Coleman A. Hatfield wrote that his father started becoming more aware of the wider possibilities of life when he spent many months in Colorado. Cap's grandson thinks it is possible that was the time when Cap began to realize that men could change their lives and that the law was one way for men to control their society, rather than the society controlling individual men.[30] In any event, Coleman A. Hatfield wrote that Cap's time in Colorado was one of the most interesting tales connected with the lives of the Hatfields.

> It was in the heyday of the roaring mining years of the 1890s in Colorado that Cap Hatfield got off the train in the town of Gunnison City. He had already visited Denver, Pueblo, and Leadville and had walked with other train passengers across the mountain of Brisbey's Pass. Along the route he had seen the monuments marking the Continental Divide.
> While in Gunnison City, he visited Aunt Magdalene Smith. That elderly lady answered Cap's knock at her door and said in a kindly way, "What can I do for you, stranger?" Cap replied, "Why, I'm Leland Smith from West Virginia." He later regretted the alias, but did not know if the wanted posters had circulated in the west.[31]

Magdalene Smith told Cap that she was a widow and was living with her daughter and son-in-law, Joe Heiner, the publisher of *The Gunnison City Cricket,* the community's newspaper. Cap then gave the lady a misleading account of his life and times:

> I'm Leland, the only son of Press Smith. My father Press, was a brother to your late husband, David Smith, who was the first clerk of Wayne County, West Virginia. He along with his brothers, Sam and Ben Smith, refused to take the amnesty oath following the Civil War. As you know, Ben went to Texas, Sam stopped in Arkansas, and, of course, your husband, Uncle Dave Smith, came here. They left behind their brothers Presley, John, and Rebel Bill, of Sandy River.[32]

The two spent the afternoon in a long conversation, during which Cap told Magdalene Smith about others in her family back east, claiming that Leland Smith had only two sisters, Eskie, who married Jocko Ellis and Nancy, who married "that rascal Cap Hatfield, who was messed up in the war with the McCoy family." The older lady accepted Cap's tale and told him about the way the family moved from Beaver County, Pennsylvania, where the family patriarch, John Smith, was raised. She also explained how John Smith served in the War of 1812, and then moved down the Ohio River to build his home in Wayne County, where the county seat was called "Fairview" in that age.

In this way, Cap ingratiated himself with Nancy Smith Hatfield's family and became accepted in the Gunnison City community. Joe Heiner, Magdalene Smith's son-in-law, told him much about that community and the state and about the possibilities in the gold mining towns of Colorado. Yet Cap did not become interested in gold mining. Instead, he became a farm hand and made a good living for a spell, as explained by Coleman C. Hatfield.

> Cap moved in with a family whose name has been lost, but who owned a substantial farm near Gunnison, according to unrecorded conversations I had with my father. The family he stayed with was an elderly couple that was childless. Since they were getting on in years, they were having trouble taking care of their farm.
>
> Cap proved himself a good farm hand and stayed out of trouble in the West. Then one evening this couple called him into the house and invited him to stay for dinner. That was an unusual practice at that time and place. Most farm hands stayed in cabins during the night.
>
> But during the course of that meal, the man and wife said, "Mr. Hatfield, we wanted to let you know that we know who you are. The tales of the feud in West Virginia have been reported in newspapers here, but you are not in any danger."
>
> They also told him that they appreciated how hard he had worked for them and then made a very surprising offer. They said they had no one to leave their farm to, but that if he would stay on and take care of their needs, they would leave him the farm. When he thought it was safe, they added, they would send word back to West Virginia so his family could join him, and they could stay there in safety the rest of their lives.
>
> I never knew why Cap did not take them up on that offer. All we know is that he decided to return to West Virginia after a few months. But my father told me that the Colorado couple was very sad when he left, and Cap himself in later years thought he may have made a mistake leaving Gunnison City.[33]

After some months, however, Cap got word that Johnse Hatfield, who had troubles of his own, had been forced to leave West Virginia and was living and working in the state of Washington as a timberman along the Snoqualmie and Snohomish Rivers, which flow together in Snohomish County, Washington.

Johnse Hatfield in the Washington Country

While Cap Hatfield was in Colorado, Johnse Hatfield became concerned that he would be arrested and taken to Kentucky, the constant fear of the Hatfield family. At about the time Cap went to Matewan for the fateful election of 1896, Johnse decided it was time to leave the feud country for a spell. Johnse consulted Anse Hatfield, who told him to go to the area around Spokane, Washington, and contact Sam Vinson, who had moved there after being accused of killing Lon McCoy. Cap told Johnse he also understood that region was good for a man looking for work as a timberman or railroad construction worker.

Soon after Johnse arrived in Spokane, he looked across one street to a saloon that advertised "fine Kentucky whiskey." Acting on the hunch that that he would learn the whereabouts of Vinson, Johnse walked into the saloon which Vinson owned. Vinson found a job for Johnse as a timberman, and Johnse disappeared from history for two years. The hovering detectives, though, had better luck and began trailing Johnse, according to Coleman A. Hatfield.

Nancy Hatfield Phillips — Johnse's first wife — guessed that he had gone to the far west and confided that information to her family. Acting on this clue, Dan Cunningham, Alf Burnett, Treve Brown, Kentucky Bill Napier, and three others set out for Washington in search of Johnse. Old Randal McCoy paid their expenses.

They went to a timbering camp on the Snoqualmie River and gave a description of Johnse. They were told there was a young, blue-eyed, light-haired West Virginian in the area who said his name was Jim Jacobs.

A young woman named Midgie Staunton McCarthy, who had become acquainted with Jacobs, wrote a note and sent it to him by a half-breed Siwash Indian. The note directed the foreman of the logging crew to "tell Jim to look out."

As "Jacobs" looked down the valley one morning, he saw seven detectives coming. He threw down his axe just in time to escape into the timberland where the Siwash guided him to the river. He concealed himself in a thicket and watched his pursuers searching the rocks and caverns in the mountains.

Johnse remarked later, "I never spent such terrible hours as I did watching them hunt for me. A big flock of Canadian birds surrounded the thicket and kept up such a chatter that anybody should have known that they were all het up about something. But the detectives never became suspicious of the birds and searched everywhere but the place where I was hidden."

When Johnse got his chance, he swam across the river and went to Seattle. There he caught a steamer to British Columbia and cut timber there for two years, though the trees were so big timbermen had to build scaffolds up above the roots to get close enough to the trees to chop them down.

The search for Johnse was so hot in Washington that Vinson contacted Hatfield and obtained a lock of his hair, sending it to Louvicey Hatfield with a note that Johnse had been killed in an accident while felling trees.

Yet while the Hatfields in West Virginia feared their oldest son was dead, Cap Hatfield learned differently. Cap learned from his wife that Johnse was someplace in the Northwest. When Cap left Colorado in 1898, he went to Oregon and Washington seeking word of any West Virginia or Kentucky men living there. He learned of one West Virginia timberman in British Columbia and relocated Johnse there. The two returned to Logan County by very different routes. Coleman A. Hatfield wrote about how Johnse's trip to the West ended.

> For two years, the Hatfields believed Johnse was dead. But one clear autumn evening late in the fall of 1898, a well-dressed stranger dismounted at Anse's gate and embraced Louvicey. Johnse had at last returned from the far Northwest.[34]

In the meantime, the era of the feud was passing rapidly — so quickly, in fact, that when another of the younger Hatfields came of age, it was as a highly respected professional doctor and an aspiring politician. He was Henry Drury Hatfield, the son of Elias, the nephew of Anse, and the double first cousin of Cap and Johnse, and he was the Hatfields precursor of the new age on the Tug Fork and Guyandot River.

The New Age Arrives In Logan County

The changes that had first affected Anse Hatfield's life swept over Logan County between 1898, the year James A. Nighbert died, and 1904, the year the Chesapeake and Ohio Railroad finally built its Guyan Valley Extension. To understand the Hatfields from that moment forward, it is necessary to understand how the changes came about in the hill country.

In 1899, the long-awaited development of a railroad between Huntington and Logan Courthouse began. Surprisingly, the line did not begin as a natural expansion of the Chesapeake and Ohio line. Instead, a group of businessmen from Huntington realized they could make a fortune from Logan County coal and created the Guyan Valley Railroad.

Those men, who later created the Dingess Rum Coal Company, underestimated how much money it would take to build the railroad. The line was extended as far as the town of West Hamlin on Guyandot River, but then the money ran out. As the Dingess Rum investors tried to solve their problem, they lucked out. The C&O took notice of the new line, and that firm's directors decided that if anyone should build a railroad to Logan County, that should be the existing railroad company.

In 1900, the C&O bought out the Guyan Valley Railroad. During the next four years, the work proceeded at a steady pace. In the meantime, the Dingess Rum investors bought up most of the land along Logan County's Rum Creek and

Dingess Run. By the time the railroad arrived, Dingess Rum Coal Company was ready to profit from the line.

Also in the meantime, there were other developments in Logan County. As mentioned before, Vicie Straton Nighbert sold her 600,000 acres of Copperas Fork of Island Creek to the creators of Island Creek Coal Company. A group of Pennsylvania coal investors sent an engineer named Harry S. Gay to Logan County. Gay bought a valuable tract of coal land from Moses Mounts and formed the Gay Coal and Coke Company. In that way, the coal leasing and producing companies were in place, waiting the arrival of the railroad.

On the afternoon of September 9, 1904, the first such train pulled into Logan Courthouse, to be greeted by a crowd of admirers who set off fireworks in its honor. *The Huntington Herald-Dispatch* of the following day noted that it would always be considered a "red letter day" in Logan County's history, marking a new era in prosperity.

Such proved to be the case. Between 1904 and 1929, the country town expanded into a fair-sized city. From 400 residents in 1890 it grew to more than 4,000 in 1910. Soon, the city was ringed by coal towns and coal camps on Main Island Creek and Copperas Fork, as well as outlying towns on Rum Creek, Buffalo Creek, Peach Creek, and Crooked Creek. Holden — Island Creek Coal Company's operations center on Copperas Fork — was hailed as a model coal town, with its partisans praising Holden as a vast improvement over the earlier coal towns along New River.

The Logan County coal industry grew at an alarming rate. There were three Logan County coal companies in 1904. By 1914 there were at least forty operating firms and more on the drawing boards. Men were hired as miners and then brought their families to the coalfield from all sections of Europe and the American South. The fairly homogeneous population of 1900 was soon a polyglot of dozens of national groups, many of whom came from the eastern European nations. African-Americans soon made a substantial part of that population.

Socially and culturally, Logan and Mingo Counties changed forever, as did Pike County, Kentucky. The educational system was forced to adapt, and the Boards of Education were challenged to build scores of new wooden frame school houses, where a mere handful had been sufficient for the older culture. Miners' families from diverse backgrounds learned from the natives and taught the mountaineers about their different lifestyles.

Because politics and economics always march hand-in-hand, important new political alliances were formed, as witnessed by the careers of the younger children of Anse Hatfield — Joe, Tennis, and Willis Hatfield. By 1920, the old political ring first created by John William Straton and then greatly strengthened by Henry Clay Ragland and James A. Nighbert was beginning to show its age. By 1930 it was gone. In its place grew a political ring financed by coal company money and headed for a considerable time by Don Chafin, one of the many cousins of Cap Hatfield.

There had been remarkably few "institutions" that normally comprise a society in Logan County in 1900. By 1920, there were four banks. In 1900, the only newspaper was Ragland's *Banner*. In 1902, Ragland retired and his paper was purchased by a group of Republicans. A competing newspaper, *The Logan Democrat* was created and soon brought the first linotype machine to the county. By 1907, a healthy and fierce competition had arisen between the two.

The competition of the two newspapers meant that public relations would become a force in the new Logan County. It was no longer practical or wise for a man to simply tell his friends what he was trying to accomplish. From 1900 forward, one could succeed only if he or she had enough allies with enough influence with the institutions like the newspapers, the coal companies, the school boards, the banks, and, most of all, the courts and other government agencies.

One young Hatfield understood all this.

The Role of Henry D. Hatfield

Henry D. Hatfield's remarkable biography began on September 15, 1875, when he was born at Elias Hatfield's home on Pigeon Creek, then in Logan County and, after 1895, in Mingo County. In 1888, when Henry D. was 13 years old, Elias moved his family to Logan Courthouse and bought a home on Dingess Street, the better to escape the violence of the feud. In his mature years, Henry D. often remembered how his father put him to work planting and harvesting corn on "Hatfield Island" and on the hillside above their home.[35]

Also in 1888, Elias Hatfield further insured Henry D.'s safety by sending his son to Franklin College in New Athens, Ohio, where he was graduated in 1890 at the age of 15. Three years later, Henry D. was graduated from the School of Medicine at the University of Louisville, Kentucky. Later he supplemented his formal education with post-graduate courses at Cornell University, Bethany College, and West Virginia University. He was awarded a medical degree by Bellevue Hospital and Medical College in New York in 1904.[36]

Henry D.'s professional career was an amazingly successful rise to influence. His first job was as a coal company doctor at McDowell County town of Eckman in 1894. His patients there later testified about his devotion to the profession, claiming that he would go out in all types of weather, at any hour, to take care of them.[37] Soon, he was hired by the Norfolk and Western Railway to take care of their emergencies at his office in the new community of Eckman.

When neither the coal companies Hatfield served, nor the railroad would provide hospital care for the increasing number of miners and railroad workers in the southern coalfields, Henry D. began lobbying the state legislature for funds for a new hospital. In 1899, when Henry D. was a young twenty-four years old, the legislature authorized the construction of the first miners' hospital in the state, at Welch. During the twelve years that followed, Henry D. treated some 18,000 patients.[38] That made his reputation secure as a man who cared about the welfare of miners and other workers, a fact of prime importance in his later political career.

In 1910, Henry D. bought part interest in another hospital at Huntington and created still another hospital in Logan in 1917 in partnership with Dr. Sidney B. Lawson. The Hatfield-Lawson Hospital evolved in time to Logan General Hospital, which later was administered by the Logan Medical Foundation in a newer building. All across the coalfield, Henry D. was becoming known as a compassionate man and an able administrator, a fact noted by and used for the benefit of his extended clan. In the words of Coleman C. Hatfield:

> Henry D.'s actions between 1893 and 1913 were as significant to the Hatfield family as anything he did as Governor of the state or as United States Senator in his later years.
>
> He was the first of the family to realize that the new coal and railroad-based economy needed professional workers who understood the traditional mountain culture as well. In this sense, Henry D. was very much a "transitional figure." He knew full well that the hill country people needed doctors, and he built a career around that knowledge.
>
> Yet I do not think it is cynical to say that he was equally aware that a man who served his people as a doctor could become a popular figure and that such popularity could be used for political advantage.
>
> If you think of Anse Hatfield as the last man who used traditional southern West Virginia alliances in a political manner, it makes sense to think of Henry D. Hatfield as the first to use the new realities of politics for his own advantage as well as the advantage of his family.[39]

In that light, Henry D. Hatfield set an example for his family. Younger Hatfields, such as Coleman A. Hatfield, who was fourteen years younger than Henry D., learned that it was as useful to the family to have trained doctors and lawyers as it was to have trained marksmen. If there was a moment when the Hatfields stopped being traditional mountaineers and started becoming men and women of the modern American age, that moment was in 1893, when Henry D. Hatfield graduated from medical school, ironically in Kentucky, where ten years previously the Hatfields had been anathema.

Johnse Hatfield and Rebecca Browning

During the same decade that Cap Hatfield was becoming a better man, thanks in large part to the importance of Nancy Hatfield in his life, Johnse Hatfield also began "settling down" under the influence of his second wife, Rebecca Browning. Coleman A. Hatfield again told that tale.

When Johnse returned from British Columbia felling the big fir and spruce trees of the Pacific Coast country, he found his way into the roughs of Guyan River, a rapid portion of the mountain stream, which lies between Clear Fork and the town of Gilbert.

He took a job cutting the virgin poplars and oak, which grew in the rugged terrain along the stream near Leatherwood Shoals, where cliffs rise in places on either side of the stream to a height of 150 feet or more.

In this picturesque section, near the logging camp, lived land-rich old Chapman Browning. Johnse was a frequent visitor during the weekends to see his daughter, Rebecca. She was the prettiest girl in the roughs of the river.

Johnse began life anew when he met smiling Rebecca Browning with her dark blue eyes and darker hair. Given that pair, you could expect nothing else but an elopement, in part because Johnse thought that old Chapman Browning would not part with his pretty daughter too easily.

After the wedding, though, Chapman came forward with a grant of three hundred acres as a wedding present for his daughter. On that land, Johnse could still swing a woodsman's axe and guide the rafts of great logs down Leatherwood Shoals as they rode the tide of the Guyan to the Ohio.

Yet Johnse did not forget the woman who had helped him escape detectives at the Snoqualmie River. The months sped away and then a little daughter arrived. Johnse was delighted to name her Midgie, in honor of the girl who saved him from Dan Cunningham and the detectives in the Spokane country.[40]

Though there would be troubles later in Johnse's life, and though he would be married two more times, his second marriage brought stability to his life that had been missing in his younger years. In 1898, when he married Rebecca Browning, Johnse was 34 years old. By then his younger brothers, Elias and Troy Hatfield, were growing up and had inherited the family's good looks. In coming years, their dramatic tales would be as important as Johnse and Cap's had been in the 1880s and 1890s.

Anse Hatfield at the Turn of the Century

From his lair at the head of Main Island Creek, Anse Hatfield was aware of the changes that were coming to his community, though he did not concern himself much with the new institutions that were growing up around Logan County.

In 1899, the year that the Guyan Valley Railroad was begun, and also the year that Henry D. Hatfield convinced the state legislature to fund a miners' hospital at Welch, Anse turned 60 years old, an age when younger fires are often exhausted in individuals. Just what Anse thought of the events happening around him has always been something of a mystery, though his great-grandson makes an interesting argument:

> You hear a lot of nonsense bandied about that Anse was some kind of a hermit, living up the head of a holler, unaware of modern times. He was nothing of the sort.
> While it is true Anse was a mountaineer and a man born to a particular tradition, it is not true that he was agog at "modern conveniences." He knew, for instance, that his children and the grandchildren growing up would deal with different conditions than those he faced as a younger man.
> Anse also was not a stupid man. He knew that if the Hatfields expected to thrive, they would have to change as the times changed.
> But one should not go to the other extreme thinking about these matters. Anse remained interested in the same things he always had been interested in. He hunted bears until he was over 75 years old. He kept bees, just as his father, his grandfather, and his great-grandfather had done.[41]

Anse never lost his sense of humor either. As the Coal Age emerged in the southern hills, it became a popular "event" for a young lawyer or politician to show up at Anse's home so they could have the experience of meeting him. The Hatfields tell an uproarious tale about such younger men.

> Anse, as you know, kept bears as pets. When one of these younger lawyer-politicians would come around, Anse would play a game with them. He would tell them that he wasn't feeling too spry that morning, though he intended to chop some firewood. He'd ask if they would be kind enough to go to his woodyard and fetch his axe.
> Such victims would go to the woodyard, happy to oblige, not expecting to run into a bear inside the fence. Anse always got a kick out of seeing how high they would jump over the fence to get away from his pet bears.[42]

Yet as the new age rolled along and as Anse amused himself playing tricks on visitors, Cap Hatfield needed to find a way to cope with the still-dangerous facts of his life. Even after the new age arrived, Cap was a wanted man, as he and Nancy Hatfield realized all too well. One way that they coped with this difficulty demonstrated that Cap may once have been a feudist, but that he could change as the times changed.

The Study of the Law

When history reached the year 1908, Nancy and Cap Hatfield realized they would never be at peace until they found a way to use the new society to their ends, just as thousands of others were doing across the hill country. Howard B. Lee, who interviewed Nancy Hatfield in the 1930s, gave her the credit for the couple's joint decision.

> At the urging of Nancy Elizabeth, Cap decided to study law, and enrolled at the University Law School at Huntingdon, Tennessee. But six months later, a renewal of the feud brought him back to the mountains. He never returned to law school, but continued his legal studies at home, and was admitted to the bar in Wyoming and Mingo counties. However, he never practiced the profession.[43]

Lee was slightly mistaken on that point. The Hatfields recall that Cap did not try many cases, but that he was active in defense of his brother, Willis, who was tried in Wyoming Circuit Court in Pineville, West Virginia, for the murder of Dr. E.O. Thornhill in 1912. Cap also helped his son organize a law firm when Coleman A. Hatfield finished his work at the Law School of West Virginia University.

The true significance of Cap's interest in the law was that he never intended to be a research attorney. Cap knew that a man who understood something about the law would be more valuable to the emerging coalfield society as a law enforcement officer than a man who lacked such training.

When the coalfields of Logan and Mingo developed, there was not a police force like one thinks about them in today's world. Instead, a man who was handy with firearms and his fists could find work as a security guard for coal companies and railroads. Coleman C. Hatfield explained Cap's attitude toward those conditions.

> Cap knew that the hill country was changing from a place of independent farms to a place where money was becoming vastly more important than it had been before. He had a reputation as a man who could take care of himself and who could control others if violence broke out.
>
> His overriding interest — just like everyone else's — was in keeping his wife and children housed, well-fed, with their other needs met, and buying them a good education. The most sensible

way he could do that was to find steady work, since mountain farming was passe in 1910.[44]

It is a little-known fact that Cap was ambidextrous, using his left hand as well as his right. The Hatfields recall that there was more than one occasion in coalfield saloons and in other dangerous situations where Cap was called in to settle the trouble. He would approach troublemakers with his right hand positioned near a holster on his hip. When he got within striking distance, Cap then would punch out the troublemaker with his left fist, thus avoiding the need to use his gun.

Another fact that historians need to face is that the Logan-Mingo-Pike coalfield was not a peaceful place between 1900 and 1960. Cap knew that his reputation as a fearsome man could be helpful stopping violence before it got out of hand. He worked as a deputy sheriff during the teens and twenties as well as a private security guard while his children came of age.

Yet this does not mean that Cap remained the same man he had been as a feudist between 1882 and 1890, when he was eighteen to twenty-six years old. Cap knew that the arrival of the Coal Age in Logan County meant there would be more law and order than there had been in the previous century. His family recalls that he did not relish the memories of the feud violence.

> Cap did not like to be reminded of those days at all. When his stepson, Joe Glenn, came back from reform school, Joe expressed interest in becoming a practicing lawyer, which he did.
>
> Cap was most pleased by that. Joe told my father that Cap told him the days were passing when a man only had his family that he could count on for protection. He said that the courts were becoming more important and that was a good thing.
>
> Joe also told my father that Cap urged him to raise his children to be gentlemen, which was a very important theme in Joe Glenn's life.[45]

Joe Glenn's sons living as this is written attest to that attitude, if not the precise details. Joe Glenn, they state, would not talk about the shooting at Matewan or its attendant events. "He wanted to put that behind him, or to leave it in the past," both Cap Glenn and John Glenn agreed. "He believed that the feud was something best forgotten."[46]

A historian who lacks evidence cannot claim Anse Hatfield thought the same way. But his actions after 1910 indicate that there were aspects of Anse's character that were more peaceful than the lingering reputation of the bloodthirsty feudist. Perhaps Dyke Garrett would have agreed.

[1] *Coleman A. Hatfield Interview*, Coleman C. Hatfield.
[2] *Coleman A. Hatfield Interview*, Coleman C. Hatfield.
[3] *Coleman A. Hatfield Interview*, Coleman C. Hatfield.
[4] *Coleman C. Hatfield Interviews*. Family lore of the descendants of Cap Hatfield claims that Johnse died with his boots on.
[5] *My Appalachia*, Howard B. Lee.
[6] *The Mountain Herald*, Hinton, West Virginia, September 7, 1882.
[7] *Coleman C. Hatfield Interviews*.
[8] *The Hatfields and the McCoys*, Virgil Carrington Jones.
[9] *Coleman C. Hatfield Interviews*.
[10] *Annabel Hatfield Goode Interview*.
[11] *My Appalachia*, Howard B. Lee.
[12] *Coleman C. Hatfield Interviews*.
[13] *The Logan County Banner*, March 28, 1889.
[14] *Cap Hatfield and the Battle of Matewan*, Coleman A. Hatfield.
[15] *Cap Hatfield and the Battle of Matewan*, Coleman A. Hatfield.
[16] *Coleman C. Hatfield Interviews*.
[17] *Cap Hatfield and the Battle of Matewan*, Coleman A. Hatfield.
[18] *Cap Hatfield and the Battle of Matewan*, Coleman A. Hatfield.
[19] *Cap Hatfield and the Battle of Matewan*, Coleman A. Hatfield.
[20] *Interview With Coleman A. Hatfield*, Coleman C. Hatfield.
[21] *Interview With Coleman A. Hatfield*, Coleman C. Hatfield. That insult was the standard way to start a fight with a Republican in southern West Virginia at the time. Apologies are due African Americans for this use of that unacceptable word. It is what the man said.
[22] *Cap Hatfield and the Battle of Matewan*, Coleman A. Hatfield.
[23] *Cap Hatfield and the Battle of Matewan*, Coleman A. Hatfield.
[24] *Coleman C. Hatfield Interview.*
[25] *Interview With Coleman A. Hatfield*, Coleman C. Hatfield. Coleman A. Hatfield was shocked by Joe Glenn's language and told his son he could not understand why the mild-mannered Glenn spoke as he had. "I hate to quote that language to you, Coley," he said. "Joe Glenn was just as good a man as you'd ever meet."
[26] *Cap Hatfield and the Battle of Matewan*, Coleman A. Hatfield.
[27] *Interview With Coleman A. Hatfield*, Coleman C. Hatfield.
[28] *Interview With Coleman A. Hatfield*, Coleman C. Hatfield.
[29] *Cap Hatfield's Jail Break*, Coleman A. Hatfield.
[30] *Coleman C. Hatfield Interviews.*
[31] *Cap Hatfield In Colorado*, Coleman A. Hatfield.
[32] *Cap Hatfield In Colorado*, Coleman A. Hatfield.
[33] *Coleman C. Hatfield Interviews.*
[34] *Johnse Hatfield in the Washington Territory*, Coleman A. Hatfield.
[35] *Coleman C. Hatfield Interviews.*
[36] *The Welch Daily News*, June 3, 1958.
[37] *The Welch Daily News*, June 3, 1958.
[38] *West Virginia: The Mountain State*, Charles H. Ambler and Festus P. Summers.
[39] *Coleman C. Hatfield Interviews.*
[40] *Johnse Hatfield and Rebecca Browning*, Coleman A. Hatfield.
[41] *Coleman C. Hatfield Interviews.*
[42] *Coleman C. Hatfield Interviews.*
[43] *My Appalachia*, Howard B. Lee.
[44] *Coleman C. Hatfield Interviews.*
[45] *Coleman C. Hatfield Interviews.*
[46] *Interview With John and Cap Glenn*. Those two men were the sons of Joe Glenn. John Glenn became an attorney in Logan, West Virginia. Cap Glenn was a retired principal of Logan High School, who has since passed away.

Chapter Nine
THE DEVIL TURNED TO STONE
Anderson Hatfield's Old Age and Death

AS THE YEARS passed by, Anse Hatfield's life became more peaceful each year, a fact that brought him great comfort, though it may have disappointed journalists and pulp fiction writers who believed the feud should have continued because it was such a "colorful" topic. Yet Anse was becoming an old man. In 1909, as his sons Johnse and Cap were settling into married life, Anse celebrated his 70th birthday, an age when even the strongest passions are apt to fade.

Similar changes happened in Pike County, Kentucky. Anse's foe, Randal McCoy, turned 85 in 1910. Though still anguished and bitter about the deaths of his children, Randal became more of a fixture around Pikeville as he managed a ferry on the Big Sandy River. Randal lost an important ally when Perry A. Cline died at age 42 in 1891.[1] During the years that followed, as the industrial age took firmer hold in the Logan-Mingo-Pike region, fewer local men and women wanted to dwell on the troubled years, believing, perhaps, that the time was best forgotten. Randal died in March 1914, the victim of burns suffered when he fell into his fireplace.

Across the region, the so-called "new age" had captured popular imagination. The people of the hill country became as enchanted as other Americans with the possibilities of making money. Coal mines opened by the scores in Logan-Mingo-Pike. Lumber firms prospered cutting wood for mine timbers and other uses. The first oil and gas wells were drilled in the region. In the nearby Kanawha Valley glass-making companies joined older coal, oil, and gas firms around the "C.O.G." city of Charleston, signaling new prosperity. By the time Randal McCoy died, Charleston investors also realized that a third fortune was waiting as the chemical industry took shape.

The political changes of that time were as remarkable as the industrial age. Hill country politics was dominated almost entirely by the family unit structure from the 1860s through the 1890s. Though some writers have argued that the family alliance system was based upon money making as well as blood kinship, there was nevertheless a marked difference in attitudes in Logan-Mingo-Pike after 1900.

New money meant new alliances. A political leader like Anse Hatfield once could have influenced his neighbors by the charm and force of his personality alone. After 1900 political leaders had another useful tool and weapon at hand. In 1905, Don Chafin, a cousin of Cap Hatfield, graduated from the business school at Marshall College — later Marshall University — in Huntington, West

Virginia. Chafin, a shrewd, ambitious, and sometimes violent man, realized that he could build a new political system in Logan County by purchasing the votes of his people. After 1912, when he was first elected sheriff, Chafin held political sway in his county until he was challenged by the younger Hatfield brothers, Joe and Tennis.

Social changes follow economic and political changes like day after night. By 1910, Anse Hatfield's old friend, Dyke Garrett, realized his fondest ambition of building a Christian consciousness in Logan County. In approximately 1893, Garrett convinced the families of Crooked Creek to build the first Church of Christ in Logan County. Soon after, two other new churches were built in Logan Courthouse. Those were the Southern Methodist and the "old church house" at the corner of Cole and Main Streets that was shared by the Baptists and the Church of Christ congregations. Both buildings were financed by James A. Nighbert.

The influence of those three churches was joined by the intellectual force of Henry Clay Ragland's first newspaper, *The Logan County Banner*. Besides arguing for industrial development, Ragland argued for more peaceful ways around the town. By the time Ragland died in the spring of 1911, he had described the type of community he wanted Logan County to become in the pages of his newspaper. Today, more than a century after Ragland's time, his vision still could serve as a blueprint for Logan's future.

The final ten years of Anse Hatfield's life are equally interesting. Journalists and others were endlessly curious about the doings of Anse and his family. As Joe, Tennis, Willis, Elliott R., and Anse's nephew, Henry D. Hatfield, became mature men, there would be much to write about the Hatfields. Some articles were vivid and dramatic. Others were simply interesting. But the Hatfields' story continued to be an American saga long after the feud ended. That point seemed particularly true when Johnse Hatfield became the focus of another tale in 1898, when he was kidnapped by McCoy partisans in Mingo County, an event which Coleman A. Hatfield called the last episode of the feud.

The Last Episode of the Feud

Sixteen years had passed since the death of Ellison Hatfield at the beginning of the feud in August 1882. Yet in 1898 the fury of the McCoys lingered. Coleman A. Hatfield wrote that here and there the echoes of former warfare sometimes rang through the gaps of the hills like shadows of the old grudges. Such was the case, he wrote, when Johnse Hatfield was kidnapped.

> Johnse Hatfield was kidnapped by six men, as he walked along the main line of the Norfolk and Western Railway, just across the river from Kentucky, in July 1898. But readers should remember that the background of the episode was trouble that grew up between Johnse and Humphrey E. Ellis.

Both men had been involved in the development of timber cutting, rafting, and marketing of the hardwood timber which grew along the Guyandot River at the Leatherwood Shoals section east of the town of Gilbert. Naturally, Ellis and Hatfield had become business rivals.

Hatfield and Ock Damron were walking along the railroad on June 18, 1898. As they emerged from a railroad "cut" three men with rifles approached them from the upper end of the opening. At the same time, three more men emerged from a hiding place at the other end of the line. No shots were fired, though Damron was carrying one of Anse's Winchester rifles and Johnse was unarmed. Johnse soon found himself on the Kentucky side of the river.[2]

Later Hatfields believed that Humphrey (Doc) Ellis had organized the ambush because Ellis fired his rifle over his head and shouted with glee when Johnse was across the river. Hatfield was taken to Pikeville and indicted on old feud charges. Johnse later received a change of venue to Floyd County, Kentucky, where he was convicted of murdering the three McCoy brothers who were slain in 1882. He was sentenced to life in the penitentiary in November 1898. Doc Ellis, however, did not remain quiet about his coup, and at least one Hatfield sought revenge.

Ellis returned to his business in the timber area and often boasted triumphantly to his friends that he had been responsible for getting rid of Johnse Hatfield. He stated that he felt no fear and that his money would see him through. He said that he had enough greenbacks to burn a blackjack log five feet in diameter.

Young Elias Hatfield, the fifth son of Anse, had grown to manhood just after the feud days of the 1880s and was employed as a bartender at Skinner's Saloon, just across Tug Fork in Kentucky. Elias was handsome. He had black hair and Scottish blue eyes which looked straight out of his smiling face. And Elias was trouble to those he perceived as enemies.

The 4th day of July 1889 was a big day in Williamson. There was plenty to eat and drink, and there were bands and marching troops as well as the oratory of local political speakers. Doc Ellis was there. He had boarded a train at Iaeger and was riding the crowded train to Williamson, where he was to be one of the masters of ceremonies that day.[3]

There was a place called Gray Yards, some 25 miles east of Williamson, just across the river from Skinner's Saloon in Kentucky. The train carrying Ellis and other passengers stopped at Gray Yards about 11 a.m. July 4, just as Elias

Hatfield crossed the river to go to the post office. The feud was not dead yet. Trouble erupted again.

> Doc Ellis came out on the platform between two passenger coaches and said, "Hello, Elias." Elias replied, "Hello, Doc. Do you think you can take me to Kentucky as easy as you did my brother, Johnse, against my will?" Elias then turned away to talk to I.J. Perrill, who was walking beside the tracks.
> There is some question about what happened next. Some think that Elias added that Ellis was an s.o.b. Whatever was said, other passengers who overheard the exchange said Ellis shouted, "I'll show you who's an s.o.b.!" and raced to the door of the passenger coach, returning with a new Winchester rifle, which he pointed at Elias.
> Like a flash of lightning, Perrill swept his hand forward and pushed young Hatfield backward as Ellis' gun went off. The shot just missed Hatfield's head. Hatfield returned the fire. His shot hit a gold cufflink on Ellis's wrist, but the bullet ricocheted upward and broke Ellis's neck. Ellis fell dying to the train platform.[4]

Elias Hatfield was arrested and tried in Mingo Circuit Court, in Williamson. There were tales that Anse Hatfield intended to gather a band of armed men and ride to the rescue of his son, though nothing of the sort happened. Instead, George Wesley Atkinson arrived in Williamson, accompanied by a man named Boggs, and convinced Elias to surrender. Elias pleaded self-defense at his trial, but no one was certain if the defense was adequate. Fearing for Elias' life, Cap Hatfield intervened, arranging for Elias' escape from jail in August 1899.[5] Coleman A. Hatfield told the remainder of that tale.

> Elias escaped and went with Cap to Oklahoma. On the way, the two decided it was best if they separated. Cap went down through Tennessee along the Tennessee River, and then on through Memphis, down through Texarkana, and on to the Cimmiron River country of Lincoln, Payne, and Pottawommie Counties, Oklahoma.
> While he was there, Cap had another experience that was remarkably similar to the one he had in Colorado. He stopped at a ranch that was owned by Tom and Ellen Harding. He milked cows and worked for them on this ranch. He told them that his name was Glenn.
> But later, when he returned to West Virginia, Cap wrote the Harding couple and told them who he was. They answered his letter, telling him that they had heard two of the Hatfields had

escaped from jail and that they suspected he was Cap Hatfield all along.[6]

No one knew where Elias went. Yet after some time he returned to West Virginia and was convicted of murder. Elias was sent to the state prison, but later paroled by Gov. George W. Atkinson, who earlier, as a lawyer, persuaded Elias to surrender to the authorities. Elias Hatfield did not make any more news until 1911, when he and his brother, Detroit, called "Troy," moved to the Fayette County town of Boomer and opened another saloon. Trouble lurked there as well. That trouble would prove fatal to Elias and Troy.

The Gunfire At Harewood

Elias and Troy Hatfield were the first of their family to fall victims to the increasingly violent world that Southern West Virginia became between the years 1900 and 1920. The younger Hatfields had moved to Boomer, one of the many raw towns that had developed along the Kanawha River as coal mining became more important in the region. Coleman C. Hatfield told how his family always thought of the deaths of Elias and Troy:

> My father did not talk much about that episode, perhaps because he believed it was a matter of shame to the family, or perhaps because he believed it was another topic that was a topic not fit for family conversation.
>
> But the impression that I have gotten by thinking about it in the light of my family's attitudes about those years is that Troy and Elias did not go out looking for trouble the day they were killed. Instead, they only wanted to talk to this man, who eventually killed them, and were caught by surprise when he began shooting at them.
>
> I think if they had meant harm, they would have been more circumspect about the way they approached the man. Certainly both would not have walked into an ambush if they had meant to start trouble.[7]

That background was not apparent in the newspaper accounts of the trouble. For that information, this history relies on *The Fayette Tribune*, which was one of the more balanced coalfield newspapers of that time. An unknown reporter for *The Tribune* wrote as follows:

> A war for supremacy in the saloon business in Falls District (Fayette County) terminated Tuesday morning in the killing of Elias Hatfield, his brother Troy Hatfield, and an Italian named Octavia Gerone.

The Hatfield brothers attacked Gerone in the kitchen of a miner's cabin at Harewood. As it is understood, Gerone had gone there to deliver some beer for his employer, Carl Hanson. The Hatfields were armed with ... pistols and Gerone carried a Colt .32 caliber. How many shots were exchanged is not known. When the firing ceased, Elias Hatfield and the Italian, Gerone, lay dead and Troy Hatfield was prostrate with wounds from which he died within two or three hours.[8]

That newspaper also reported an account of the shooting witnessed by Angelo Valenzalo, the only eyewitness of the incident, who told his tale to Fayette County Assistant Prosecutor Sam Love. The newspaper reported:

According to Valenzalo, Elias Hatfield, at an earlier hour in the day, had attacked Hanson's driver and, after whipping him, sent him down the road.

At about noon, he appeared with his brother Troy, and together they went to Valenzalo's cabin in search of Gerone. They found him in Valenzalo's kitchen.

Gerone opened fire upon Elias and put three bullets in him. Elias then retreated out of the front door and went around the house by the back door, leaving Troy inside. In the meantime, Gerone emptied his revolver into the body of Troy Hatfield.

Troy returned the fire, sending three bullets into [Gerone's] body, [any] one of which would have proved fatal. After being shot, the Italian left the house through the kitchen door and fell on his face in the back yard. After he fell, Elias Hatfield came on the scene, and placing his pistol at the back of the Italian's head, sent a bullet through his brain.

After the shooting, Elias and Troy sat on the back porch and discussed their wounds. They realized that they had been mortally wounded, but discussed the incident calmly and without excitement.

Elias lived about seven or eight minutes. Troy lived for half an hour.

Valenzalo had been put under arrest. Joe Hatfield came on the scene, intent on assaulting Valenzalo, who was presumed to be implicated. Troy Hatfield told his brother that Valenzalo was innocent, that the man who had killed them was dead.[9]

Many years later, Willis Hatfield, Elias and Troy's younger brother, reflected on the killing. "They were money crazy," Willis said. "That's what got them killed."[10] Though true enough, the remark was incomplete because it did not tell the background to the incident. *The Fayette Tribune's* reporter wrote more details.

> According to the story, there had been a bitter rivalry on between the Hatfields and others who ran saloons in that neighborhood. As is known, Elias Hatfield has had the only saloon...between Cannelton and Gauley Bridge, which assured to his place a tremendous business.
>
> Lately, however, a saloon was established across the Kanawha River at Eagle. Another one is in operation across the Kanawha County line, near Cannelton. Both of these saloons have been bidding for the trade where Hatfield had a monopoly.
>
> The proprietor of the Eagle saloon has been maintaining a river ferry between Boomer and the Black Diamond, which has been cutting in on Hatfield's trade. But the opposition that worried most was the Kanawha Saloon, owned by Carl Hanson.
>
> Hanson cut the price on beer from $3 per case of three dozen to $2.25 per case and employed the Italian Gerone to solicit orders and make deliveries....
>
> *The Tribune* informant says that Hatfield has several times put his competitor to rout by forcible means and driven him away by threats and menaces. There being no other motive apparent, it is judged that the Hatfields were after Gerone Tuesday morning for the purpose of setting him back over the Kanawha County line.[11]

Writers of the time were prone to relate every event in the lives of any Hatfield to all other Hatfields. The writer for *The Tribune* was not an exception to that rule. His account of the deaths of Troy and Elias ended with a reminder of Hatfield family history.

> Since they came to Fayette County, the Hatfield boys, four of them, have been employed generally as special officers, guards, railroad detectives, and so on. They are all men of remarkable courage and well-adapted to the work that they cut out for themselves ...
>
> Born of a fighting family, the Hatfields were always counted ready at the drop of a hat ... They are sons of "Devil Anse" Hatfield, whose participation in the feud with the McCoys on the Kentucky border was so well and widely known a generation ago.[12]

Yet one remarkable fact connected with the way the Hatfield family has been treated by historians is that unwary readers often do not realize that the Hatfields changed as individuals between 1882 and 1912, a period of thirty years. Young Elias Hatfield, for instance, was 21 years old when he shot Doc Ellis at Gray Yards. Elias was 33 years old when he was killed with his brother at Boomer. Yet some histories convey the impression that the incidents happened back-to-back, though there is sometimes a vast difference between individuals of those two ages.

Anse Hatfield's Baptism

The persistent idea that the death of Troy and Elias led Anse Hatfield to baptism seems misleading in the light of Coleman A. Hatfield's research and other careful research that shows Anse was baptised some three weeks before his sons were killed. Coleman C. Hatfield recorded his family's recollection of that matter.

> No one who loves his or her children ever fully recovers from such deaths. But the stage play *Hatfields and McCoys* that is performed in the summer in Beckley, West Virginia, did not get the tale exactly correct, when it shows Anse as devastated and seeking the comforts of religion when he learned about the gunfire at Boomer.
>
> Troy and Elias Hatfield were not killed until three weeks after Anse was baptized. So the stage play contains that chronological error. You have to look in another direction to understand what Anse was thinking and feeling when he agreed to be baptized.
>
> My impression is that Anse knew he was getting along in years. He already had lived a Biblical three score and ten. I think his larger concern was that if he intended to make peace with the Lord, the time had come to do so.[13]

As much as a writer may appreciate drama, the Beckley play contains another important error. The play depicts "Preacher Anse" (or "Good Anse") Hatfield as the one who baptized "Devil Anse" in Island Creek. Dyke Garrett, however, is actually the one who performed the baptism, a fact confirmed by a letter from one Lewis Chafin printed in *The Logan Democrat* on October 5, 1911. Many sources identify Dyke as a Baptist preacher, with some adding the adjective "hardshell." That, too, is incorrect. Dyke was a preacher for the Church of Christ, a system of independent community churches that seeks to restore "First Century Christianity."

Mary (Molly) McDonald Justice was a daughter of Scott McDonald of Crooked Creek and a close personal friend of Dyke Garrett. Before she died in February 1971, she left memories of how Dyke Garrett was affected by Anse Hatfield's decision and how proud Dyke was of his actions at that time:

> I can remember it like it happened today. Dyke had a clear voice that carried a long way, and he was a good singer. He was fond of the hymn "Honey in the Rock." There was a large rock on the old river road that ran from Logan Courthouse to Pecks Mill. Dyke would get up on that rock and sing a hymn to let my mother know he would be at our house for supper.
>
> That day he came to supper and said grace for us. Then he turned to me and smiled and said, "Well, Molly, I baptized the Devil today!" Dyke had a wonderful sense of humor and laughed when he said that. And he talked about it until the end of his own life.[14]

Coleman C. Hatfield added pertinent thoughts to that tradition, which do more to explain how Anse's mind was working in 1911. He said that Anse had told Crawford that Hatfields belonged to "the devil's church." But Anse knew that some writers, especially those that interviewed him after 1888, according to Coleman C. Hatfield, took his joke out of context.

> I think one important point at work here is how close Anse and Dyke were as friends. It is true that Anse would go hunt a bear with anybody, but he seemed particularly fond of going hunting with Dyke. Anyone who has had a close friend, who is also a fellow hunter, will understand the respect that develops between such friends.
>
> I think Anse's decision to be baptized was made because Dyke urged it on him. Anse never lost his sense of humor, but he respected Dyke a great deal. And Dyke may well have convinced Anse that he was interested in the welfare of "the Devil's" soul. However it happened, the family tradition is that Anse never regretted his decision.[15]

Historians must note with regret that Coleman A. Hatfield neither wrote an account of Anse's baptism nor left a recollection with his children about that matter. Yet Mary McDonald Justice remembered that Dyke was particularly fond of the Bible verse Acts 2:38, which says, "Peter said unto them, 'Repent, and be baptized every one of you in the name of Jesus Christ for the remission of sins, and ye shall receive the gift of the Holy Ghost.'" She added that Dyke used that scripture at every baptism she ever saw him perform. Coleman C. Hatfield agrees that it would be remarkable if Dyke did not use that text the day he baptized Anse.

The only record of the ceremony is a photograph taken that day that shows Anse's extended family on the banks of Island Creek. Such a large gathering may indicate that the family was pleased that Anse made his decision. Another indication of that attitude is found in the fact that Anse sent Joe Glenn, by then a young attorney, to Pikeville to see if the McCoys would agree to abandon the old feud indictments. Nothing came of that, though Glenn met with Jim McCoy, who assured him that he no longer sought revenge.[16]

Anse's Motion Picture

As the decade between 1910 and 1920 passed by, the tales of Anse Hatfield became more of a stock item in regional newspapers, though there were fewer events to report. One of the most interesting of such stories was that which circulated in *The Hinton Independent Herald, The Raleigh Register, The Fayette Tribune*, and other newspapers in the spring of 1915. That story told of Anse playing himself in a motion picture about the feud. The tale was told again by Coleman A. Hatfield.

> Anse Hatfield was visited by Emmett Dalton of Oklahoma about the year 1914, who had hopes of making a film about the troubles of the 1880s and 1890s. Dalton was the lone survivor of "The Dalton Gang" of Oklahoma, who were involved in a Wild West shootout at Coffeyville, Kansas, in the nineties.
>
> At Dalton's proposal, Hatfield entered into an agreement to reproduce certain scenes and events of the feud along the borderline that had occurred thirty years before that time. The pictures were to be shown, along with scenes of the doings of the Dalton brothers during the time they were active in Oklahoma.
>
> Showing of the pictures looked pretty good financially to the old feud leader and scenes of the feud were exhibited to audiences through southern West Virginia for several months. After the pictures were shown, some of the friends of Anse met him and spoke confidentially with him, manifesting their interest in his part in the picture business.
>
> They said, "Anse, you have a history in the feud story, but both Hatfields and McCoys were never known to molest strangers. We think it is not consistent for you to be identified with any show that tells of those who took advantage of any individual, bank, or railroad company, or robbing money."
>
> Anse looked steadily into the faces of his friends and said, "You know, I never thought of it in that way. I'm right now through with the picture business." And that was the day that Anse quit.[17]

An interesting sidelight to that tale is the question of what happened to the pictures. There are still photographs that show a scene that some feud historians believe is Anse's reenactment of the McCoy brothers' death in 1882. There is also a posed photograph that shows Anse with a rifle in hand, wearing gunbelts. That photograph may date to the time that Dalton's motion picture was made.

There were also stories of the movie told in and around Logan County. One such tale in *The Logan Democrat* of August 12, 1915, claimed that the motion picture was shown in Logan's Star Theater that week. As the movie was shown, Anse and his boys marched in carrying rifles to make sure they were presented respectfully. A similar tale circulated in Pike County about the McCoys doing the same thing.

The significance of such tales is found in the fact that Anse Hatfield was being reinterpreted by the regional press, though much of the information was faulty. As early as August 1895, *The Hinton Independent Herald* reported that Anse planned to move his family to Cabell County.[18] Cap Hatfield began giving interviews to newspapers in following years, notable examples being those printed in Hinton's newspaper on May 26, 1904, and in *The Wyoming Mountaineer* on April 2, 1908.[19] Another newspaper quick to take notice of Hatfield doings was *The Huntington Dispatch*, which reported on March 16, 1905, that Anse had killed "a monster bear" in the hills above Island Creek.[20]

Anse's hometown newspapers were equally quick to print articles about the Hatfields. *The Logan Democrat* of October 9, 1913, contained the improbable (and eventually false) story that Anse planned to open a vaudeville show and tour the nation.[21] All this was very remote from Anse's character. He preferred simply to live out his years in peace, though he welcomed visitors who were not a threat to his or his family's safety.

Instead of seeking limelight, Anse preferred to go about his business of timbering, farming, and hunting when he could get the chance. One great-grandson is fond of telling the stories of how Anse kept bees at his hill country refuge, just as Big Eph Hatfield, Valentine Hatfield, and Eph-of-All Hatfield had done during their times. Beekeeping, Anse believed, was as profitable as it was interesting, since beeswax could be sold in river market towns.[22] That, along with his continued interest in hunting bears, was more typical of Anse's old age than any feud activities.

Anse's Bear Hunting

Anse's bear hunting expeditions became the stuff of legend. During the trial of the peddler murderer, Anse testified that he had killed three bears one winter after he was 65 years old. Attorney John Marcum questioned that point sharply, but Anse invited Marcum to the Hatfield home to inspect the bear hides for himself. Coleman A. Hatfield saved another tale of Anse's keen interest in hunting that persisted into the feudist's old age.

> One November some neighbors had dropped by Anse's home to "set a spell," but there was more going on than talking about the weather. Bear signs had been seen at an old wooden

dam on lower Dempsey Branch, and the evening callers were anxious to tell Anse about that.

One said, "We followed him a long way around the ridge into the hills of Dempsey Branch, but then he turned right around and backtracked hisself to a yellow pine tree just under the top of the hill where he gnawed the bark off one side. It's right there, fresh-gnawed for you to look at."

Old hunter Anse said, "Why, boys, that limb-found bear is startin' to go to the hole, and I'll bet you the ears off my head that he's right in his hole now for the winter. When you see a bear backtrackin' hisself, you can just be sure he's tryin' to throw you off his path.

"Furthermore, I know he's goin' to hole up for the winter because the last thing a bear eats is pine bark so he can get pine tree sap and rosin to make a plug in the lower part of his insides. After he does that, he drinks a lot of water and goes to his hole."[23]

The men agreed to go hunt the bear, which they caught. Three weeks later, Anse told the rest of the tale to his grandchildren, explaining how they jumped the bear before he got to his hole for the winter. Coleman A. Hatfield quoted Anse saying:

All the men were posted along the creek before we jumped the bear. I knowed that the bear would circle in order to try to lose the dogs. That bear struck out around the ridge in a southern direction and crossed Dempsey Branch just below the three forks of the creek, then took to the north hill, all the time battling the dogs.

I come around the upper bench of the mountain as he headed north. After traveling three miles along the upper bench of the mountain, he come down a long 'pint.' You know, when you're followin' a bear that's on the move, he never gets on low ground but keeps close to the top of the hill. When he does come off, he generally follows a high 'pint' where he can get the wind of any men or dogs that are comin' in either direction.

We six followed that bear for eleven days. The trail got so cold that I had to depend on my dog, "Old Brindle Watch." He kept on the trail, and then on the eleventh day when it was spittin' snow, we crossed Rich Creek Mountain and dropped down to the horse road path that goes over to Conley Branch.

That day we found the bear in an old log that had laid there for years. My dogs started whiffling around that log and raising their bristles on their backs like a mad boar hog. The first thing you knew they commenced barkin' into the hole in the end of that log, and I knowed my bear meat was in there.

Me and the boys went right on up as fast as we could, and I looked back in that log about thirty feet. What do you know, I could see that varmint's eyes a-shinin' like two brass buttons. But I didn't want to shoot him in that log.[24]

Anse's four dogs — Old Tiger, Colonel, Bull, and Old Brindle Watch — worried the bear out of the log. Anse fired back of the bear's head and his shot went through the bear's neck. The bear retreated back into his log, but Anse shot twice, killing the "varmint." He said later it was the fattest bear he ever killed.

Such fireside tales remained more typical of Anse's life than any of the newspaper stories that circulated through the hill country during Anse's final ten years. The real family news was being made by the young Hatfields by that time.

Anse Tracks The Peddler's Murderer

Another indication that Anse was becoming as much a man of the bygone era was the tale of the peddler's murderer, which proves that Hatfield did not lose his skill as a woodsman, even in his old age. That also was a tale that indicates that Anse remained a citizen of his community, even though the feud had taken a terrible toll on his life.

In early September 1890, two peddlers called at the gate of David James, who was one of Anse's neighbors. The travelers rested there and ate a good meal, and then went ahead to an abandoned log cabin a half-mile below the James' home. As they passed the cabin, the peddlers heard a voice call out, "Come in. I want to buy a shirt." One salesman turned toward the door, while the other waited beside a chestnut tree.

A shot rang out. The second peddler rushed back to the cabin and found his partner dying with a bullet hole in his back and his head crushed by a heavy stone. James' neighbors, including Anse Hatfield, gathered to see if they could help find the suspected murderer. Tom Chafin told Anse what happened and said if anyone could track the accused killer, Hatfield could. Anse told the crowd to stay ten steps behind him while he tracked the suspect.

The accused killer — whose name has not been saved in the Hatfield records — was arrested shortly afterward and taken to trial before Judge John B. Wilkinson in Logan Circuit Court. Anse's testimony as preserved by his grandson tells the way the accused murderer was tracked down with his help.

> "Well," Anse began, "I was just picking off apples when Greene Meadows came riding up and said, 'Uncle Anse, a man's been killed down the road, and they want you to come help find who done it.'

"I got on my horse and we rode back as soon as possible and found nearly two dozen men and boys there. Nobody seemed to know who done it. It wasn't long 'til I looked over at the foot of the hill and saw what looked like fresh dirt where a body had made a quick step in going up the hill.

"I went up over a steep place and started along the 'pint'. I got down on my knees to look up at the leaves where they had been stepped on, and I laid aside the upper leaves one at a time that had been kicked up a little. The lower leaves next to the ground, where it was solid, showed that somebody had walked on them with big-headed tacks in their boots.

"I picked up one or two of these leaves and went on slow ahead and laid some other leaves away and picked up the damp leaves next to the ground and found where they had also been cut with shoe nails. I kept on following the tracks as I could tell by the leaves which had been cut with nails.

"After a while I reached a hollow beech tree, and I noticed two or three spots on the side of the tree, as if somebody had rested his fingers near a hollow place. The spots looked like a man's fingers with blood on them.

"There were some pieces of dead wood piled up inside the hollow beech, and I took out a jeweler's case that the peddlers carry rings and watches in. I looked at the ground then and saw that the footprints became heavier, leaving deeper marks in the ground, like a bear does when it is running from you. You see, when a bear is running, his front toes cut deeper than when he is just walking on the leaves."[25]

John Marcum, who was the attorney for the defense, objected to Anse's testimony at that point, claiming that a hunting tale had nothing to do with a murder indictment. But Judge Wilkinson said that Anse should continue with his testimony, which Anse did, according to his grandson.

"Yes sir," Anse continued. "I left that beech tree after I handed the boys the jeweler's case, and I went on as I had, following the tracks through the leaves. And I found where some sticks had been stepped on and had been broken fresh, and I knowed I was p'inted in the right direction.

"Then I come to a fence, and it was where no path had been before, and I saw where somebody had put their feet upon the fence rails and climbed over it. The tacks had cut little 'nicky' places on the rails and they were fresh cut, just like a bear's claws.

"After I got over the fence and started around back of the fence through the timber, I saw weeds which had been parted like where somebody walks through. I also got down and picked up more leaves and got some more that were cut with shoe tacks.

"As I was going around a field, I come to some dead logs and noticed somebody had climbed over two or three of these logs because the shoe tacks had scraped them. The other fellers were following me, and I told them to watch for the things that I was finding.

"Pretty soon I come to a rocky branch where there was a flat rock. Somebody had stood on this rock not long before and left white specks on the rock where the shoe nails had made spots. I couldn't tell where they had gone up the hollow or down, so I looked down on some more flat rocks and saw where someone had spit tobacco juice that had spranged down toward the hollow. I knowed he was walking the way he spit.

"I followed on down over the rocks where the branch had run before it went dry, and there was two or three rocks which showed a step on each one which had a nail missing on the bottom of one boot about where the right big toe would be."[26]

Coleman C. Hatfield said his father told him that by that time the judge, the attorneys for prosecution and defense, the jurors, and the spectators present were listening with amazed expressions on their faces, even though Anse was just telling "a hunter's tall tale."[27] Anse's testimony, as recorded by Coleman A. Hatfield, then told the rest of the story.

"I found another track on a rock further down, which showed that one of the nails had been bent down and was cutting the rock with a little sharp groove and not striking on the head of the tack," Anse said.

"After we got back to where the man was killed, just about all of the boys and men in the whole neighborhood were gathered there, and nobody seemed missing. I figured that whoever done this trick was in the crowd, so Uncle Tom Chafin and me had all of them sit down on a long log.

"We walked by and looked at the bottom of their feet as they held them up, and it was Levi who had a nail missing on the sole of his shoe just under the big toe, and it was Jack who had a nail bent down on the toe of his foot where the edge of the nail had cut a long mark on the rock instead of a round mark.

"I should have explained that after finding the footprints on the rocks in the hollow, and before we got out of the woods, we kept on following the trail and the tobacco spit kept p'inting in the direction of the old log house that stood up in the woods and that had the roof nearly all off of it and the rain had beat in. I looked inside the door, and I saw a board from the roof and a piece of board that had been moved."[28]

John Marcum for the defense objected again, asking how Anse knew the board had been moved. Anse replied that the "puncheon" floorboards where the roof boards had lain were a different color from the rest of the puncheon boards. Anse also said he raised the first puncheon board and found two pair of bloody pants, two jackets and two shirts under it. The clothes were entered as evidence.

Defense attorney John Marcum then cross-examined Anse, asking first if he was "Devil Anse" Hatfield. Anse replied, "You don't see any horns on my head, do you?" Marcum repeated the question, and Anse asked, "Aren't you the one they call 'Soda Head' John Marcum?" The lawyer then asked if Anse was the man who led the Hatfields against the McCoys for twenty years. Anse replied, "Yes, but we never killed and robbed one another or beat one another's brains out for money."

Marcum then turned to questions that tried to show Anse was only telling a hunter's story. When those questions led nowhere, Marcum asked the court to send the jury out of the room while he made a motion to exclude Anse's testimony. Coleman A. Hatfield then quoted the court records about how that matter was handled:

> The counsel for the defense said, "Your honor, I want to move the court to strike out the evidence of this witness as being immaterial, irrelevant, and having no bearing on this case. Why, your honor, this witness has gone on the stand and told a bear-hunting story. What has that got to do with this case? How much is this court concerned with whether a bear has five toes or six, or whether he cuts the leaves with his front claws deeper when he's running than when he's walking? The whole of this witnesses' testimony should be stricken out."[29]

The court disagreed, Coleman A. Hatfield wrote:

> Judge Wilkinson said, "This witness has clearly demonstrated that he has a long experience in woodcraft and that he has a keen insight into matters with which we are concerned. Without his experience, as disclosed by this evidence, the state would not have a clue as to the identity of the guilty parties.
> "He has qualified himself as being able not only to follow animals, but to follow human beings by the signs which they leave behind them, the tracks they make over leaves, stones, logs, and fences, and can even tell you the way a man is

traveling by the direction that his spit whizzes. The motion will be overruled, and the bailiff will bring the jury back into court."[30]

Coleman A. Hatfield did not indicate if the accused man was convicted or not. He just wrote the tale to show that Anse had not lost his keen sense of the outdoors, and how those skills could be valuable, even after the times had changed.

The Politics of Henry D. Hatfield

As Anse Hatfield enjoyed his life as a renowned woodsman and "colorful" Logan County "old timer," his nephew, Henry D. Hatfield continued a remarkable rise to power and influence that began in 1910 and did not end until he was defeated by Rush Holt in a reelection bid for United States Senator in 1934. Henry D.'s younger life and his role as a mountain land doctor were explained earlier in this tale.

Yet in Henry D.'s career, a careful reader also can see how the Republican Party was becoming more important to his family, a fact marked by Henry D.'s first vote for President William McKinley in the election of 1896.[31]

Henry D.'s turn to politics was not surprising to those who knew him or who knew the Hatfield family. Though it is true that Henry D.'s first priority was to establish his career as a physician, which he did between 1893 and 1908, he always had the idea in mind that he would win fame, protect his family, and change the state for the better. *The Welch Daily News* of June 3, 1958, told of Hatfield's first political actions, though that newspaper made the common error of thinking Henry D.'s actions were not thought out ahead of time. That newspaper told first of his career in McDowell County politics:

> His first public office in McDowell County was that of Commissioner of the Board of Education in Browns Creek District. It was through his efforts as Commissioner of Education that teachers in McDowell County received what was then one of the highest salaries in the state. Chiefly through his influence, the educational system of the county rose to the front ranks in the state.
>
> After his tenure with the Board of Education, he was elected to the McDowell County Court. Dr. Hatfield instituted a system of working county prisoners on the county roads, thereby giving McDowell County some of the best roads in the state.[32]

West Virginia's county commissions — once called "county courts" — are the most powerful agencies in local government because they control all fiscal matters and because programs mandated by the state and even the federal governments are instituted by the commissions. By serving as a county commissioner in McDowell County, Henry D. was in position to go to a higher office, as he did in the election of 1908, according to that newspaper:

> Dr. Hatfield's entry into state politics was accidental. A candidate for the State Senate on the Republican ticket withdrew shortly before the election of 1908 and Hatfield's name was substituted. He was elected and, three years later, as a result of an historic incident, he emerged as President of the Senate and the leader of his party.
>
> The legislative session of 1911 had a stormy start. An overwhelming Democratic majority had been elected to the house, but the senate was evenly divided with 15 Democrats and 15 Republicans.
>
> However, the election of two of the Republicans was contested and required confirmation by the house before they could be seated. The Democrats were anxious to get the legislature organized, for there were two vacancies from West Virginia in the U.S. Senate and, at that time, the legislature was privileged to elect both senators.[33]

The Republicans of West Virginia knew that the election of the U.S. Senators was a foregone conclusion, but sought to make the best deal they could. Because the president of the state senate succeeds to the governorship if the sitting governor dies, and since Republican Gov. William Glasscock was in poor health, the Republicans argued that it was fitting for a Republican to be next in line. *The Welch Daily News* added:

> The Republicans feared that if the senate met with the house without an agreement on the matter, the house might refuse to confirm the doubtful Republican senators. This would make a Democratic senate president assured by a 15-13 majority. Therefore, the Republican senate members refused to meet and allow organization of the senate until they were promised the senate presidency.
>
> For several days, the legislature had to mark time because it could not begin business until the senate was organized. Finally, Robert F. Kidd, Democratic senator from the tenth district, who was presiding at the organization sessions, issued warrants for the arrest of the Republicans.
>
> But the 15 Republicans took a special train to Cincinnati, where they remained beyond the jurisdiction of the legislature until they received the promise that the Republicans would be

seated and a Republican elected senate president. The presidency fell to Dr. Hatfield when the compromise was effected.[34]

Presidents of the West Virginia Senate have as much power on the state level as county commission presidents have on the local level. In the legislative session of 1911, Henry D. Hatfield exercised his power by naming the chairman of the standing committees, who then determined which bill would receive favorable treatment and which would be defeated in the committees. At the end of the session, the senators bought a silver tray and gave it to Hatfield in tribute to the even-handed manner he used as senate president. That left Henry D. in good position to run for governor in 1912.

To understand that campaign and Henry D.'s career as governor, however, it is important to know more about West Virginia's coal-mining history. The surface events reported by newspapers do not help such understandings. The pain and abuse suffered by West Virginia miners during the years between 1870 and 1912 are poorly understood and often neglected by American historians. While a biography of Anse Hatfield and his family cannot dwell at length on that topic, it should be noted when one studies the role of the Hatfield family in history, particularly during the final years of Anse's life and Henry D.'s rise to fame.

The Hatfields' World and the Miners' Union

Southern West Virginia coalfield historian Jerry Bruce Thomas once wrote that before the industrial age, the borderline country where Mingo and McDowell Counties border Pike County was the scene for families like the Hatfields and McCoys, whose chief concerns were making corn liquor and feuding. Though that is a misunderstanding of the region, it is possible to understand how Thomas reached his conclusion.

Logan-Mingo-Pike was not the home of a large population before mining began there. There were no good schools. There were not many churches. There were few institutions characteristic of a settled area. When the railroads penetrated the region during Coleman A. Hatfield's youth, the region grew at an astounding pace. When the mines opened, the miners were brought to the region. And with mines and miners came the great struggle for control of wealth. Thomas had meaningful words to write about that era:

> The rapid rise of the West Virginia coalfields in the nineties proved disruptive to an already troubled industry. With the supply of coal constantly outstripping demand, miners' organizations and operators elsewhere sought to cooperate in stabilizing the bituminous industry, but West Virginia operators refused to participate in interstate wage agreements, which they believed destructive to their interests. The United Mine Workers resolute efforts to bring West Virginia into the interstate system

and the equally determined resistance of the Mountain State operators resulted in protracted disputes which embittered labor-management relations for decades.[35]

Thomas wrote that there were almost no union-organizing drives in West Virginia before the 1890s, though Thomas Nelson Page claimed that the alleged "Mollie McGuires" of the northeastern Pennsylvania anthracite coalfield made an attempt to enter West Virginia. The Knights of Labor had a few local chapters in the hill country before the organization of the United Mine Workers of America on January 23, 1890.

The UMWA had a good beginning, but the depression that began in 1893 wrecked any chances for labor-management agreement in the Central Competitive Field of western Pennsylvania, Indiana, Ohio, and Illinois. National miners' wages fell 23 percent in three years, setting off the strike of 1894, the first that affected southern West Virginia. Coal operators in the nonunion fields of Virginia and West Virginia were not affected, and coal from those regions forced the end of the strike, but convinced UMWA leaders that a southern field organizing drive was needed.

The union's strike of 1895 was caused in part by the failure of efforts in 1894, but another factor at work was the collapse of the N&W Railroad, which had overextended its finances building the Ohio Extension. In that unusual strike, the mine operators encouraged the miners to quit work as the operators sought to force the railroad to keep a guaranteed high price of coal shipped to Tidewater, Virginia.

The operators and the railroad came to terms later in the spring of 1895, but the miners remained on strike, despite pleas from operators to Gov. William MacCorkle to send troops into the coalfields to maintain order, which MacCorkle refused to do. The strike eventually was broken as the operators brought in replacement workers of the type that embittered miners labeled "scabs."

The battle was fought again in 1897 when the UMWA workers struck the Central Competitive Field in an effort to keep wages from falling any lower. Again, the strike failed because enough coal from the southern fields met the demand of consumers.

The following year, representatives from management and the union met in Chicago to extend their working agreement into the coalfields of the Midwest. In the wake of that meeting, UMWA Vice President John Mitchell — "Johnny da Mitch" — rose to fame, taking on the effort of organizing West Virginia. Though his first effort failed, Mitchell became more prominent in the autumn of 1898, when UMWA President Michael Ratchford resigned and Mitchell became the union's new leader.

Also in 1898, at a meeting in Pittsburgh, mine operators of the Central Competitive Field told Mitchell and other union leaders that they would cooperate with the union only if the workers succeeded in organizing West Virginia. To West Virginia coal operators, this was a red flag. They argued that

Central Competitive Field operators meant to destroy the West Virginia industry, convincing many state politicians that the "Pennsylvania conspiracy" was also a threat to the prosperity of the state. Thus the stage was set for the strike of 1902.

Though 1902 marked the first time the federal government under President Theodore Roosevelt acted as a mediator between labor and capital in the coalfields, that strike was the UMWA's third great failure because West Virginia continued to produce coal. Despite the end of the strike, however, New River miners remained off work until February 25, 1903, when U.S. Deputy Marshall Dan Cunningham led an eighty-man force against strikers at Stanaford in Raleigh County, crushing the last resistance of the strikers.

Cunningham appeared earlier in this tale as one of the many detectives who stalked the Hatfields during the feud years. His role as a deputy marshall is another reflection of the fact that many men were turning to law enforcement as a livelihood as the coal industry developed in the hills. However important Cunningham's career was at that point, there are more significant ideas connected to the recurring strikes.

One aftermath to the strike of 1902 was the creation of private security companies that served the interests of the coal operators. New River and Pocahontas field operators began thinking they could not count on the state government to use its force to control miners. That belief led directly to the organization of the Baldwin-Felts Detective Agency under Thomas L. Felts, whose war against the union miners contributed to the troubles in McDowell, Mingo, and Logan Counties during the final ten years of Anse Hatfield's life. That firm also caused much grief in the Kanawha coalfield just before and during the administration of Gov. Henry D. Hatfield.

West Virginia thus became virtually a closed field to UMWA organizers, especially after 1907, when in a federal court case in northern West Virginia known as *Hitchman Coal and Coke Company v. Mitchell, et al.*, the court banned union organizers from approaching miners. The Hitchman ruling was still in effect in 1912, when Henry D. Hatfield was elected governor, facing the worst coalfield violence before the 1920s in the Paint and Cabin Creek strike of 1912-13. The history of the coalfields thus gave a sharp edge to the conclusion reached by Jerry Bruce Thomas:

> The struggle between the UMWA and West Virginia coal operators from 1894 to 1910 shaped the attitudes of a generation on both sides. For decades, uncompromising hostility characterized the relationship. Labor-management embroglios in the Mountain State coalfields became notoriously brutal affairs, as the coal operators' truculent attitudes and the mine guards' arrogance were met by the miners with armed violence. The effect of such a strained atmosphere on the area's development can only be surmised, but little economic or sociological sophistication is required to suggest that it was pernicious.[36]

Henry D. Hatfield and the Kanawha Strike

For all the troubles the miners had experienced between 1894 and 1910, there were some gains recorded. In the strike of 1902, for example, some of the Kanawha County coal operators signed union contracts that were still in force in 1912. Yet other sections of that county, Paint Creek and Cabin Creek in particular, remained nonunion. In 1912, the union miners were still anxious to bring fellow workers into the general system that held sway in the Central Competitive Field.

In May 1912, many Paint and Cabin Creek miners went on strike and were promptly evicted from their company-owned houses, a move which forced the miners to take refuge in hideous tent colonies. Strikebreakers were soon imported, and gunfire became common in the hills above the two creeks. As such gunfire erupted, some of the Kanawha County coal executives and "law" enforcement officials decided that enough was enough for them. They organized a train, known to history as the infamous "Bull Moose Special," filled it with armed mine guards and shot up the tent colonies, killing at least one striking miner.

In the rage that followed, Governor William Glasscock — bitterly denounced by the famous labor organizer Mary Harris (Mother) Jones — was powerless. Clearly, a change was needed. Equally clearly, a more humane individual was needed at the head of state government. Henry D. Hatfield seized the opportunity to run for governor, was elected in 1912, and began a healing process that made the opening days of his administration justly considered in some ways one of the most far-sighted administrations of America's progressive era.

Hatfield's first goal was to bring peace to the Paint and Cabin Creek area. He was inaugurated on March 4, 1913. The next day, packing only his doctor's bag, Hatfield began his famous journey by train to the coalfield. West Virginia historian John Alexander Williams wrote that this was symbolic because Hatfield "wanted to heal in both the literal and figurative senses of the word."[37]

Hatfield spent two days on the creeks, ministering to the ailing "Mother" Jones and talking to the miners. He promised he would settle the strike in a way that was fair to both sides. When he returned from the strike zone, Hatfield called Kanawha coal operators in for conferences. A few weeks later, he announced a framework to settle the strike. The miners believed the so-called "Hatfield agreement" was too one-sided because the operators lost little under its terms. Yet eventually the strike was settled on Hatfield's terms, though he displayed a regrettable temper in shutting down *The Labor Argus*, a pro-labor newspaper printed in Huntington.

With the strike behind him, Hatfield then turned his attention to the long-term health care issues that he believed were in West Virginia's best interests. John G. Morgan, biographer of the state's governors, wrote that Hatfield's pioneer efforts establishing the nation's first workers' compensation program, was Hatfield's finest hour. Coleman C. Hatfield agreed:

> When I was a youngster in the mid-1930s, Henry D. spent part of his time as a doctor in the Hatfield-Lawson Hospital, as Logan General Hospital still was known at that time.
>
> He said he was always proudest of the Workman's Compensation Act, which was passed early in his administration. He said that he had seen too many cases in the Welch hospital of miners, railroad workers, and others fearfully injured at work without any hope of providing for their families.
>
> Henry D. also said that the law he and his allies drafted was considered a model for the nation, and all the governors of the states wanted a copy of it to write similar legislation in their sections of the country.[38]

Under Hatfield's administration, the state also created the state health department, hygienic laboratory, public service commission, labor bureau, state road bureau, and "Blue Sky Department" to enforce a speculative security act. Another achievement was the primary election law, which ended the nominating conventions of bygone days.[39]

Hatfield's administration ended in the spring of 1917. By that time, it was apparent to far-sighted observers that the United States would become involved in the First World War. Hatfield entered the army as a physician and served until the end of the war in November 1918. Feeling the need to work at his profession, Hatfield was politically inactive for the following ten years, returning to public life during the election of 1928.

That year, Hatfield defeated Matthew M. Neely for the United States Senate and served one term in Washington as a confidant of President Herbert Hoover. The great depression that began in the fall of 1929, the coming of President Franklin D. Roosevelt, and Hatfield's opposition to the New Deal ended his political career in Washington, although he remained an elder statesman for West Virginia's Republican Party until his death at home in Huntington on October 23, 1962.[40]

The Gunfire At Mullens

Yet as Henry D. Hatfield labored to bring order and reason to the state and its coalfields, other Hatfields made other news, some of which recalled the violence of the feud era. The authors of *West Virginia USA* who interviewed Willis Hatfield in the mid-1970s described Hatfield as a tall, white-haired, and charming man with a twinkle in his eyes. That description was accurate, just as the added information that Willis had never lost his "appreciation for the ladies."[41] Yet there was also a violent episode in Willis' life, one that he regretted very much in his later years. It was an episode that recalled the violence of the feud era, but also showed that the industrial age was even more violent. *The Fayette Tribune* reported the story on January 4, 1912, just after Henry D. Hatfield announced his intentions to run for governor.

> Willis Hatfield of Herberton emptied all six chambers of his pistol into the body of Dr. E.O. Thornhill at Mullens Sunday afternoon, killing him instantly.
>
> Hatfield had been drinking during the day, and his supply of whiskey ran down. He went to Dr. Thornhill and asked him to give him a prescription for some whiskey so that he could procure it at a drug store.
>
> Seeing that he did not need it for medical purposes, Dr. Thornhill declined his request.
>
> Thereupon Hatfield began cursing and abusing Thornhill and the latter, offended, slapped him in the face. This enraged Hatfield so greatly that he drew his six-shooter and emptied its contents into the body of the physician.
>
> Dr. Thornhill died instantly.
>
> Hatfield was immediately arrested and taken to jail at Pineville, the county seat of Wyoming County. The officer was accompanied by four men to make sure that Hatfield did not escape.
>
> Dr. Thornhill was a young man of great popularity in the neighborhood. He was the physician for the Ritter Lumber Company at Maben. A brother of his, Dr. R.T. Thornhill, is the physician for the Tams Colliery on Winding Gulf. Their home was formerly in Appomattox County, Virginia.
>
> Willis Hatfield is a brother of Elias and Troy Hatfield, who were recently killed in a pistol duel at Boomer. He has been connected with the saloon at Herberton for two years, where he made his home. His wife and baby are living there.[42]

Other family members, such as Cap Hatfield, were trying to escape their violent past, fearing that new arrests would be planned, fearing also that they would not be able to live down the troubles of the eighties. Yet Cap, who had become a lawyer, rallied to Willis' defense. Cap sought temporary admission to the Bar in Wyoming County and helped defend Willis in the only known court case of Cap's life. Coleman C. Hatfield saved the memory of that time.

> Cap thought that Willis had brought on unnecessary trouble for the rest of the family, but Willis was, after all, Cap's brother. Cap did what he could to keep Willis out of prison, but the facts were pretty well known.

That was something else my father was not fond of talking about very much. Willis killed Dr. Thornhill just as Henry D. Hatfield was beginning his campaign for governor. My father had much respect and affection for Henry D. and did not like to talk about facts that embarrassed his cousin.

I think my father believed that Willis got off with a lighter sentence than he deserved, given the facts. But to my knowledge, my father never talked with Cap Hatfield about the trial or anything else connected with that episode.[43]

The known facts of Willis Hatfield's trial were reported, again most notably by *The Fayette Tribune*, whose editors showed a remarkable willingness to avoid making editorial comments about such developments. That report claimed:

After some deliberation, the jury in the case of State vs. Willis Hatfield, charged with killing Dr. Thornhill at Mullens, returned a verdict of voluntary manslaughter. Judge Miller sentenced Hatfield to serve four years in the penitentiary.

The trial was started at Pineville Friday morning, and it required until Saturday afternoon to complete the testimony. During all of the time that it progressed, the courthouse was crowded with spectators.

The arguments consumed about three hours, the principal speeches being made by Hon. John McGrath of Mercer County for the State, and Hon C.W. Osenton of Fayette County for the defense. Cap Hatfield, brother of the prisoner, made a speech of a half-hour's duration, in which he pled for the life of his brother.

The jury returned its verdict at an early hour Sunday morning.

In many respects, the trial was one of the most sensational and spectacular that has ever been witnessed in the state. All of the Hatfields, including "Devil Anse" were there.

"Devil Anse," the father of the boys, was present, and with rifle lying on his knees, sat in a commanding position throughout the trial. All of the Hatfields were said to have been heavily armed, as were most of the others who were interested in the trial.

Even the innocent bystanders are said to have had their shooting-irons where they could readily lay their hands on them.[44]

Willis served his four years peacefully and returned home. He lived the rest of his life in a private manner, taking little part in the political activities of his more famous brothers, Tennis and Joe Hatfield, who soon were in the midst of Logan County's notorious political and economic life, which took national attention again during the mine war of 1919 through 1921.

War Along the Ridges

The younger generation of Hatfields and Chafins and other mountaineer families had come into their own during the First World War, while Henry D. Hatfield was away in the Army. Among such younger mountaineers were Sid Hatfield of Matewan and Don Chafin of Logan. The two may have been distant blood kin. They may not have been related. But in the changing nature of the Logan-Mingo-Pike general area, it would be hard to find two more dissimilar men.

Sid Hatfield was gregarious and happy-go-lucky. No one would claim he was an angel, and he may not even have been a Hatfield. There are doubts about just whom Sid Hatfield's biological parents were. What was beyond doubt was that this Hatfield was a popular man with miners and their families who had gathered in and around the neighboring towns of Red Jacket and Matewan, Cap Hatfield's old stomping grounds.

Part of Sid Hatfield's popularity was his personal charm. He was jug-eared and jaunty, and his willingness to flash a grin that was enhanced by the gold fillings in his teeth gave him the nickname "Smiling Sid." The other reason for Hatfield's popularity was his politics. Sid defended the interests of the miners. In some ways this made him a forerunner of the politicians who thrived in the region after the New Deal of the 1930s. Yet in 1920, his brand of politics was practically unheard of in the region.

Don Chafin was the other extreme. A cousin of Louvicey Chafin Hatfield, Anse's wife, Don Chafin had come to power because he promised the Logan County Coal Operators Association that he could keep the United Mine Workers of America out of Logan County. He was as good as his word. The union made very little headway in that county between 1912 and 1928, when Chafin's power was at its zenith.

Chafin used a variety of methods to rise to power. He convinced miners that he could rid Logan County of the hated Baldwin-Felts detectives. This allowed him to win his first term as sheriff in the election of 1912. Chafin kept that promise. He ran the Baldwin-Felts out of Logan County, but then replaced them with his own force of deputies, loyal only to Chafin's access to money.

The usefulness to history of the biographies of Sid Hatfield and Don Chafin lies in the fact that the two men personified the explosion that was waiting just over the rim of history at the end of the world war. Men would shoot each other in the coalfields because of what they believed about Hatfield and Chafin. And in such feelings also lay the seeds of the mine war that began in 1919 at Matewan.

When the world war ended in November 1918, the coalfields had been quiet for nearly two years. This was because the federal government had established a working agreement with coal operators and miners to support the nation while the war lasted. Few if any miners wanted to tell Uncle Sam where to go. The result was that coal company profits soared while wages remained fixed. At the end of the war, the miners wanted their loyalty rewarded with pay raises. This they did not get. So the strike began in the spring of 1919.

The strike went on and on. Spring, summer, fall, and winter passed until the spring of 1920 arrived. The Red Jacket Coal Company wanted rid of the striking miners so replacement workers or "scabs" could begin mining coal again. They called on the Baldwin-Felts to evict miners from company-owned houses at the town of Matewan. The detectives did their work in summary fashion and returned to Matewan to wait a train back to their base in the city of Bluefield. History had reached Wednesday, May 19, 1920, the day of the Matewan Massacre.

Matewan Police Chief Sid Hatfield approached the detectives and asked what authority they had in his town. He told them he had a warrant for their arrest. Al Felts replied that he had a warrant of his own for Sid's arrest. No one is very sure who fired the first shot, but seconds later Matewan Mayor C.C. Testerman lay dying with a bullet wound in his stomach and Al Felts was dead with a bullet in his head. Before the massacre was over just minutes later, ten men were dead. The list included detectives Al Felts, Lee Felts, A.J. Boorher, C.B. Cunningham, J.W. Ferguson, Troy Higgins, and an unidentified Baldwin-Felts agent. The other dead men were miners Bob Mullins and Tot Tinsley, and C.C. Testerman.

Many miners were jubilant. Someone had faced down the mine guards. A year passed. The strike wore its way to an end with the miners no better off in May 1921 than they had been the previous year. Sid Hatfield was tried for the murder of the detectives, but then cleared of the charge. Don Chafin had tightened his grip on Logan County. Tom Felts, head of the detective agency, was still bitter about the death of his brothers. Sid Hatfield was indicted in McDowell County on charges of shooting up the coal town of Mohawk and was to go on trial in Welch on August 1, 1921. But Hatfield would not live to go to trial.

The courthouse at Welch sits high on a knoll overlooking the town's main street. There is a sharp turn in the stone stairway that leads up to the courthouse, and there is a steep rise up to the courthouse door. A man walking up the stairs could not see another man positioned there to tell if he was armed. As Sid Hatfield and fellow defendant Ed Chambers walked up the stairs that morning, they saw a crowd of men that included C.E. Lively. Hatfield reached out his hand and said, "Hello, boys." Those were his last words.

Lively and a rough dozen Baldwin-Felts agents shot him dead.[45]

In the month that followed, at least two thousand miners gathered in and around the Kanawha County town of Marmet with the avowed purpose of marching southwest through Boone County to Logan and Mingo Counties to organize the coalfields, hang Don Chafin, and avenge Sid Hatfield and Ed Chambers. The armed march in southern West Virginia that followed has been called the greatest armed insurrection in United States history between 1865 and 1932.

The march failed its purpose. Don Chafin organized a defensive force that occupied the Logan County hills from Blair Mountain on the county's northeastern border to Crooked Creek on its southeastern border. Men on both sides died there, fighting for what they believed was right. The United States Army was called in at the frantic request of Governor Ephraim Morgan to halt further bloodshed. The union movement in southern West Virginia was shattered and did not recover until the New Deal of the 1930s.

Yet perhaps the most important result as far as the Hatfield family was concerned was that Don Chafin would never hold public office in Logan County again. Though Chafin remained a political force, he was detested by many miners. This fact gave the Hatfield brothers Joe and Tennis their chance to wreck Chafin's political machine, which they did in short order. In that way, the Hatfields recovered much of the political power that they had lost after Henry D. Hatfield left the state to go to the army during the world war.

The City in the Coalfield

By 1919, the year that Anse Hatfield became eighty years old, Tennis and Joe Hatfield were thinking about political careers, Cap had become a lawyer, Johnse was living a very private life, and Anse's brothers and sisters had become elderly men and women.

The community had changed as well. Between 1910 and 1920, Logan County had undergone a hothouse growth, propelled by the growing fortunes of the coal companies, if not the miners. The change of the buildings in the city of Logan were a good indication of what was happening.

In 1912, there was a disastrous fire in the city that was sparked in the trash bin behind one of the stores on the south side of Main Street. The high winds blowing that night carried the flames over to the courthouse, which was destroyed that night, taking some records with it, though not all legal papers. A new courthouse was built in short order, and the new building that stood between 1912 and 1964 became a symbol of the new city.

Gradually, the older frame buildings of Logan were replaced by brick structures. The first churches of the town — one used jointly by the Church of Christ and the Baptists, and the other that belonged to the Methodist congregation — were replaced by new brick or stone buildings. Specialty stores opened for business. Supply houses were needed by the growing mining industry. The older, rather quaint newspapers were replaced by more modern-appearing publications which also were housed in new brick buildings.

In March 1928, an unknown photographer crossed the river to the hillside site of Hatfield-Lawson Hospital and took a famous photograph of the city. Instead of the rustic village that Anse Hatfield had known in his youth, there was an impressive-appearing city, which thought it was destined to become the growing center of the regional coal industry.

History proved that was a mistaken assumption. The mine wars of 1912 and 1921 may have been an apparent victory for the coal operators, but the bitterness lingered. In time, the continued battles of miners and coal company owners would undercut the power of both sides, leaving the energy market to the petroleum industry that first took root in Britain, the Netherlands, and the United States, and then became a global concern.

In a similar way, the railroads that appeared so important to the region during the youth of Coleman A. Hatfield lost their hold on the United States after 1908, when the first Model T Ford automobiles began chugging along the highways. Autos quickly became so important that West Virginia politicians like Henry D. Hatfield became enthusiastic backers of the so-called "Good Roads Movement" which sought to replace West Virginia's primitive roads with modern highways that would link all the county seats.

The First World War brought other social changes. At least fifty men named Hatfield entered the armed service in 1917 and 1918. A popular song written a few years after the war told how hard it was to keep younger men content with the lifestyle that had developed in the hill country after they had served in the war. In many ways, the First World War was the precursor to the Second World War, which intensified American social mobility, though of course that experience did not happen during the lifetime of Anse Hatfield.

Anse died just as radio was entering its infancy in the United States. Yet the national communications revolution that began with improving newspapers and magazines at the start of the Civil War was already making its power felt in the hill country when Anse died. Within a few years, for example, Scott McDonald, who was born the same year as Anse's brother, Elias Hatfield, was enjoying the humor of radio comedians whose broadcasts were conveyed to Logan County by radio stations in Charleston.

Electricity, auto transportation, radio communication — all made the feud seem very distant. As Cap Hatfield, Jim McCoy, and the other younger men who had fought the feud became older men, the mountaineer lifestyle was lost in time.

Perhaps that was just as well. The new age was no more peaceful than the older time, but its positive benefits made the thought of a mountain feud ludicrous. If the violence of the 1880s was characterized by the image of a small band of mountaineers armed with single-shot weapons approaching an enemy's home by stealth at midnight, violence of the 1920s seemed characterized by inner-city hoodlums driving by speakeasies, shooting up such places with machine guns. That was a different world. One has the thought that Anse Hatfield was not overly impressed with the changes.

And so the old age passed. From the later perspective, West Virginia's history seems to tell the tale of how a mountain farm became a timber camp, which became a coal camp, which became a chemical plant, which is yet to become something new. In a similar way, American itself changed from a dense forest to a rural landscape to a Civil War battlefield to an industrial colossus to a communications empire and so on to the unknown. Anse Hatfield died in the middle of powerful changes.

The Death of Anse Hatfield

As the bitter year 1921 began in Mingo County, and as tensions spiraled again in the coalfields, Anse Hatfield's life came to a quiet end. The irony of that fact should not have been lost on anyone, though it seems to have been on the editors of *The Logan Banner*. The world that Anse lived in was in a turmoil, and there was so much hatred loose in the coal towns that the newspaper paid scant attention to the passing of the region's most legendary figure, one whom many once considered the devil incarnate, and one whom many once thought of as the most dangerous and violent man of his era. The obituary printed in *The Logan Banner*, which follows, was almost understated.

> Anderson Hatfield was buried Sunday. He had been ill for several months, but his health was of such a state that nearly everyone thought that he would live to pass through the coming year. Therefore his death came as a surprise to this community.
>
> He was 81 years old last September. Anderson Hatfield was born on Mate Creek of this county. He was a soldier in the Confederate Army, being a captain of Company A, 45th Virginia Infantry. After the war he was the leader of the Hatfield clan during the world-famous Hatfield-McCoy Feud. This feud lasted 15 years, and 35 men and one woman were killed as direct result of it. The killing of Ellison Hatfield, brother to Anderson Hatfield, was the cause of the feud between the Hatfields and the McCoys.[46]

Showing a better sense of history, *The New York Times* printed a longer obituary, one that summarized the events of the feud and seemed to make the point that Anse's passing ended the older era in Appalachia. During the years that followed, this sense doubled as many writers wrote interpretations of the feud, all which sought to define Anse's character. Yet it would take time — decades, in fact — before that complex man would be described as an individual in history, rather than the hoofed and horned "devil" of popular imagination.

Cap Hatfield's branch of Anse's extended family believes that Anse would have liked to be remembered as a great hunter and a man who cared for and protected his family. There is rather more realism in their attitude than there is in the many paragraphs written to describe Anse as the personification of a mountain feud.

For all that, however, one poet may have been closer to the meaning of Anse's life than his biographers. Stephen Vincent Benet wrote such a telling passage about the men and women of the hills in his epic poem about the American Civil War, *John Brown's Body*. He wrote that when the last moonshiner bought a radio and the last "wild rabbit of a girl" bought a mail-order dress, the spirit of the older and wilder American would be lost forever.

Historians who look at the photographs of the somber Hatfields gathered around Anse's coffin or the thousands of mourners who met that day might have had the same feeling. When Anse was laid to rest on his hillside, his children, their children, and then the successive generations of Hatfields would never know the freedom that Anse had known. The only remembrance of the era would be the feelings of those who stood at his graveyard statue watching the autumn leaves dancing in the wind.

---

[1] Feud: Hatfields, McCoys and Social Change in Appalachia 1860-1900, Altina L. Waller.
[2] The Last Episode of the Terrible Feud, Coleman A. Hatfield.
[3] The Last Episode of the Terrible Feud, Coleman A. Hatfield.
[4] The Last Episode of the Terrible Feud, Coleman A. Hatfield.
[5] Coleman C. Hatfield Interviews.
[6] Coleman A. Hatfield Interview, Coleman C. Hatfield.
[7] Coleman C. Hatfield Interviews.
[8] The Fayette Tribune, October 19, 1911. The actual shooting happened on Tuesday, October 17, 1911.
[9] The Fayette Tribune, October 19, 1911.
[10] Willis Hatfield Interview.
[11] The Fayette Tribune, October 19, 1911.
[12] The Fayette Tribune, October 19, 1911.
[13] Coleman C. Hatfield Interviews.
[14] Conversation with Mary McDonald Justice. A writer should be honest with his readers. I do not have a tape recording of this matter. The conversation took place when I was about sixteen years old. But this is how I remember it now. Perhaps my memory is faulty. Perhaps my memory is too good and I have improved this somewhat. But it is an essential truth.
[15] Coleman C. Hatfield Interviews.
[16] The Hatfields and the McCoys, Otis K. Rice.
[17] Anse Hatfield's Reputation, Coleman A. Hatfield.
[18] The Hinton Independent Herald, August 22, 1895.
[19] The Hinton Independent Herald, May 26, 1904. The Wyoming Mountaineer, April 2, 1908.
[20] The Huntington Dispatch, March 16, 1905.
[21] The Logan Democrat, October 9, 1913.
[22] Coleman C. Hatfield Interviews.
[23] Bear Caught In A Log, Coleman A. Hatfield.
[24] Bear Caught In A Log, Coleman A. Hatfield.
[25] Anse Tracks The Peddler's Murderer, Coleman A. Hatfield.
[26] Anse Tracks The Peddler's Murderer, Coleman A. Hatfield.
[27] Coleman C. Hatfield Interviews.
[28] Anse Tracks The Peddler's Murderer, Coleman A. Hatfield.
[29] Anse Tracks The Peddler's Murderer, Coleman A. Hatfield.
[30] Anse Tracks The Peddler's Murderer, Coleman A. Hatfield.
[31] The Welch Daily News, June 3, 1958.
[32] The Welch Daily News, June 3, 1958.
[33] The Welch Daily News, June 3, 1958.
[34] The Welch Daily News, June 3, 1958.
[35] Coal Country, Jerry Bruce Thomas.
[36] Coal Country, Jerry Bruce Thomas.
[37] West Virginia: A Bicentennial History, John Alexander Williams.
[38] Coleman C. Hatfield Interviews.
[39] West Virginia Governors 1863-1980, John G. Morgan.
[40] West Virginia Governors 1863-1980, John G. Morgan.
[41] West Virginia USA, Jerry Wayne Ash, Stratton L. Douthat, Bill Kuykendall, and Harry Seawell.
[42] The Fayette Tribune, January 4, 1912.
[43] Coleman C. Hatfield Interviews.
[44] The Fayette Tribune, March 14, 1912. The trial began Friday, March 8, 1912, and ended Sunday, March 10, 1912.
[45] Thunder In The Mountains, Lon Savage.
[46] The Logan Banner, January 14, 1921.

Epilogue
THE DEVIL'S HISTORIAN
The Lifework of Coleman A. Hatfield

ON JANUARY 12, 1912, three months after Dyke Garrett baptized Anse Hatfield in the waters of Main Island Creek, a fire burned the courthouse in the city of Logan. The following year, a new stone structure was built which became the symbol of the law in the county. Fifty-three years later, in the spring of 1965, after the rebuilt courthouse had outlived its usefulness, a new courthouse was constructed and Coleman A. Hatfield was asked to say a prayer at the dedication ceremony. In his prayer, Hatfield asked his Lord to continue to dispense justice among men.

There were few events in the long life of Coleman A. Hatfield that were more symbolic. He came of age just about the time that Anse was baptized and the courthouse was rebuilt. His life was centered around his deep religious faith and his belief in the law as a force for good. His eighty-one years spanned the era when the reputation of his family changed from being roughnecks to being civilized and humane men and women. More than any other Hatfield of his time, Coleman A. represented those values.

Coleman A.'s life also continued and expanded a subtle process that began when Henry D. Hatfield, his cousin, fourteen years older, decided to become an educated and professional doctor. Coleman A. chose the law for his profession because it provided a good life, but also because it reflected his love of education that had been instilled by his parents.

In one of his manuscripts of Hatfield family history Coleman A. wrote that the Hatfields needed time, education, and the effects of the religious spirit to move the family from the days of the feud to the peaceful days of his own old age. Nothing could be a better description of the work he did to understand the family in history.

For these reasons, it is important to understand his life.

The Childhood of Coleman A. Hatfield

Coleman A. Hatfield began telling the tale of his own life to his son, Coleman C. Hatfield, one evening in the late 1950s. He began the account in a manner easy to understand: "I was born about a mile above Thacker, West Virginia, or about five miles above Matewan, at the mouth of Grapevine Creek, on Tug Fork on February 25 in the year 1889."[1]

Though Coleman A. did not mention the fact in that interview, he could have told his son that the year of that birth was the worst year to be born in the

Hatfield family. The unrelenting pressure from the government of Kentucky, the activities of the men Coleman A. contemptuously called "mail order detectives," the very real threat of the long-dreaded McCoy "invasion" of West Virginia, and the fears that haunted Nancy Smith Hatfield should have made Coleman A.'s childhood a nightmare.

Curiously, the realities of 1889 did not scar him for life. Though it is true that children are more resilient that they often are given credit for being, Coleman A. recorded memories fifty years later that showed he was quite aware of what was happening around him, but that he developed an abiding respect for his land and curiosity about the industrial events of the Tug Valley. The point should be recalled that he had an "eidetic" memory that retained a lasting impression of such events.

Those who want to understand Coleman A.'s childhood also are referred to the most famous photograph of his family, the one that shows the Hatfields sitting or standing in three rows, with nearly all of them holding a rifle or another weapon. Coleman can be seen holding a pistol between his brother Shepherd and sister Levicy (or Pinkie), with a child's serious expression. Though one should not judge too much from a single photograph, that seriousness seemed to become an abiding part of his personality.

In common with many people, Coleman's life should be studied in relation to its major events. His first fourteen years must be understood in the light of the terrible pressure brought to bear on Cap and Nancy Hatfield. Then Cap Hatfield sent his son to Concord Normal School, later renamed Concord College, in Athens, Mercer County, West Virginia, to obtain a good education.

Cap Hatfield was on the run during the years, 1889 to 1903. The fact should be remembered that his second son, Shepherd Hatfield, died at that time, a victim of malnutrition. Later in his life, Coleman A. recalled that sad time during a conversation with his son.

> In February 1897, the last day of February, I believe it was, we moved from the mouth of Grapevine Creek on Tug Fork, across to Island Creek. My earliest recollections are on the head of Island Creek, where we lived in a little log house that was known as the old George Steele place.
>
> And we lived there while my father was on the run out in Oklahoma that time he helped Elias escape from jail. He came home at the end of October 1898, but my brother had died while he was gone.
>
> Shephard had mastoid trouble. He was two years younger than I was. And I am convinced now that he was undernourished because we were poor. We did not have enough to eat, and I am convinced more than anything else that he died of malnutrition and undernourishment and privation, such as we suffered in those terribly hard days. I was nine when my little brother died.

He was buried up at the old cemetery where his grandfather, Anse, is now buried.[2]

Naturally, a child such as Coleman A. Hatfield would have an incomplete understanding of what was happening. He learned the importance of silence, of course. But he also learned to cope with events as they happened. There is another tale from his childhood. Though its significance may be minor, since it is only the tale of a small boy, the story does indicate how quickly Coleman A. needed to start growing up.

Nearly all hill country families of the nineties had cooking implements called "gritters." It was not practical to make frequent trips to a corn grist mill, such as Pecks Mill eight miles down the river from Logan Courthouse. So families fashioned a "gritter" from a strip of tin, driving a nail through one side to make many jagged holes on the reverse. The tin strip was mounted on a board with supporting strips under the outer edges of the tin.

With that implement, corn was "gritted" off the cobs after it had been boiled until it was soft. A type of corn bread could then be made in a skillet with buttermilk and grease for seasoning. As often as not, that was the only food Cap and Nancy's children would have for days at a time. Coleman A. recalled many years later that, "We used to think we were poor with nothing but hot, brown, crusty cornbread baked in the skillet and then buttered up and eaten with sweet milk."[3]

Like Joe Glenn, who wanted his sons to be somewhat sheltered from the realities of the 1890s, Coleman A. wanted his four children to know that life could be sweeter than growing up in the midst of violence. Though he did not fill in many painful details of the feud years for his children, a reasonably intelligent person can figure it out.

Coleman A. spent much of his childhood keeping a mountain farm, just as had Cap, Anse, Big Eph, Valentine, and Eph-of-All Hatfield. That was a terrible burden for a child. It is difficult to imagine a nine-year-old boy plowing, sowing, and caring for crops in the hot summers of the nineties, and then facing the chores of harvesting the crop in the autumn. Though he no doubt had help, that was a rough way to grow up. The fact that only meager education was at hand did not help.

Education in the Logan-Mingo-Pike region was not much to brag about between 1889 and 1903. The schools were still the pioneer one-room log structures that later writers have romanticized. Though one could become aware of literature, basic math, and the rough outline of United States history in such mountain schools, the idea of a well-rounded education was quite unknown.

Many teachers were idealistic, but it was common enough for "educators" to be the same type as old Charlie Carpenter, who did so much to get the feud started in 1882. There were as many untrained or merely partly trained instructors as there were scholars. Even with that, Coleman A. Hatfield's early education was limited, as he explained to his son.

> I was thinking just the other day about the years that I missed schooling. I went two months when I was five. And the next year I went to a full term of school. The next year I missed. The next year I went some to school. The next year I missed. And it was that way up until I was about fourteen. Then I went up to Concord. But I didn't have any training in anything much except reading and spelling.[4]

Stated a different way, Coleman A. had one full year and a few scattered months in school between 1894 and 1903. A liberal education may have seemed to him something for people in other sections of the world.

Another powerful influence on youngsters is the adults and older children whom they know and admire. Those adults who influenced Coleman A. in his childhood were a powerful collection of individuals, but historians have to wonder just how he was inspired to study law later in his life.

The dominant figures in his childhood were, of course, his parents, Cap and Nancy. Others were his Hatfield grandparents, Anse and Louvicey. A sensible way to understand who else mattered to young Coleman A. is the list of those who appeared in the famous photograph of the armed clan that was taken at a logging camp on Beech Creek.

In the first row of that photograph we see Tennis, Midge, and Willis Hatfield. (Midge was the daughter of Johnse and Rebecca Browning Hatfield.) In the second row there is Mary (with infant daughter Vicie) Anse, Louvicey, Nancy (with Bob), Louise, Cap, Shepherd, Coleman, Levicie (Pinkie), and a man named Borden, who arranged for the photograph to be taken. In the third row there is Rose, Troy, Elizabeth, and Elias Hatfield, Tom Chafin, Joe Hatfield, and Ock Damron.

In that group, the only fully adult Hatfields are Anse, Vicie, Nancy, and Cap. It is safe to think Tom Chafin, Ock Damron, and Borden had little influence. Troy, Elias, and Joe Hatfield were beginning to grow up, but they were still adolescents.

When the photograph was taken in 1897, Cap Hatfield, at age 33, was not yet the man he would become when he had more education, though he was interested in seeing to it that his children were educated. Cap would become the most important figure in his son's life, and Coleman A. would spend years understanding Cap's role in the feud and in the development of the Hatfield family.

Young Coleman A. could have learned from Anse such practical matters as how to handle livestock, horses, and guns. Anse was 58 years old in 1897. Yet the fact that Anse loved his offspring does not cancel the fact that Anse was not the type of man from whom a boy could learn to be a lawyer or a schoolteacher. That simply was not Anse's character, though there are many of Anse's other attributes Coleman could and did admire.

Writers cannot assume that Louvicey Hatfield had no effect on young Coleman, but historians simply do not know the nature of that relationship. Louvicey would have been described in the 1950s as a housekeeper. Later day feminists may interpret that as a slur, but it is not meant to be an insult. The fact is that she was concerned with providing food and shelter for her family, which is something at which no one should sneeze. But she was not a model for Coleman A.'s life.

That leaves Nancy and Cap as the persons most likely to have encouraged Coleman's ambitions to become an educated gentleman. He may have learned from them that a man who knew "book learning," especially the law, stood a better chance of influencing his society than a man lacking such knowledge.

Though Coleman's immediate chances for education were slim, that could change quickly if the family moved from danger to a more secure position. One fact to Cap's credit is that in 1902 he made just such a move. Coleman C. Hatfield explained the circumstances.

> It was in 1900, I believe, that Cap took his first steps to improve his family's safety when he was free of the troubles that began with that Matewan shooting affair in 1896.
>
> There is a small town just across the border between Virginia and West Virginia called War Eagle. Cap moved Nancy and his children there and opened a saloon. They were free of the immediate dangers from Kentucky, and I am not sure that very many people knew they had moved there.
>
> But for some years, Cap was able to make a living for them in a more settled manner. It was at that time as well that he took the law course that we have discussed, so that when he moved back to Logan County some years later, he was a more respected figure.[5]

Another development during those years was that the coal industry had fully developed in Logan County. It was becoming apparent to the young Coleman A. Hatfield that coal would be the future, rather than timbering or associated activities.

Yet before leaving the subject of Coleman A.'s childhood, the role of another important person in his young life should be explained. Joe Glenn, his half-brother, friend, and ally throughout Coleman's life had been sent to the reformatory at Pruntytown after the shooting at Matewan in 1896, the year that Coleman A. was seven years old.

Though that was a fact that later Glenns need not feel ashamed, Pruntytown had a remarkable effect on Joe Glenn. When he returned to Logan County some four years later, he was a more sober and serious man. Coleman C. Hatfield and others recall that it was Joe Glenn who gave Coleman A. the first Bible that he ever owned.

Glenn also told Coleman A. about his Pruntytown experiences, warning him of the importance of living a respectable life to avoid such consequences. Glenn himself set about getting more education and also eventually became a respected and noted attorney. Thus Coleman A.'s life was already improving by 1903, the year Cap decided to send him to Concord Normal School.

Coleman A. Hatfield's Education

Coleman A. Hatfield was fully aware of the difficulties he would face getting a formal education. Those problems involved money and his inadequate experience in what today would be called a grade school education. Many years later, he told his son, "I had not advanced any beyond reading, spelling, addition, multiplication, division, and subtraction."[6] Hatfield's first challenge when he went to Concord Normal School was to discover what higher education was.

The question naturally arises about why Coleman A. chose Concord for his education. An immediate answer is that it was the best education available that he could afford. A more detailed examination of the type of education he sought is needed, however, because it sheds further light on the type of individual Hatfield became later in his life.

Concord was an institution called at that time a "state normal school." In his ground-breaking study, *A History of Education in West Virginia*, Charles H. Ambler described the background of such schools and why they were important to youngsters like Hatfield. He wrote that the schools were the product of the fertile imagination of Thomas Jefferson.

> Since colonial times, the need for better teachers for Virginia youth was a matter of concern to her leaders. Influenced by their experiences, Thomas Jefferson's proposal for the establishment of public free schools emphasized the need for trained "masters."[7]

The Virginia General Assembly acted on that idea and even the communities in the western section of the state that became West Virginia in 1863 acted vigorously to establish such institutions. Mercer County was not as quick as some other sections to act on that matter, but by 1872, the town of Athens was ready to support higher education.

Ambler wrote that the establishment of Concord Normal School was the result of local politics in Mercer County. Princeton was the county seat on May 1, 1862, when Confederate troops under Colonel W.H. Jenifer burned the courthouse to prevent supplies from falling into the hands of a Union Army.

There was little need for a courthouse until 1865, but the court was reestablished by Judge Nathaniel Harrison that year. He called court into session in Princeton, but quickly moved it to Concord Church, as Athens was known then, because Princeton was hostile to Union sympathizers like Harrison. In 1870, Harrison resigned to avoid impeachment charges being considered by the House of Delegates, then controlled by Democrats. Ambler wrote of the events that followed that decision.

> With this turn of events, relocation of the county seat was again taken up. By resort to a "masterpiece of political strategy," by which the voting strength of the northern portion of the county was reduced in 1871 by the formation of Summers County, supporters of the Princeton location were able to turn the decision in their favor. Accordingly, the county court, after ten years, erected a courthouse on the present site.
>
> The quickened hopes and ambitions of Concord were not, however, to be thus thwarted. It, too, had friends, and their day under the new state government was at hand. Taking advantage of these facts, Major Wm. M. Reynolds, Mercer County delegate in the state legislature, presented to that body a petition from residents of Concord Church, asking that a branch of the State Normal School be located there, and on February 28, 1872, the legislature passed, "An act to locate a Branch State Normal School at Concord, in the County of Mercer."[8]

There was considerable give and take about the way the new normal school would be funded and administered, as was quite common during those years. Yet by the end of the 1870s, Concord was as ready as any other institution of education in the state for the era Charles H. Ambler called "the transition," which took place between 1880 and 1909, or the era when Coleman A. Hatfield attended Concord.

Unfortunately, Ambler's book did not include a detailed account of what was happening at Concord during those years. He did, however, write of the general trends in higher education. It is relatively safe to think that Hatfield's education was influenced by those trends.

Ambler wrote that there were differences between those who believed in strong executive control of the schools and those who believed in faculty control of the institutions. This contention retarded progress at those institutions. He added that despite those facts there was "a large degree of individual worth and earnestness of purpose" as faculty members began to appreciate scholarship and good teaching, while administrators began to help evolve workable systems for the various schools.

There were, as always, conservative elements in the state who did not trust free thinking, but such voices were countered by those who understood that human curiosity is not repellant. "On the other hand," Ambler wrote, "thanks largely to the printing press and the Chautauqua, the plain folk were beginning to entertain more liberal views than they cared, and in some cases dared, to express." Added to this was the fact that West Virginia was becoming somewhat wealthier and hence, more open to "outside" influences.[9]

If these ideas are accepted as a realistic view of what was happening in West Virginia's system of higher education, it is easier to understand the type of man Coleman A. Hatfield became. Though his religion was then, and remained to be, a vital part of his character, he followed the ways first explored by Henry D. Hatfield and became the second of his family to analyze and use the new society that had taken shape in the state and the Logan-Pike-Mingo region. His son had important ideas about Coleman A.'s mind.

> My father achieved what we think of today as a liberal education. He began to learn and appreciate such abstract ideas as history, literature, and elocution at Concord, believing knowledge of those ideas was essential to a teacher.
>
> Concord did much for him. He had not had the opportunity for much education in his childhood, but Concord introduced him to the wider world of ideas. One of the characteristics of his later life, which I feel sure came from his experiences at Concord, was that life should be enhanced by as much education as someone could absorb.[10]

Thus educated, Coleman A. Hatfield was ready for the challenges which lay ahead — including practical experience in teaching, then his days as a Chautauqua speaker, and then on to Law School at West Virginia University.

Coleman A. had entered Concord as a youngster of 14 years in 1903. His first formal education ended in 1909, when he was 20 years old. In the meantime, he had married his college sweetheart, Mossie Caldwell, on May 12, 1907. He had done so well as a student that he was offered a job as a teacher by Mercer County's Rock District School Board, a job which he kept until January 1917, when he resigned to go to work for a Chautauqua company.

Before leaving the story of Coleman A. Hatfield in Mercer County, however, there are two other tales that told of Coleman's memories of Anse Hatfield. Anse traveled there to see how Coleman A. was getting along. Anse met Coleman A. with several of the grandson's friends and chatted for some time. Anse had a letter with him, but was unable to read. He asked Coleman A. to read it for him. But, seeking to avoid embarrassing the younger man, he asked Coleman A. to read it to him because he had forgotten his spectacles at home.[11]

On another occasion, Anse is thought to have heard from some acquaintance that one "Mooney" Hatfield was being hazed by other youngsters at Concord. Anse went to Mercer County to find out about the matter and sufficiently impressed the people living there that they should leave Hatfields alone.

Shortly after that, Coleman A. began his work with a Chautauqua company, which were firms that hired speakers and entertainers to travel throughout the nation, bringing some sense of a larger world to isolated communities. A biographical sketch of Coleman A.'s life written for *The Logan Banner* preserved some details of that experience.

> In January 1917, he signed a contract with the Lyceum Bureau of America under whose auspicies he lectured fifteen months, traversing seventeen different states. He was at first attached to the Colt Lyceum Bureau and Colt-Aber Circuit of Cleveland, but was later transferred to the Mutual Bureau of Chicago, and then with the Dixie Lyceum Bureau of Dallas, Texas.[12]

Coleman A.'s son adds more details to that sketchy picture of what happened, indicating that his father was trying to explain the meaning of the feud, even before Coleman A. started the detailed research that became his main effort in that direction. Coleman C. Hatfield recalled:

> Father was trying to give people in other sections of the country a better idea of what people of the Tug Fork and Guyandot Valleys were like. He knew that hill country people were more complex than they had been depicted before 1917, and he wanted others to understand our history.
>
> But I think he was frustrated in that effort. The Chautauqua companies billed him as one of those "awful" Hatfields who had fought the feud, and the companies tended to emphasize that connection, rather than the more serious presentation that he wanted to give the audiences. That is why he gave up that work.
>
> I have the feeling that his Chautauqua days were rather like the experiences of Sitting Bull, the Sioux warrior. Do you know that story?
>
> Well, Sitting Bull was hired by the Chautauqua people to give lectures on the Indians, though he spoke only the Sioux language. As he gave serious speeches on the plight of the Indian nations, a translator was standing by who gave a lurid account of the battle of Little Big Horn, when General George A. Custer and his men were killed.
>
> I think my father believed he was treated the same way. He wasn't interested in titilating people. He wanted to teach them the deeper meaning of the feud, but he was disappointed in the end.[13]

After his fifteen months on the road, Coleman A. returned home to Logan County and became employment manager and real estate agent for the Main Island Creek Coal Company. Those were the days between the end of the First World War and the Mine War of 1921. Though that was good work, Hatfield still longed for more education and was admitted to the law school at West Virginia University in 1921.[14]

Coleman A. had chosen to study law at a most interesting time. Anse Hatfield, his grandfather, had passed away in January of that same year, perhaps indicating to Coleman A. that a new age had arrived. That summer, the Mine War was fought in the hills that surrounded the Logan County towns of Blair, Clothier, and Hughey (which served the mining camps along Peach Creek and Crooked Creek).

Part of Hatfield's reason for seeking admission to the WVU Law School may have been that he thought his community needed lawyers as much as it did doctors, miners, coal company officials, and schoolteachers. Doubtless another reason for the decision was personal finances.

Even at that date, law schools were expensive, and it is not likely that Coleman A. could have paid his way through the WVU program, if he had not had the help of his wife, Mossie Caldwell Hatfield, who generously agreed to teach school until Coleman A. obtained his law degree. That was a fact Coleman A. acknowledged in later interviews with his son.[15]

Another reason Coleman A.'s timing was interesting was that the university law school was being reorganized at the time, in keeping with the era of transition described by Charles H. Ambler. The key figure in the change of that school seems to be H.C. Jones of George Washington University, who became dean of the law school on July 1, 1914. That was the year the program was admitted to the Association of American Law Colleges. Ambler wrote of the changes that affected the school just before Hatfield was enrolled:

> The period from 1909 to 1914 witnessed important changes in the law curriculum. Beginning in 1909-10, the course leading to the B.L. degree was reduced to three years, which might consist either of one year of academic work and two years of law or of three years of law alone. The standard course was, however, three years. If a student elected to attain the degree by offering one year of academic work and two of law, he might attain the M.L. degree by the successful completion of the third year in law.[16]

There are no records to indicate which option Coleman A. Hatfield chose, which is an annoying omission from his biography. There is the possibility that he chose to do one year of academic work because of the stiff requirements for admission to the law that the university required at that time, according to Ambler's history.

> Fifteen units of preparatory work were required for admission to the college, but students who lacked only one hour of the necessary preparation might be admitted conditionally.

> Beginning in 1912, nothing was said in the catalogue about admissions to the state bar through examinations conducted by the College of Law, but the practice was resumed in 1913 under an order of the state supreme court of appeals. In 1912 the requirements for the LL.B. degree, beginning June 1, 1913, were fixed at one year of 38 hours in the College of Arts and Sciences and three years, or a total of 96 hours, in the College of Law. Moot court, revived in 1913-14, was supplemental to the regular course work.[17]

From that history, it is clear that Coleman A. had given himself another tough row to hoe. On September 1, 1921, about the time Coleman A. went to Morgantown, Dean H.C. Jones resigned from the college and was replaced by Dr. J.W. Madden of Ohio State University. Madden did much to raise the reputation of the college, according to Ambler, and he was the guiding light of the program while Hatfield was enrolled there.

There is a rather touching story connected with Coleman A.'s years at West Virginia University that also involves Dr. Madden. On one occasion, the professor asked Hatfield to remain after class. Feeling some dread that he may be asked to leave law school, Coleman A. waited while other students left.

Dr. Madden then asked Coleman A. if Mossie Hatfield was his wife, and if she was a teacher in the school system that served Morgantown, to which Hatfield replied that she was. Dr. Madden then threw his arms around him and told him the Maddens did not know how they would ever repay the Hatfields. Dr. Madden's son had trouble learning to read, though the child had been tested and had no discernable learning disability. It seemed that somehow Mossie Hatfield had gotten through to the boy and taught him how to read, much to their relief.

Coleman A. finished his work and won his LL.B. degree in 1924, just before the requirement for admission to the law college was raised from one to two years of preliminary instruction. Then Hatfield returned to Logan County once again, just in time for the angry election of 1924, in which he played a minor role, as the Republican Party won control of the county for the first time in many years, an event caused in no little part by his uncles, Tennis and Joe Hatfield.

Lawyer In Logan County

The time when Coleman A. Hatfield returned to Logan County as a young lawyer was a most interesting time, and it is useful to look at the community from the eyes of newcomers at that time to understand what it was like.

In the summer of 1923, a young man named Pierce Lee Johnston moved to the city of Logan to find a new home and better work. Like J. Cary Alderson, who had arrived about thirty years before that time, Johnston was a keen observer and left memories about Logan County. During the forty years that followed his arrival, Logan became the best place to live it ever would be — and the worst it ever was. More than anything else, it was vital and busy. "Oh man, it was working alive," Johnston recalled:

> They were running buses up all these hollers, and the buses would be full all the time. The mines were working. And downtown it would be crowded on a payday. I've seen it so crowded that you couldn't get up and down the sidewalk at all. On payday night and especially on weekends — Friday and Saturday evenings — you couldn't get up and down that street.[18]

Of course, that "Kingdom of Logan County" was no paradise. The community was undercut with bitterness resulting from the attempts of the coal miners to win decent pay and safety conditions, and the coal operators' intransigent resolve to keep the United Mine Workers out of the field. For all that, the mining companies and the people were in a generally optimistic mood about the future of their community. In this active and industrious place, newcomers found a way to live.

The town those men and women saw was far different from the collection of wooden buildings of the 1900s. It had become a place of stone and brick. Instead of the town of 1902, with its square brick courthouse, old frame churches and wooden jail and schoolhouses, Logan in the 1920s had brick-paved streets, a stone courthouse with a high dome, and a new Logan High School building made of bricks and situated in east end. If in the early 1900s there was a small bar association of lawyers who decided the legal problems of the community by informal discussions in the brick courthouse, by the late 1920s there were fifteen different law firms practicing in the circuit court, and there was a city manager government for the city.

There were 52 coal companies working at least 160 mines by the end of the decade. Buffalo Creek and Main Island Creek were dotted with mines that had names like Berkeley, Phillips, Daisy, Avis, Donald, Wilson and Josephine. The mines of the Gay, Amherst, and Island Creek Coal Companies were pouring out thousands of tons of coal. Work was progressing on highways to keep the county businessmen in touch with their customers. Mary Hurst wrote that the first graded road was built in 1921, and by 1928 hard-surfaced roads had brought the cities within one hundred minutes of each other.

Life had expanded in the county seat, as well. By the end of the 1920s there were automobile dealers, dry good and grocery stores, restaurants, a soft drink plant, barber shops, music stores, bakeries, drug stores, insurance agencies, public utilities, shoe stores, pool rooms, home appliance stores, medical specialists, banks, and scores of other concerns. Logan was as varied as any other city of its size during that time.

It also is true that Logan County politics have received most of the attention that the community got through the years. Johnston was certainly aware of that fact when he moved to town in 1923. Yet with his talent for practical construction work and partly because of his political outlook, Johnston had little trouble in Logan.

> I was walking up the street one morning and someone hollered over at me, "Hello, Johnston. I know you!" But I didn't think he knew me from a soldier. That was Don Chafin. Now he has an awful name, but he wasn't half as bad as people let on like he was.
> He was the sheriff when I came here. I'd bet a dollar that he gave away a million dollars in cash right here in Logan. Just hand it to fellows wanting money. He never turned them down. Some few would pay it back.
> One time a fellow handed him maybe ten or twenty dollars and said, "Here, Don. Here's what I owe you." And Don said, "Do you owe me?" The fellow said, "Yeah, I owe you. You take it." And Don took it and thanked him. He was thataway.[19]

There are, of course, those who think that Chafin had one of the most baleful influences on Logan County's development. Miners loyal to the United Mine Workers of America, for example, think Chafin was a brutal and calloused man. Be that as it may, Chafin was in his heyday in the late 1920s, and it was his politics that gave Logan County its popular reputation.

It is important, therefore, to understand the community on that basis. But it was also more complex than many realize. To understand what Logan County became after the Great Depression of the 1930s, one must know it as it was just after the Mine War. The best place to begin is in the pages of *The Logan Banner*, which had become a very different newspaper than Henry Clay Ragland's older paper, *The Logan County Banner*. And that newspaper soon had an interesting tale to tell concerning the Chafins and the Hatfields.

One of the mysteries of Logan County history is whether or not Don Chafin had any actual involvement with the Blue Goose — the place at Barnabus to buy liquor during the prohibition years. Chafin himself denied the allegation, though he was convicted of that charge in the U.S. District Court for West Virginia before Judge George W. McClintic. The conviction was based on information supplied the court by Tennis Hatfield, who admitted being part-owner of the saloon.

Despite the later decision to grant parole to Chafin, it was important news in Logan County in October 1924 that Chafin had been found guilty of that charge. On October 17, 1924, *The Banner* reported that Chafin had been sentenced to a two-year term in the Atlanta Federal Prison and was fined $10,000. The newspaper added that this was the maximum penalty provided under law. Chafin appealed the conviction, but Logan County erupted into one of its classic political battles.

Joe and Tennis Hatfield sought to establish their own political control over the county while Chafin was in prison, and largely succeeded in doing so, though as Republicans instead of Democrats. In the long run, that did not matter because traditional Logan County politics is based more on personal loyalties and family ties than it is on political parties. After the election of 1924, there were in effect two political parties in Logan County, one loyal to Don Chafin and his successors, the other loyal to Tennis and Joe Hatfield and their successors.

The role that Coleman A. Hatfield played in this change is not thought to be too significant. Instead, he sought to establish a good life for himself, his wife, and his growing family. The first child of Coleman A. and Mossie Hatfield, Elizabeth Aileen Hatfield, was born on August 21, 1908, and grew up to become the first Logan County woman admitted to the Bar Association when she graduated from law school in 1932.

Elizabeth Aileen was followed by Christine, Coleman C., and Annabel Hatfield, who were born, respectively, on December 28, 1915, September 25, 1926, and February 13, 1929. Coleman A.'s main concern was to feed his "younguns". To that end, he established a law firm with his father, though Cap Hatfield did not practice law too often. The Hatfields were helped by two other attorneys, Ira P. Hager, who stayed with the firm for one year, and N.D. Waugh, who joined the firm in 1925.

It was about that time that Coleman A. also made a significant friend. In the election of 1925, a young lawyer named Cush C. Chambers ran a winning campaign for mayor of the city of Logan. Chambers was a complicated man. In later years, he would run unsuccessfully for the state legislature and stage the unsuccessful 1932 defense of Clarence Stephenson, the accused killer of Mamie Thurman in Logan County's most sensational court trial.

Chambers would remain very active in politics, once comparing President Franklin D. Roosevelt to Jesus Christ, before Chambers was elected judge of the Logan Circuit Court in 1936, after a heated and controversial contest with former Judge Robert Bland. Chambers remained on the bench 32 years after his first election and would become steadily more conservative through the years, enjoying his reputation as a tough, uncompromising jurist.

In the meantime, as the younger lawyers of Logan formed their alliances and started their businesses, there were many changes in the Hatfield family. Frank Phillips, the most uncompromising McCoy ally of the feud era, passed away in the middle of December 1926. Phillips had fallen on hard times after the Battle of Grapevine Creek. In his later years, he suffered a grievous injury to one of his legs, which had to be amputated. Some Logan historians tell a tale that Phillips' life was saved on that occasion only because Henry D. Hatfield personally performed the amputation.

Be that as it may, the feud was passing into distant memory. On July 13, 1928, the Logan newspaper printed an article that told how Sheriff Tennis Hatfield had gone to Pikeville, Kentucky, on some minor matter. While he was there an acquaintance pointed to an aging man and told Tennis, "That's Uncle Jim McCoy."

Tennis insisted on greeting McCoy. The two shook hands as an enterprising photographer took the picture of the event that became world famous. The following September, Cap Hatfield himself praised Jim McCoy as one of the best of his family, adding that he and few other, if any, Hatfields bore any resentment of Jim McCoy. Time was healing the wounds. Time was removing those with personal memories of the feud.

In March 1928, Louvicey Hatfield joined her husband in eternity. Anse's sister, Emma Roush, followed her in April 1929. Then in July 1930, Cap was taken to a local hospital, suffering from the effects of his ancient wound he received at the Christmas Eve frolic of 1880. On August 19, 1930, the Logan newspaper reported he had been taken to Baltimore to be treated by a cancer specialist. The newspaper of August 22, 1930, reported that Cap had died in his 65th year.

As these sad events marked the years of the Hatfield family, Logan County and its surrounding region were approaching one of the United States' watershed events, the Great Depression that began with the collapse of the stock market in New York in October 1929 and did not end until the United States was pulled into the Second World War at the end of 1941. Though the biography of one man or one family cannot be used to explain an overwhelming event like that one, the stories of individuals and families can serve as prisms that capture and divide the stream of light as it flows through time.

History is lived going forward but is understood looking backward. So the events that affected the southern West Virginia coalfield and the life of Coleman A. Hatfield can be reorganized into meaningful patterns with the perfect vision of hindsight.

The era when the Republican Party dominated the Logan coalfield can be dated roughly between May 1924, when Tennis Hatfield was elected the Republican sheriff of the county, until November 1930, when the old Don Chafin Democratic machine rose from its ruins and overwhelmed the Republicans at the county level.

That was an explosive history. Though Tennis was elected sheriff in 1924, he could not take office until 1926 because the election was challenged. When the Republicans did take the reins of office in 1926, *The Logan Banner* reported party members went wild with joy. The Republican domination of local politics was short lived, however, because the Democrats were able to rally their forces after the stock market crash of October 1929. That was why the election of November 1930 was so crucial to Logan County's history.

We know more about that era than we do the earlier years because *The Logan Banner* — the only historical document of the county not concerned solely with court cases — began twice weekly publication on June 18, 1926. Though its concerns included much news of crimes and punishments, there were stories printed that could have served as warnings that the times were a-changing again.

On July 27, 1926, *The Banner* printed a news article on one of its inside pages that should have been taken very, very seriously by Logan County coal operators, as well, of course, as their many fellows and competitors across the nation. That was the news that German chemists working in the aniline dye industry's "community of interest," known as I.G. Farben, had succeeded in producing synthetic petroleum from coal.

That was an enormously complicated development. Broken down to its utmost simplicity, the Germans realized at the beginning of the First World War that they needed powder to fire their cannons. Germany is notoriously poor in all natural resources except the coal of the Ruhr Valley. Walther von Rathenau, a leading figure in the aniline dye industry, convinced the German government to release chemists from military service so they could develop the processes that made synthetic nitrate, which is basic to powder. For his trouble, von Rathenau was later murdered because he was a Jew.

After the war, Fritz Haber, another of Germany's leading chemists, applied the same techniques to coal and found that it would make oil. Thirteen years later, much of Europe fell to Adolph Hitler's armies because German tanks and airplanes and other motor vehicles had the fuel they needed to crush the nations of that continent.

This was also a significant moment in world history because the world's petroleum companies realized that sooner or later they could replenish their supplies of oil, if they ever ran short, by processing coal into petroleum. So began the long process by which the oil companies bought out the coal companies. This would come home to Logan County in the last years of Coleman A. Hatfield's life.

Two years after *The Banner's* article told about this most significant event, there was another article which indicated the shape of the future for those who paid attention. This was an interview with T.B. Davis, the president of Island Creek Coal Company, whose office was located at 26 Broadway in New York, the most famous business address in the world at that time, the address of the Rockefeller family.

Davis' interview was first printed in William Randolph Heart's newspaper, *The New York American*, one of the most sensationalistic newspapers in the nation's history. Yet that article was wide-ranging and far-sighted, telling, as it did, how the coal industry needed to change if it expected to survive.

Davis said that the problem was that there were too many mines and too many miners. His solution was to turn to industry-wide consolidations. If there were fewer mining companies, those firms could offer miners steady work at reasonable pay, to the benefit of everyone. T.B. Davis also proposed using West Virginia as a model for the consolidations he suggested.

The plan did not take shape in West Virginia. Then the Great Depression wrecked the idea's chances for success anywhere. But the idea survived and became the underlying principle for the gradual shrinking of the coal industry after the Second World War, as well as the turn to mechanized mining that accompanied that development.

Thoughtful readers are asking themselves at this point just what all this had to do with a lawyer living an individual life in a small city of southern West Virginia. The answer is easy enough. *Fortune* magazine once likened Island Creek Coal Company to a large frog trapped in a drying pond. So too was Coleman A. Hatfield. He needed to feed his children. His world was changing under him.

One symptom of that was the role of the Republican Party in Logan County. The Republicans were jubilantly dominant between 1926 and 1930. They were perhaps fatally impaired at the local level in the election of 1930. They were crushed in the election of 1932. They lost their last local office holder, Judge Naaman Jackson in the election of 1936. This means that between 1930 and 1980, Logan County Republicans did not have a role in local politics except in individual cases when Republicans ran for office as "Democrats" and were elected from time to time.

This was important to Coleman A. Hatfield because he followed his father into the Republican Party and was loyal to it. He once served as chairman of the Logan County Republicans and sought to improve its chances for success. He resented those who became "Democrats" for self-interested reasons.[20] And he sought to fight for his values through the agency of his political party.

There is a deeper significance to this that will withstand the stress of two paragraphs. Individuals possessed of insight know that many ideological differences of opinion are an illusion. There is much apparent contradiction between American "liberals" and American "conservatives." Yet they need one another. The past is valuable as the seed of the future, while the future is valuable as the flower of the past.

Because Logan County did not have a working Republican Party for fifty years, it did not enjoy the benefit of the caretakers of the past, so it lost its chances to see the beauty of the future. Coleman A. Hatfield knew this fact. A close-at-hand illustration of the point was the later career of Henry D. Hatfield, his first cousin.

Before leaving the tale of Coleman A. Hatfield in these vital years, it is also a painful duty to leave a record of his personal tragedy. He did not get the chance to aid the Republican Party and his community as much as he would have liked because he went blind in a gradual fashion between 1924 and 1940. His affliction was retinitis pigmentosis, an inherited disease that has its most devastating effect on young adults. For that reason, Coleman A. depended on the aid of secretaries for much of his life as he recorded his account of the Hatfield family.

That research seems to have begun as the nation entered its crisis during the Great Depression. Coleman A. Hatfield's life also became more complex and more interesting at that time. After his daughter Elizabeth Aileen Hatfield graduated from West Virginia University Law School in 1932, and became the first woman admitted to the Logan County Bar Association later that year,

Coleman A. immediately made her a partner in his firm, which improved their financial condition somewhat.

That income was needed. In 1929, Coleman A. and his wife bought a house at 306 Guyan Street, in the city of Logan. That was a heavy burden during the Depression years. Coleman A. told his son that he was forced to take out a homeowner's loan, which took many years to pay. He also sold some of the Hatfield family land to keep a roof over his family's head.[21]

When the Depression hit full force, the Hatfields' troubles multiplied, the same condition faced by everyone else in the coalfields. By then, however, the political conditions were changing that, paradoxically, made life better for the Hatfields than it might have been.

In 1930, Cush C. Chambers was reelected mayor of the city of Logan. He named Coleman A. one of the city's police court judges, which helped Hatfield's financial position. Then in 1936, Chambers was elected judge of the Logan Circuit Court and appointed Hatfield one of the divorce commissioners. This gave him a reliable income, if not a large one. With his family's help, his income was sufficient to ride out the Depression.

More interestingly, it was during those years that Coleman A. began writing his account of the feud. The year 1932 marked the fiftieth anniversary of the death of Ellison Hatfield at the hands of the McCoy brothers on Election Day in Kentucky, August 1882. That is the most appropriate moment to begin telling of Coleman A.'s research.

Coleman A. Hatfield's Research

What follows is intelligent guesswork, which is supposed to be anathema to historians, but which is the only way to tell how Coleman A.'s remarkable work was accomplished. The research seems to fall in four general categories — Hatfield's work as a lawyer in legal documents of West Virginia, Kentucky, and Virginia; his correspondence with friends and relatives; his conversations with friends who could recall the feud era; and his dictation of memories to a series of secretaries, some of whom he trained personally and who became valued aides.

The trouble with telling how that was done is that we do not know chronological sequence. The letters are dated, but there is no clear record of when the manuscripts were written or when the legal documents were compiled. The only approach that historians can take that makes any sense is to summarize the documentation by the four categories Coleman A. used.

One such document that Coleman A. seems to have located fairly early was a land record in Deed Book Number Two of Russell County, Virginia, that told some of the land transactions of Ericus Smith, who was the father of Mary Hatfield and thus, the father-in-law of Eph-of-All Hatfield. Coleman A. copied this information from that document.

> This deed discloses that Mary Hatfield and Ephriam Hatfield, Rachel Hatfield and Joseph Hatfield, together with Andrew Smith, joined as grantors in a deed to Ely Smith and Ericus Smith to a tract which aggregated two hundred acres of land lying on Thompson Creek, New Garden District, County of Russell, deed dated in the year 1786.
>
> A court order entered in the records of the court discloses that in the year 1784, Ericus Smith was declared to be the owner of a tract of two hundred acres of land as described above, by reason that he had settled the same in 1774 and had resided there, held possession, and paid taxes for a period of ten years, which vested title.
>
> It is assumed that Ericus, the father of this family, died between the years 1784 and 1786, and that his widow, Rachel Smith, together with her two daughters, Mary Hatfield and Rachel Hatfield, joined in dividing the land between two of the Smith sons.
>
> The court order referred to contained several entries where the court allowed bounties paid for hunters killing wolves. It is found among these records that John Hatfield and Valentine Hatfield are named as having received bounties for killing wolves.
>
> It is assumed that this Valentine Hatfield was probably a brother of John. It is also assumed that Ephraim (Eph-of-All) later had a son whom he named for the Valentine Hatfield mentioned in the Russell County records in 1791 as having received a bounty for killing a wolf.[22]

In that work, Coleman A. Hatfield also sought to clear up the confusion about whom Eph-of-All Hatfield's parents were. The point should be recalled that Coleman A. thought that frontier militia hero Andrew Hatfield had a brother named Joseph, who served as a scout for the army commanded by George Washington during the American Revolution. In Coleman A.'s view, this Joseph Hatfield's wife was Rachel Hatfield, who moved to Campbell County, Tennessee, and died there at age 96 in 1851.

Coleman A. then hired a genealogist named Will Daniel of Huntington to try to trace down the facts. The matter was still unsettled at the time of Coleman A.'s death in 1970, but he recorded his impression of how difficult that work was.

> A local genealogist by the name of William H. Daniel, Huntington, West Virginia, has undertaken to place Ephriam as the son of Joseph, the revolutionary scout, and it is my belief that this attempt is to make Ephraim and his descendants eligible to membership in the Sons of the Revolution.

> This is a mighty fine idea, and I would be glad to know that such is true. However, I cannot believe it and I am not willing to stretch the facts to this extent. Ephraim might or might not have served in the Revolution. If he did, well and good. If he did not, there is one thing sure. I believe myself to be the lineage of Ephraim, whether or not he has a military record.[23]

Coleman A. then asked himself how closely connected Eph-of-All may have been to Captain Andrew Hatfield. He thought the connection might be very close, using as evidence recurring family names down the generations of the Hatfields.

> I wish to refer to Captain Andrew Hatfield of Montgomery County, Virginia, who served in the Revolution and is mentioned in Revolution annals. He was sent out, together with Jonas Hatfield, in a company commanded by a Captain Hale in the year 1793 and was stationed at the mouth of Elk River, now the present site of Charleston, West Virginia. The object was to guard the Virginia settlement against encroachment of the Indians from the Ohio Valley.
>
> Captain Andrew Hatfield then took up land, a tract of seven hundred and fifty acres on the Guyandot River near the present site of Barboursville, where he died in 1809. He left descendants in Cabell County, including sons Isaac Hatfield and (I believe) Adam Hatfield.[24]

Coleman A.'s questions were if it could be possible that Valentine Hatfield named his twin sons born in 1813 after John (who would have been Valentine's grandfather) and Andrew, for Captain Andrew Hatfield of Montgomery County, Virginia. He also asked if Captain Andrew and John Hatfield were brothers, one from Russell County and the other from adjoining Montgomery County.

This question occupied much of Coleman A.'s time during the following thirty-five years. At various times, accompanied by his son and daughters, he made trips to Kentucky and Virginia in search of the records. He studied tax books, other deed books, and court records, including both county administrative courts and legal or circuit courts. In one document, Coleman A. recorded his frustration at the lack of evidence.

> It is a well-known historical fact that the British Army burned the capitol at Washington in 1814. In doing so, they destroyed the census of 1790, which George Washington ordered. The census of 1800 and of 1810 were likewise destroyed.
>
> This destructive and warlike act on the part of the British has deprived historians and genealogists of much information which had been recorded up to the time of that war.

> For instance, in 1782, after the close of hostilities between the colonies and the British, all citizens in every county of Virginia were required to list themselves and their slaves, horses, and cattle. Sometimes the slaves of a family or the family sons under 21 years were listed as so many "black tithes" or "white tithes."
>
> It was imperative that all white males between the ages of 16 and 21 should be listed by the father for the purpose of establishing military information, in order to know the potential strength of the states for the purposes of war. It was also important to know the extent of the land in case food was needed in a hurry for an army.[25]

To locate information about the Hatfields, Coleman A. turned to those tax records. In them, he found one of the most persuasive arguments that some of the Hatfields descended from a John Hatfield, who was a mature man in 1786. That information also came from the tax records of Russell County, Virginia:

> The next Hatfield that appears on the tax records of Russell County, in the year 1786, is John Hatfield, with 100 acres. It may also be assumed that John was the head of a family and had arrived at that age in life where he owned his home and a substantial acreage of land to cultivate and to raise livestock. He also may be assumed to be of the age of George and Joseph Hatfield, and it is possible these three who have been mentioned were brothers.[26]

Since he was not content with guesswork, Coleman A. Hatfield also bought research from the Media Research Bureau of Washington, D.C. That firm's work indicated that there were several Hatfield emigrants to Virginia, including Thomas Hattfield of Charles River County, who arrived in 1637. Others were Thomas Hatfield (or Hatfeild) of Gloucester County in 1653, and Grace Hatfield (or Hatfeild) of New Kent County in 1655. That document was a dead end, however, because the firm could find no definite records of their families or descendants.

One interesting aspect of the Media Research Bureau's work was that it seemed to disprove the recurring contention that Hatfield is a corruption of the German name Hatzfeld. Instead, the firm argued that all of the Hatfields that researchers could find in the new world came from England. The report stated:

> The name of Hatfield is believed to have been derived from the residence of its bearers at a village or parish of that name in England. It is found in ancient English records in the various spellings of Hatfeild, Hitfield, Heathfield, Hithfield, Haytefeld,

Haytfield, Hatfeield, Hatfeld, Hatfully, Hattfield, Hatfield, and numerous others, of which the form last mentioned is that most generally used in America today.[27]

As Coleman A. Hatfield strove to find the source of his family in America, however, he also became interested in leading other writers to source material or correcting mistakes in the history that appeared in other writings and broadcasts. Between 1959 and 1961 there were at least four occasions when Coleman A. wrote to such writers or broadcasters.

On November 6, 1961, Coleman A. sent a letter to Lowell Thomas, who was then doing reports for the Columbia Broadcasting System. Hatfield learned that one such broadcast concerned the mining area around Gunnison, Colorado. He then corresponded with Thomas in the interest of finding out more about Gunnison because Cap Hatfield spent some time there away from the feud country. The letter states:

> I am writing you for perhaps a lead to some information relative to a story or stories written of the mining days around Gunnison, Colorado, and other places in that state.
>
> During the Hatfield-McCoy Feud of the 1880s, my father, Cap Hatfield, left the West Virginia-Kentucky border and sojourned for a time in Colorado in and around Gunnison, Pueblo, Leadville, and Denver.
>
> He has now been dead for more than thirty years, and while I remember many things which he told me in my boyhood regarding his travels in Colorado and even to Washington state, which was a territory at that time, I have often regretted that I did not find out more of his personal experiences in the mining areas of Colorado.[28]

We do not know if there was a direct connection established, but Coleman A.'s collection of materials contains postcards and other photographs of the Colorado mining town. There is a possibility that Thomas led Hatfield to that information.

At another time, erroneous information began circulating about the death of Elias Hatfield, the brother of Anse and the father of Henry D. Hatfield. Though its date, unfortunately, was not preserved, a "By The Way" column written by Charles D. Hylton for *The Logan Banner* told that tale:

> Like the death of Mark Twain, attorney Coleman Hatfield says the demise of one of the kin has been slightly exaggerated, and he has given us some facts to set the record straight.
>
> Mr. Hatfield said he heard a few months back a story on a radio program about the death of Elias Hatfield. According to the

program, "Old Prater," as Elias was known, was stabbed to death by a couple of McCoys on Blackberry Creek in Pikeville, Ky., at the outbreak of the famous feud between the two families.

This is not correct, the venerable attorney says, and he offered the following background on Old Prater:

Some of our oldest citizens who lived in and around Logan at the turn of the century will remember Elias Hatfield, who was jailer under Sheriff Jim Henderson. He was known by his relatives as 'Uncle Lias,' but most of the old-timers knew him by the familiar name of 'Prater Hatfield.'

"Old Prater, whose home stood on what is now Dingess Street at the railroad crossing, had to give way to the coming of the railroad when his home was moved back from what is now the right-of-way line. He sold part of the property for a hospital site after the railroad came through and his residence was moved back by the side of the hospital. The house was destroyed by fire in 1925.

"No, 'Old Prater' was not whittled to death on that fateful August day in 1882 by the McCoy brothers. He was quite active in local politics in Logan County in the early part of the century and saw the first train come into Logan. He was here when the telephone and telegraph lines came in and saw the first coal shipped down the Guyan Valley.

"He lived for more than a quarter of a century after the time, according to the radio story, which said he was cut down in the early feud days."[29]

At about the same time, Kermit Hunter, who was then living at Hollins College, Virginia, heard the tale from Kyle McCormick that Anse Hatfield had terrorized individuals around Athens, West Virginia, who supposedly had abused one "Mooney" Hatfield. Hunter wrote an article about the matter, which appeared in print. Coleman A. then wrote a letter to Hunter's family objecting to the story.

Hunter replied on August 24, 1959, from Welch, apologizing for the matter and claiming that he was proud of his West Virginia background, meaning no offense or disrespect to the Hatfield family in particular.

A third controversy flared at the end of 1961, when Shirley Donnelly of Beckley wrote tales about the feud in a column titled "Yesterday and Today." In his reply to Donnelly, Coleman A. Hatfield added much information about his family which did not appear in his collection of manuscripts. Though the reply was rather longer than most of Hatfield's correspondence, it is reprinted here because the material may be valuable to future historians:

Dear Mr. Donnelly:

In your "Yesterday and Today" column published on the 14th instant, I wish to call your attention to the fact that part of your statements are erroneous with reference to the estrangement of the brothers, Johnson Hatfield and William A. (Cap) Hatfield, the two eldest children of Anderson "Devil Anse" Hatfield and Levicy Chafin Hatfield.

I am not writing this letter in order to be critical, but merely for the sake of the record. As the eldest grandson of Anderson Hatfield, I feel that I am in a position to state facts relative to the family history through the past three score and ten years, since my friends say I have a good memory.

Anderson Hatfield was born on September 10, 1839, on Mate Creek in what was then Logan (now Mingo) County. He trained with a company of Virginia Militiamen known as the "Logan Wildcats" from about 1856 until 1860. In the journal which was kept for the company by Dr. Joseph Hinchman, Hatfield was allotted a certain area on the Tug Fork of Sandy River, all of the soldiers within the allotted area being led by Hatfield as their captain. The remainder of the county which now comprises both Mingo and Logan was divided up in like manner so that each "captain" had a parcel of the territory and all soldiers in training were led by the respective "captains" from the various areas of the entire county. They trained at regular intervals at Logan Courthouse in those days.

Johnson Hatfield and Cap Hatfield, his next younger brother, were born in 1862 and 1864, respectively, and could well have inherited the spirit of fiery conflict which raged in the borderline country where they were born and grew up. I am not informed where you got your information as to the estrangement of these two brothers, but the facts were that all down through their lives they were as inseparable as David and Jonathan. Johnse was more daring and less cautious than Cap, and Johnse was often a care to his mother when she feared that he would go into dangerous places, particularly the time when he slipped down the bed sheets from his upper window without his mother's consent and rode away across into Kentucky to see Roseanna McCoy. But in all of these episodes and many others, "Cap," his next younger brother, always rushed to the rescue.

It was always true throughout their lives when either was in trouble, you could expect the other to dash to his rescue, just as it was in 1914, when Johnse, as constable, led a posse in pursuit of payroll robbers who shot down Dr. Amick and two of his companions and took the payroll at Glen Alum in Mingo County.

Johnse was a foreman at the tipple, and with four others, including Red Jess Browning, Jim Mounts, John Turk, and Jake Grow, grabbed their rifles and went in hot pursuit up the Spring Fork of Ben Creek, where the bandits were cornered in a rocky ravine behind logs and boulders.

Jake Grow was shot through the body, John Turk had his thumb shot off, and Jim Mounts was shot through the thigh while Red Jess Browning and Johnse Hatfield held the robbers at bay.

Although Johnse was behind a hickory tree and in such position to keep the bandits from escaping, yet he was unable, for his own safety, to change his position for hours. Word came to Cap Hatfield at War Eagle that the robbers had shot two or three of Johnse's companions and that he was saving his own life by keeping a hickory tree between him and the bullets.

Cap gathered a crowd at War Eagle and crossed the mountain, and it was there later that citizens, as well as the sheriff, Greenway Hatfield, and sheriff's deputies converged upon the area and all of the robbers were carried out by the undertaker and the money recovered.

That was eight years before the death of Johnse Hatfield and throughout most of the remainder of that period, Cap and Johnse both lived at Stirrat, West Virginia, at the large mining plant of the Main Island Creek Coal Company, where they often saw each other and were the best of friends, as brothers should be.

In their last years, both realized the mistakes of their youth in the score of years which followed the Civil War, but both realized that they had been victims of the tragic times during the last quarter of the 19th century, so that during their last years, they endeavored to be good citizens, and both served as officers of the law.

Johnse was elected in Mingo County and served a term as constable while Cap served for a time as Deputy United States Marshall in Logan County, as well also deputy sheriff under his brother, and under the latter's successor, Joe D. Hatfield.

Another error in your review of the conversion of Anse Hatfield is that you say that he "turned to the Primitive Baptist faith." It is true that within the last decade of his life Anderson Hatfield was baptized in the then clear waters of Main Island Creek by Uncle Dyke Garrett.

These two men had served in the Southern Army. Uncle Dyke was not of the "Primitive Baptist faith," but, on the other hand, was a preacher in the Christian Church which is commonly spoken of in connection with the Restoration Movement of Thomas Campbell and his son, Alexander Campbell, in which the work of the latter resulted in founding of the Movement of the Christian Church and the college at Bethany, West Virginia.

Uncle Dyke was a fellow minister with Alexander M. Lunsford, one of the earliest preachers to bring the Restoration Movement to Logan County. He was commonly known as "Daddy" Lunsford. He died some fifty years ago at Logan, West Virginia.

Phil Conley, the West Virginia historian, wrote a gripping story of Uncle Dyke and his wife, Aunt Sally, in which Conley told of his visit to the veteran minister's mountain home, and in this story, which was published several years ago, Uncle Dyke was rightfully called the "Shepherd of the Hills" of his native Logan County.[30]

In all this writing, Coleman A. Hatfield's concern was that the truth be told faithfully and without embellishment. Through his lifetime there were many books of so-called "pulp fiction" printed about the feud, though he is not known to have reacted to them. Rather more information is known, though, about Coleman A.'s reaction to several books that were published between 1930 and 1970. His attitude toward those writings should become part of the record.

Coleman A. Hatfield and the Writers

Coleman A. Hatfield deplored inaccuracy like that which marred Shirley Donnelly's work, but worse examples were at hand. In 1930, just before Coleman A. began writing his manuscripts, John L. Spivak's book, *The Devil's Brigade*, was printed. Though it was called a novel, the book was about Anse Hatfield and his times. If African Americans are rightly offended by the view of their people presented in the movie "The Birth of a Nation," Hatfields and Appalachians have an equal right to be offended by Spivak's work.

The diatribe began with the introduction to *The Devil's Brigade*:

> This is the story of the longest, most bitter, and most dramatic vendetta in American history — the Hatfield-McCoy scrap which involved the two most powerful families in West Virginia and Kentucky for fourteen years, the echoes of which, in a diverted form, are still rumbling today. If the killings traceable indirectly to the clan hatreds are considered, the trouble actually lasted some forty years.
>
> The feud started over a tragic love affair between Roseanna McCoy and Jonse Hatfield and immediately drew into its web

hundreds of people, and for a period threatened a civil war between West Virginia and Kentucky. A good many of the killings were committed with the tacit approval of the legal authorities of each state. Everybody seemed to have enjoyed it.[31]

Reread and note well that last sentence. *"Everybody seemed to have enjoyed it."* To say the least, that is an odd statement. One questions if Randal McCoy actually enjoyed knowing that five of his children had been murdered. One wonders if Anse and Cap Hatfield enjoyed living in desperate fear.

The remainder of Spivak's novel follows a similar course. The love affair of Johnse Hatfield and Roseanna McCoy is presented with much invented dialogue, as is the election day fight of Ellison Hatfield and the three McCoy brothers, which, in Spivak's hands, is presented as a fight started by Ellison Hatfield.

Though Coleman A. Hatfield did not find a copy of the novel during his lifetime, his son did find one and gave his own opinion of it in the light of Coleman A.'s better research:

> Spivak's work is not as bad as T.C. Crawford's was, but neither can be accepted as anything close to the truth about Anse's family or the events of the feud.
>
> I think it is very unfortunate that Spivak quoted people without having any idea what they said in particular circumstances. His presentation of the killing of Ellison Hatfield is ludicrous, even by the standards of pulp fiction.[32]

Coleman A. did buy a copy of Virgil Carrington Jones' 1948 study, *The Hatfields and the McCoys,* and had a rather higher opinion of it, though he again objected to the reconstructed conversation of men and women who had been dead many years. Coleman C. Hatfield recalled:

> My father thought that Jones came closer to the truth that other accounts he had read. But Jones was not a native of the region and failed to understand that there were more complicated reasons for people acting as they did than were apparent on the surface.
>
> For example, he failed to understand that the trial about the hogs was not a contest of will between Anse and Randal. The dynamic of that situation was that Bill Staton offended Randal by testifying against McCoy. Staton was a brother-in-law of Ellison Hatfield, but he was also a relative of Floyd Hatfield's wife.
>
> This meant that Randal was angrier at one of his near kin than he was at any of the Hatfields at that time, as I understand the situation and as my father understood it. The Hatfields only

became the focus of Randal's temper after Ellison Hatfield testified against Paris and "Squirrel-Hunting" Sam McCoy, after they were accused of killing Bill Staton.

You can find many such examples of misunderstanding in Jones' book. But that does not mean he totally misunderstood the feud and our community. He came closer to the truth than many other writers.[33]

Though most of the smaller books written about the feud contain serious distortions, occasionally one finds a book written while feudists were still living that comes closer to the events. Such a book was L.D. Hatfield's 1944 account of the troubles, with the cumbersome title, *The True Story of the Notorious Feud Between the Hatfields and the McCoys in the Hills of Kentucky and West Virginia.*

L.D. Hatfield's book missed many of the key points, but those he wrote about were in line with the more careful research of Coleman A. Hatfield, Otis K. Rice, and Altina L. Waller. L.D. Hatfield wrote:

The actual feud between these two families started on the first Monday in August in the year of 1882....

It was a hot day and Ellison Hatfield was lying in the shade of a tree, and having heard of the argument between Elias Hatfield and the McCoys, arose and jestingly offered the McCoys his big "Sun-down" straw hat and told them to forget the argument, and he would give them the hat to make feed for their cattle. The McCoys were already angry and infuriated, so they did not take the offer of the straw hat as a joke in the way Ellison had intended. Having a score to settle with Ellison anyway, Tolbert McCoy walked up to Ellison and said, "I'm h— on earth." McCoy drew back seemingly to strike Ellison with his fist, but instead he had his knife open in his hand and he stabbed Ellison in the abdomen, cutting him for several inches and severed his liver.

At this instant Ellison struck McCoy with his fist, knocking him down and fell on top of him. McCoy managed to wriggle clear and he had his two brothers stab Ellison twenty-five times in the back and then shot him with a revolver injuring him fatally....

The wounding occurred on Monday and Ellison died on Wednesday. The next morning, after the death of Ellison, the three McCoys were found tied to some pawpaw bushes on the Kentucky side of Tug River and all three had been killed.

There were no witnesses who would testify that the Hatfields killed the McCoys, and on this technicality "Devil Anse" escaped punishment for the killing.[34]

Coleman A. Hatfield did not live long enough to see the publication of the histories of Otis K. Rice or Altina L. Waller, though his son expresses admiration for both. As the years pass, it is likely that scholarly books like Rice's and Waller's will overtake the fiction written by Crawford and Spivak and the incomplete account written by Jones. Coleman C. Hatfield expressed the hope that his father's manuscripts would "draw out" other Hatfields and McCoys like L.D. Hatfield and that the growing collection of accurate information would allow the feud to be studied in its entirety.

Yet Coleman A. Hatfield's concern for the truth was not exhausted by his work writing his manuscripts and answering the many questions posed in letters from friends and relatives. In a speech to Hatfields and Musicks who gathered near Honaker, Virginia, on August 7, 1960, to honor the memory of families of David Musick and Eph-of-All Hatfield, Coleman A. had some meaningful words to speak:

> We are not believers in ancestor worship, but we pity the man today who feels that the traditions of the past and the memory of those who have gone on before have left us no patriotic, moral, or spiritual heritage. Such a concept would afford little interest in what the future holds in store for this generation.[35]

Such concerns were characteristic of Coleman A. Hatfield during the final twenty years of his life, and they lay at the root of his final writings during those years.

Logan County at the End of Coleman A. Hatfield's Life

The main theme of Logan County's history was the impact that the coal industry had on the mountain people. Though this remained unchanged after the Second World War, the nightmare of the Great Depression and the energy aroused to win the war brought more changes to the county.

Mine operators had experienced a crushing defeat during the Depression and were determined to hold their share of the energy markets after the war. When fuel oil began cutting into their markets, they fought back hard and ruthlessly. The war brought the mine owners enough prosperity to experiment with new ways of mining coal. The mining companies of the Appalachian region turned to highly-mechanized production, which brought a new set of problems to the area.

An important theme of local coal history was that fewer miners were needed for higher production as the mines were mechanized. As the men were forced out of work, they moved with their families to northern cities like Detroit, where other employment could be found. By the end of the 1950s, the county's population shrank back to a level it had passed decades before.

There were other issues that came to the surface during that time. Miners' health and retirement needs became important political issues. Strip mining — which was thought to be a more efficient mining method than underground mining — soon began to scar the mountains, thus helping bring on the environmental movement.

With these economic realities at hand, there were also political facts that were faced. Traditional Logan County politics were challenged by the need to bring reform in the fields of education and community betterment. These concerns flowed naturally into the zeal of the 1960s, which at first seemed to hold the promise of a better community until war in the Far East darkened the scene.

The last fifty-plus years of Logan County's history have been the most interesting by far. The times have been built, like many decades before them, around the themes of failure, success and hope. If both the achievements and the evils of the times are clearer, that is because more is known about the community.

One commonplace thought of that time that finds frequent expression is the idea of a curse that says, "May you live in interesting times." Those who lived in Logan County between 1950 and 1970 experienced such times to remember them as they will. In the year 1960, it seemed at times like the community was about to collapse. The migration of the mining families north in the 1950s, Logan County's reputation as a place of violence and corrupt politics, the destruction of the land by clear-cutting timber operations and strip mines, all took a toll on the county's reputation.

Yet there was another trend of the times that made the era fascinating to some persons who lived then. That final decade opened with the tragic mine disaster at the Holden 22 operation in 1960. That same year, John F. Kennedy brought his presidential campaign to West Virginia, and much attention was focused on Logan County, where one faction of Democrats used Kennedy's money to drive another faction from power.

John F. Kennedy's life and his presidency ended in his assassination, but as Lyndon Johnson followed him in the White House, much public attention was focused on the Appalachian region. For some time before Johnson's presidency was destroyed by the war in Vietnam, it looked as though federal money would help end the chronic problems of the region and that Logan County would be renewed by economic improvements.

As the 1960s ran smoothly into the 1970s, the mining economy demonstrated improvements that led some to think that the energy concerns of the mid-1970s would bring the local economy back to life. Yet in other ways, that belief was deceptive, because the energy crisis did not last as long as many thought it would, and because the dynamics of the energy economy did not change.

Another characteristic of the time, however, was that Logan County citizens began understanding that their history, though troubled, was vastly fascinating. As the Second World War faded into history, the community at large began trying to understand how its past had taken shape. Older citizens, such as Coleman A. Hatfield, were consulted to find out the truth of Logan County's tale.

In 1952, many county citizens thought it would be a good idea if the community celebrated the one hundred years of development that began when Anse Hatfield was a youngster of 14 years. A historic drama, "The Aracoma Story," about the supposed daughter of Shawnee war leader Cornstalk, was written. Pageants and various contests were organized, and some community old-timers were asked to share their understandings of the way the county developed.

Coleman A. Hatfield was one who contributed his memories to the centennial booklet that was published that summer. As we have noted before, this was a careful, cautious summary of some of the key events that concerned the Hatfield family. Yet Coleman A. must have known that a colorful ceremony only scratched the surface of history.

He continued his research and writing but also thought deeply into the nature of the events happening around him. Ten years after the centennial events, Coleman A. wrote a letter to the editor of *The Logan Banner* that was printed in the aftermath of the terrible flood of that time. He asked that the newspaper use the pseudonym "Old-Timer." But the letter, as much as anything, reflected Hatfield's love of his land:

> This letter would not be written you regarding the flood which struck Logan County on February 27th, were it not for the varying experiences which the writer recalls with reference to flood waters on the Guyandot during the past sixty years.
>
> It is recalled that at the turn of the century, timber industry was being developed along the Guyandot and its tributaries throughout Logan and Wyoming Counties, all the way to its headwaters at the Devil's Fork and Winding Gulf near the source of the stream.
>
> Millions of hardwood logs were floated down to market at the cities and towns on the Ohio. In carrying on the industry during those years, splash dams were built on the smaller streams. Water was backed up to be released at the proper time for carrying logs down to deeper water. Mighty dams were opened, releasing hundreds and even thousands of logs which went tearing down the channels destroying the trees along the bank, eroding the land, leaving exposed rock bars and widening the channels along the narrow tributaries of the Guyandot.

No regard was had for the condition of the landscape or the resulting erosion and shifting of the channels of the streams.

Previous to the coming of the timber industry, it is recalled that the channels of Guyandot tributaries were narrow and deep. Mother Nature, when undisturbed by *civilized* man and his encroachment, will regulate the conservation of rainfall and the release of the same in perfect order.

Old timers often speak of deep snows which fell back in the eighties and nineties, the likes of which have never been seen since. All this is true. The mighty forest trees with their lofty branches interlocking shaded the ground from the sun's rays.

Early snows that began to fall in November never melted, and then would come another snowfall and another throughout the winter months, and then it was that the snow pack melted with the "spring thaw," and the ice went out about the beginning of spring.

In those years, the virgin forests held the moisture, and their shade prevented radiation and the melting of the winter snow. The summer season's leaves and dying vegetation over millions of acres of our watersheds acted as a reservoir, and the rains and melting snow were released gradually to feed the streams throughout the summer season.

But what has become of these potential reservoirs in these modern years of industrial development along the Guyandot?

Careless, *civilized* man again permits our forests to be burned out and that which would be a reserve of water supply from rain and snows of winter is released in sudden floods to rush down the ravines and valleys.

Civilized man, in his quest for gold (and we are all guilty) has not only negligently permitted the beds of our small creeks and branches to be filled, clogged, and ruined, but he has actually aided and abetted in filling them (and we are all guilty) with slate, slag, cinder, garbage, cast-off lumber and all other waste from our industrial and domestic life along our valley.

Just three score years ago, the trees grew down near the edge of the streams and held the banks. It will be remembered that this was true in the area round the mouth of Mud Fork, Trace Fork, and Main Island Creek, and that in the locality of Cherry Tree, White's Addition, and all the way up Main Island Creek — the channel was deep, the water was clear, and many fish were in the stream.

Sixty years ago there were potholes of water seven to ten feet deep where bass and other fish were abundant. Under the hide-away boulders at these holes of water, bass measuring from twelve to fourteen inches were often caught throughout the summer.

Now what do we find? The bank-lining trees and bushes are gone. The channels are spread out and barren to the drying summer sun, and the dumping of the trash, garbage, slate, slag, and other refuse still goes on.

There is your problem, people of the Guyan Valley. You need cleaner banks, and channels to be cleaned out deeper. If you would bring back the old-time esthetic appeal which Mother Nature furnished a half century ago, then deepen your channels, clean the banks, encourage the growth of trees, not only along the streams, but on the mountain sides and hilltops as well.

Protect the forests. Give us the beauty which God intended Mother Nature to furnish the people of our state and those who travel our highways as they cross the hill country....

Appropriate action to forestall the results of raging floods in Logan County will make for the safety of life and property, as well as the beautifying of our countryside along the highways of our streams and valleys, and will save tax dollars in meeting flood disasters and its attendant emergencies in the years to come.[36]

Such were Coleman A. Hatfield's final words to the community he loved so much and which he had served so well by trying to understand its history and guard its future.

The Death of Coleman A. Hatfield

The final eight years of Coleman A. Hatfield's life were a blend of the joys and sorrows that many aging individuals know so well. Among his joys was the knowledge that he had completed his life's work of writing a full account of the feud as seen by his family.

He had grouped the tales together in three general sections. The first told the tales of Anse Hatfield, from his youth in isolated Logan County through the years of the Civil War and the feud, on to Anse's peaceful old age, when he was called as an expert witness in at least one law case.

The second group of tales that Coleman A. wrote told of his father, Cap Hatfield, from the time of the Christmas Eve 1880 "frolic" that left Cap suffering from a serious wound, on through Cap's life story and his final years.

The third set of Coleman A.'s tales told of the "heroes and hard cases," many of whom contributed to the history of the feud one way or another, or who were friends and allies of the Hatfields during the years between 1880 and 1920.

Along with this major accomplishment, Coleman A. also went with his son to visit aged Charlie Harrison, who gave the Hatfield pair a rare and valuable interview about Anse's character and some of the events of the feud years. The work was valuable because Charlie Harrison was at the time the last living feud participant.

Coleman A. also kept his law practice in good order, taking care of his clients until he was in his final days. One grandchild recalls that on his last day, Coleman A. went to his office to take care of a few letters and other matters concerning his law practice. He did not suffer the sad decline that many aged persons experience as they face diminished capacities and the other frailties of old age.

There were, of course, sorrows in his life. On March 25, 1946, Elizabeth Aileen Hatfield, his eldest daughter and a brilliant human being, died after suffering for several years with severe depression. Then on May 6, 1963, Mossie Caldwell Hatfield, Coleman A.'s wife, whom he described as "his best friend," also passed away.

Despite such sorrows, he loved his surviving children and the success they enjoyed. He seemed particularly fond of spending time with his son, making certain the family history would be preserved. During his late seventies, Coleman A. left his collection of manuscripts and interviews in the care of Coleman C. Hatfield and his sister Annabel, telling them that though an attempt to have a book published had not been successful, the tale might still somehow become part of history in the years to come.

As the 1970s began taking shape in Logan County, there was a sense, noted all over West Virginia by state historian John Alexander Williams, that many believed the "bad old days" were at last coming to an end. Williams wrote that the sense of an improving West Virginia was buoyed by a popular song of the time, and by younger people searching out the meaning of the state's history by interviewing "old timers."

It was during that time that Coleman A. Hatfield passed away. The circumstances were again touching. Coleman C. was due to drive home from Chicago, where he was teaching at the Illinois College of Optometry. On Friday, July 10, 1970, Coleman A. spent the day in his law office, and the next day asked his part-time housekeeper, a Mrs. Young, to prepare enough food for the family's visit.

A grandchild recalled that he told Mrs. Young a humorous story he had just heard, and they had a good laugh. Then he told her he thought he would go take a nap. She went to awaken him before she left to see if he wanted her to do anything else, but found that he had died peacefully in his sleep — the best way of all to leave this world — on Saturday, July 11, 1970.

THE END

Green Are The Woods

This song was composed and sung by Elder Abner Vance, under the gallows at Abingdon, Virginia. It was provided to the news media by Rev. A.M. Lunsford on October 14, 1897. Rev. H.L. Marcum published it on July 30, 1918:

Green are the woods where Sandy flows
And peace it dwelleth there.
In the valley the bear they lie secure,
The red buck roves the knobs.

But Vance no more shall Sandy behold
Nor drink its crystal waves;
The partial judge pronounced doom,
The hunter has found his grave.

The judge he said he was my friend
Tho' Elliott's life he had saved;
A juryman I did become
That Elliott he might live.

That friendship I have shown to others
Has never been shown to me;
Humanity it belongs to the brave,
And I hope it belongs to me.

'Twas by the advice of McFarlin
Judge Johnson did me call,
I was taken from my native home,
And confined in a stone wall.

My persecutors have gained their request
Their promise to make good,
For they oftime swore they would never rest
Till they had gained my heart is blood.

Daniel Horton, Bob and Bill,
A lie against me swore.
In order to take my life away
That I might be no more.

But I and them together must meet
Where all things are known;
And I will rest on Abraham's breast,
While they roll in the gulf ís below.

Bright shines the sun on Clinch's hill,
Soft the west wind blows;
The valleys are covered all over with bloom
Perfumed by the rose.

But Vance no more shall Sandy behold
Nor smell its sweet perfumes;
This day his eyes are closed in death,
His body confined in the tomb.

Farewell my friends, my children dear,
To you I bid farewell,
The love I have for your precious souls
No mortal tongue can tell.

Farewell to you, my loving wife,
To you I bid adieu,
And if I reach fair Canaan's shore
I hope to meet with you.

---

[1] Interview With Coleman A. Hatfield, Coleman C. Hatfield.
[2] Interview With Coleman A. Hatfield, Coleman C. Hatfield.
[3] Interview With Coleman A. Hatfield, Coleman C. Hatfield.
[4] Interview With Coleman A. Hatfield, Coleman C. Hatfield.
[5] Coleman C. Hatfield Interviews.
[6] Interview With Coleman A. Hatfield, Coleman C. Hatfield.
[7] A History of Education in West Virginia, Charles H. Ambler.
[8] A History of Education in West Virginia, Charles H. Ambler.
[9] A History of Education in West Virginia, Charles H. Ambler.
[10] Coleman C. Hatfield Interviews.
[11] Coleman C. Hatfield Interviews.
[12] The Logan Banner, June 14, 1938.
[13] Coleman C. Hatfield Interviews.
[14] The Logan Banner, June 14, 1938.
[15] Interview With Coleman A. Hatfield, Coleman C. Hatfield.
[16] A History of Education in West Virginia, Charles H. Ambler.
[17] A History of Education in West Virginia, Charles H. Ambler.
[18] Pierce Lee Johnston Interview.
[19] Pierce Lee Johnston Interview.
[20] Coleman C. Hatfield Interviews.
[21] Interview With Coleman A. Hatfield, Coleman C. Hatfield.
[22] Research Into Russell County Records, Coleman A. Hatfield.
[23] Research Into Russell County Records, Coleman A. Hatfield.
[24] Research Into Russell County Records, Coleman A. Hatfield.
[25] Hatfield Pioneers, Coleman A. Hatfield. One of the many purposes of the present study is to reorganize Coleman A. Hatfield's various notes so future historians can find their way around his documents. Hatfield Pioneers is such a collection. Coleman C. Hatfield asked me to make slight additions to the work for the sake of clarity. The final sentence of this quotation is such an addition.
[26] Hatfield Pioneers, Coleman A. Hatfield.
[27] The Name and Family of Hatfield, Media Research Bureau Report.
[28] Letter to Lowell Thomas, Coleman A. Hatfield.
[29] "By The Way" in The Logan Banner, date unknown. There have been slight corrections to the original copy, which errs in some particulars, such as calling it a "faithful day" instead of a "fateful day" and other changes to the final sentence.
[30] Letter to Shirley Donnelly, Coleman A. Hatfield.
[31] The Devil's Brigade, John L. Spivak.
[32] Interview With Coleman C. Hatfield.
[33] Interview With Coleman C. Hatfield.
[34] The True Story of the Notorious Feud Between the Hatfields and the McCoys in the Hills of Kentucky and West Virginia, L.D. Hatfield.
[35] Address At Musick Reunion, Coleman A. Hatfield.
[36] Letter To The Editor, Coleman A. Hatfield. Coleman C. Hatfield warns that his father was not to be mistaken for a 1970s era environmentalist because he also appreciated the need for money-making concerns. If so, the language about saving mountains and forests still seems very familiar.

Bibliography

Ambler, Charles H., and Summers, Festus P., *West Virginia: The Mountain State* (Second Edition) © 1940, 1958 by Prentice-Hall, Inc., Englewood Cliffs, New Jersey. Also by Ambler, *A History of Education in West Virginia*, ©1951, Standard Printing and Publishing Company, Huntington, West Virginia.

Annals of America, © 1976 by Encyclopedia Britannica.

Ash, Jerry Wayne, and Douthat, Stratton L., *West Virginia USA*, © 1976 by Seawell Multimedia Corporation, printed by Waverly Press Inc., Baltimore, Maryland.

Brockenbough, W.H., *Joseph Martin's New and Comprehensive Gazetteer of Virginia*, published by Joseph Martin and printed by Moseley and Tompkins, printers, in 1835.

Callahan, James M., *A Semi-Centennial History of West Virginia*, © 1913, The Semi-Centennial Commission of West Virginia.

Chambers, Cora, *My Sketch Book*, no copyright, printed by The Logan News Printers, 1955. (This was a book of personal memories printed as a gift for friends and relatives.)

Crawford, Theron C., *An American Vendetta: A Story Of Barbarism in the United States*, © 1889, Belford, Clarke and Company, New York, San Francisco, and Chicago.

Cubby, Edwin A., *The Transformation of the Tug and Guyandot Valleys*, © 1961 by the author; a dissertation for Syracuse University, Syracuse, New York, University Microfilms, Inc.

Deskins, William David, *Pike County: A Very Different Place*, © 1994 by the author, Printing By George, Pikeville, Kentucky.

Draper, Lyman C., *Border Forays*, a part of the Lyman C. Draper Collection, Historical Society of Wisconsin. (Microfilm Copy used at the West Virginia State Archives.)

Hatfield, L.D.: *The True Story of the Notorious Feud Between the Hatfields and the McCoys in the Hills of Kentucky and West Virginia*, © 1944 by the author, printed by Jarrett Printing Company, Charleston, West Virginia.

Hurst, Mary B., *A Social History of Logan County, West Virginia*, no copyright, a masters degree thesis done at Columbia University, New York. (A personal copy of this work was given to Robert Y. Spence by Mary Hurst in 1974.)

Jones, Virgil Carrington, *The Hatfields and the McCoys*, © 1948, University of North Carolina Press.

Lancaster, Bruce and Plumb, J.H., *The American Revolution,* reprint of *The American Heritage Book of the Revolution*, © 1971, American Heritage Publishing Company.

Lee, Howard B., *My Appalachia*, © 1971 by the author.

McCoy, Truda Williams, *The McCoys: Their Story*, © 1976 The Preservation Council Press of the Preservation Council of Pike County, Kentucky.

Morgan, John, *West Virginia Governors*, 1960, Newspaper Agency Corporation, Charleston, West Virginia.

Parkman, Francis, *Montcalm and Wolfe*, Library of America edition, 1983.

Pauley, Michael J., *Unreconstructed Rebel: The Life of General John McCausland, C.S.A.*, © 1992, Pictorial Histories Publishing Company, Charleston, West Virginia.

Ragland, Henry Clay, *History of Logan County*, no copyright, printed as a newspaper serial Spring 1896 in *The Logan County Banner*.

Rice, Otis K., and Brown, Stephen W., *West Virginia: A History*, 1993 by The University Press of Kentucky, Lexington, Kentucky. Also by Rice, *The Allegheny Frontier: West Virginia Beginnings, 1730 - 1830*, © 1970, University Press of Kentucky, Lexington, Kentucky. Also by Rice, *The Hatfields and the McCoys*, © 1982 by the University Press of Kentucky, Lexington, Kentucky.

Savage, Lon K., *Thunder In The Mountains*, © 1984, Jalamap Publications, Inc., South Charleston, West Virginia, and Summersville, West Virginia.

Scott, J.L. and H.E. Howard, *36th Virginia Battalion*, © 1987, H.E. Howard, Lynchburg, Virginia.

Spence, Robert Y., *The Land of the Guyandot: A History of Logan County*, © 1976 by the author; Harlo Printing Company, Detroit, Michigan.

Spivak, John, *The Devil's Brigade* © 1930 by the author, published by Brewer and Warren, Inc., New York, New York.

Swain, George T., *Lest We Forget*, no copyright, printed by *The Logan Democrat,* Logan, West Virginia, 1916.

Thomas, Jerry Bruce, *Coal Country: The Rise of the Southern Smokeless Coal Industry and Its Effect on Area Development 1872 -1910*, © 1971 by the author. This was a dissertation prepared at West Virginia University, available through University Microfilms, Inc.

Waller, Altina L., *Feud: Hatfields, McCoys, and Social Change in Appalachia 1860 -1900*, © 1988, University of North Carolina Press, Chapel Hill and London.

Ward, Geofftey C., Burns, Ric, and Burns, Ken, *The Civil War: An Illustrated History*, © 1990 by American Documentaries, Inc, published by Alfred A. Knopf, Inc.

Weaver, Jeffrey C., *45th Battalion Virginia Infantry*, © 1994 H.E. Howard, Lynchburg, Virginia.

Williams, John Alexander, *West Virginia and the Captains Of Industry*, 1976, the West Virginia University Foundation, printed by McClain Printing Company, Parsons, West Virginia. Also by Williams, *West Virginia: A History*, © 1976 by the American Association for State and Local History.

Those tremendous lines from T.K. Whipple's *Study Out The Land* about everyone in American living connected in dreams to the Wilderness Road were found on the flyleaf of Larry McMurtry's wonderful novel, *Lonesome Dove*. None of us knew exactly how to cite that in a bibliography, but we feel the debt to both gentlemen.

Brief Index

Chafin, Don, 230, 239, 264, 265, 266
Chambers, Cush, 284, 288
Ford, Henry, 89
Garrett, Sallie Smith, 70
Garrett, William Dyke, 94, 97, 157, 240, 246, 247, 271, 295
Hatfield, Andrew, 34
Hatfield, Cap (William Anderson), 81, 90-94, 107, 108, 169, 170, 172, 173, 174, 177, 178, 179, 182, 183, 239, 242, 243, 249, 262 – 264, 266 – 268
Hatfield, Ellison, 115, 116, 118-123, 128, 139, 144, 146, 153, 154, 166, 168, 169, 183, 213, 221, 240, 266, 268
Hatfield, Ephraim, (Eph-of-All), 31, 35, 288 – 290
Hatfield, Ephraim (Big Eph), 17, 18, 20-22, 25, 28-30, 35, 56, 76, 77, 102, 107, 109, 110, 115 - 117, 120, 121, 125, 127, 128, 130-132, 159
Hatfield, Henry D., 27, 212, 144, 148, 231, 232, 234, 255 – 257, 259, 260 – 264, 267
Hatfield, Joe, 230, 240, 244, 248, 264, 266, 274, 281, 284, 295
Hatfield, Johnse, 13, 120, 125 – 127, 129, 139, 169, 170, 182, 183, 211, 212, 214, 217, 227 – 229, 232, 233, 235, 239, 240 – 242, 266, 274, 294, 295, 297
Hatfield, Louvicey "Vicie" Chafin, 58, 145, 175, 220, 212, 214, 228, 229, 274, 275, 285
Hatfield, Mossie Caldwell, 278, 280, 281, 304
Hatfield, Nancy McCoy, 90, 91, 102, 111, 112, 125 – 127
Hatfield, Nancy "Nan" Elizabeth Smith, 63, 84, 115, 117, 159, 212, 226, 272
Hatfield, Nancy Vance, 17, 18, 21, 23, 31, 91, 102, 159
Hatfield, Tennis, 217, 230, 240, 264, 266, 274, 281, 283 – 285, 295
Hatfield, Willis, 154, 217, 230, 235, 240, 244, 261 – 263, 274
Kennedy, John F., 300
Jefferson, Thomas, 276
McCoy, Randal, 13, 23, 25, 57, 77, 82, 83, 84, 86, 115 – 117, 120, 123 - 127, 130, 138, 139, 140, 160, 161, 171-174, 211, 213, 228, 229, 297
McCoy, Roseanna, 13, 115, 125, 126, 128, 294, 296
Mitchell, Henry, 165, 166
Mounts, Ellison, 170, 174, 176, 182 – 184
Nighbert, James Andrew, 76, 148, 152, 158, 159, 179, 180, 215, 217, 229, 230, 240
Phillips, Frank, 137, 138, 139, 158, 161, 176, 284
Pulitzer, Joseph, 132, 142, 149
Ragland, Henry Clay, 44, 47, 48, 94, 98, 99, 129, 148, 159, 160, 215, 216, 217, 223, 230, 240, 283, 284
Ragland, Louisa Goins, 129
Thurman, Mamie, 284
Vance, Abner, 50-52, 58, 84
Vance, Jim, 13, 57, 64, 70, 80, 84, 85, 139, 163, 164 – 167, 172, 184, 211, 215
Wilson, E. Willis, 137, 139-142, 157, 158, 174, 175, 181

— Also From Woodland Press —

Arch
The Life of Governor Arch A. Moore, Jr.

By Brad Crouser

— Also —

West Virginia Tough Boys

By F. Keith Davis

Book resellers / bookstores: If you would like to carry Woodland Press titles, contact:

West Virginia Book Company
Telephone (888)-982-7472
1125 Central Avenue, Charleston WV 25302
(www.wvbookco.com) e-mail: wvbooks@verizon.net

Or Contact
Woodland Press LLC
www.woodlandpress.com
BookWorld Services
www.bookworld.com

Watch For Our Upcoming Woodland Press Titles.

Appalachian Stories.
Appalachian Authors.
Appalachian Pride.

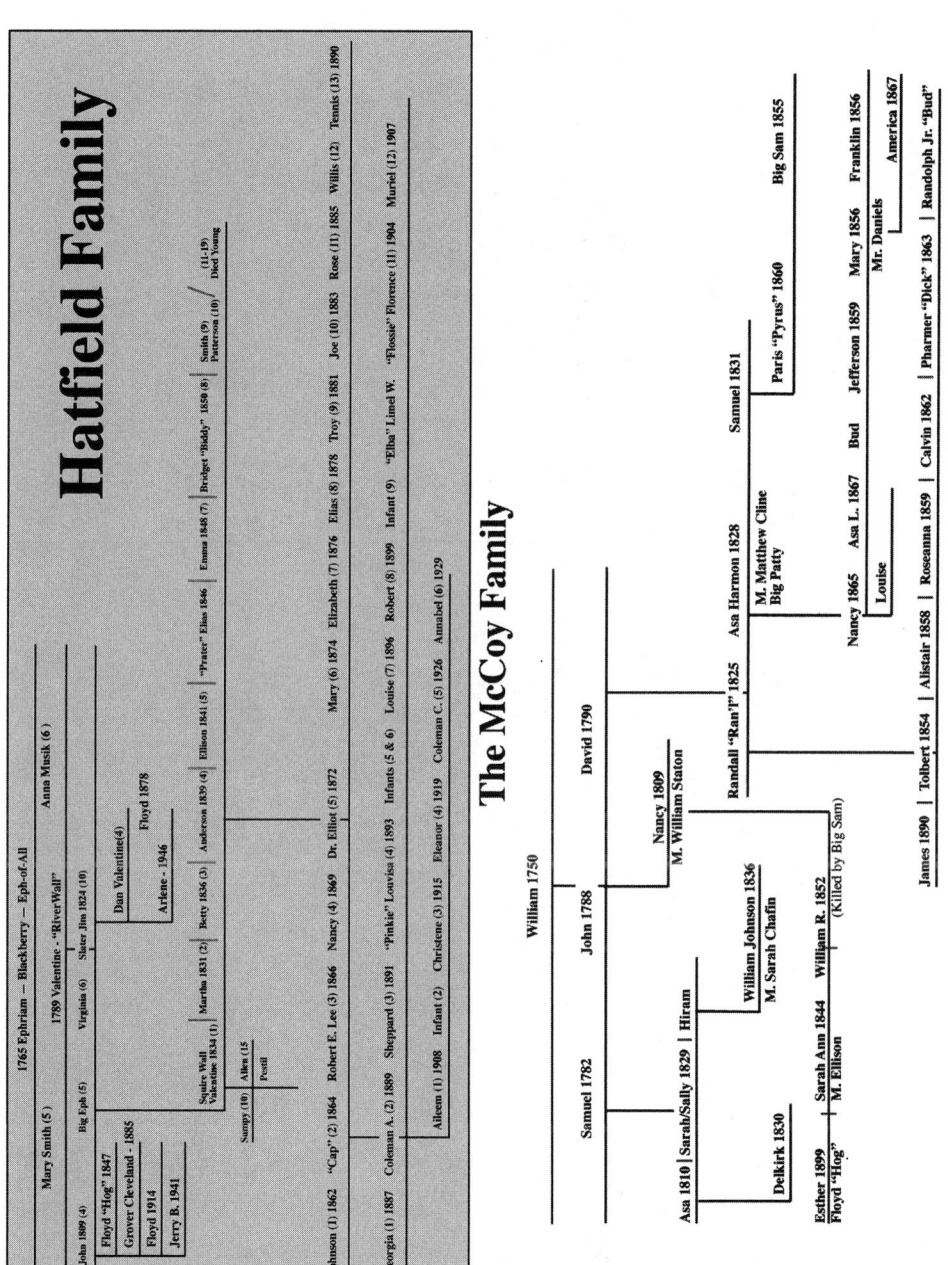

THIS WORN CABINET CARD shows the Hatfield couple, Devil Anse and Louvicey, in their elder years at their home. — Dr. Coleman C. Hatfield Collection

THE END OF AN ERA, this rare photograph portrays "Ole Ran'all McCoy," patriarch of the Kentucky McCoy clan, in his elaborate coffin at his homestead. He died on March 28th, 1914. In contrast, Devil Anse Hatfield lived until 1921. — Courtesy of Robert Spence Collection

AT LEFT, DETROIT "Troy" Hatfield is shown, along with his brother, Elias Hatfield, at right. These are two of Devil Anse Hatfield's sons. Both Troy and Elias were reported involved in a saloon business and were shot to death in Boomer over a liquor dispute, on October 17, 1911. — Courtesy of Robert Spence Collection

PREACHER UNCLE DYKE Garrett and Mrs. Willis Hatfield. It was Uncle Dyke who baptized "Devil Anse" Hatfield in 1911. — Courtesy of Robert Spence Collection

CAP HATFIELD, ELDEST SON of Devil Anse, is shown in his Logan County deputy uniform. Cap also studied law, and was considered one of the most wanted and dangerous of the feud participants.— Courtesy of Dr. Coleman C. Hatfield Collection

IN THIS TATTERED PHOTO, Devil Anse and Louvicey pose for this snapshot on their front porch. On the back row are Taylor (left) and Willis (right), both looking quite intimidating as they pack high-powered rifles. Below, the Hatfield family again poses on the porch at Sarah Ann. In the photo is Louvicey and Devil Anse (center), Ossie Browning (granddaughter), Rev. Uncle Dyke Garrett (back), and Rossie Browning (left).